Anonymous

The Risings on the north-west Frontier

Anonymous

The Risings on the north-west Frontier

ISBN/EAN: 9783337146337

Printed in Europe, USA, Canada, Australia, Japan

Cover: Foto ©ninafisch / pixelio.de

More available books at **www.hansebooks.com**

THE
RISINGS
ON THE
North-West Frontier.

———⁂———

Being a complete narrative, with specially prepared maps, of the various risings of the Frontier Tribes in the Tochi Valley, the Swat Valley, the Country of the Mohmands and Mamunds, and the Country of the Afridis and Orakzai; and of the several punitive campaigns undertaken against these tribes, as well as the two minor expeditions sent against the Utman Khels and the Bunerwals: the whole covering a period extending from the middle of June 1897 to the end of January, 1898.

(Compiled from the Special War Correspondence of the "Pioneer.")

———⁂———

Allahabad
Printed and Published at the Pioneer Press
1898

CONTENTS.

INTRODUCTION.

THE AREA OF DISTURBANCE.

PART I.

THE RISING IN THE TOCHI VALLEY.

CHAPTER.	PAGE.
I.—The Maizar Outrage	1—9
II.—The Official Account	10—17
III.—The Punitive Expedition	18—22
IV.—The Work of Destruction	23—27

PART II.

THE RISING IN THE SWAT VALLEY.

I.—The Attack on the Malakand	29—33
II.—The Situation in the Swat Country	34—37
III.—Renewed Attacks on the Malakand	38—44
IV.—The Malakand Field Force	45—47
V.—The Relief of Chakdara	48—51
VI.—Further events in the Swat Country	52—54
VII.—The Action at Landaki	55—58
VIII.—Concluding Operations in the Swat Valley	59—63

PART III.

THE RISING OF THE MOHMANDS AND THE MAMUNDS.

CHAPTER.	PAGE.
I.—The Raid on Shabkadr Fort	65—68
II.—Prompt Reprisals	69—74
III.—The Mohmand Expedition	75—79
IV.—With General Jeffreys's Brigade	80—90
V.—With General Wodehouse's Brigade	91—94
VI.—With General Elles's Division	95—98
VII.—Further Operations against the Mamunds	99—106

PART IV.

THE RISING OF THE AFRIDIS AND THE ORAKZAI.

I.—The Brewing of the Storm	107—112
II.—The Capture of the Khyber Forts by the Afridis	113—116
III.—The Rising of the Orakzai	117—123
IV.—The Relief of the Kurram Valley Forts	224—131
V.—The Attack on our Samana Forts—Saragheri and Gulistan,	132—142
VI.—The Tirah Punative Expedition	143—149
VII.—The Attitude of the Amir	150—157
VIII.—Crossing the Samana—The Capture and Abandonment of Dargai	158—166
IX.—The Re-capture of Dargai—Gallantry of the Gordons	167—173
X.—Lifting the Purdah from Tirah	174—184
XI.—Guerilla Warfare—a Heavy Casualty List	185—199
XII.—The Plan of Campaign further developed	200—210
XIII.—The Plan of Campaign completed	211—227
XIV.—The Re-occupation of the Khyber and the Expedition into the Bazar Valley	228—238

PART V.

Two Minor Expeditions.

CHAPTER.	PAGE.
I.—The Utman Khel Expedition	239—244
II.—The Expedition against the Bunerwals	245—250

APPENDICES.

	PAGE.
I.—The Rewards for Maizar	i & ii
II.—The Tochi Field Force	iii—v
III.—The Tochi Valley Despatches	vi—vii
IV.—The Malakand and Swat Valley Despatches	viii—xvi
V.—The Mohmand and Mamund Despatches	xvii—xxvi
VI.—The Tirah Field Force	xxvii—xxxv
VII.—The Samana and Kurram Valley Despatches	xxxvi—xliii
VIII.—The Tirah Despatches	xliv—lxii
IX.—Casualty List	lxiii

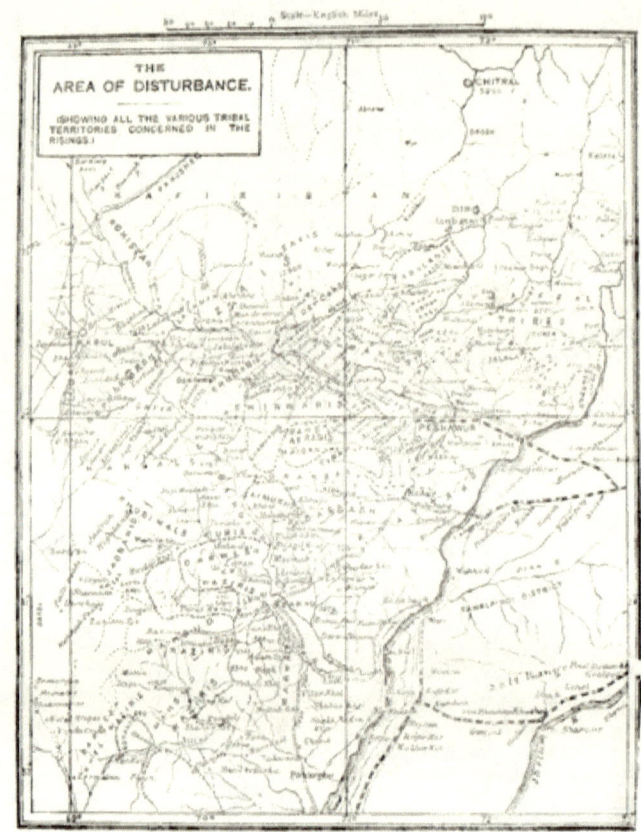

INTRODUCTION.

THE AREA OF DISTURBANCE.

IN the extent of the area affected, more obviously than in any other respect, the Indian Frontier disturbances of 1897-98 differ from all previous border troubles. From Waziristan on the left to Buner on the right a stretch of more than 400 miles of our borderland, inhabited, as Sir George White said in a speech at the United Service Club in Simla, by 200,000 first-rate fighting men, has been involved in the outbreak, and the dates of the various risings indicate an identity of design and a unity of purpose never before discernible in the history of frontier disturbances. "The disturbed area on the true frontier, namely, the one which we guard and protect," wrote Sir Robert Low in an article in the *National Review*, "commences with the mountains on the right bank of the Indus near Dirbund, where the river emerges from the hills into the plains. From this point the frontier line follows the line of mountains: it takes a long sweep to the north and then bends round to the west and south, enclosing the Peshawar Valley, and it completes a rough semicircle at Kohat. From Kohat our frontier goes west to Thull and then north-west up to the head of the Kurram Valley. The tribes which immediately face us on this frontier line, commencing at the top of the semicircle at Dirbund, on the Indus, are, taking them in their order, the Bunerwals, the Swats, the Utman Khels, and the Mohmunds; then come the Khyber Pass and the Afridis, and lastly, on the northern flank of the road from Kohat to Thull, the Orakzai. There are many other minor tribes and sections of the larger ones with different names, but to mention them is only confusing. The above are our immediate neighbours, and are the principal tribes, and they led the others with them to a great extent in such risings as we are dealing with.

"Our positions for the defence of this line,—(prior to the outbreak)—taking them from the top of the semicircle, have been 'Hoti Mardan,' the head-quarters of the Corps of Guides; in advance of it in the hills the Malakand position with its outpost at Chakdara; then, further round the semicircle, the forts of Abazai, Shabkudhr and Michni, and then Peshawar with its outpost of Jamrood guarding the entrance of the Khyber Pass; then, crossing the spur of the hills which run down towards the river Indus, we come to the station of Kohat with its outposts on the road to the Kurram Valley at Hangu and Thull, and the flanking position of Fort Lockhart and minor posts on the Samana Range. These posts were all occupied by troops or police, while beyond them, the road to Chitral, the Khyber Pass, and the Kurram Valley were held by tribal levies."

The map facing the first page affords a comprehensive view of the whole affected area. The actual tribal outbreaks and their dates were as follows:—

The Maizar outrage on the 10th of June; the attack on the Malakand and Chakdara positions on the 27th July; the attack on Shabkudhr on the 9th August: the threatening attitude of the Afridis and Orakzai on the 18th August, and the attack on the Khyber Pass on the 23rd August. Thereafter the narrative of events turns from tribal aggression, and follows the punitive operations of the Government of India's forces.

PART I.
THE TOCHI VALLEY AFFAIR.

PART I.

THE TOCHI VALLEY AFFAIR.

CHAPTER I.

THE MAIZAR OUTRAGE.

The Frontier disturbances of 1897 began, as has been briefly shown, on the 10th of June, when a startling outrage was committed on a British party in the Tochi Valley. Naturally enough the first account of the affair which reached head-quarters in India from the Tochi gave but scanty details, but it was unfortunately certain that the casualty list was a heavy one; three British Officers, twenty-two men of the native ranks and two followers being killed, while three other British Officers and twenty-four men were wounded. The three Officers killed were Colonel A. C. Bunny, 1st Sikhs, Captain J. F. Browne, R.A., and Lieutenant H. A. Cruickshank, R.A., both of No. 6 Bombay Mountain Battery; while the wounded were Lieutenant A. J. M. Higginson and Surgeon-Captain C. C. Cassidy of the 1st Sikhs, and Lieutenant C. L. Seton-Browne, 1st Punjab Infantry.

It appeared that Mr. Gee, Political Officer in the Tochi Valley, left Datta Khel on the morning of the 10th June, with an escort of 300 men from the 1st Sikhs and 1st Punjab Infantry, two guns of No. 6 Bombay Mountain Battery, and twelve sowars of the 1st Punjab Cavalry. Colonel Bunny, commanding the Tochi Column, was in charge of the escort. The object in view was to fix a site for a new outpost beyond Sheranni, nine miles beyond Datta Khel, and also to realise a fine which had been imposed upon the local tribesmen some months back. The party got as far as Maizar, which is somewhat to the south of Sheranni, and halted. What exactly occurred there was not explained in the first hasty despatches, but Mr. Gee, in a short preliminary report, stated that a cowardly and treacherous attack was made at 2 P.M., when the troops were at rest, and the little force was suddenly rushed by a large body of tribesmen. A desperate fight followed, the escort had to beat a retreat, and they were followed for four miles along the road to Datta Khel. Captain H. A. Cooper, 1st Sikhs, was in command at that post, and the first news he received was at 5 o'clock, when a sowar arrived, who stated that the troops had been attacked, their British Officers killed or wounded, and that their ammunition was running short. Captain Cooper ordered out two companies of infantry with a fresh supply of ammunition, and sent with them the only two British Officers who, with himself, had been left at Datta Khel. These reinforcements enabled the retirement to be completed, the tribesmen desisting from the pursuit and not venturing near the post.

Until more complete information arrived it was not possible to judge how it came about that an escort of such a size was surprised. The Political Officer's reference to the cowardly and treacherous manner in which the original attack was made, pointed to a species of tribal tactics not uncommon on the border, namely, the appearance of headmen professing friendliness, the gathering of tribesmen about the camp, and then the sudden rush of others lying hidden near at hand. Judging from the casualties, the British Officers seemed to have been the first to be attacked, for all six were killed or wounded. The losses among the native rank were distributed as follows :—1st Punjab Cavalry, 2 sowars wounded; No. 6 Bombay Mountain Battery, 2 killed, 3 wounded; 1st Sikhs, 12 killed, 13 wounded; 1st Punjab Infantry, 8 killed, 6 wounded. Two followers were also killed, and one other was wounded. The mountain battery had four mules killed and five wounded, but the guns were brought safely into Datta Khel. Nineteen commissariat mules were lost, while the cavalry detachment had three horses killed.

The tribesmen concerned in the affair belonged entirely to the Madda Khel sub-section of the Darwesh Khel Waziris. They hold the country at the western end of the Dawar Valley, through which the Tochi River runs. The Darwesh Khel Waziris had hitherto behaved extremely well, and as portions of the tribe dwelt in British territory, it was not expected that they would give trouble. During Sir William Lockhart's expedition against the Mahsud Waziris, they showed no disposition to join with their fellow-tribesmen. Conjecture was therefore rife as to why the men of the Madda Khel should so suddenly have committed themselves. Meanwhile it was clear that their punishment would have to be an exemplary one. True, the season was not very favourable for the movement of a large force, but it seemed quite possible to carry out punitive measures with a small column. For the moment it was decided to immediately reinforce the garrison of Tochi with one battalion of native infantry, and to move an additional regiment to Bannu. The following moves were therefore ordered :—33rd Punjab Infantry, from Bannu to Tochi Valley ; 3rd Sikhs, from Kohat and the 14th Sikhs from Ferozepore to Bannu ; 2nd Punjab Infantry, from Abbottabad to Kohat.

Within twenty-four hours of the receipt of the first intelligence the following further particulars arrived regarding the disaster :— Mr. Gee, the Political Officer, with his escort, arrived at Maizar, as already stated, on the morning of the 10th June, nothing having occurred on the road from Datta Khel to excite suspicion regarding the attitude of the tribesmen. He was met at Maizar by Sadda Khan, Malik of Sheranni, and other local headmen, whose bearing was quite friendly. The troops were halted near the village, and Mr. Gee, with only the cavalry detachment (12 sabres), proceeded to Datoi, a few miles away, accompanied by some of the maliks. The visit was an uneventful one, and the party returned to Maizar. Sadda Khan had meanwhile provided food for all the British Officers and also for the Mussalman sepoys in the escort. This was partaken of, and such a show of hospitality threw the party off their guard, as even among the Pathans the lives of guests are usually held sacred for the time being. At 2 o'clock, just as the Officers had finished their lunch, fire was opened upon them from the village towers, and all six were shot down, almost at once. At the same time a continuous fire from all sides was directed against the sepoys, some five hundred tribesmen joining in the attack. The position was apparently unsuitable for defence, and the troops began to retire over the hills in the direction of Sheranni. The number of their assailants rapidly increased, and it was calculated that a thousand men were engaged in the pursuit before the river bank was reached opposite Sheranni. It was clearly established that the tribesmen had planned the attack beforehand, as fresh parties appeared from the hills between Sheranni and Datta Khel. The troops did not reach the latter post until 11 o'clock at night. Their march was necessarily a slow one, as a running fight had to be maintained for four miles, and they were encumbered with their dead and wounded. Nine rifles only were lost, which spoke well for the sepoys. The Waziris were said to have lost ninety killed and a considerable number wounded. Among the former were four mullahs and a malik. It was satisfactory to learn that the wounded Officers and men were on the whole doing well. Lieutenant Higginson was severely wounded in the left arm; Lieutenant Seton-Browne had a flesh wound in the thigh; Surgeon-Captain Cassidy was hit in the knee.

Later information received at Army Head-Quarters from the Tochi fully confirmed the first estimate of the behaviour of the troops in the affair at Maizar. It appeared that Lieutenant-Colonel Bunny, though mortally wounded, almost immediately the tribesmen opened fire, managed to issue orders under which the retirement from the neighbourhood of the towers and walls of the village was effected. The men had to fall back two miles, as no defensive position offered, but thereafter they quite held their own against the attack. Shortness of ammunition alone compelled further retirement, but this was made without disorder. Not only so, but when reinforced by the two companies from Datta Khel, bringing up more ammunition, the troops faced about and shelled Sheranni village.

Thus, from a number of separate reports, a fairly complete idea of the circumstances of the disaster was now obtainable, but the following simple, straightforward account of the affair from one of the few survivors of the little party of Officers presented the events in a more connected form and in a clearer light:—

"The recent attack on the military escort which accompanied Mr. Gee, Political Officer, Tochi, to Sheranni and Maizar was the work of the Madda Khel section of the Utmanzai Darwesh Khels. The Madda Khels occupy the Tochi Valley from Sheranni, nine miles above Datta Khel, up to the Amir's boundary, and a portion of them who were not, as a tribe, concerned in the attack live in the Kazha, which is a northern tributary of the Tochi. Sheranni and Maizar are on the main Tochi route from Birmal or Ghazni to Bannu, and the tribe is under agreement to keep this road open. Maizar, which is the name given to a collection of villages at the mouth of the Shawal Algad, eleven miles from Datta Khel Camp, had already been fixed on as the site of the most westerly levy post in the Tochi, and it was mainly for the purpose of finally selecting the site for this post that the Political Officer proceeded there on this occasion. He had also arranged to meet all the Madda Khel Maliks of the Tochi there, to discuss the question of the distribution of a fine which was outstanding against the tribe.

"The escort consisted of 200 rifles 1st Sikhs, Lieutenant-Colonel Bunny in command, with Lieutenant Higginson, 100 rifles 1st Punjab

Infantry under Lieutenant Seton-Browne, four guns No. 6 Bombay Mountain Battery under Captain Browne, R.A., with Lieutenant Cruickshank, and 12 sabres 1st Punjab Cavalry, and Surgeon-Captain Cassidy, Medical Officer. The escort marched from camp Datta Khel at 5 A.M., and after halting twice on the road reached Maizar at 9-30. Maizar consists of a number of cultivated terraces gradually sloping down to the Shawal Algad, and the men were halted on the highest terrace at an open space under some trees not far from a *kot* belonging to the Drepilari section of the Madda Khels. This spot was pointed out by the maliks themselves as the best place to camp, as there was plenty of room, and water was available near. The guns were placed close to a garden wall in a field clear of the trees. The approach to this camping ground is over a small kotal and down a narrow lane through fields bounded by low stone walls. The lane runs straight from the kotal to the camping ground, which is close to a threshing-floor and then curves round to the north to the *kot*. The men were ordered to keep their arms with them and not to pile them. All necessary precautions were taken—guards, pickets and sentries placed were considered necessary. As soon as this was settled Mr. Gee and Captain Browne, R.A., taking the sowars, 1st Punjab Cavalry, and accompanied by some of the maliks, visited Datoi, which lies a few miles further on in the Tochi, while those left behind made themselves comfortable under the trees.

"The Political Officer returned about 12 o'clock; the question of the fine was said by the maliks to have been settled amicably; food was provided by the leading maliks for all the Mussalman sepoys, and there was not the slightest suspicion of unfriendliness on the part of the tribesmen. After lunch, about 2 P.M., Colonel Bunny ordered the pipers to play for the villagers to listen to, and they played one tune. Just as they began another, a man was seen waving a drawn sword on a tower in the Drepilari *kot*, and the villagers suddenly cleared off towards the village. A single shot was fired, apparently as a signal, and a fusillade at once commenced, directed at the British Officers, who were together under a tree, and the Sikhs. This was taken up on all sides, the sepoys in the meantime falling in at once and taking up positions. Lieutenant Seton-Browne was hit in the leg at the second or third shot, and Colonel Bunny was mortally wounded almost immediately after. The guns then opened fire and did great execution among a party of men who attempted to rush them, but as they were in an exposed position the two British Officers afforded an easy mark for the men in the *bagh*.

Captain Browne was hit at about the fifth shot and Lieutenant Cruickshank shot dead almost directly after. This was all within five minutes of the first shot, and as the enemy's fire did not slacken, and the guns had expended their ammunition, a movement was made back towards the kotal, the guns limbering up and going first up the lane.

"As the Infantry retired, the Waziris came out in great numbers from all sides, but a stand was made round the corner of the *bagh* to allow the wounded men to retire. In the meantime Lieutenant Higginson was shot through the arm and Surgeon-Captain Cassidy in the knee. The Waziris were, however, successfully held in check by a mixed party of 1st Sikhs and 1st Punjab Infantry, and the latter retired up the kotal when every one was over. Successive positions were taken up on the six ridges which stretch from Maizar to the plain above Sheranni, a distance of about two miles, and though the Waziris followed up in a most determined fashion and occupied all available positions on the hills round, the retirement was orderly and time was given for all the wounded to get safely out on to the plain. Lieutenant Higginson was shot in the arm a second time while crossing the hills. The force eventually took up a good position about a mile from the last ridge about 5-30 P.M., and waited there until reinforcements (two companies of the 1st Sikhs) with more ammunition under Lieutenant deBrett, R.A., arrived from Datta Khel. These reinforcements covered nine miles in $1\frac{1}{2}$ hours and arrived at 6-15 P.M.

"The tribesmen had been in the meanwhile kept thoroughly in check, and the guns were now got to work again, and the heights and the village of Sheranni were shelled. This put an end to the business and no further opposition was met with. The Khiddar Khels, who live on the Tochi below Sheranni, behaved well, bringing out water for the sepoys and supplying *charpoys* for the wounded. The rear-guard reached camp at 12-30 P.M. Colonel Bunny and Captain Browne died on the road. One Subadar (1st P. I.) and 22 men were killed and 25 wounded. Nearly all these were Sikhs and not Mussalmans. The enemy are reported to have lost 90 killed and many wounded.

"The causes of this treacherous attack are not at present clear, but all the circumstances point to its being premeditated. It is known that some of the maliks were implicated, and one or two of them were killed. Once the affair commenced it no doubt became a matter of 'ghaza' but it does not appear that the mullahs had previously worked up the tribesmen. The fact that they attacked a party who had just eaten food with them—contrary to all Pathan codes of honour—renders the matter additionally hard to explain."

To complete the story the following roughly written notes of the action at Maizar were received privately from Datta Khel:—

"The enemy held a nullah in front in great strength and had lined the village walls and a 10-foot high wall on the right, the latter with picked marksmen. They also held the rising ground and some huts on the left, and a tower in the rear. Our troops were rested on the ground between. The 1st Sikhs and the 1st P. I. and all the Officers were under the trees to the left front near the nullah, and 60 to 70 yards from the walls on the right. Pickets were out at the front and rear, and the guns were unlimbered at the right rear 10 yards from the 10-foot wall. The mules were unsaddled. At the set-off Captain Browne and Lieutenant Higginson were hit by the first volley and Colonel Bunny was struck shortly afterwards while talking to Mr. Gee. Captain Browne and Lieutenant Cruickshank doubled to the guns and Captain Browne was hit immediately by a marksman on the wall. The guns opened fire with case shot on the nullah. Lieutenant Cruickshank was hit by a marksman on the wall, but raised himself up on one knee and continued directing the fire on the nullah till hit a second time and killed. The guns fired reversed shrapnel when the case shot was exhausted, and were commencing common having exhausted shrapnel, when orders were received to retire. In limbering up a wheel a mule was shot, but Havildar Amardin ran back under fire and picked up both wheels, 72lbs. each, and started to rejoin the Battery. He was shot dead and the wheels were not recovered. Cruickshank's orderly picked up a gun weighing 200lbs. single-handed and carried it to the gun mule. The mule was shot dead, so he carried it to the relief mule. Then he went back and brought in Lieutenant Cruickshank's body. One N.-C. O. of the battery was hit by a ·450 express bullet. Surgeon-Captain Cassidy was hit by a man in the tower. The ammunition and hospital mules stampeded, so 4,000 rounds of M.-H. ammunition, the field hospital, and the Veterinary stores fell into the enemy's hands. The enemy also captured a helio which they now flash from the top of a hill. Subadar Narain Singh, 1st Sikhs, conducted the retirement till the arrival of Lieutenant deBrett who threw 28 shells into Sheranni. One shell struck a mosque, blowing up the mullah, who was waving a green flag, into the air. All the bodies were brought in by friendlies.

Sikhs and Pathans were alike mutilated. Mr. Gee rendered great assistance throughout and conveyed the order to the guns for the retirement, but escaped being hit. He has it that over 100 of the enemy were killed, and their wounded are reported to be dying daily."

All was now known that could be known of the main incidents of the outrage, but as the details emerged there was much to say of the gallantry shown by the troops. Colonel Bunny, though mortally wounded at the outset, directed the retirement. Captain Browne, R.A., though faint from loss of blood, owing to a severed artery, looked carefully after the withdrawal of his guns. Lieutenant Cruickshank, R.A., after being shot down, staggered to his feet and fought his guns until hit by a second bullet which killed him. As to the men with the section of the battery, they were Sikhs and Punjabis, and their conduct was beyond praise. There were only sixteen shells for each of the two guns, and these were quickly expended as the tribesmen were within a hundred yards. In order to prevent a rush while the mules were being got ready the native gunners fired powder charges. It has already been related how the gunners carried a gun and limber when the mules were wounded. Havildar-Major Mahomed Ismail and Havildar Nehal Singh particularly distinguished themselves. The native drivers vied with the gunners in their gallantry. They assisted in carrying off the wounded, and some of them even began coolly loading up spare mules with the over-coats of the detachment in spite of the heavy fire, but Captain Browne ordered them to lead the mules away as the risk of casualties was too great. One of the Salutris of the battery, named Kewal, did his best to dress Captain Browne's wound, regardless of the enemy's approach. As to the infantry, Subadar Narain Singh, 1st Sikhs, must come first on the list not merely for personal gallantry, but for the military qualities he displayed. No sooner had the attack begun than he recognized the immense importance of saving the reserve ammunition (ten boxes, each containing 600 rounds), as he knew the sepoys had only twenty-two rounds in their pouches. He told off seven men to fetch the boxes, and they succeeded in carrying six back to the firing line. These were opened and the packets at once distributed among the two companies of the regiment. Sepoy Shiv Singh made two journeys for this ammunition and was twice wounded. Narain Singh, as senior Native Officer, had the burden of carrying out the details of the retirement, under orders issued by Lieutenants Higginson and Seton-Browne who were both suffering severely from their wounds. He did his work admirably. Subadar Sundar Singh, 1st P. I., must be bracketed with Narain Singh. He, with his brother Sundar and Jamadar Sherzad, 1st Sikhs, formed up a party of sepoys to cover the retirement, and not a man budged until the order was given that they might fall back. The enemy closed with them, hand-to-hand fighting taking place, but the tribesmen could not force their way through this small body of determined men. It was here that the great majority of the casualties occurred. Sundar Singh was killed, sacrificing himself in order to give more time for the retirement to be effected. He was a young Officer, having entered the service in 1883. Jamadar Sherzad surely earned the Victoria Cross if such a decoration were given to the Native Army. He first of all carried Lieutenant Higginson away, then possessing himself of a rifle he covered by his fire a party of three men carrying Surgeon-Captain Cassidy to a place of comparative safety, and finally he shared in the desperate rear-guard fight. Subadar Nawab Khan, 1st Sikhs, was among the last to leave the ground. He was twice shot in the leg, but his wounds did not interfere with his cool discharge of duty on the way to Datta Khel. Coming now to the rank and file the gallantry shown was so universal that it is difficult to single men out. Chief among those who distinguished themselves were Lance-Naik Ishar Singh, 1st P. I., who killed several of the enemy with the bayonet, himself escaping untouched; Bugler Bala Singh, who first assisted in saving the reserve ammunition, then with a rifle taken from a dead man doing some fighting, and afterwards distributing packets of cartridges among the sepoys whose supply was running out; Sepoy Allayar Khan, 1st P. I., who carried Lieutenant Seton-Browne to the first defensive position taken up; Lance-Naik Assa Singh, 1st P. I., who assisted the same Officer when the enemy were pressing closely upon the troops during the retirement; and last, but not least, Sepoy Nurdah, 1st P. I., who drove off a party of tribesmen by shooting two of them at close quarters and then with a few comrades charging them with the bayonet. He was severely wounded in the affray.

CHAPTER II.

THE OFFICIAL ACCOUNT.

FINALLY there was the official version of the affair, contained in the report of Mr. Gee, the Political Officer in Tochi, which may be given in full:—

Maizar is the name given to a group of Madda Khel villages situated above the junction of the Shawal Algad and the Tochi, and not the name of one single village. It consists of a number of broad cultivated terraces sloping down to the stream, and is occupied by Drepilari, Khoji Khel, Ali Khan Khel and Macha sections of the Ger portion of the Madda Khel tribe. It lies two miles beyond the village of Sheranni, and is about eleven miles distant from Datta Khel Camp.

The main road to Birmal and Ghazni, which the tribe is under agreement to keep open, runs through it, and it forms part of that tract of the Upper Tochi in which a more extended influence was contemplated as compared with the hill tracts of Darwesh Khel country. As long ago as September 1896, I had visited Sheranni and Maizar with the view of examining possible sites for the Sheranni levy post, and you had concurred generally with me that the post should be somewhere between Sheranni and Maizar.

My chief object in making the present visit was to select a final site for this post, as the building season was already far advanced and the sanctioned plan and estimate were expected back from the Public Works Department, and, if possible, to establish a temporary post there for the Sheranni levies, who since our occupation of Datta Khel have been kept close to camp. I had asked Colonel Bunny to accompany me in order that he might give me his advice in the final selection of the site. In my letter, dated 15th June 1897, I have explained the circumstance connected with the realisation of the fine in Honda Ram's case, and my intention of discussing the details of distribution with all the maliks concerned on my visit to Maizar. This was an additional reason for going up the valley, though the fact that I asked the *jirgah* to meet me at Maizar was merely due to my intention to halt there as being the most convenient place.

Under ordinary circumstances, with the valley quite peaceful, as we believed it to be, an escort of sowars and maliks would have sufficed to visit Maizar, as the road lies through open country, and the kotal above Maizar is visible from Datta Khel Camp. I asked Colonel Bunny if he would mind taking out the same number of men as were employed on my recent visit to the Kazha. That visit had an excellent effect on the Kazhawals, and as I had not visited Maizar for some time, I was of opinion that the sight of a large escort would have a good effect there too, especially in view of the early commencement there of the levy post. Lieutenant-Colonel Bunny agreed to my proposal.

The following is the detail of the escort that accompanied me :—

200 rifles 1st Sikhs with Lieutenant-Colonel Bunny and Lieutenant Higginson.

100 rifles 1st Punjab Infantry under Lieutenant Seton-Browne.

2 guns, No. 6 Bombay Mountain Battery under Captain Browne, R.A., and Lieutenant Cruickshank, R.A.

12 sabres 1st (P. A. V. O.) Punjab Cavalry.

Surgeon-Captain Cassidy, 1st Sikhs.

The 9th was originally fixed for the visit, but owing to rain it was postponed till the 10th. Sadda Khan and Alambe had been sent on one day in advance to make what preparations were required and collect the local maliks for the purpose of discussing the distribution of the fine in Honda Ram's case.

A start was made from Datta Khel at 5 A.M. and Maizar was reached at 9-30. I was accompanied from Datta Khel by Khan Bahadur Ghulam Muhammad Khan, Assistant Political Officer, Maliks Nabbi Khan, Sabil and his son Dande and Khanadin of the Kazha ; Shadam Khan, brother of Malik Sadda Khan, Mozammil Khan, his nephew, at present officiating as Levy Jamadar, and Kotan Khan, Kabul Khel. At Ziarat village I was joined by the Khiddar Khel Maliks, Salehdin, Gul Samid, Syad Khan and Khan Wazir, and at Sheranni by the Madda Khel Maliks, Khan Habib and Zer Makhmad. Sadda Khan and Alambe were already at Maizar, and met me there.

Sadda Khan showed me the place where he wanted the troops to camp and where a number of *charpoys* had been placed in readiness. This was under some trees on the topmost terrace, close to a threshing floor and not far from the Drepilari *kot* of Modai, a small malik. I showed the place to Colonel Bunny and the troops were halted there.

I went on at once with most of the maliks who had come with me and the cavalry so as to inspect Datoi, and came back before it was very hot. Before going, however, I and the Assistant Political Officer saw some of the Maizar Maliks, and they were told with reference to the fine in Honda Ram's case that I would have them all up and discuss the matter on my return. Sadda Khan and Alambe stayed in camp by my order. Captain Browne, R.A., and Lieutenant Higginson accompanied me towards Datoi and we returned to camp at 11-30, when we all had breakfast. The people of the villages round at that time appeared perfectly friendly, and talked freely to the Pathan sepoys. Everything required in the way of grass and wood had been supplied; and about midday food which had been cooked in one of the Maizar *kots* was brought down for the sepoys, and a special point was made of the British Officers partaking of some of it. I then made enquiries as to whether the local *jirgah*, which had been sitting under some trees near for some time, were ready to come and see me, and I was told by the Assistant Political Officer that they had come to an amicable agreement by themselves and that all that was necessary was that they should come up later and make a formal statement before me. This was what Malik Sadda Khan had led Ghulam Muhammad Khan to believe; but if the evidence available is to be trusted, Sadda Khan's statement was a deliberate lie, for at that very time the Maizarwals had refused, as they had the day before, to be bound by Sadda Khan's proposals and must have been preparing for the outbreak. Had Sadda Khan given us the slightest information of this attitude on the part of the Maizarwals, which he, as well as the other Madda Khel Maliks, who had been there all day, must have been perfectly well aware of, there would have been plenty of time to prepare for an attack.

The attack actually did not take place till a little while after this, about 2 P.M., when we had just finished lunch. I was preparing to go round with Captain Browne and look at sites for the post. The pipes had begun to play at the request of the maliks, for the villagers to listen to, and the sepoys and ourselves were seated under the trees. The pipes played one tune and had just commenced a second, when suddenly all the villagers cleared off towards the Drepilari *kot*. It was seen that something was wrong and the order to fall in was given, but at the same moment a signal shot was fired which was followed by an irregular volley apparently aimed at the Officers under the tree. Lieutenant Seton-Browne was hit in the thigh at the second or third shot, and

Surgeon-Captain Cassidy carried him to a place of comparative safety by a small *bhusa* stack and tied up his wound. Colonel Bunny and myself had meanwhile gone towards the trees where the men were, but the Colonel was mortally wounded in the stomach just as he got there, and Lieutenant Higginson was shot in the left arm almost at the same minute. The firing had now become general from all the *kots* round.

The guns then opened fire with case and did great execution among a body of men who had come out of the Drepilari *kot* and attempted to charge them. As they were not protected by any cover, the two Royal Artillery Officers afforded an easy mark for the men who were shooting from towers around, and Captain Browne was hit in the arm at about the fifth round from the battery, and Lieutenant Cruickshank was shot very soon afterwards, first in the arm and then in the chest, the second wound being fatal. It is much to be regretted that no medical aid was available for Captain Browne. The bullet had severed the artery, and had a proper tourniquet been applied, his life would have been saved, but Surgeon-Captain Cassidy was shot in the knee while going towards the kotal and could give no assistance.

After about five minutes from the commencement of the attack, the guns having expended all their ammunition limbered up, and Colonel Bunny gave orders for a general retirement towards the kotal. This was effected along the lane which had low walls on either side of it. As far as the kotal we were exposed to fire on both sides, and practically all the casualties occurred before the kotal was reached.

A fine stand was made at the corner of the garden by the lane, with the result that the battery and the wounded men were all safely over the kotal before the position was evacuated. It was here that the greatest loss in men occurred, including Subadar Sundar Singh, 1st Punjab Infantry, and many individual acts of gallantry were performed which will be duly brought to the notice of Government by the Officer Commanding Tochi Valley. The retirement was then continued across the six ridges which extend from the kotal above Maizar to the sloping plain above Sheranni, which is a part of the Tsirai plain. A position was taken up on each ridge in succession, and the retirement was conducted in an orderly manner, time being given for all the wounded to get safely out on the plain, a distance of about two miles. Directly Maizar itself was evacuated, the tribesmen came on in large numbers, which were constantly being increased by reinforcements from every village round including Sheranni. They followed up the force closely and persistently and also occupied all the heights they could along the line of retirement. They were unable to do much damage owing to the steady behaviour of the rear-guard, and they must have lost a good many men themselves. Lieutenant Higginson had the misfortune to be shot again in the left arm while crossing the hills.

The force eventually took up a good position about a mile from the last ridge at 5-30 P.M., and waited there for reinforcements from Datta Khel, which arrived at 6-15 P.M., under Lieutenant deBrett, R.A. Some sowars of the 1st Punjab Cavalry had been despatched as soon as possible to fetch them and warn the camp. These reinforcements covered a distance of nine miles in one-and-half hours. They consisted of two companies of the 1st Sikhs and extra gun and rifle ammunition.

The tribesmen meanwhile, whose numbers had probably increased to well over 1,000, had been kept thoroughly in check, and as soon as the gun was got to work (the second gun had lost its wheels) the gathering began to disperse. The heights all round, which had been crowded with men, were shelled, and then Sheranni village, from which I had myself seen large parties issuing to intercept our retirement. This was continued until I received a message from Khan Bahadur Ghulam Muhammad Khan who had escaped *viâ* the Tochi with a few maliks, to the effect that he had arrived close to the village and was in danger of being hit.

No further opposition was met with. The Khiddar Khels of Ziarat village gave us great assistance in bringing out water for the men and *charpoys* for the wounded, and though a few of them undoubtedly joined the Madda Khels, the maliks, who had gone straight back from Maizar when the attack began, were entirely successful in preventing the tribe from joining.

Captain Browne, R.A., had by this time died from loss of blood, and Colonel Bunny did not live to reach camp. The rear-guard reached camp at 12-30 P.M. Khan Bahadur Ghulam Muhammad Khan also came in the same night.

It appears that when the outbreak occurred, Sadda Khan had just come over to him from the *jirgah* with Kotan Khan and stated that the fine had been arranged for and would be paid up in five days, and almost directly afterwards the firing began. Ghulam Muhammad Khan had just gone down to a lower terrace to perform his ablutions, and he was at once joined by Nabbi Khan, Khangai Macha, Ahmad Madda Khel, Wadin Saidgi and the Khiddar Khel levies and Border Police. His munshi and clerk were also with him. This party was afterwards joined at different times by Sadda Khan, Shadam Khan, Dande, his brother, Khan Habib, Zerin and Mozammil Khan and they went down the Shawal Algad to the Tochi and took refuge on the other side of the Tochi in Tarmori Kila, the inhabitants of which were just preparing to join the fight. From there Sadda Khan was despatched to Sheranni to keep the people quiet, and he returned after two hours, saying he had dispersed the lashkar and the road was clear. Nothing could have been further from the truth. In consequence of what he stated, Ghulam Muhammad Khan started down the Tochi, and, as already stated, arrived at Sheranni when it was being shelled. Mozammil Khan and Alam Shah, the Madda Khel Daffadar of Kazha, were the only Ger Madda Khels who came on with the Assistant Political Officer to camp.

The next day I called the Khiddar Khel Maliks in and asked them to arrange to bring in the dead, and this they eventually did with the assistance of Kotan Khan, Kabul Khel, and I think great credit is due to them for the performance of this service, especially as the bodies were much mutilated, Mussalmans and Sikhs alike.

The following is the list of casualties on our side :—
Three British Officers killed. Three British Officers wounded.
Native ranks killed—
One Subadar and seven men of the 1st Punjab Infantry.
Twelve men and a Kahar of 1st Sikhs.
One Havildar and one driver, No. 6 Bombay Mountain Battery.

It is a significant fact that of the above total 17 were Sikhs, though the force was composed of nearly an equal number of Sikhs and Mussalmans.

Wounded—
1st Punjab Infantry—Two men severely, two men slightly.
1st Punjab Cavalry—One man slightly.
1st Sikhs—Twelve men severely, one mule-driver dangerously, eight men slightly.

No. 6 Bombay Mountain Battery—Two men severely, one man slightly, one Kahar slightly.

The Waziri loss in killed has been put at 100 by the maliks, from whom enquiries have been made, and as it is probable that a good many have died since of their wounds probably a total of 100 is not very wide of the mark.

This is also the opinion of Native Officers who had the best means of judging. A large number (some 30 or 40) are said to have been killed outside the Drepilari kot by the case shot, and very nearly as many were killed at the corner of the garden where the stand was made. All along the line of retirement the tribesmen pressed close, and a number of them were shot down.

* * *

Here ends the Political Officer's report. The narrative of the Maizar outrage however cannot properly be closed without mention of the rewards granted to those who had taken part in the action connected with the outbreak.

The military reports received from Lieutenant-Colonel Gray regarding the Maizar affair were published as despatches. The Commander-in-Chief placed on record his appreciation of the heroic conduct of Officers and men, and declared that "the action was a deed of arms second to none in the annals of the British Army." The Government of India "most heartily endorsed this view."

The two surviving British Officers who were present at Maizar, Lieutenant A. J. M. Higginson, 1st Sikhs, and Lieutenant C. L. S. Seton-Browne, 1st Punjab Infantry, both of whom were severely wounded, were recommended for the Distinguished Service Order.*

With regard to Mr. Gee, Colonel Gray, in his report on the Maizar affair, thus referred to the Political Officer whose escort was attacked: "Though it is not my business to report on Civil Officers, it would be unjust to omit mentioning that Mr. Gee's exertions and presence of mind were of great value in the help he rendered during the retirement and in sending to call up the reinforcements."

On the recommendation of General Corrie Bird, supported by the Commander-in-Chief, the three principal Native Officers with the troops engaged in the Maizar affair were given the Order of Merit at once as a reward for their gallantry. Subadar Sundar Singh, 1st Punjab

---

* Lieutenant Higginson did not live to receive this award, and Surgeon-Captain Cassidy had already succumbed to his wound.

Infantry, who was killed, was also gazetted to the Order of Merit, so as to enable his widow to draw a larger pension. Subadar Narayan Singh, 1st Sikhs, whose coolness and gallantry were so noticeable, was admitted to the Order of British India, with the title of Bahadur ; 23 Non-Commissioned Officers and men were given the Order of Merit ; Jhanda Singh, cook of the 1st Sikhs, was also admitted to the Order of Merit, though a non-combatant, for having carried off a box of ammunition under heavy fire. The widows of eight men killed were admitted to a pension of the 3rd class of the Order of Merit. Later on there was published in the *Gazette of India* a full list of rewards for the Non-Commissioned Officers and men. This list will be found among the appendices.

There is only one more fact to chronicle. An impression gained ground, when the news of the outrage was first published, that the Madda Khel had singled out the Sikhs for attack and that the Mahomedan sepoys escaped lightly. This was altogether erroneous. No such distinction was made, and indeed in the mêlée it would have been impossible. It is sufficient to mention that of five sepoys killed in the splendid defence at the garden wall three were Mahomedans and that both Sikh and Mahomedan bodies were afterwards found mutilated in the horrible manner peculiar to the frontier tribes.

A special *Gazette* was subsequently issued, containing a despatch in which the gallantry of Lieutenant de Brett, R.A., on June 10th, near Sheranni, was warmly acknowledged. This Officer, it appeared, in his keenness to keep his battery in continuous play, rammed the charges home in a mountain gun with a sepoy's rifle without sponging out between the rounds—a most dangerous thing to do.

CHAPTER III.

THE PUNITIVE EXPEDITION.

As it appeared imperative to punish without delay the villages of Maizar and Sheranni, which were immediately concerned in the treacherous attack on the Political Officer's escort, the Government of India arranged within the next two or three weeks for a punitive column to move into the offending country from Datta Khel.

The expeditionary force consisted of two Brigades. Major-General G. Corrie Bird, then commanding the Punjab Frontier Force, was given the chief command, and the principal members of his staff were as follows :—Assistant Adjutant-General, Major J. Wilcocks, D.A.A.G. at Nagpore ; Assistant Quartermaster-General, Lieutenant-Colonel J. E. Nixon, 18th Bengal Lancers ; Ordnance Officer, Major C. H. Wilson, R.A.; Intelligence Officers, Major G. V. Kemball and Lieutenant G. K. Cockerill of the Intelligence Branch at Army Head-Quarters ; Superintendent, Army Signalling, Captain G. W. Rawlins, 12th B. C.; Field Engineer, Major I. Digby, Madras ; Assistant Field Engineers, Captain A. L. Schreiber and Lieutenant W. D. Waghorn ; Principal Commissariat Officer, Major G. Wingate, Peshawar ; Transport Officers, Veterinary-Major G. J. R. Rayment and Captain H. James, Mian Mir ; Provost Marshal, Captain P. Malcolm, 4th Gurkhas ; Principal Medical Officer, Surgeon-Colonel R. H. Carew.

The two Brigades were composed as follows :—

1st Brigade : Colonel C. C. Egerton, Corps of Guides, Commanding ; D. A. A.-G., Captain H. B. B. Watkis, then at Army Head-Quarters ; D. A. Q.-M.-G., Major F. Wintour, Allahabad ; Commissariat Officer, Lieutenant E. A. R. Howell, Sialkot. Troops :—The Peshawar Mountain Battery, the Argyll and Sutherland Highlanders, the 1st Sikhs, the 1st Punjab Infantry, and the 33rd Punjab Infantry.

2nd Brigade : Brigadier-General W. P. Symons, Sirhind District, Commanding ; D. A. A.-G., Captain J. MacN. Walter, Devonshire Regiment, then on the Staff at Lucknow ; D. A. Q.-M.-G., Major M. H. S. Grover, then D. A. Q.-M.-G., Punjab Command. Troops :—No. 6 (Bombay) Mountain Battery (4 guns), the 3rd Battalion Rifle Brigade, the 14th Sikhs, and the 25th Punjab Infantry. The two squadrons of the

1st Punjab Cavalry already in the Tochi Valley and No. 2 Company Bengal Sappers and Miners were also ordered to form part of the expeditionary force.

Fuller details of General Corrie Bird's staff and of the staffs of the two Brigades, as well as of the composition of the force, are added in an appendix.

Full political power was vested in Major-General G. Corrie Bird during the operations in the Tochi Valley. Mr. Gee was appointed Chief Political Officer attached to the General, while Mr. Lorimer and Mr. Kettlewell were Assistant Political Officers, each attached to a Brigade. A proclamation was at once issued notifying to the tribesmen in and about the Tochi Valley the reason for the expedition.

While the concentration of the Tochi Field Force was yet in progress, speculation was rife as to the nature and strength of the opposition which our troops would be likely to encounter at and beyond Datta Khel. News received from native sources mentioned that a gathering of tribesmen in strength was contemplated at Sheranni and Maizar. The Mahsud Waziris, who were then lying to the south, were said to be sending a contingent to join the Madda Khel, while another tribal force was reported to be moving from Birmal in Afghan territory. As against this, the Darwesh Khel in the Upper Tochi Valley were certainly not unanimous at that time in the matter of further hostilities: the Khiddar Khel sub-section had brought in the bodies of some sepoys killed in the retirement from Maizar, and their headmen were holding aloof from the Madda Khel. It seemed improbable also that the tribesmen of Birmal, who are subjects of the Amir of Kabul, would cross into British territory. It was quite likely, however, that restless spirits among the Mahsud Waziris would join their kinsmen in Tochi. Later news from the Waziristan direction stated that the Khiddar Khel and the Sadgis from Birmal were helping the Maizarwals to remove their goods into Afghan territory, thus giving the tribesmen a free hand for fighting. The latter, however, showed no desire meanwhile to assume the offensive against the Datta Khel post.

At this early period there appeared upon the scene a figure of some note—an old acquaintance, the Mullah Powindah—whose movements thenceforth became a matter of considerable interest to our Intelligence Department in Tochi. The tactics of the Mullah up to the time of the preliminary concentration of our troops at Bannu were however of a kind which showed that his influence over the Mahsud Waziris as a body was not as great as three years previously. He at first tried to induce the tribesmen to send a contingent to help the Madda Khel, but there was such a faint response to his appeal that he promptly changed his ground and wrote into our Political Officers in the Tochi offering to mediate between the Government and the people of Maizar and Sheranni. This step was, of course, taken by him in order to increase his prestige in Waziristan and the adjacent country: it was a clever move, but the Government could not recognise his position in any way. The Madda Khel are a section of the Darwesh Khel Waziris, and with the latter the Mullah had nothing whatever to do. He had, in fact, no status, and it would have been most unwise to have any dealings with him. As a possible enemy he had to be watched: as a friendly mediator he was put aside. Mediation moreover was not called for. The Madda Khel had deliberately planned the attack on Colonel Bunny's detachment and had carried it out in the most treacherous way. Their offence was clearly defined and their punishment would need to be exemplary. A tribal rising of the ordinary local kind, or a raid upon an outpost, is not of material consequence in the borderland. Such disturbances are more or less expected whenever our troops occupy positions beyond the old frontier line. But the Maizar affair was of an entirely different complexion, for it involved a breach of hospitality and could only have been successful by cunningly contrived treachery. The Mullah Powindah himself was said to have denounced its treacherous character, but probably if he did so at all he only did it when he found that the Mahsuds would not obey his summons to raise a force to help the Madda Khel.

From all that could be learnt it seemed that the great majority of the Darwesh Khel, many of whom held lands in British territory, were as little disposed as the Mahsuds to commit themselves to hostilities. Lest, however, in view of these facts and in the light of subsequent events it should be thought that the Field Force was too large for the work before it, it may be at once said that the Government of India were anxious not to set the whole frontier from Kurram to the Gumal in a blaze by sending up a small force which would invite attack, and it was expected that large military preparations would have the effect of checking the fanaticism of any clans who might be hesitating whether they should join the malcontents in the Upper Tochi Valley. It was known that the Madda Khel against whom the Tochi Valley Force were about to move, could muster only 1,200 fighting men, but it was impossible to say with certainty that no other section of the Darwesh and Mahsud Waziris would join them, and hence the necessity for being prepared for more than a mere promenade to Maizar, Sheranni and Datoi. The Dawaris also, who hold the greater part of the Tochi Valley, were known to be an ill-conditioned and fanatical lot, who might give trouble along the line of communications in case of any check to our troops beyond Datta Khel. The Kabul Khel of Birmal, who were said to have made common cause with the Madda Khel, are a section of a big clan of the Utmanzai, and they were in a position to fight with the comfortable assurance of being able to get away whenever they had had enough, for Birmal is in Afghan territory and is only a day's journey from Sheranni. It was therefore impossible to foresee that General Corrie Bird's force would find no enemy when the advance was made from Datta Khel. As had been proved at Wano, 5,000 or 6,000 tribesmen can assemble so quickly, and their movements are made so secretly, that their presence is first announced by a rush of swordsmen on our pickets. Waziri tactics are, as a rule, based on surprise, and valleys which may have been empty of men in the morning may swarm with thousands after nightfall. If opportunity offers for striking a sudden blow the tribesmen do not generally hesitate to deliver an attack. The affair at Wano itself was but a repetition of that at Palosin in 1860, when our losses were 63 killed and 166 wounded, in addition to 60 casualties among the levies. Any force which moved up the Tochi Valley had to be prepared for attack, not only from the south but from the north also, for there was no guarantee that the tribesmen from the Kurram border to the Gumal would not suddenly be infected with a spirit of hostility.

And now to follow the actual course of events. The concentration of the troops was carried out as rapidly as possible consistent with the collection of supplies and transport. Bannu being the base, Datta Khel was fixed upon as the advanced base from which the force would only have to advance about 13 miles to reach Maizar and Sheranni, and 6 miles further to reach Datoi (some tribesmen of which participated in the Maizar outrage). To ensure the safety of Bannu itself and to keep the peace on the border the following additional moves were ordered:—200 sabres of the 3rd Punjab Cavalry and the whole of the 3rd Sikhs from Kohat to Bannu; the 2nd Punjab Infantry from Abbottabad to Kohat, and 250 of the 4th Sikhs from Dera Ismail Khan to Jandoula, Sarwakai and Haidari Kach on the Mahsud frontier. As a special precaution against the effects of the heat the British soldiers in the Tochi Field Force were provided with sola topees in lieu of helmets and with sun glasses. It is probable that this thoughtful measure saved many casualties that would otherwise have occurred from sunstroke and fever.

The concentration at Bannu was of course uneventful, but the advance to Datta Khel *viâ* Saidgai, Idak and Boya was not made quite so serenely, as shots were repeatedly fired into camp, a sentry being killed in this way at Datta Khel.

The Engineers *en route* from Bannu had rendered valuable service in cutting a good road, partly through solid rock, all the way to Boya, and in constructing (in twelve days) a crib and trestle bridge, 600 feet wide, over the Tochi River at Boya. As a result the march to Datta Khel was accomplished with the minimum of difficulty, and the Field Force was then within striking distance of the doomed villages.

CHAPTER IV.

THE WORK OF DESTRUCTION.

WITHOUT a blow being struck or a shot being fired, Sheranni was occupied by General Egerton's Brigade of the Tochi Field Force on July 20th. General Bird and his Staff accompanied the Brigade. The rear-guard saw a body estimated at about 500 men some 2 miles from the road who disappeared into the further hills.

On arrival at Sheranni the cavalry reconnoitred the scene of the action at Maizar and found one man who was brought in prisoner. The carcases of five mules and two ponies were seen lying where they had been shot down, and about five yards from the wall of one of the *kothis* an ordnance pack saddle and one or two other articles of Government property were found and brought in.

Sheranni itself was quite deserted. Its wood wall was torn down to serve for firewood for the troops, as the hills in the vicinity were barren of vegetation. There was a certain quantity of *bhusa*, barley and clover about in the village, and the fields around were fairly advanced in cultivation. After the *bhusa* had been gathered and sufficient wood accumulated the destruction of the village was begun.

A few shots were fired into camp that night by a band of about 10 to 20 men, but no large body of the enemy was anywhere discernible. This absence of opposition was variously explained. The Madda Khel tribesmen in a body, with their families, were reported to have crossed the Afghan frontier into Birmal, leaving only scouts to watch the approach of General Corrie Bird's force. As Birmal is a tract which usually yields only sufficient supplies for its ordinary population, the position of the Madda Khel, if this report were true, threatened to become a very awkward one. In another direction it was reported that the Mullah Powindah had assembled 7,000 Mahsud Waziris near Razani in the adjoining Khaisora Valley to the south, and that his intention was to attack Boya or Datta Khel after the advance from the latter post to Sheranni had been made. As a precautionary measure two companies were ordered from Miran Shah to Boya. Boya is the post on the line most exposed to Waziri raids, as a fair road is said to exist to it from Khaisora, but it had been strongly entrenched by the Sappers and was believed to be impregnable against any tribal attack.

When all defensive arrangements had been completed news was received that the Mullah Powindah had abandoned his intention of attacking our troops in the Tochi Valley, and that his gathering of Mahsuds had dispersed. Every precaution, however, was still taken at Datta Khel, Boya, Idak, and Miran Shah to guard against possible surprises, while all convoys were strongly guarded. Reports from Wano showed that southern Waziristan was quiet, and no demonstration seemed likely to be made in that quarter; in fact the Mahsuds as a body had apparently shrunk from committing themselves to helping the Madda Khel. Later news made it almost certain that the Mullah Powindah had returned to his own village in Waziristan, and it was further ascertained that there was no large gathering of Mahsuds at Razmak. The Tochi Field Force had therefore little prospect of getting any fighting worthy of the name, unless some totally unexpected tribal combination occurred.

The night of the 25th of July witnessed the successful destruction of the towers and fortified houses of Sheranni. The next day parties from each corps went out to Maizar to destroy the fortified houses and towers of the villages. The defences of Drepilari *kot* were destroyed by the Highlanders and Sappers. The towers were blown up, and after the troops had left, smoke was seen rising from the direction of Drepilari, the result probably of some woodwork catching fire after the explosions necessary to demolish the towers. As a high wind was blowing, and the *kot* contained a large quantity of *bhusa*, most of it was probably burnt. The troops were again occupied on the 27th of July in destroying the *kots* in the Maizar settlement to the north of the village of Drepilari. The village itself, which caught fire, was already pretty well destroyed. On the 28th July the *kots* to the south of it were destroyed, as also were those in the village of Tormor, which lay some two miles up the stream of Sheranni on the left bank of the Tochi.

With the exception of intermittent and ineffectual sniping, varied by small seizures of straggling camels and donkeys, there was nothing all this time to suggest the presence of an enemy in the neighbourhood, and the position eventually became very tiresome. Finally, on the 5th of August, letters were sent to all the leaders of the Madda Khels, inviting them to come in under safe conduct and hear what the terms demanded by the Government were. It was, of course, well understood beforehand that nothing less than the surrender of the ring-leaders and the payment of heavy fines could well be exacted by General Bird. When first summoned the maliks hung back and apparently placed no reliance on the safe conduct promised them. General Bird, however, utilized the services of some of the headmen of the neighbouring tribes, and on the 16th of August three Madda Khel Maliks came in. The following afternoon General Bird held a Darbar at which some Kazha Khel and Tori Khel Maliks were also present. It was announced that Government demanded the return in good condition of the property which had been lost at Maizar, the surrender of some 18 headmen, the payment of a fine still outstanding for the murder of a Hindu writer there, and a further fine of Rs.10,000 for the outrage. Ten days was given them in which to take the terms to the tribe and discuss them and to give an answer. The Darbar did not last more than half-an-hour, and the people were told that no discussion was to be permitted; they had been sent for merely to receive the orders of Government.

On the 22nd of August the tribes were reported to be still discussing the terms imposed on them, and thereafter news from the Tochi Valley became very scant and infrequent. On the 2nd of September there was said to be a probability that the sons of the Madda Khel Maliks would come in that day and give their answer to the terms imposed by the Government, but the expectation was not realised. The same day a column, under the Hon'ble Montagu Curzon, consisting of the Rifle Brigade, the 1st Punjab Infantry, two guns, and a company of Sappers, marched to Landi Khel to make a road along the right bank of the Tochi River to Datoi, and was fired at on arrival and also at night when in camp. The next evening a belated reconnoitring party under Major R. M. Maxwell, while returning to Miran Shah from towards the Khaisora Valley, was also fired at in the dark by parties from both sides of the river near the village of Argun; but no mischief was done.

In this uneventful manner the Tochi Valley punitive operations, for want of an enemy to punish, came to be generally regarded as at an end. The aspect of affairs was not enlivened when, on the 14th of September, the Madda Khel definitely refused to accept the terms offered them, for as they still carefully avoided a collision with our troops by remaining in Afghan territory their contumacy only converted a position of perplexity into an absolute deadlock. It was perhaps rather sanguine to expect that at this stage any frontier tribe would agree to give up leaders whose execution was admittedly a foregone conclusion. Our troops meanwhile could do nothing. There was no enemy to fight and it did not seem in the least likely that there ever would be one. Nevertheless, the Government of India decided to leave the Tochi Force in occupation for a time with the general idea of their continuing to overawe the Waziris.

At the end of September the political situation was much the same. The Madda Khel showed no signs of submitting to our terms, and were still over the border. It was stated that the Amir had offered them land and water, but in Turkistan, and that they could not make up their mind whether or not to accept the offer. No doubt they hoped by staying out to wear down the patience of Government, and so be re-admitted to their own land on terms less severe than those already deliberately imposed on them for their conduct.

A month later—October the 29th to be exact—five headmen belonging to the villages of Tormor, situated about two miles above Sheranni, came in and surrendered themselves to General Bird. On the 31st of the month Khan Saheb and three other Sheranni Maliks came in, followed shortly afterwards by Sadda Khan and his brother Shadam, the headmen of the Madda Khel tribe. It was decided to try them by a tribunal to be specially assembled for that purpose. On the 14th November General Bird received the submission of the whole of the Madda Khel tribe unconditionally, and among those who surrendered were four more of the seventeen men who were demanded by name for their share in the affair at Maizar. A good many of the proscribed headmen, whose families took refuge in Afghan territory, were said to be experiencing a difficulty in getting away from their asylum and in removing their families. Five of the proscribed men for instance were ready to come in and surrender unconditionally on the 13th November, but during the night received news that their families had been detained beyond the border, and they naturally went off to obtain their release before surrendering to General Bird, which they had sworn on the Koran before their whole *jirgah* to do.

General Corrie Bird proceeded to Datta Khel on the 15th November, taking with him his prisoners and the *jirgah* of friendly tribes, for the purpose of finally deciding the question of assessment and distribution of fines among those concerned, and of obtaining proper security for payment. These points were duly settled, and it was understood that the tribe as a whole would be admitted back to its territory at once. The work assigned to the Tochi Field Force was accomplished, and the Tochi Valley no longer formed part of the "disturbed area."

It is but fair to add here that though the force only experienced desultory opposition on the part of the enemy, it had to fight against an unhealthy season in the hottest time of the year, and against difficulties which only those who are actually acquainted with the Tochi Valley can properly appreciate. Moreover, the expedition has been productive of at least one permanently useful result outside the scope of its strictly military purpose: a very large extent of country, the whole of it in fact that lies between the Tochi Valley and the Kurram River at Thal, has been accurately surveyed and mapped by Lieutenant Pirrie, the Survey Officer with the Tochi Force. The gazetteering and reconnaissance work was done by Major Kemball, who on one day reached the village of Biland Khel which is only some three miles from Thal.

* * *

In order to preserve the continuity of what is to some extent a separate narrative, we have carried events in the Tochi Valley uninterruptedly from the Maizar outrage in June to the submission of the castigated tribesmen in November; and have made no mention of the graver occurrences which were being enacted the greater part of this time in other territories on our North-West frontier. Thus, while General Corrie Bird's punitive force was engaged towards the end of July in destroying Sheranni and Maizar, the Malakand position was being fiercely assailed by thousands of Swatis; and to this stirring period the story now reverts.

PART II.

THE RISING IN THE SWAT VALLEY.

PART II.

THE RISING IN THE SWAT VALLEY.

CHAPTER I.

THE ATTACK ON THE MALAKAND.

An outbreak no less sudden than that in the Tochi Valley, and infinitely more serious in its extent and sustained ferocity, began at the Malakand on the 26th of July when our strategical position at the head of the Pass was attacked by about 2,000 tribesmen, mostly belonging to the Swat country. The assailants were for the moment driven back with great losses, but also not without a severe loss to the garrison, one British Officer being killed and four others wounded, in addition to several casualties in the native rank and file.

From all the information ultimately available it appeared that on the morning of the day in question, which was a Monday, news reached Malakand that a disturbance had taken place at Thana, a village a few miles to the north-east, opposite Chakdara (the outpost of our Malakand position) where the suspension bridge crosses the Swat River. It did not then seem that anything very serious had occurred, but later in the day further reports were received to the effect that the "Mad Fakir," a mullah who had gained much notoriety locally, had gathered some hundreds of tribesmen about him and was bent upon mischief. In the evening the levies employed on the road to Chakdara came flying into camp, their report being that the Swatis had risen *en masse*, and that the "Mad Fakir" was marching down the valley with the intention of attacking Malakand. Colonel Meiklejohn, Commanding the Malakand Brigade, decided, after consultation with Major Deane, the Political Officer, to send out a column at 3 A.M. in order to disperse the tribal gathering. But the mullah and his following anticipated this action by attacking the camp at half-past ten o'clock at night, a most unusual hour for Pathans, who usually wait until just before dawn.

At 9-45 P.M., while the troops were engaged preparing for the march at daybreak, a levy jamadar arrived with the news that the

"Mad Fakir" and his force had passed Khar* and were advancing up the Buddhist and graded roads, and that the hillsides east of the camp were covered with Pathans. The alarm was at once sounded, all the pickets were doubled, and the regiments fell in on their alarm posts. Lieutenant-Colonel McRae, who was commanding the 45th Sikhs, taking as many men as he could get together, at once doubled up to the point where the old Buddhist road reaches the top of the hill, and arrived at the narrow gorge through which the Buddhist road passes just in time to meet a mass of several hundred Pathans creeping silently up the road. In another few minutes they would have been in the camp. He gave them a very hot reception, holding this gorge for about 20 minutes, and finally falling back, as the enemy took possession of ground commanding the gorge, to a very strong position completely barring the road, which he held the whole remaining time. Colonel McRae's prompt action and the stubborn resistance which he, aided by Major Taylor and his small party, offered to vastly superior numbers, undoubtedly saved the camp from being rushed on that side. As Colonel McRae fell back to the more easily defensible position he was reinforced by Lieutenant Barff, and thenceforth that night they held in check immense odds, fighting unremittingly till daybreak. Major Taylor was wounded in the side by a bullet early in the fight, and was carried away to hospital, knowing that he could not recover.

In the centre and left of the camp, on the alarm sounding, Lieutenant Climo, with a company of the 24th Punjab Infantry, had manned the walls of the bazar commanding the approaches from the graded road and the gorge below it. Another company of 24th Punjab Infantry under Lieutenant Costello had manned the walls of the commissariat and hospital enclosures facing the gorge from the North Camp, and a third company of the same regiment supported the pickets on the left. The remainder of the regiment was held in reserve in their camp. No. 5 Company Sappers and Miners had fallen in at the walls and abattis surrounding their own camp.

It was a pitch dark night, and at about 10-15 the first shot was fired. The enemy made a vigorous rush at the Abbott Road picket and overpowered it. Dashing through the opening thus made they gained

---

* There are two places, quite distinct from each other, so named, and both obtain mention in different parts of the narrative. The Khar now referred to is situated on the road between Malakand and Chakdara. The other Khar lies on the northern confines of the Mohmand country.

the high ground behind the Sappers' lines and surrounded their camp and the commissariat godown. Colonel Meiklejohn, with his D.A.A.-G., went at once to the 24th Punjab Infantry camp and ordered Lieutenant-Colonel Lamb to bring up another company of this regiment to strengthen the Sappers, and proceeded with them to the Sappers and Miners' camp. Lieutenant Climo's company was now also ordered into this enclosure, as the enemy were getting round his left flank and in his position he partially masked the fire which Lieutenant Costello could bring to bear on them. In these positions the troops remained all night.

The enemy came on with great determination, charging the abattis defended by the Madras Sappers and Miners over and over again. The corps behaved splendidly, driving their assailants back and holding their own manfully under a hailstorm of bullets and rocks showered on them from the rising ground close in front of their abattis. Twice, however, the enemy got through, once taking possession of their quarter-guard, in which was all the ammunition of the corps and some spare rifles. In trying to check this charge Lieutenant Watling was wounded by a ghazi, who leapt the abattis, but whom he ran through as he got in. The man struck him across the shoulder and neck first, but apparently with the back of his sword, and then as he fell cut him again above the heel. Sergeant Byrne of this company was killed here. Colonel Meiklejohn was at this time watching the defence on the south and south-east faces of the enclosure, to which place Lieutenant Watling was carried, and where Major Herbert, who had also been shot, was being attended to by Surgeon-Captain Langston. Lieutenant-Colonel Lamb, commanding the 24th Punjab Infantry, was leaning over Major Herbert, asking him about his wound when he himself was struck by a bullet above the knee, shattering the bone. Colonel Meiklejohn, on hearing that the quarter-guard had been taken, at once decided that it must be retaken, and getting together 10 or 15 men with Captain Holland and Lieutenant Climo, led them on to the attempt. As they got near they made a dash, Colonel Meiklejohn leading. Almost immediately two Sappers were shot and fell at his feet, his orderly was cut down at his side and a Pathan struck him across the chest with the flat of his sword. This was really the gallant Colonel's second escape, for the bullet which had wounded Major Herbert had first passed through Colonel Meiklejohn's gaiter. Captain Holland was shot here, the bullet passing across his back, going under both shoulder blades, but missing his spine, leaving four holes. The reception that this party got caused a slight check, but Colonel Meiklejohn, who was now standing ahead alone, was immovable, shooting down his assailants with his revolver as they came for him. The check was only momentary, and the sepoys, cheered on by Lieutenant Climo, dashed up to him and into the guard, driving the enemy from the enclosure and saving the ammunition.

Some of the enemy had at the commencement got into the commissariat enclosure and into the room where Honorary-Lieutenant Manley, Commissariat Officer, and Sergeant Harrington were. Lieutenant Manley went for them with his revolver, shooting two, and was then killed. Sergeant Harrington had a wonderful escape: he had no weapons. the room was dark, and he stood with his back to the wall as still as he could. The ghazis walked round the room feeling the wall, but just missed him, and thinking the room was empty left. As they came in he had heard them say in Pushtoo: "There should be two here," showing that the men knew the place well and expected to find him there. The attack was carried on for the rest of the night with great vigour, and the enemy, having possession of commanding ground on two sides of this enclosure, brought a severe cross fire to bear on the defenders, and continually charged right up to the abattis. It was so dark that, although their yells and shrieks could be heard, they could not be seen till within five yards of the men's rifles. At 2-30 the sound of pipes and "tom-toms" coming up the graded road indicated reinforcements coming to the enemy, and Colonel Meiklejohn therefore ordered Lieutenant Rawlings, 4th Punjab Infantry, to go up to the fort and bring down 100 men to this enclosure. The enemy were pretty well all round the enclosure, and it was a risky thing to be asked to do, but Lieutenant Rawlings, accompanied by one orderly, did it gallantly and, shooting a ghazi who attacked him on the way with his revolver, returned safely with the reinforcements.

At 4-30 A.M. the enemy withdrew, taking most of their dead with them, but some 40 bodies were picked up in the camp, most of which were recognised as those of men who had been in the habit of bringing wood, grass, milk, eggs, etc., for sale into camp.

One very unfortunate incident of the fighting was that the enemy succeeded in looting 19 boxes of ammunition containing 10,400 rounds. After the Madras Sappers had been attacked, these boxes, belonging to their reserve supply, had been loaded upon mules ready to be taken up to the fort. The animals were standing in the lines when the tribesmen temporarily captured the quarter-guard, and in the confusion mules and ammunition disappeared.

A brave deed was performed by Lieutenant E. W. Costello. During the hottest part of the fight, while the football ground was overrun with the enemy's swordsmen and swept by a heavy fire from both the enemy and our own troops, Lieutenant Costello dashed out upon the ground from the hospital enclosure and, with the assistance of two sepoys, brought in a wounded Lance-Havildar who was lying 60 yards away in the open. For this he was, on the 9th November, awarded the Victoria Cross.

Our losses on this the first night were—British Officers :—*Killed :* Honorary-Lieutenant L. Manley, Commissariat Department ; *wounded dangerously :* Major W. W. Taylor, 45th Sikhs ; *wounded seriously :* Lieutenant-Colonel J. Lamb, Commandant, 24th Punjab Infantry ; Major Herbert, D.A. and Q.-M.-G. ; Captain H. F. Holland, 24th Punjab Infantry ; Lieutenant F. W. Watling, R.E., Madras Sappers and Miners. British N.-C. Officer :—*Killed :* Sergeant Byrne, Madras Sappers and Miners. Native ranks :—*Killed*, 21 ; *wounded*, 31. It may be added that two days later Major Taylor died of his wound, and on the 23rd of August Colonel Lamb also succumbed.

CHAPTER II.

THE SITUATION IN THE SWAT COUNTRY.

THE rising in the Malakand was totally unexpected. Since the time when the Chitral Campaign came to an end the Lower Swat Valley had been singularly peaceful, and the people seemed well content with the new order of things. Trade had expanded, the Chitral road had been kept open without any difficulty, and splendid crops were expected in the valley. Everything in fact seemed to make for peace. Suddenly the "Mad Fakir" appeared on the scene and quickly gathered about him a large fighting force, whose boldness in attacking a stronghold like Malakand showed with what desperate courage they were inspired. He chiefly had with him men from Upper Swat, Mian Guls as they are called, from their adherence to the principles inculcated by their great Akhund who died some years ago. These tribesmen are noted for their fanaticism, but another motive for their action was the resentment excited by the Khan of Dir's attempts to extend his authority over them. Once the "Mad Fakir" had succeeded in making a disturbance at Thana, he was joined by the Lower Swatis, carried away by the rising tide of enthusiasm, and as the news of the movement spread the lawless Utman Khels from the west and a section of the Bunerwals from the south-east also sent contingents.

The suddenness of the attack on the 26th July illustrates the marvellous rapidity with which the tribesmen on our borders can be mustered for warlike projects. The few hundreds who assembled in the first instance at Landaki had their numbers swollen by men from Thana, Aladand and Khar, as the "Mad Fakir" made his way down the valley; and by nightfall the gathering was so large that the mullah was able to attack the Malakand at once. But for the news brought by the levy jamadar the pickets might have been rushed before they had been doubled, and the regiments would not have had time to reach their posts. The tribesmen apparently waited until after sunset before beginning their stealthy movement along the hills, and this further accounts for their sudden and unexpected appearance. Their numbers on this first night were fortunately smaller than on subsequent nights; otherwise, with the troops broken up into two parties—in the North

Camp and on the Malakand Ridge—the losses of the garrison must have been very great.

Fanaticism did not entirely account for this determined rising in a country which had been singularly peaceful for two years. The "Mad Fakir" was, undoubtedly, a power in the country at that time, but his fiery preaching was not the sole incentive which made the villagers of Swat leave their rice-fields at a moment's notice, swarm about the Malakand, fighting with a heroic disregard for their lives, and when repulsed turning with savage fury (as will afterwards appear) upon the isolated garrison at Chakdara.

When the *purdah* was lifted from Swat in April 1895, the people of the valley fought one action on the Malakand and then quietly made their submission. At the close of the campaign they accepted willingly enough, as it appeared at the time, the new conditions which were established. They were formally brought within the sphere of British political influence, though permitted to manage their own tribal concerns ; their headmen were subsidised in return for the levies which they provided ; they benefited materially by the demand for supplies required by the troops left in occupation of the Malakand and Chakdara ; the trade of the valley developed rapidly, owing to the improved road to Bajoar and Chitral and the bridging of the Swat and Panjkora Rivers ; and, to add to all this, some of the material benefits of civilisation were placed within their reach. Major Deane, the Political Officer to whom their interests were entrusted, was acceptable to them, and they showed marked anxiety to refer their disputes to him for decision. No resentment was openly mainfested at the presence of our troops in the country ; the relations between the sepoys and villagers were of the most friendly kind ; and not a single disturbance occurred. The annual relief of the Chitral garrison was carried out in 1896 and again in 1897 without a shot being fired in Swat, and the Government of India might fairly have congratulated itself on the peaceful outlook beyond the Malakand.

We have spoken so far only of Lower Swat, through which the Chitral road runs. In Upper Swat the same contentment did not altogether prevail, though no danger was anticipated from that quarter. The reason for unrest in the upper country was the growing power of the Khan of Dir, the man whom Umra Khan had driven into exile among the Swatis, but who rose as the Chief of Jhandoul fell. Mahomed Sharif Khan, after the campaign of 1895, had all the prestige which attaches to a border chief directly supported by the British Government, and he began to extend his authority over that portion of Upper Swat which adjoins Dir. Further, the people in the Talash Valley beyond Chakdara were made to feel that he might possibly claim to exercise control over them. Exactly how far he pursued a forward policy is not for the present purpose worth inquiring into, but it is certain that the Upper Swatis grew alarmed at his pretensions. The Mian Guls, the four grandsons of the old Akhund, began to fear that such power as they had might disappear, and it was difficult to reassure them. A man calling himself Mohamed Ibrahim appeared in Simla at the beginning of July bringing a letter addressed to the Lieutenant-Governor of the Punjab from one of the grandsons of the late Akhund of Swat. It was an attempt to play a trick which is common enough in the East. Those who employed him had addressed Major Deane direct regarding their grievances and had simultaneously sent the emissary to make a separate representation at head-quarters. They hoped to obtain conflicting orders and thus to weaken the authority of the Political Officer on the spot. Their scheming was so transparent that it was seen through at once, and their emissary was referred back to Major Deane. This was the situation in the Swat country when the "Mad Fakir" appeared on the scene.

According to tribal reports this man is a native of Swat, who, in his earlier years, travelled to Central Asia and eventually settled in Mazar-i-Sharif, the Amir's chief cantonment in Afghan Turkistan. He lived there for ten years and then moved to Kabul. During the summer of 1897, he visited Bajour, the Utman Khel* country and Buner, preaching the necessity of waging war against all enemies of the Faith. He was in league with Hajab-ud-din, the notorious Mullah of Hadda, whose fanatical hostility to the British Government was already notorious and who was destined to play an active part in subsequent frontier troubles. When the "Mad Fakir" appeared in Upper Swat in July, the fame of his preaching spread far and wide. He gradually worked his way down the valley, with a huge rabble of men and boys at his heels, and on July 26th was at Landaki within hail of Chakdara. It was not

---

* This name is also borne by several unimportant subsections of other and quite distinct tribes. In this part of the book it refers only to the clan dwelling between Swat and Bajour.

till then that he took the final step which brought about the rising. He claimed to be inspired to work miracles; the Heavenly Host were, he said, on his side; and he announced that with or without help from his listeners he would sweep our troops from Chakdara and the Malakand in eight days. His excited appeals to the fanaticism dormant in every Pathan were responded to in a manner little short of marvellous: his progress from Landaki to Thana and thence to Aladand, both villages in view of the Chakdara post, must have been a triumphal one; the villagers flew to arms; our levies hastily retired, except such as joined his standard; all the headmen, with one solitary exception, were carried away by the popular enthusiasm, and by nightfall a resolute body of tribesmen were on the move to attack the Malakand, while another party turned their attention to Chakdara. The mullah had roused the whole valley, and his standard afterwards became the rallying point for thousands of fighting men from Upper Swat, Buner, the Utman Khel country, and even more distant parts.

CHAPTER III.

RENEWED ATTACKS ON THE MALAKAND.

Soon after daybreak on the 27th of July, in fact immediately the enemy had withdrawn after the repulse of their initial attack on the Malakand, Colonel Meiklejohn, in accordance with his original idea, sent out a column consisting of four guns of No. 8 (Bengal) Mountain Battery, one squadron of the 11th Bengal Lancers, and the 31st Punjab Infantry. These troops were ordered to pursue and break up any gathering in the Swat Valley and open up communication with Chakdara. They found themselves opposed to large bodies of tribesmen, but the cavalry pushed on towards Chakdara. The guns and infantry, however, had to return to Malakand. It then became clear that the rising was serious and Colonel Meiklejohn wired down south to Mardan ordering the Corps of Guides up with all possible speed. He withdrew the troops from the North Malakand Camp, concentrating his brigade in and about the entrenched position on the Kotal, where they could best be utilised in repelling any attack in strength. At the same time he telegraphed to the head-quarters of the Punjab Command at Murree asking that reinforcements might be sent. During this same day (July 27th) bodies of tribesmen appeared on the hills about the Malakand position, but did not venture upon any determined advance. They were fired upon when within range. The Guides arrived in the evening, though they had received the order to proceed to Malakand only at 9 P.M. the night before. They thus completed the march of 32 miles, with a long climb of seven miles at the end of it, in most oppressive heat, in something like 16 hours. It was a march to be proud of. They dropped a detachment of infantry at Dargai* at the foot of the hills so as to keep the road open.

The garrison in the Malakand at that time consisted of one squadron of the 11th Bengal Lancers, No. 8 Mountain Battery, No. 5 Company Madras Sappers, the 24th and 31st Punjab Infantry, and the 45th Sikhs, or something under 3,000 men. Of these, 25 cavalry and 200 infantry were ordinarily detached to hold the outpost at Chakdara and the

---

* This place will not be confused with the now famous heights of the same name on the Samana Range.

bridge-head on the Swat River. The Chakdara post was considered to be impregnable, and was armed with Maxim guns which could sweep the bridge. As ample supplies and reserve ammunition are always stored there, not the least fear was entertained regarding the safety of the post itself. In response to Colonel Meiklejohn's demand for reinforcements the following movements of troops were promptly ordered from Murree :—No. 7 British Mountain Battery from the Murree Gullies, the 35th Sikhs from Peshawar, the 18th Dogras from Nowshera, to Malakand ; three squadrons 11th Bengal Lancers from Nowshera, and the 22nd Punjab Infantry from Jhelum, to Mardan ; the 37th Dogras from Sialkote to Peshawar ; and one Native Infantry regiment from the Bengal Command to Nowshera, where there was only a small detachment of British troops, as the Argyll and Sutherland Highlanders were absent on service in the Tochi Valley.

When Colonel Meiklejohn evacuated the North Camp on Tuesday afternoon, July 27th, the tents in the camp had to be left standing, as no camel transport was available to move them and they were too heavy for the mules, being of the pattern known as "European private's." The enemy burnt them, and as the conflagration must have been visible for miles, the tribesmen from a distance flocked in to see how far successful the Swatis had been. The numbers of the enemy were thus greatly increased, and at 8-30 P.M. they again attacked Malakand on all sides.

The Malakand force had by this time been redistributed, the 24th Punjab Infantry with two guns holding a conical hill on the north side of the camp commanding the approaches from the North Camp direction, and the 31st Punjab Infantry with two guns and the main body of the Guides occupying the central enclosure ; two guns and 100 of the Guides were sent to strengthen the 45th Sikhs on the right, while a party of 50 men were sent from the Fort to Maxim Point to close that side of the camp and command the water-supply. The attack commenced at 8-30 P.M. and was carried on with the same determination as on the night before, but this time the enemy did not penetrate. They, however, succeeded in capturing the Serai, which was outside the line of defence, and in which 25 men of the 31st Punjab Infantry had been placed. The enemy attacked it with great vigour, and eventually mined it and set fire to the door. The picket held on manfully as long as they could, but ultimately had to let themselves down by the back wall and retire to the enclosure, in doing which they lost ten men. The 45th Sikhs and

24th Punjab Infantry were equally vigorously attacked, but they drove off the enemy with great loss. As day dawned the enemy began pressing the 24th Punjab Infantry, and Lieutenant Climo, who was in command of the regiment, decided to deliver a counter-attack. Accordingly with 100 men he advanced up the spur to the east to meet them and delivered a tremendous fire. The enemy drew off, but were pursued and driven from crest to crest in grand style, losing about 90 killed. Lieutenant Costello was wounded in this brilliant little counter-attack, and our losses altogether on the second night were :—Lieutenant Costello slightly wounded ; native ranks, 10 killed, 45 wounded.

All day during Wednesday, the 28th July, desultory fighting was going on in every direction round the camp, and large bodies of the enemy could be seen collecting from all directions and joining our foes on the hills. At 10 o'clock in the evening they attacked again from all sides, and with the same vigour as they had shown both nights before. The distribution of the troops remained the same as on the 27th. The attack commenced on the enclosure in which were the Sappers and Miners, the 31st Punjab Infantry and the Guides—and the brunt of the fight fell on this position all night, the enemy continually charging in the dark right up to the abattis and breast-works, but they did not penetrate. The 31st Punjab Infantry suffered heavily, the 45th Sikhs also had a very severe time, but they must have killed at least 200 of the enemy. The fighting was incessant all round the camp, and lasted till 3 A.M. It was impossible then to estimate the total losses of the enemy ; they were certainly very large, and in the early morning the tribesmen could be seen dragging away bodies over the hills. The troops, however, had been fighting now for about 60 hours without sleep, and were too exhausted for pursuit, with the risk that they might have to fight again the following night. Our casualties on this the third night were : British Officers—Lieutenant Ford, 31st Punjab Infantry, seriously wounded ; Lieutenant Swinley, 31st Punjab Infantry, slightly wounded ; Lieutenant Maclean, Guides, slightly wounded. Lieutenant Maclean had a narrow escape, the bullet going into his mouth and coming out of his cheek. Native ranks—2 killed, 16 wounded.

Signalling communication was re-established with Chakdara on the 29th, when it was ascertained that they also had been attacked twice by day and three times by night but were holding their own. Lieutenant Minchin, Political Officer at Chakdara, signalled that large bodies of men were streaming down the valley, the number being calculated at

5,000, and that another attack might be expected on the Malakand that night. The determination of the tribesmen in their repeated attacks at night showed how large was the gathering, for their losses had been so heavy that unless fresh men were constantly arriving the attacks could not have been renewed.

All day during Thursday, the 29th July, the troops at Malakand were employed strengthening the defences, clearing the field of fire of huts, trees, and anything that could give cover to the enemy, and in arranging bonfires to light up the approaches over which the enemy were bound to advance to reach the central enclosure. The force was augmented in the afternoon by one squadron 11th Bengal Lancers, under Major Beatson, who were taken into the Fort.

The same night the garrison was attacked by a very much larger force than had appeared on the three previous nights; the attack was delivered on both flanks and in a most determined manner. Apparently the enemy did not like the idea of crossing the belt of light given by the bonfires in front of the Sapper enclosure, and consequently this portion of the camp had a less severe night of it than before. The 24th Punjab Infantry on the left and the 45th Sikhs on the right had to bear the brunt of the fighting this time, and it seemed to be carried on with even greater ferocity than before. The guns of No. 8 Bengal Mountain Battery, commanded by Lieutenant Wynter, which had been working almost incessantly for 84 hours, played great havoc with the enemy and rendered valuable assistance to the defenders. The attack began at 9-30 and was pressed vigorously all night, culminating with a tremendous effort from 2 to 2-30, when it suddenly ceased, and the enemy drew off. The increased fury of the attack this night turned out to be due to the presence of the "Mad Fakir" himself. On the three previous nights he had sent his infatuated followers on to fight, saying that he would stay behind and pray. After three nights of defeat, and having suffered very heavy losses, the believers began to feel a little dissatisfied with the efficacy of their leader's prayers, and suggested that he should come himself and lead them and then perhaps the heavenly hosts which he professed to be able to call to his aid would come down and assist them. It was an argument that he dared not resist and so he came. His followers, firmly believing that the "infidels" were now to be delivered into their hands and that the heavens would be opened and crowds of armed spirits would descend and help them, dashed on to our ranks, led by the Fakir himself and his first lieutenant and faithful companion. The latter was killed and the Fakir himself wounded. This probably happened at 2-30, when the enemy withdrew, the Fakir himself flying back to Landaki. The accident to their leader considerably shook the belief of his followers in his divine power and his rapid retirement to Landaki was no doubt regarded by them as a proof that he had not a very strong belief in himself. At any rate, the fighting, though again resumed the next night, was no longer pushed with the same spirit as hitherto. Our casualties that night (July 29th) were : British Officer— Lieutenant Costello, seriously wounded. He had already been shot in the arm, but insisted on going on with his duty, and was again shot in the other arm, the bone being fractured. Native ranks—killed one, wounded 17.

A curious fact afterwards came to light which illustrates the kind of reverence felt by the tribesmen for their mullahs. The " Mad Fakir's " wound necessitated the amputation of two joints of one of his fingers, and these joints were buried with great ceremony, a standard being placed over them and a shrine erected. But the most amusing thing was that the Fakir gave out that anyone who had a wish or want had only to pay a visit to the shrine in order to get it fulfilled—and he was believed.

The four night attacks on Malakand had been made with the greatest determination, and the total losses resulting had been very heavy. They amounted to 36 killed and 106 wounded, including 15 followers killed and 11 wounded, mostly in the first attack. The casualties among the British Officers were the noticeable feature of the affair, two having been killed and nine wounded. The regiments being short of Officers, the control of the fire could not be so good as it would have been with a full complement, and the repeated and long night attacks caused an enormous expenditure of ammunition, but fortunately the supply was in excess of the regulation number of rounds, which would ordinarily have been 400 per rifle.

All was pretty quiet during Friday, the 30th July, but a very large organised gathering was seen to have joined the enemy, and it was evident that though the two leaders were *hors de combat* the tribes had no intention of giving up the fight yet, and the garrison prepared for another attack in the night. It began at 9-30, but was not delivered with the same energy as before. A heavy thunderstorm broke over the scene in the middle of the night, and the enemy, taking advantage of the greater darkness, the noise of the thunder and the rain, attempted to rush the 15th Sikhs. They were met, however, with the same perfectly cool and steady resistance which this gallant regiment had opposed to them night after night since the fight began, and were bayoneted in considerable numbers. The enemy withdrew at about 3 A.M.; our casualties being only 2 sepoys wounded.

The next day, Saturday, July 31st, the 35th Sikhs and 38th Dogras arrived in camp after a most trying march, the heat on the road being intense, and they were a most welcome reinforcement to the garrison. All was quiet during the day and nothing but sniping into camp occurred that night, so the troops had comparative rest.

On Sunday, the 1st of August, Colonel Meiklejohn decided to take with him 1,000 infantry, one squadron of cavalry and 2 guns, and also 50 Sappers and try to relieve Chakdara. At 11 A.M. the cavalry went down to the plain by the short road to the North Camp. This move was at once discovered by the enemy, who turned up in swarms from every direction. The cavalry, composed of the Guides Cavalry under Colonel Adams and one squadron 11th Bengal Lancers under Major Beatson, charged them in grand style, and got well into them once, but the difficult nature of the ground and the skill with which the enemy availed themselves of it prevented their going far, and they had to fall back, having accounted for nearly 100 of the enemy. They returned into camp under cover of the fire from the infantry and guns, their casualties being: British Officers:—Captain Baldwin, Guides, severely wounded, and Lieutenant Keyes, Guides, slightly wounded. Native ranks:—1 killed, 12 wounded. Colonel Adams had his horse shot under him. It was now so late in the day and the enemy were evidently in such numbers, that it was thought impossible to get to Chakdara that night, with the probability of having to fight three fights on the way, one in getting out of the kotal, another at Batkela and the third at Amandara Pass. The attempt was accordingly put off till the next day.

At Chakdara itself, the attacks upon the fort had been almost continuous, and it looked as if the assailants intended to wear out the garrison, and, if possible, cause them to exhaust their ammunition. Practically, it was impossible for the enemy to capture the fort until the troops holding it had no cartridges left, and even then storming parties might be beaten back with the bayonet, as the fort stands on a scarped, rocky eminence of great natural strength. A heliograph message had however been received at Malakand from Chakdara with the two words "Help us" and great anxiety was consequently felt for the little force. A heliograph had been sent in reply "Expect us to-morrow morning. Is the bridge standing?" But no reply to the question had come back. It was imperative therefore to relieve the post at all costs. How this relief was carried out at a critical moment will presently be related.

CHAPTER IV.

THE MALAKAND FIELD FORCE.

Owing to the serious aspect of affairs in the Swat Valley orders were issued from Army Head-Quarters for the troops at Malakand, together with those moving up, to be formed into a Division for field service, the command of which was given to Brigadier-General Sir Bindon Blood (then commanding the Bundelkhand District), with a complete staff. The 1st Brigade, under Colonel Meiklejohn, was to be composed of the Royal West Kent Regiment, the 24th Punjab Infantry, the 31st Punjab Infantry and the 45th Sikhs. The 2nd Brigade, under Colonel Jeffreys, then officiating in command of the Sirhind District, was to be composed of the Buffs, the 35th Sikhs, the 38th Dogras and the Guides Infantry. The Divisional corps were to be No. 1 and No. 7 British and No. 8 Bengal Mountain Batteries, No. 5 Company Madras, and No. 4 Company Bengal Sappers and Miners, the Guides Cavalry and one squadron of the 11th Bengal Lancers. Colonel Aitkin was given the command of the Royal Artillery. Lieutenant-Colonel Schalch, 11th Bengal Infantry, was made Base Commandant at Nowshera.

The following was the full staff of the new Malakand Field Force :—

Commanding, Brigadier-General Sir B. Blood ; Assistant Adjutant-General, Major H. H. Burney, Gordon Highlanders ; Assistant Quartermaster-General, Lieutenant-Colonel A. Masters, Central India Horse ; Deputy Assistant Quartermaster-General, Intelligence Department, Captain H. E. Stanton, R.A. ; Field Intelligence Officer, Captain H. F. Walters, 24th Bombay Infantry ; Signalling Officer, Captain E. W. M. Norie, Middlesex Regiment ; Principal Medical Officer, Surgeon-Colonel G. Thomson ; Commanding Royal Artillery, Colonel W. Aitkin ; Adjutant, Royal Artillery, Captain H. D. Grier ; Field Engineer, Major E. Blunt ; Assistant Field Engineers, Lieutenants C. M. F. Watkins and H. O. Lathbury ; Ordnance Officer, Captain W. W. Cookson, R.A. ; Chief Commissariat Officer, Major H. Wharry ; Assistant Commissariat Officer, Lieutenant A. S. Cobbe, 32nd Pioneers; Divisional Transport Officer, Captain C. G. B. Thackwell ; Assistant Transport Officer, Captain F. H. Hancock, 26th Punjab Infantry ; Veterinary

Officer, Captain H. T. W. Mann ; Provost Marshal, Captain C. G. F. Edwards, 5th Punjab Cavalry.

1st Brigade Staff :—Commanding, Colonel W. H. Meiklejohn ; Deputy Assistant Adjutant-General, Major E. A. P. Hobday, R.A. ; Deputy Assistant Quartermaster-General, Captain G. F. H. Dillon, 40th Pathans; Commissariat Officer, Captain C. H. Beville ; Brigade Transport Officer, Captain J. M. Camillery ; Regimental Transport Officer, Lieutenant R. Harman, 4th Sikhs ; Veterinary Officer, Captain W. R. Walker.

2nd Brigade Staff :—Commanding, Colonel P. D. Jeffreys ; Deputy Assistant Adjutant-General, Major E. O. F. Hamilton, Queen's Royal West Surrey Regiment ; Deputy Assistant Quartermaster-General, Major C. H. Powell, 1st Gurkhas ; Commissariat Officer, Captain G. A. Hawkins ; Brigade Transport Officer, Captain D. Baker, Bombay Grenadiers ; Regimental Transport Officer, Lieutenant G. C. Brooke, Border Regiment ; Veterinary Officer, Lieutenant T. W. Rudd.

Base and Line of Communication :—Base Commandant, Colonel V. A. Schalch, 11th Bengal Infantry ; Staff Officer at Base, Captain H. Scott, Royal Sussex Regiment ; Section Commandant, Captain O. B. S. F. Shore, 18th Bengal Lancers ; Commissariat Officer, Captain S. W. Lincoln ; Assistant Commissariat Officer, Lieutenant E. G. Vaughan ; Transport Officers, Lieutenants R. S. Weston, Manchester Regiment, and E. F. Macnaghten, 16th (Queen's) Lancers.

Brigadier-General Sir Bindon Blood was given the temporary rank of Major-General while commanding the Malakand Field Force, and Colonel W. H. Meiklejohn and Colonel P. D. Jeffreys were given the temporary rank of Brigadier-General while commanding the 1st and 2nd Brigades respectively under Sir Bindon Blood.

Orders were also issued for the immediate formation of a Reserve Brigade for the Malakand Field Force. This was composed as follows :—Commanding, Brigadier-General J. Wodehouse, R.A. Troops :— The Highland Light Infantry from Cawnpore, the Gordon Highlanders from Rawalpindi, the 2nd Battalion 1st Gurkhas from Dharmsala, the 10th Field Battery from Rawalpindi, and No. 3 Company Bombay Sappers from Kirkee.

The formation of this Reserve Brigade was due to further information received as to the attitude of the tribesmen in the Swat Valley. It was by this time clear that four sections of the Bunerwals were in the field, and though the Malakand position was no longer in danger there were ten or twelve thousand of the enemy on the hills to the north, the north-east and the south-west, as well as in the Swat Valley itself.

Sir Bindon Blood arrived at Malakand in advance of some of his troops on Sunday, August 1st (the day when Colonel Meiklejohn made his ineffectual attempt to relieve Chakdara), and at once assumed command. After inspecting the Malakand defences and the garrison, he reported to Army Head-Quarters that all the arrangements made by Colonel Meiklejohn were admirable in every way, and the position absolutely secure. He described the spirit of the troops as excellent, all showing eagerness to be led against the enemy. He warmly praised "their soldierly bearing and keenness after the almost continuous fighting of the week, with little rest at night and exposure to sun during the day." With such troops there could no longer be any lack of confidence in assuming the offensive and in relieving Chakdara, as the Malakand garrison now comprised more than four thousand infantry, five or six hundred cavalry, one company of Sappers and a mountain battery.

The heliograph, it will be remembered, had already told the Malakand garrison that help was urgently needed at Chakdara. On the evening of Monday, July 26th, almost simultaneously with the first assault on the Malakand, Chakdara had been invested by a large force of Pathans, who attacked from all sides. The garrison of four British Officers, two companies of the 45th Sikhs, and 25 sowars of the 11th Bengal Lancers, was augmented on the Tuesday, under circumstances already described, by two Officers and 40 sowars of the 11th Bengal Lancers from Malakand. Communications in the fort were commanded from nearly all sides by the enemy, who sniped from cover at from 100 to 200 yards distance. Frequent attacks were made on the Tuesday and Wednesday, the enemy bringing ladders and bundles of grass to get over the wire entanglement. All this time the garrison could get no rest, not being able to tell when or where the enemy's attack would next take place. On the Thursday night a desperate assault was made on the isolated signal tower, garrisoned by 16 men, but was repulsed with great loss. On the Friday, the strength of the enemy in men and Martini-Henry rifles was very much increased, and they so closely surrounded the fort that no one could leave cover. This critical condition of affairs continued till the Sunday night when the tribesmen made another fierce onslaught, which was still in progress the following morning when the relieving force from the Malakand dashed victoriously upon the scene.

CHAPTER V.

THE RELIEF OF CHAKDARA.

THE relief of Chakdara was carried out by Colonel Meiklejohn in brilliant style on Monday morning, August 2nd. In order to clear the way for the relieving column, it was necessary at the outset to disperse the enemy on the hills to the east and north-east, as they commanded the road leading into the Swat Valley. This task was assigned to Colonel Goldney, who took with him two mountain guns, the 35th Sikhs and the 38th Dogras, these two regiments being quite fresh, as they had had two days' rest after arrival at Malakand. At the very first streak of dawn Colonel Goldney silently advanced from the position his troops had held at night to within rushing distance of the enemy's position without firing a shot. He charged the position with the bayonet, taking the enemy completely by surprise. They fired a few wild shots and then fled in every direction, disappearing like rabbits among the huge rocks and boulders with which the whole side of the hill down to the foot of the graded road is covered. Their exact casualties were never ascertained, but seven dead bodies were found and one prisoner was taken. At the same time that Colonel Goldney started, Colonel Meiklejohn also moved off with his force, and he got three-fourths of the way down the graded road before a shot was fired at him. Those of the enemy, however, who had fled from Colonel Goldney's attack had carried the alarm down to the villages and encampments at the foot of the hill, and Colonel Meiklejohn soon saw swarms of men with many banners running out of the villages and down the hillsides to prepare to oppose him. They took up a position across the road; their right being strongly posted on a conical hill west of the graded road, their left resting on a high spur running from the main mountain and completely commanding the road. Colonel Meiklejohn immediately deployed to his left, sending a party to seize the levy post, which was about 600 yards in advance of the enemy's position. It was grand to see the way the troops advanced. They had longed for this opportunity, and they went at it with a determination that the enemy doubtless appreciated.

The fire was brisk on both sides, but there was no delaying our troops. They rushed the hill occupied by the enemy's right and drove them from it. The enemy fled up the hills to the east, and in the directions of Khar and Butkela, where they were met by a friendly stream drawn from Butkela by the noise of the firing. The fleeing and advancing portions of the enemy met where the road crosses the saddle of the Dogras Hill, and here they re-formed, taking up a position on Dogra Hill. Colonel Meiklejohn, without wasting a moment, advanced on this second position, covered by the fire of his guns, sending his cavalry round the north point of the hill, so as to be in a position to cut off the enemy from Khar and Butkela. The enemy, however, would not wait to be attacked. Many of them probably had a remembrance of the Guides' charge over the same plain in 1895, and they fled. They were too late, however, for in a few minutes the cavalry were on them, through them, and beyond them to the villages of Khar and Butkela, leaving our polo ground and the whole plain dotted over with what appeared to the garrison left behind in Malakand Fort only little black heaps, but were in reality Swatis, Bunerwals, and others who would fight no more. The cavalry scoured the whole plain, and only those escaped from them who took to the broad stretch of rice-fields on the banks of the river.

This sudden dart from the Malakand spread terror in the valley and people could be seen hurrying in every direction from the village to the river bank, carrying away what they could. Colonel Meiklejohn's force, however, had another and more pressing object in view than in cutting these men off, and so the cavalry resumed their direction straight for Chakdara, having first dismounted a third of a squadron, and given the gathering on the banks a few rousing volleys. Colonel Meiklejohn, having taken Dogras Hill, resumed his march, and disappeared from the view of those who had watched with admiration the brilliant and dashing manner in which the previous week's score was being wiped out.

Covered by the cavalry, Colonel Meiklejohn's force advanced on Butkela, which was occupied by the enemy. The cavalry got beyond the village without a shot being fired at them, and galloped on to the Amandara Pass, holding it with dismounted men, and then cut off the enemy's retreat. The infantry came up rapidly and attacked Butkela. The enemy made next to no resistance and fled across the rice-fields to the river, where the cavalry could not pursue them. As soon as the infantry came up to the Amandara Pass, the cavalry dashed on towards Chakdara, where, from the noise and smoke, it was evident that severe fighting was going on. The cavalry reached Chakdara at 9 A.M. The bridge was intact, but the enemy were occupying the Civil Hospital and the terraces of the hill on which the signalling tower is and also innumerable *sungars* all over the level ground and rice-fields round the north and east sides of the fort, from which they kept up a heavy fire. The cavalry at once crossed the bridge, part of the garrison moving out to cover their crossing, and on reaching the north bank they at once moved out against the enemy in the open, getting among those on the hard ground and attacking those in the *sungars* in the rice-fields with dismounted fire, while the fort supported them with fire from their 9-pounder guns and Maxims. They killed a great many of the enemy, who began to retire at once, some towards Uch, others up the valley to Upper Swat. In many of the *sungars* light scaling-ladders were found, with which the enemy had evidently intended to get over the walls of the fort.

The Chakdara garrison were in good spirits and holding their own magnificently. The party in the signalling tower were suffering most, not having had any water for two days. The only casualty that morning among Officers was Lieutenant Rattray, severely wounded in the neck, who was hit in coming out to cover the passage of the cavalry to cross the bridge. Other casualties among the garrison were very slight. The fort had proved itself practically impregnable and the garrison had behaved gallantly. They had been fighting with hardly any sleep for seven days.

Colonel Meiklejohn arrived with the infantry at 10, by which time the fighting had ceased. It may be added here that in addition to the troops already spoken of the Chakdara Relieving Column included No. 5 Queen's Own Sappers and Miners. The casualties in Colonel Meiklejohn's force in the morning's operations were :—Native ranks, 4 killed and 26 wounded. No British Officers were hit.

As for the enemy, their losses had all along been enormous. The following were sent in as reliable estimates for the week's fighting at Malakand and Chakdara :—At Malakand, 700 ; at the fighting with Colonel Meiklejohn's force on its way to Chakdara, over 500 ; at Chakdara, 2,000. The Maxims and 9-pounder guns at Chakdara did great execution. One discharge of grape from the 9-pounder smooth-bore is supposed to have accounted for 80 men. Another shot, which happened to land in the mosque at Chakdara while the enemy were at prayer, killed a considerable number. Several stories are told of the individual courage of the Pathans, and the following is an instance of their extraordinary vitality, as recorded by an eye-witness. One of the Bengal Lancers ran a Pathan through with his lance, and being unable to extract the lance left it and passed on. The Pathan pulled the lance out, threw it away, and attacked the next man who came up to him, wounding his horse with his sword. He then attacked an Officer of the 11th Bengal Lancers, who shot him through the head.

CHAPTER VI.

FURTHER EVENTS IN THE SWAT COUNTRY.

So completely was the aspect of affairs changed by the relief of Chakdara that the lately beleaguered troops had now actually to move out and search for the enemy, who had vanished as quickly as they had appeared. Sir Bindon Blood was determined not to give his demoralised foe any breathing time to rally, and to this end, after doubling the Chakdara garrison and replenishing its stores, he arranged, in concert with Major Deane, a plan of action under which flying columns were to be sent out to sweep the whole of the disturbed country and enforce submission. The full strength of the field force, on the completion of the concentration at Malakand, was: two regiments of cavalry, three mountain batteries, two companies of sappers, and ten regiments of infantry (not counting the garrison of Jellala); in all between 8,000 and 9,000 men. This was quite sufficient for immediate purposes, more especially as the Bunerwals, who lay on the flank of any force moving into Upper Swat by the river route, seemed inclined to disown the hostile action taken by the Salarzai* section of their tribe during the recent fighting. It was known that the Utman Khels, the Kanazai, the Lower Swatis and a certain number of Upper Swatis were implicated; not to mention the Dushi Khels, the Adinzai, the Showazai, the Shomizee, the Nekbe Khels and other sub-sections, whose names are only worth repeating by way of showing how general was the rising; but the whole strength of the enemy actually in the field at that time was not believed to be much more than twice as numerous as the full field force. Sir Bindon Blood accordingly issued the following orders on the 4th August regarding the disposition of the troops:—The 1st Brigade, consisting of the Royal West Kent Regiment, the 24th and 31st Punjab Infantry, the 45th Sikhs, with a proportion of sappers and artillery, to concentrate at Amandara; the 2nd Brigade, consisting of the Buffs, the Guides Infantry, the 35th Sikhs, the 38th Dogras, with the Divisional troops, to be placed on the Malakand and at Khar. These orders were quickly carried out and the two brigades then stood ready to move in any direction at the shortest notice, equipped with ten days' supplies.

---

* There is also a Salarzai section of the Bajouris.

The rising of the tribes about the Malakand did not seem to have infected those further to the north with any excitement or restlessness. Communication between Gilgit and Chitral was still open, and the last letters received from Chitral, dated the 17th July, spoke of nothing unusual, though this was of course long antecedent to the Swat outbreak. Again, Major Rundle, D.S.O., and Captain Walker, 4th Gurkhas, had just arrived in Gilgit, having come up by way of the Babusar Pass and Chilas with an escort of police levies of the Agency, and had found all quiet on the route; and the Chilas revenue had been duly paid in to Captain Godfrey, the Agent at Gilgit. Nor were there as yet (August 6th) any signs of further outbreaks elsewhere along the frontier. The Indus Kohistan, the Mohmand country, the Khyber, Kohat and Kurram all seemed to be undisturbed. With regard to Bajour satisfactory news was received from the Nawab of Dir that the Bajouris had remained quiet. The tribes on the border of Peshawar district—with the exception of the Utman Khel, who are always ready to turn out when a prospect of loot offers—had also remained quiet. The Mohmand headmen sent in word that their clans had not participated in the rising. The Buner frontier on the Hazara side continued undisturbed, while no signs of unrest were apparent on the Black Mountain border. The quickness with which Malakand was reinforced had doubtless exercised a strong effect upon all the tribes who might have been inclined to join the Swatis. It was the Lower Swatis, who had generally been despised as fighting men, who really formed the bulk of the recent attacking force. Thus the Khan of Aladand, whose conduct had been exemplary since the Chitral Campaign, and who had provided a portion of the levies, receiving a subsidy in return, was among the enemy killed in one of the attacks. Villagers who had been in the habit of furnishing supplies for the past two years, and who were perfectly well known to the garrison, shared in the *ghazu*, fighting well too.

The only disquieting frontier news was to the effect that a number of mullahs with a following of fanatical tribesmen had left Ningrahar, Tagao and other districts about Jellalabad to join either the Mullah of Hadda[*] or the "Mad Fakir."

Jirgahs now began to come in to Major Deane from the offending country beyond the Swat River, and these submissions were expedited when Sir Bindon Blood with the 1st Brigade under Brigadier-General

---

[*] *Vide* Part III, Chapter I.

Meiklejohn moved up the left bank of the Swat River into Upper Swat. The Lower Swatis generally submitted unconditionally and were allowed to return to their villages.

The strength of the 1st Brigade was increased for the purpose of the advance by one field and two mountain batteries, the Guides Cavalry and a detachment of the 11th Bengal Lancers, as well as by No. 5 Company Queen's Own Sappers and Miners; and as the tribesmen always dread both artillery and cavalry, especially the former, it was not expected that the progress of this formidable force would be seriously resisted. The Bunerwals who were on the right flank of the advancing force were not expected to make any demonstration; but to guard against possible trouble with them, the 1st Reserve Brigade at Mardan under Brigadier-General J. H. Wodehouse was raised to the full strength by the addition of the Highland Light Infantry and the 2nd Queen's Regiment from Rawalpindi. General Wodehouse then moved out in force to Rustam, 20 miles north-east of Mardan, to watch the southern border of the Buner country, having with him one squadron of the 10th Bengal Lancers, the Highland Light Infantry, and the 39th Garhwalis. The appearance of this force at Rustam was very timely as it reminded the Bunerwals that they could be attacked both in front and in rear. The Musa Khel, holding the country between Landaki and Barikot, had already submitted in haste before the 1st Brigade started marching.

While Sir Bindon Blood was preparing for his advance, orders were issued from Simla on the 13th August for the concentration at Rawalpindi of two additional Reserve Brigades to be known as the 2nd and 3rd Reserve Brigades of the Malakand Field Force. The new brigades were constituted as follows :—

2nd Reserve Brigade :—2nd Oxfordshire Light Infantry from Ferozepore ; 2nd Royal Irish Regiment from Jubbulpore and Saugor ; 1st Battalion 3rd Gurkha Rifles from Almora ; 12th Bengal Infantry from Bareilly ; No. 3 Mountain Battery from Jutogh ; 18th Bengal Lancers at Rawalpindi ; No. 4 Company Bombay Sappers from Kirkee.

3rd Reserve Brigade :—1st Northamptonshire Regiment from Secunderabad ; 1st Dorsetshire Regiment from Bangalore ; 9th Gurkha Rifles from Lansdowne ; 1st Battalion 2nd Gurkha Rifles from Dehra Dun ; 3rd Field Battery from Saugor ; 3rd Bengal Cavalry from Fyzabad ; No. 4 Company Madras Sappers from Bangalore.

CHAPTER VII.

THE ACTION AT LANDAKI.

MAJOR-GENERAL SIR BINDON BLOOD moved out from Thana on the left bank of the Swat River at 6-30 on Tuesday morning, August 17th. As already forewarned by a reconnoitring party, he found some three thousand tribesmen gathered near Landaki to oppose his advance up the valley, and to clear these away an action became necessary. The 10th Field Battery got to work without delay, its twelve-pounder guns making excellent practice, and the Royal West Kent Regiment attacked on the left, while Brigadier-General Meiklejohn, with two regiments and six companies of native infantry and a mountain battery, advanced on the right, to make a turning movement and so cut off the enemy's line of retreat to the hills on the right. The advancing force also included No. 5 Company Queen's Own Sappers and Miners. The tribesmen would not wait until this movement was developed, about two thousand retiring rapidly over the Morah Pass into Buner. These were apparently a contingent of the Salarzai Bunerwals. The remainder stood their ground for some time, but were driven from their position, and by 11 A.M. the action was over, the enemy being in full retreat.

The following are the details of the fighting:—

On the enemy being sighted at 8 o'clock the force moved steadily up to the foot of the long spur which runs down towards the Swat River from the range on the right, and the attack was commenced by the West Kents driving back skirmishers from the small spur in front, where they were presently reinforced by No. 7 Mountain Battery under Major Fegan, who kept up a galling fire on the main body of the enemy, assisted by No. 10 Field Battery from the plain below. The guns had come up to their position over ground which was very difficult for wheeled artillery. Meanwhile the main attack under Brigadier-General Meiklejohn was developed on the right. The 24th Punjab Infantry, supported by the 31st Punjab Infantry, with the 45th Sikhs in reserve, worked their way up the hill to within 500 yards of the crest line, where they opened a heavy fire on the position. By this time No. 8 Bombay Mountain Battery, commanded by Captain Birch, had joined the firing line and came into action at a range of about 500 yards. The resistance offered here was slight, and the troops soon won their way to the summit of the ridge. They now wheeled to the left, and swept the crest of the hill before them for a short distance, when they were joined by the West Kent Regiment. The battery (No. 8) opened fire on a small stone fort at a range of 600 yards and after shelling it for about ten minutes it was rushed by the West Kents. Resistance had practically ceased, and the enemy were seen streaming away across the plain below in the direction of Butkela and were harrassed by shrapnel from No. 8 at a longish range.

All this time the Guides had been anxiously awaiting their opportunity. A narrow causeway commanded by the enemy's fire prevented them from passing round the end of the ridge into the plain beyond, but when at last the Sappers had cleared the way both of the enemy and of the obstacles placed in the road, they at once advanced and were seen from above moving rapidly towards the village of Kotal. The retreating tribesmen had reached a point about a mile beyond this village and were already close under the hills. Passing the village the Guides broke into a gallop; but to those watching from the hills it became plain that the fugitives could reach shelter before it was possible for the cavalry to overtake them. The heavy rice-fields soon told on the troop horses, and a few, better mounted than the rest, singled themselves out from the advancing line of horsemen and bravely forged ahead many yards in front of their corps. Then occurred a most regrettable incident. The two leaders, Lieutenant Greaves and Captain Palmer, were met by a heavy volley—the former was shot dead and Captain Palmer's horse was killed and he himself shot through the right wrist. Colonel Adams and Lord Fincastle, who were close behind, at once dashed up to rescue their fallen comrades, who were now surrounded by a crowd of *ghazis*—both their horses were shot under them and they found themselves on foot under fire at a distance of about 20 yards. By this time Lieutenant MacLean with a few sowars had arrived on the scene and the little party dashed in most gallantly to the rescue of the Officers. Lieutenant Greaves' body was safely removed, but meanwhile Lieutenant MacLean was shot through both thighs and bled to death almost immediately. Colonel Adams and some of his men again charged into the hornets' nest at the risk of their lives and bore away his body. The cavalry now took up their position in a neighbouring clump of trees, which they defended until relieved by some infantry and No. 8 Mountain Battery. This closed the operations of the day, and the enemy retreated over the hills. Other casualties were Colonel Adams, Guides, slightly wounded ; three sepoys, 24th Punjab Infantry, wounded ; one sepoy, 31st Punjab Infantry, wounded ; one sepoy, 45th Sikhs, wounded ; two followers, wounded. As some of the Bunerwals who had been engaged in the fight were retreating into their own country over the Morah Pass, they were pursued and routed by Major Delamain with two squadrons of the 11th Bengal Lancers who had been left behind at Thana, and who now accounted for some 20 or 30 of these tribesmen.

As must almost necessarily happen after a desperate fight, some rather conflicting accounts were subsequently received as to the details of the Guides' charge. To publish all these would not perhaps make the story any clearer, but room may be found for an extract from a private letter of an Officer with the 1st Brigade, the publication of which set at rest the controversy as to the exact manner in which Lieutenants Greaves and MacLean met their deaths :—" When the 1st squadron of the Guides Cavalry debouched from the causeway, the enemy were already taking a position on a hill about 1½ miles away up the valley. Colonel Adams thereupon directed the squadron to move across the plain to a tope of trees, about 150 yards from the enemy's position. Captain Palmer meanwhile had got separated from his men, owing to the ground being intersected by *nullahs*, and Colonel Adams was unable to make him understand his intended movements. Shortly afterwards Captain Palmer, looking round and seeing Colonel Adams with the squadron following, thought he meant to charge the enemy's position. He therefore kept ahead, followed by Greaves who seemed to have a difficulty in holding his horse. Lord Fincastle meanwhile had been following the cavalry on one flank, but hearing Colonel Adams shouting to Palmer he closed up towards the former and rode towards the tope with him. On nearing the tope Palmer and Greaves made a dash for some standards at the foot of the hill which was now occupied by some four or five hundred *ghazis*. They were at once attacked, Greaves falling at the foot of the hill, and Palmer's horse being shot down. The latter, on being dismounted, at once engaged in a hand-to-hand conflict. Colonel Adams called out ' Follow me,' and he and Fincastle went straight for Greaves who was now surrounded by *ghazis*. Fincastle's horse was killed a few yards off, and he ran up on foot, Colonel Adams having already got up. The latter dismounted, but Fincastle shouted to him to get up again, which he did, while Fincastle tried to get Greaves, who was still alive, on to Adams' horse. The *ghazis* poured in a heavy fire, and Adams' horse was wounded, while Greaves was shot dead in Fincastle's arms as he was being lifted, and the latter's scabbard was smashed by a bullet. Two sowars meanwhile had ridden out to Palmer's assistance, who was severely wounded, and got him back to the tope. These two sowars then came on to help Adams and Fincastle—on whom the *ghazis* were closing—and one had his horse killed. Lieutenant MacLean came out a minute later, having dismounted the remainder of the squadron in the tope, whence they kept up a heavy fire on the enemy; he arrived just in time to check the enemy as they were preparing to rush these two Officers. MacLean brought three sowars out with him, two of whom had their horses shot under them. Meanwhile Adams and Fincastle had been carrying Greaves nearer the tope. MacLean was shot through both thighs as he was helping Fincastle to lift Greaves' body on to his horse. Adams and Fincastle then got back safely to the tope with the dismounted sowars who supported the bodies of MacLean and Greaves on MacLean's horse. This tope was held for about a quarter of an hour until the infantry arrived, the enemy's fire being exceedingly hot as our troops were practically attacked on three sides."

Lieutenant R. T. Greaves belonged to the Lancashire Fusiliers and, being on leave from his regiment, was acting as special correspondent of the *Times of India*. Lieutenant H. L. S. MacLean belonged to the Guides; he had been wounded in the previous fighting at Malakand but had rejoined his regiment. Lord Fincastle belonged to the 16th Lancers and was acting as the special correspondent of the *Times* with the Malakand Field Force: in recognition of his heroism General Blood at once attached him to the Guides Cavalry for duty.

On November 9th Lieutenant-Colonel R. B. Adams and Lord Fincastle were gazetted for the Victoria Cross.

CHAPTER VIII.

CONCLUDING OPERATIONS IN THE SWAT VALLEY.

The force continued its march into Upper Swat on the 18th August, leaving Landaki at sunrise. No opposition was encountered on the way, and the troops camped near the village of Ghalajai. Here Major Deane received a letter from the Mian Guls and other tribes in general terms of submission to the Government. This included all the tribes of Upper Swat. The "Mad Fakir" was said to have moved off in the direction of Buner. The next day, August 19th, the force moved up the valley to Mingaora, a large village on a tributary of the Swat River, and camped there for five days. The Swatis appeared to have completely settled down, and were sending in every day their submissions and their arms, some of them even assisting Major Deane in forwarding *daks* to and from Chakdara. Over 800 guns and rifles were collected, including some Government rifles stolen from the Malakand Fort. The Guides Cavalry made a number of peaceful reconnaissances, and survey parties did some work in perfect security. In short, the object of the advance up the Swat Valley seemed already to have been fully accomplished, and on the 25th August Brigadier-General Meiklejohn's Brigade started to retrace its steps.

We may pause here for a moment to describe in greater detail this march of the Field Force under General Sir Bindon Blood up the Swat Valley, as it had been one of great interest to all who had taken part in it. The greater part of the country travelled over was previously quite unknown to Europeans except from the reports of natives; and the map compiled from various sources by the Intelligence Branch, although in the main correct as to names and intermediate distances, proved to be considerably out as regards the general direction of the valley, which keeps a more easterly bearing than had been estimated.

From Chakdara the valley runs straight, general direction E.-N.-E., as far as Barikot, a distance of some 12 miles, whence it turns sharply almost due north for a short way, and then again resumes its easterly bearing, running about N.-E. for some 20 miles. Numerous side streams join the Swat River at various points, and the whole valley is of wonderful fertility—at that time of the year it was green with luxuriant crops of growing rice and Indian corn. Villages are thickly scattered along each side of the main stream, and around them are the invariable graveyards, shaded by groves of trees, which form such a characteristic feature in the scenery of this part of the world. Numerous remains of Buddhist "stupas," monasteries and other buildings are passed, which would afford an interesting field for investigation to the archæologist. Most of these remains are of great antiquity, as is proved by the writings of the Chinese traveller Hiuen-Tsiang, who ascended this valley some 1,400 years ago, and whose remarks upon prominent features and objects of religious interest were verified in numerous instances by Major Deane, Political Agent, who took a number of interesting impressions of Pali inscriptions, and also of the footprints of Buddha, which latter and their exact location are accurately described in the manuscript above referred to. Even at this early date Hieun-Tsiang speaks of the remains as "old and ruined."

As one advances up the valley the scenery becomes wilder and more mountainous. The hills, which rise to heights of 3,000 or 4,000 feet above the river bed, become more rugged and bolder in outline, while the snowy peaks of the Kohistan are seen towering in the far distance. These rise to altitudes of 16,000 or 17,000 feet and form a fine background to the vista of the river winding sluggishly along through its green level valley bounded on either side by bare rocky hills on which the pines begin to show themselves at elevations of 4,000 to 5,000 feet.

The furthest point reached by the cavalry reconnaissance on the 21st August from Mingaora (the present capital) was Gutibagh, about 12 miles higher up, where a halt was made on the summit of a small eminence opposite to the junction of the Arnawai River with the Swat. From here the view extended some 5 or 6 miles further, beyond which point the river appears to trend in a more northerly direction towards the Kohistan or hill-country proper—the valley itself still fertile and thickly populated. Between Mingaora and this point the village of Manglaor was passed : this was the former capital and is surrounded by numerous Buddhist remains. Here, and for a few miles higher up, the valley widens, instead of narrowing as was expected, and broad stretches of cultivation are found on both sides of the Swat.

The reconnaissance to the Karakar Pass on the 25th August lifted the "purdah" of another hitherto unexplored country. This pass leads from Barikot in the Swat Valley into the Salarzai portion of Buner, and is one which is much used for the export of grain from Upper Swat southwards to Rustam and other Indian marts. The pass is an easy one, some 4,500 feet in height above the sea level, and from its summit a fine view is obtained of this portion of Buner. The general character of the country appeared to be similar to Swat, that is to say, a mountainous country with wide, level river beds which are fertile and highly cultivated. Immediately below the pass is an open valley, now green with growing crops, drained by a stream which makes its way through a break in the hills into a larger valley beyond. Mountains rise in the background, beyond which lies the Indus, and on the nether side a river of considerable size (the Barundu) is seen winding its way south and east through a broad fertile valley.

Thus the expedition had served to reveal some 40 miles of new country of a highly interesting character. The Swat Valley is of great fertility throughout. The principal crops are Indian corn, wheat, barley and rice: fruit trees are scarce, although doubtless they would flourish if once planted and cared for. Vines, tomatoes and water-melons are grown and ripen well. The villages are of the usual Pathan type, flat-roofed, built of stone and rubble, the household utensils few and rude, with grain stored in bins made of earth and straw, or else buried in the ground. The old Buddhist road, flagged in places, is still the principal means of communication up and down the valley, and is good enough except at those places where spurs run down from the hills and dip steeply to the river. Here the roadway is generally very bad, being rough, stony and uneven, and it was such a place that delayed the Guides in their pursuit of the enemy after the action at Landaki.

As regards the Swatis themselves both Upper and Lower are of pronouncedly Semitic type with aquiline noses, thin lips, and sharp gleaming eyes. Most of the elder men are bearded, and many of the faces show signs of strong individuality and character. They are powerfully built, and wonderfully active on the hillside. As regards the women few or none (except old hags and quite young girls) were seen, as they had all been removed to safe retreats among the hills during Sir Bindon Blood's occupation of the valley.

On the 27th August the 2nd Brigade, under Brigadier-General Jeffreys, marched out to Thana, to relieve the returning 1st Brigade which was ordered to rest at Khar, Sir Bindon Blood and his staff and the Royal West Kent Regiment proceeding to Malakand. This move was thought at first to prelude an advance into Buner—a measure by no means uncalled for in view of the fact that the Salarzai section of the Bunerwals retained some twenty rifles and a large amount of Martini ammunition captured at the Malakand. But the idea, if it was ever entertained, was relinquished, greatly to the disappointment of the now idle Field Force ; and the following moves were ordered :—"The 2nd Brigade, with divisional troops, will march back past Khar to Golagram to await orders ; the 1st Brigade remaining at Khar. A small force of all arms will proceed to Uch to support the Khan of Dir in settling the right bank of the Swat. The 1st Reserve Brigade, henceforth styled the 3rd Brigade of the Malakand Field Force, will withdraw from Rustam and concentrate at Mardan.

Colonel Reid was given command of the force moving to Uch, which was composed of the 10th Field Battery, all the 11th Bengal Lancers available except one squadron, the 38th Dogras, and the 22nd Punjab Infantry. Uch is situated about six miles from Chakdara on the Dir Road. On the 29th August the troops composing the Uch force concentrated at Chakdara, and moved off to Uch the following day, when they were joined by Major Deane. The work of disarmament there was at once begun, and large quantities of firearms were readily brought in, showing that the spirit of the Swatis to the north was thoroughly broken. These were the clans which suffered such severe losses at Chakdara. The Khan of Dir was then at Uch, and he was well pleased to see the policy of disarmament being carried out so thoroughly.

The 2nd Brigade under Brigadier-General Jeffreys, which had been marched back to Golagram to await orders, was now directed to move out against the Utman Khels, starting on the 30th August ; and Captain Walters with one troop of the 11th Bengal Lancers was sent on in front, two days ahead of the brigade, to reconnoitre the passes. The Inzari Pass, 12 miles from Khar (which is not to be confused with the pass of the same name in the Mohmand country), was reached by General Jeffreys without opposition, but there the advance came to an abrupt end, the brigade being at once recalled to Khar

There were two reasons for this sudden cancellation of the movement against the Utman Khels. In the first place, the Mohmands on the Peshawar frontier had risen in force in front of Shabkadr (under circumstances which will presently be related) ; and the whole of Sir Bindon Blood's Division—that is to say, General Jeffreys' Brigade moving against the Utman Khels, General Meiklejohn's Brigade resting at Khar, and General Wodehouse's Brigade watching the Buner frontier at Rustam—was required to be available at Khar to co-operate at any moment with General Elles's Division at Peshawar, in case it should be decided to advance into the heart of the Mohmand country and deal a knock-out blow at the new rising. The second reason for recalling General Jeffreys' Brigade from the Utman Khel passes was connected with events transpiring or at least impending in the direction of Uch. The Hadda Mullah, of whom much will have to be told in subsequent pages, and whose Mohmand army just alluded to had already been severely chastised by General Elles's troops, was apparently bent on retrieving his fortunes in a new direction ; in other words, he was reported to be preparing an attack upon the Khan of Dir. News was brought in that the mullah had succeeded in collecting a large force of Western Mohmands for this purpose, and that he was trying to persuade the Utman Khels and Bajouris to join him. It was therefore considered advisable to keep General Jeffreys' Brigade in hand at Khar, instead of losing it for a time in trivial operations against a comparatively small clan like the Utman Khels, so that in the event of the Khan of Dir being seriously threatened the brigade could be promptly despatched to join Colonel Reid's Column at Uch. From Uch to Sado on the Panjkora River is one march only, and a force placed there could check any hostile movement against Dir.

It has been mentioned that the 3rd Brigade under Brigadier-General Wodehouse was withdrawn from the Buner frontier to Mardan in order to be at hand for possible employment with General Elles's Division against the Mohmands. The move was no sooner carried out than the brigade was further ordered to Uch (instead of General Jeffreys' Brigade) to join Colonel Reid's force. The march was quickly accomplished, and on assuming command of the united forces at Uch, General Wodehouse at once sent out a small force to take possession of the Panjkora bridge from the Dir levies which was effected without opposition, though only just in time to forestall the Mohmands.

On the 5th September orders were issued for the 2nd and 3rd Brigades of Sir Bindon Blood's Field Force to move to Nawagai on the northern confines of the Mohmand country and then turn southwards right through the heart of the Mohmand country according to circumstances, with the view to eventually effecting a junction with the force under General Elles which would advance from Shabkadr on the southern side of the Mohmand country to meet Sir Bindon Blood.

* * *

And now it will be convenient to leave the Malakand Field Force temporarily and to turn to those events at Shabkadr which added the Mohmand country to the "disturbed area" on our frontier.

PART III.
THE MOHMAND RISING.

PART III.

THE MOHMAND RISING.

CHAPTER I.

THE RAID ON SHABKADR FORT.

WHILE in the early part of August Sir Bindon Blood was preparing for the advance up the Swat Valley which led to the fight at Landaki and to the subsequent subjugation of the Swat tribes, another grave outbreak of tribal fanaticism was disturbing that portion of our border which faces the Mohmand territory.

The facts are briefly these. About four o'clock in the afternoon of Saturday, August 7th, some four or five thousand Mohmands made a sudden incursion into British territory near Shabkadr Fort, 18 miles north of Peshawar. They moved upon the Hindu village of Shankargarh, which is the bazar of Shabkadr, and burnt it, killing two men who had remained there. The rest of the villagers, having been warned of the approach of the raiders, had already sought refuge in the Fort, held by a detachment of the Border Police. Shabkadr itself was not very fiercely assailed, but some sort of an assault upon it did take place, and the Border Police fired on the raiders, killing and wounding a number of them.

On the news of this outbreak reaching Peshawar, the same evening, Brigadier-General E. R. Elles, commanding the Peshawar District, took out a reinforcing column consisting of four guns of the 51st Field Battery, two squadrons of the 13th Bengal Lancers, four companies of the Somersetshire Light Infantry, and the whole of the 20th Punjab Infantry. The cavalry went on ahead, and arrived at Shabkadr at 6 A.M. The guns and infantry were a good deal delayed in crossing the Kabul River, having to be ferried over. By this time the raiders had disappeared and were reported to have hurriedly retired across the border on the approach of the reinforcing troops.

Shabkadr Fort was built by the Sikhs. It stands on a mound and has walls fifty feet high, so is practically impregnable to any force without artillery. Shankargarh was an old Sikh Cantonment bazar, inhabited chiefly by rich Hindu money-lenders, who had very profitable dealings with the tribesmen on both sides of the border, which is only three miles distant. At the time of the raid Shabkadr was held by forty or fifty Border Police, and the attack lasted from about 4 P.M. to 5 A.M., the little garrison accounting for some forty of the tribesmen without loss to themselves.

This raid, it may be said at once, though the fact was not learnt till afterwards, was the direct work of the notorious Mullah of Hadda, Najib-ud-din, who has already been alluded to in these pages, and who was at that time a great power among the more fanatical tribesmen in the Mohmand country, as well as in Bajour and the Utman Khel districts. It was this mullah who tried so hard to create trouble for us during the Chitral Campaign, and it was he again beyond all doubt whose plotting had indirectly hepled to bring about the recent rising in the Swat Valley. He lived at the supposed village of Jarobi* at the head of the Bohai Valley, in that part of the Mohmand country which is under the Amir of Kabul, and was known to have intimate relations with the Sipah Salar, General Ghulam Hyder Khan† Karki (commanding the troops in Eastern Afghanistan, with head-quarters at Jellalabad). While the recent attack on the Malakand was proceeding the Hadda Mullah had collected a body of men and sent them to help the Swatis. A few days before the present raid on Shabkadr the mullah had succeeded in stirring up the fanaticism of the Northern and Western Mohmands, and had gathered a considerable body of men about him. This force advanced down the Bohai Valley, crossed the Nahaki Pass, and then entered the Gandab Valley, and so into British territory at Shabkadr. The raid was doubtless designed to effect a diversion in favour of the Swatis, still suffering from their failure to capture the Malakand or Chakdara. If the Hadda Mullah had timed his effort so that Shabkadr should be attacked on the same day as the Malakand, he would have done a clever stroke of business, and widespread uneasiness would have been caused all along our Peshawar frontier. As it was, our troops (as already shown) had swept the Lower Swat clear of tribesmen, and two full brigades in the Malakand were now ready to

---

* The mystery enveloping this place was dispelled a couple of months later when General Elles lifted the *purdah* of the Bohai Valley (*Vide* Chapter VI).

† Since dead.

operate in any direction, while a reserve brigade had been formed at Mardan which could move at a few hours' notice into the Peshawar Valley.

As for the Mohmand tribes, a few words will suffice to tell all that needs to be stated here about them. They hold the country bounded on the south by the Kabul River from Jellalabad to its entrance into British territory, and on the north by Bajour. They extend westwards to the hill country above the Kunar River, and in the east they touch the Peshawar border and the Utman Khel country lying about the junction of the Swat and Panjkora Rivers. Under the Durand Treaty they came partly under the political influence of the Indian Government and partly under that of the Amir of Kabul. The actual demarcation of the zones of influence has never been carried out, the attempt to form a Boundary Commission having come to nought a few months previously. The following is an official description of the Mohmand territory: "The country of the Mohmands is divided naturally into two parts, the rich alluvial lands along the bank of the Kabul River from Jellalabad to Lalpura, and the country to the east of Lalpura, consisting of a network of hills and valleys. The principal of the latter are the valleys of Shilman, Gandab and Pandiali. They are, as a rule, dry and arid water-courses, raging torrents in heavy rain, but usually presenting a stony and shingly bed, from which slopes of barren ground lead to the rocky spurs and ranges that flank them." As the Durand boundary runs from Landi Kotal eastwards of Lalpura and then along the watershed separating the basins of the Kunar and Panjkora Rivers, the most considerable portions of the country are within the British zone. The fighting strength of the whole tribe is put at between 17,000 and 18,000, the Baizai accounting for one-half of the total. These hold the eastern part of the country adjacent to Bajour and the Utman Khel border. The Mohmands had never been accounted an enemy of much importance in previous conflicts with our troops. In 1880 they made but a poor resistance, when some 5,000 of them, who had crossed the Kabul River near Dakka, were attacked by a column 850 strong under Colonel Boisragon. On an earlier occasion, in 1879, a small detachment of 170 men of the Merwara Battalion, under Captain O'Moore Creagh, successfully held a position near Kane Dakka against several thousand Mohmands who attacked for six hours. As a tribe, the Mohmands are split up into six clans: the Baizai, already mentioned, good fighting men; the Tarakzai, (including the Is Khel and Barhan Khel), 2,800; the Halimzai, 2,600; the Khwaizai, 1,800; the Dawezai,

800 ; and the Utmanzai, 400. There is a comparatively easy route into their country from Matta, a few miles north of Shabkadr, over the Inzari Pass.* This is known as the Alikandi route, and it might have been used by the Chitral Relief Force in 1895 in preference to that over the Malakand, but it was thought desirable not to enter the Mohmand country at that time.

---

* Another pass bearing this name, situate in the Afridi country, comes into the narrative later.

CHAPTER II.

PROMPT REPRISALS.

THE report regarding the retirement of the Mohmand raiders after the arrival at Shabkadr of strong reinforcements from Peshawar was true only in part. They withdrew to the low hills which run from the main ranges to within a mile of the Fort, which is three miles from the border line. Here they remained out of gunshot range. Their numbers increased on Sunday night, August 8th, the presence of the Hadda Mullah serving to attract contingents from all the Mohmand clans, with the exception of the Tarakzai.

On Monday morning, August 9th, at daybreak, Lieutenant-Colonel Woon, 20th Punjab Infantry, who had been left in command at Shabkadr by Brigadier-General Elles, moved out his troops to the attack. He had at his disposal four guns of the 51st Field Battery, two squadrons of the 13th Bengal Lancers, two companies of the Somersetshire Light Infantry, and the whole of the 20th Punjab Infantry 600 strong, or a total of between 1,100 and 1,200 men. The enemy's line was about two miles in length, some 6,000 men, at least, being assembled. Their right rested on the high hills, their centre extended across the low hills, while their left stretched into the cultivated ground in the plain itself. Colonel Woon began his attack with the infantry, shortly after 6 o'clock, but could make no impression on the position, and his small force was outflanked by the Mohmands, who streamed out into the plain on either hand. To guard against the infantry being completely enveloped, Colonel Woon began to withdraw towards the Fort.

At this period of the action Brigadier-General Elles arrived on the scene and took command. He had had to return to Peshawar on the previous day to arrange the disposition of the garrison there (weakened by the sudden call upon it) and to report by telegraph to Army Head-Quarters the state of affairs on the border. He left Peshawar again early that morning, taking with him two companies of the 30th Punjab Infantry. On arrival at the ferry over the Kabul River, he heard the sound of heavy firing at Shabkadr and at once pushed on, leaving the infantry to follow.

General Elles reached the scene of action at 8-40 A.M., by which time most of the enemy had swarmed down from the low hills and were engaged with our infantry in the open, and he at once saw the favourable opportunity offered for using his cavalry. He first concentrated the fire of the four guns upon the enemy's left, and then directed the two squadrons of the 13th Bengal Lancers to charge from right to left along the whole line of tribesmen. This charge was brilliantly carried out under the leadership of Major Atkinson, commanding. The two squadrons of Lancers swept right along from end to end of the line, rallying and re-forming on the left of the infantry. Their losses were few, but Major Atkinson and Lieutenant Cheyne had their horses shot. By this time the two companies of the 30th Punjab Infantry had come up, and an infantry attack was ordered against the enemy before they could recover from the effects of the cavalry charge. The Mohmands were driven back, and pursued to the foot of the high hills, on which they took refuge. Had an additional cavalry regiment been present they would, in General Elles's opinion, have been almost completely cut off, but as it was, their losses were very heavy, as the dead they left on the ground showed. The action was over by 10-30 A.M.; General Elles not considering it desirable, with the small infantry force at his command, to push further into the hills, particularly as his men had been hotly engaged for four hours. The Mohmands, however, had received a sufficiently sharp lesson, and they began to retire over the hills when the troops returned to Shabkadr, and by two o'clock not a man was to be seen. The Hadda Mullah, who was present during the fight, had evidently seen that his defeat could not be retrieved.

Our casualties in this affair were 12 killed and 52 wounded; not heavy losses considering how sharp was the fighting, and the number of the enemy. *Severely wounded :* Major Lumb, Somersetshire Light Infantry, bullet wound in the neck; Captain Blacker, 51st Field Battery, bullet wound in the leg. *Slightly wounded :* Lieutenant Cheyne, 13th Bengal Lancers. The details of the casualties were as follows :—Somersetshire Light Infantry: 4 men killed, 8 wounded severely, 1 slightly; 20th Punjab Infantry, 7 killed, 20 wounded severely, 1 slightly; 13th Bengal Lancers, 1 killed, 8 wounded severely, 6 slightly.

Another account of the fight gave the following additional details :—
" Our infantry attacked in front, the cavalry and artillery on the right being thrown forward for the advantage of the ground, and to threaten

the enemy's line of retreat. The enemy changed front to meet this, and swarmed on both flanks under heavy rifle fire from our left, and they pressed hard to cut us off from the Fort, distant about 2 miles. Most of our casualties occurred at this time, but the artillery kept the enemy off on our right. General Elles with his Staff arrived at this moment, about 9 A.M., and took over command. He lengthened and threw back our left and ordered the cavalry out to the right front. Captain Blacker of the Artillery here received his wound. The cavalry charged down the enemy's line, rolling it up, and in spite of the heavy ground and bad going, the charge was brilliantly executed by Major F. G. Atkinson, Lieutenant A. G. B. Turner, and Lieutenant Cheyne and two squadrons of the 13th Bengal Lancers, supported by the artillery fire directed ahead of the cavalry line. The enemy immediately fled to the tops of the foot hills, and remained watching in groups. Shells dispersed the groups, but our force was too small to enter the hills in pursuit. On our side the total number engaged was just 800, and with these were only 15 British Officers, including General Elles and Staff, and four of these were wounded in addition to the Medical Officer. The latter was struck by a stone knocked up by a bullet, and incapacitated for a short while, but he insisted on returning to duty. Certainly first aid to the wounded was efficiently performed, and in this case saved many lives. None of the wounded have yet died, and none apparently are in bad case. Seventy-seven were killed or wounded, a loss of about 10 per cent." A curious fact worth mentioning is that the ground on which the action was fought was practically the same as that on which Sir Colin Campbell in 1852 with 600 men met and defeated 6,000 Mohmands, and where again in January 1864 Colonel A. Macdonnel, of the Rifle Brigade, with 1,750 men, defeated a body of 5,000, who held the low hills facing Shabkadr. The success of the latter, like that of General Elles, was due to the cavalry, the Mohmands being tempted into the plain and then charged. A squadron of the 7th Hussars on that occasion made three successive charges which enabled the infantry to act with decisive effect against the enemy's broken line.

Having withdrawn the troops to the neighbourhood of the Fort, General Elles returned to Peshawar, and immediately ordered up to Shabkadr the remainder of the Somersetshire Light Infantry and 250 of the 37th Dogras, so as to be ready to assume the offensive if the Mohmands should reappear. At 2 o'clock, however, a heliographic message was received from Shabkadr stating that no enemy could be seen even on the distant hills.

As it was impossible to say how far the excitement extended along the border, General Elles called up three companies of the 8th Bengal Infantry from Nowshera, and at the same time asked for one battery of artillery, a regiment of native cavalry and one of native infantry, it being important to have a garrison at Peshawar. The Gordon Highlanders, under orders from Army Head-Quarters, had been despatched from Rawalpindi by train at midnight on Sunday, August 8th, and reached Peshawar on the Monday afternoon; the 2nd Queen's from Jullundur replacing them at Rawalpindi as part of the Reserve Brigade of the Malakand Division. The arrival of the Gordon Highlanders filled the gap at Peshawar caused by sending the Somersetshire Light Infantry to Shabkadr. The troops now watching the Mohmand Frontier were the 51st Field Battery (four guns), two squadrons 13th Bengal Lancers, the Somersetshire Light Infantry (740 strong), the 20th Punjab Infantry (600 strong), the 30th Punjab Infantry (300), and the 37th Dogras (250); a handy force of about 2,200 men.

A reconnaissance was made on Tuesday, August 10th, five miles into the hills from Shabkadr without any enemy being seen. The Mohmands, however, were reported as intending to return to the attack after replenishing their ammunition and food supplies. They were said to have lost between three and four hundred killed and several hundred wounded in the action on the 9th August.

The reinforcement of the Peshawar garrison was most promptly carried out. In addition to the Gordon Highlanders from Rawalpindi and the three companies of the 8th Bengal Infantry, the 2nd Battalion 1st Gurkhas arrived on the scene. The Gurkhas had been intended for the Reserve Brigade at Mardan, but on arrival by train at Nowshera they were sent straight on. The 9th Bengal Lancers and the 57th Field Battery from Campbellpore were also ordered up. These reinforcements enabled General Elles to send the whole of the 13th Bengal Lancers to Shabkadr, thus raising the strength of the force there to about 2,500 men. Apart from this detached column General Elles eventually had the following troops in Peshawar itself : one section of the 51st Field Battery and the whole of No. 57 Field Battery, No. 5 Company Bengal Sappers, 9th Bengal Lancers, the Devonshire Regiment, the Gordon Highlanders, the 2nd Battalion of the 1st Gurkhas, five companies of the 30th Punjab Infantry, six companies of the 37th Dogras, and three companies of the 8th Bengal Infantry.

As the general situation on the North-West Frontier now presented itself, however, it was obviously wise to still further strengthen the garrison of Peshawar so as to have a second column ready to take the field in case the tribal excitement should spread. The Government of India therefore ordered up the following troops :—4th Dragoon Guards and " K " Battery Royal Horse Artillery, from Rawalpindi; the 26th Punjab Infantry from Jullundur, and No. 3 (British) Mountain Battery from Jutogh, Simla Hills.

For the next five days or so phenomenally heavy rains came down and made matters extremely uncomfortable for the Peshawar and Shabkadr garrisons. The fair vale of Peshawar almost disappeared under water, and the roads were turned into bogs, the one to Shabkadr being a veritable slough of despond to Transport Officers. The new bridge over the Kabul River, which runs midway between Peshawar and Shabkadr, was a triumph of engineering skill. The current at that time was coming down with a roar at a speed of from ten to twelve knots an hour, and was generally level with and sometimes overflowing the banks ; but the bridge, which was held by wire hawsers, splendidly withstood the flood : it consisted of country boats, pontoon system, and its length was about two hundred yards.

Fortunately the floods did not interfere with any urgent military operations, for the reason that no immediate operations were possible without an enemy ; and the Mohmand warriors, imitating the beaten Swatis at Chakdara, had completely disappeared. The Mullah of Hadda was so discredited that he had retired temporarily to his haunt in the Bohai Valley. The "Mad Fakir" in Swat, in replying to a message from the Hadda Mullah asking for congratulations, was reported to have sent the answer—" Dog, you have done nothing !" which indeed was the plain truth. On August the 22nd, however, about a fortnight after the action at Shabkadr, it was reported at Peshawar that the Hadda Mullah had again worked up the Mohmands, and that he intended to attack both Shabkadr and Michni, one tribal column coming down the Gandab Valley and another by the more northerly Alikandi route. This demonstration was announced as arranged for Monday, August 23rd. If it had actually taken place the Mohmands would have had a warm reception, as more cavalry were now on the scene with General Elles than were available on the 9th of the month ; but the still smarting tribesmen were apparently not to be thus easily inflamed a second time. As a matter of fact many of them were attending peacefully to their fields, the recent heavy rains having rendered agricultural work a necessity ; added to which the war council of the tribe was for the moment hopelessly torn by internal dissensions.

* * *

While General Elles was awaiting permission from head-quarters to press home retaliation upon the Mohmands, signs of restlessness were being reported day by day from the Afridi and Orakzai country, and at length on Tuesday, August 24th, the smouldering embers of fanaticism in this new direction burst suddenly into flames, and a fierce attack was made upon our Forts in the Khyber Pass. This new rising, however, and the grave events which succeeded it, require separate narration, and are only mentioned here for the sake of chronology, and because they influenced the Government of India in deciding upon the further exemplary operations against the Mohmands now to be described.

CHAPTER III.

THE MOHMAND EXPEDITION.

DURING the first week in September the welcome announcement was received in Peshawar that the Government of India had sanctioned extensive punitive measures against the various tribes on the Peshawar border, and that the Mohmands would be the first tribe to be taken in hand. Definite orders followed for the immediate concentration at Shabkadr of two brigades under the command of General Elles, the troops to be drawn from the force already in and about Peshawar. The Peshawar force at that time numbered something like 9,000 men, although it had just been depleted by the despatch to the disturbed Afridi and Orakzai frontier of the 6th Bengal Cavalry, the 1st Battalion 2nd Gurkhas, and the 30th Bengal Infantry.

The proposed movement against the Mohmands was well timed, as the Hadda Mullah was once again reported to be on the war-path, this time with 4,000 Baizai Mohmands, his intention being to re-visit Shabkadr. His other ambitious plan (already described) for attacking Dir and cutting round to Chitral had come to nought, owing to the rapid movement across the Panjkora River of the Uch force under Brigadier-General Wodehouse, and owing also to Sir Bindon Blood's promptness in recalling Brigadier-General Jeffreys' Brigade from the Utman Khel Expedition. Everything pointed to the operations of our troops being short and decisive, as two powerful forces were about to move upon the condemned country from opposite directions. Sir Bindon Blood, with the two brigades of the Malakand Field Force under Brigadier-General Wodehouse and Brigadier-General Jeffreys, was acting from the north and east, while General Elles, with two brigades (commanded by Brigadier-General Westmacott and Brigadier-General Macgregor), would move forward from Shabkadr on the southern side.

The composition and staff of the Mohmand expeditionary force from Peshawar were as follows:—

Commanding : Brigadier-General Elles with the rank of Major-General; A.-D.-C., Lieutenant E. Elles ; A. Q.-M.-G., Major P. Sulivan, R.E. ; Commanding Royal Artillery, Colonel A. E. Duthy ; Adjutant, R. A., Captain W. K. McLeod ; D. A. Q.-M.-G. for Intelligence, Captain

F. A. Hoghton, 1st Bombay Grenadiers; Field Intelligence Officer, Lieutenant C. E. E. F. K. Macquoid, Hyderabad Contingent; Principal Medical Officer, Surgeon-Colonel E. Townsend; Field Engineer, Major Kelly; Assistant Field Engineers, Lieutenants W. A. Stokes and C. B. L. Greenstreet; Ordnance Officer, Major F. E. Rowan; Chief Commissariat Officer, Captain G. R. C. Westropp; Divisional Transport Officer, Captain F. C. W. Rideout; Commissariat Officer for the Base at Shabkadr, Lieutenant E. G. Vaughan; Veterinary Officer, Veterinary-Captain F. W. Forsdyke; Provost Marshal, Major H. S. Massy, 19th Bengal Lancers.

1st Brigade:—Commanding, Brigadier-General Westmacott. Troops: Somerset Light Infantry, 20th Punjab Infantry, 2nd Battalion 1st Gurkhas.

2nd Brigade:—Commanding, Brigadier-General C. R. Macgregor. Troops: Oxfordshire Light Infantry, 9th Gurkhas, six companies 37th Dogras.

Divisional Troops:—13th Bengal Lancers, No. 3 British and No. 5 Bombay Mountain Batteries 28th Bombay Pioneers, and one regiment of Imperial Service Infantry.

The Maharaja of Patiala and Sir Partab Singh of Jodhpur joined General Elles's personal staff as extra Aides-de-Camp; Major W. J. Bythell, R.E., accompanied the Mohmand Expedition in charge of the survey.

It will be noticed that certain Imperial Service Troops were included in the expeditionary force, and the following notification on the subject, which was issued from the Foreign Department on September 5th, affords all the explanation that is necessary :—"The tribal disturbances on the frontier have prompted the ruling Chiefs in all parts of India to come forward with their wonted loyalty to press upon the Governor-General in Council the services of their Imperial Service Troops. The Governor-General in Council has resolved that the time has come when the assistance of the troops so loyally prepared and maintained may be accepted from the Chiefs of the Punjab, and when they may be allowed to co-operate in punishing those who have made and are making persistent efforts to disturb the peace of that Province. It is impossible to employ cavalry to any great extent in the expeditions which have now to be undertaken; the Governor-General in Council has therefore decided to accept from the States in the Punjab the service of four battalions of infantry and of two companies of Sappers and Miners. These troops will immediately proceed to the front. It has also been determined to utilise the services of the Gwalior and Jaipur transport trains which did such good work in the Chitral Expedition, and which the patriotic action of His Highness the Maharaja Sindhia and His Highness the Maharaja of Jaipur places again at the disposal of the Government of India. Orders have been given that the thanks of the Government of India should be conveyed to all the Chiefs from whom offers of troops have been received. The urgency and unanimity which characterise the action in this respect of rulers of States in India emphatically testify to the spirit of loyalty which animates them."

The plan of campaign, already outlined, may now be more fully unfolded. During previous border wars the custom in attacking hostile tribes had been to march straight into their country on one line of advance. This had always enabled the tribesmen to gather at a single point, generally a pass, offering a good defensive position, thus compelling our troops to storm breastworks before making good their entrance into the country. In some instances heavy losses had been incurred by our troops in this way, and progress had necessarily been slow. The present expedition was being conducted on very different lines. Our possession of Lower Swat and the opening out of the road to Chitral through Dir permitted of a strong flank movement being made against the Mohmands, pending the development of which General Elles would not move out from Shabkadr. Sir Bindon Blood had crossed the Panjkora River at Sado, and was marching rapidly due west up the Ushiri Valley to Mandia, the route followed by Sir Robert Low in the Chitral Campaign. From Mandia a road leads south-west up the Khalnzi Valley to the high range which separates Bajour proper from the Mohmand country. This range Sir Bindon Blood intended to cross by a pass overlooking Nawagai, the head-quarters of the Khan of that name, who had assumed a particularly friendly attitude towards the British *Raj*. This Chief is an old rival of Umra Khan's and his territory in the south touches the Mittai Valley, a tract about which there had been a dispute between the Government and the Amir of Kabul. From Sado to Nawagai is about 50 miles. When our troops reached Nawagai, they would be in rear of the Mohmands and could march to any point in their country. A caravan route leads due south to the Peshawar border and this would perhaps be the best to follow as it passes through Lokerai in the Bohai Valley, where the Mohmands have many villages. The Mohmands, on the appearance of Sir Bindon Blood's Division at Nawagai, would be obliged to gather their fighting-men to oppose his advance southwards. They had never been attacked from the north before, and would clearly be taken at a disadvantage. But at the very time at which their attention would be turned to Nawagai, their scouts would bring in news that another big force had entered the country from Shabkadr and was pressing forward through the Gandab defile upon Lokerai. This place is 30 miles from Nawagai and about 50 from Shabkadr. As each division was 5,000 strong, and as the total strength of the Mohmands was only 17,000, of which one-half had to be furnished by the Baizai clans to the extreme west, the tribe was not likely to make much of a fight against the two forces. The Mohmands are a poverty-stricken race, and, unlike the Afridis, were badly armed, as they had never been able to purchase breech-loading rifles. In the raid on Shabkadr they were assisted by the clans which owe allegiance to the Amir, but help could not, it was believed, reach them from this direction now, as Abdur Rahman * had shown that he would not permit his subjects to join in the fighting on the border. As our two divisions moved to meet each other in the Bohai Valley, the tribesmen would probably flee to the hills, though they might make some show of resistance at the outset. Their villages would lie open to the troops, and columns could be sent out in various directions. Jarobi, the head-quarters of the Hadda Mullah, would doubtless be visited, as it lies at the head of the valley and could readily be reached. This then was the plan of operations, and predictions were not wanting that within a week the Mohmand operations would be over, the four brigades being then free to move against the Afridi and Orakzai combination. As a matter of fact, the expedition (as will be shown) occupied more than a month, and to at least a portion of the troops engaged afforded quite as much fighting as even a keen soldier could desire.

No proclamation was issued to the Mohmands before our troops moved into their country. Our Political Officers, however, made known that the visit was not made in order to deprive any tribe of its independence, but because the British Government were determined to "take such measures as would insure its border against being attacked in the future." Further, the Mohmands were informed that if any opposition

---

* The attitude of the Amir towards the various tribes breaking the peace on our frontier is alluded to more fully in a later chapter.

was offered, those who engaged in hostilities would be followed up and punished.

On Saturday, the 11th of September, Major-General Elles and the Divisional Staff moved out from Peshawar to Shabkadr, and Colonel A. Gaselee, then commanding Cawnpore station, took over the command of the Peshawar District with the temporary rank of Brigadier-General. On Monday, the 13th September, the whole force was concentrated on the Shabkadr-Michini road, and after a delay of two days marched off. This short delay, it is worth explaining, was due to causes affecting General Blood's further advance upon Nawagai. Major Deane, before leaving General Blood and returning to Swat, desired to secure the complete submission of the Utman Khels, who had apparently been wholesomely alarmed by the march of our troops. All their *jirghas* were anxious to come in, and General Blood at Major Deane's request halted his division for two days for that purpose. Hence the date of General Elles's advance was changed from the 13th to the 15th September, as it was most important that the combined advance of the two divisions should be so timed that the enemy could be caught between the two armies approaching simultaneously from north and south. It was now expected that General Blood and General Elles would join hands at Lokerai on the 18th September: whereupon Sir Bindon Blood would assume supreme command of both divisions with full political power.

The advance from the Shabkadr side was uneventful enough. On Wednesday, September 15th, General Westmacott's Brigade marched through the Khorappa* defile into the Gandab Valley. Half of General Macgregor's Brigade followed in support. The Hadda Mullah was reported to be in the Gandab Valley just ahead with a gathering of tribesmen belonging to the Khwazai and Utman Khel sections, the numbers being unknown. No enemy, however, was seen on the march, which proved to be a difficult one. The remaining troops of the division followed in due course, and General Elles soon found himself in an advanced position in the enemy's country, practically unchallenged.

. . .

Leaving the Shabkadr Division thus marching on unopposed, the narrative has now to follow the more chequered fortunes of the two brigades under Sir Bindon Blood on the opposite borders of the Mohmand country.

* Another place bearing this name is mentioned in later pages dealing with the Orakzai rising.

CHAPTER IV.

WITH GENERAL JEFFREYS' BRIGADE.

GENERAL WODEHOUSE'S Brigade, accompanied by Sir Bindon Blood, reached Nawagai on Monday, September 13th, the camp having been sniped at the previous night at a place called Lhamshak. No *jirgahs* had come in, and evidently the natives were hostile, as small parties armed with Martinis had fired the previous day on two squadrons of the 11th Bengal Lancers reconnoitring the Mohmand Valley. But the Khan of Nawagai was friendly, and while the troops remained in his territory, collected grain and supplies for them. No large body of the enemy being in sight, instructions were issued to the Survey Officers with the force to examine the Mittai Valley closely, with a view to the settlement of its boundaries. This was an important step to take, as the Amir of Kabul, when he claimed the valley the year before, had sent troops to occupy it. The country could now be surveyed without interruption (as it seemed), up to the Durand Border, after which the brigade could swing round and march due south *viâ* Lokerai upon Yakhdand, in order to unite with General Jeffreys' Brigade entering the Mohmand country by the route east of Nawagai which leads direct upon Yakhdand. But neither General Wodehouse nor General Jeffreys was able to adhere strictly to these plans, owing to the difficult position of the one and the resolute opposition encountered by the other.

While in the neighbourhood of Inayat Kili on the 14th September a determined attack was made at night on General Jeffreys' camp and the firing lasted for nearly six hours, two British Officers being killed, and one dangerously wounded, while nine men in the rank-and-file were hit, and about 80 horses and transport animals lost. The tribesmen attacking were Mamunds[*] and Salarzai, who inhabit the valleys of south Bajour west of Munda. It has just been mentioned that a day or two previously a cavalry reconnaissance in the Mohmand Valley was fired upon by tribesmen, but Sir Bindon Blood did not stop to punish them as there was no large gathering to be found. These tribesmen were Mamunds, and seeing one brigade thus pass on harmlessly to Nawagai

---

[*] A clan of the Bajouri tribes, not to be confused with the Mohmands.

they seem to have thought they could harass the troops which still remained south of the range of hills separating Bajour from the Mohmand country. General Jeffreys had intended crossing this range the following day, September 15th, and had sent the Buffs and Sappers to hold the crest for the night. His camp, with the transport animals, was in the best position available, and it was guarded by shelter trenches, which the 35th Sikhs and the 38th Dogras lined when the enemy opened fire. The tribesmen must have got the range accurately, judging by the results of their fire, but they made no attempt to rush the entrenchments. Firing began at 8·15 P.M. on the face of the camp occupied by the Guides Infantry. At 10 o'clock there was a lull, but at 10·30 heavy firing recommenced on the face occupied by the 38th Dogras and the 35th Sikhs, and Brigadier-General Jeffreys proceeded thither to direct the fire. The attack was continued until 2·15 A.M., when the enemy retired carrying their dead with them. The disproportionate loss among the British Officers was due to the fact that they walked about without cover, conducting the defence, while the men were protected by shelter trenches. The enemy were extremely well armed, and creeping along various nullahs, gained positions whence a most galling fire was delivered. The troops were directed to avail themselves of cover, but the necessity of sending messages involved exposure, principally of Officers, resulting in the losses already mentioned. All lights were extinguished, yet such tents as stood were pierced by bullets. The enemy were everywhere repulsed. Our casualties in detail were :—British Officers—*killed :* Captain W. E. Tomkins and Lieutenant A. W. Bailey, 38th Dogras : *dangerously wounded :* Lieutenant H. A. Harrington,* 26th Punjab Infantry, attached to the 38th Dogras. Natives—*killed :* one havildar, No. 8 Bengal Mountain Battery, one sepoy, 38th Dogras, and two followers ; *wounded,* 5. Seventy-six horses and mules were hit. Captain Tomkins and Lieutenant Bailey were buried the next morning with military honours. Lieutenant Harrington's condition was hopeless from the first, the bullet having penetrated the brain.

That same morning, as soon as light allowed, a squadron of the 11th Bengal Lancers, under Captain E. H. Cole, went out and overtook the Mamunds at the foot of the hill, killing 21, with the loss of one horse killed and one wounded.

---

* Died of his wounds a fortnight later.

The enemy, however, did not appear to be disheartened, and though they were quiet the next night, they had boldly declared their intention of returning after resting. Clearly they had not been punished sufficiently. General Jeffreys accordingly recalled the Buffs and Sappers from the crest of the Rambat Pass, and proceeded to visit the valleys whence the enemy had come. The idea of joining General Wodehouse's Brigade at Yakhdand was given up in favour of punitive operations in the Mamund (or Watelai) Valley. How far these operations would delay the movement of the brigade into the Mohmand country was not yet plain; but in any case Sir Bindon Blood with General Wodehouse could carry out the plan of joining hands with General Elles. The incident showed the wisdom of having sent large forces forward from the Swat Valley. If there had been only one brigade on the northern Mohmand borders, the plan of the Mohmand Campaign would have fallen through. Now, however, General Jeffreys could comfortably devote his attention to the two sections of the Bajouris which had thus unexpectedly assumed a hostile attitude, and in the event of this task occupying a considerable time he could return to the Swat Valley *viâ* Sado, as the troops already in the Mohmand country would be sufficient to deal with any possible Mohmand combination.

Sir Bindon Blood, on hearing what had happened, ordered another squadron of the 11th Lancers at Nawagai to join General Jeffreys, seeing that the cavalry already in the Watelai Valley had been used against the Mamunds to such good purpose.

The Mamunds and Salarzai were plainly in a sullen temper, but whether they would be able to gather in any great strength seemed doubtful, as the Bajour clans as a whole had not made common cause with them. In order, however, to be prepared for possible complications, the 1st Brigade under Brigadier-General Meiklejohn, which since its return from subjugating the Swat Valley had been awaiting developments, was moved from Sarai to the Panjkora River, a depôt being established at Sado on the river bank.

On Thursday, September 16th, General Jeffreys' Brigade fought the important and in some respects memorable action of the Mamund Valley, which began at 7·30 in the morning, continued throughout the day, and did not finally cease till after midnight. In this severe engagement nine Officers, including the Brigadier himself, and 140 men were either killed or wounded. This was the greatest loss that had occurred in frontier warfare in a single day since the Ambela Campaign. The facts are these: After the night attack on General Jeffreys' camp on the 14th September the brigade moved from Inayat Kili to the head of the Watelai Valley, to punish the Mamunds by burning several of their villages near at hand. To expedite the work of destruction General Jeffreys divided his attacking force into three columns, each of which was to operate independently of the other two. The right column under Lieutenant-Colonel F. G. Vivian consisted of the 38th Dogras, a section of Sappers and two guns. The centre column under Colonel P. H. Goldney consisted of one squadron 11th Bengal Lancers, four guns, the 35th Sikhs and the Buffs. The left column under Major F. Campbell included the Guides and was instructed to operate in the neighbourhood of the camp. At 7-30 the cavalry with the centre column came in contact with the enemy, and firing began. The tribesmen retired slowly, taking advantage of cover, and shooting accurately. Five companies of the 35th Sikhs belonging to the same column now arrived and cleared the enemy from the hillside, reaching a village, which they partially burned, the tribesmen ascending the hills. At 12 o'clock only a few snipers were visible, and the retirement of the column was ordered. As soon as this had begun, large numbers of the enemy appeared showing great courage, and being armed generally with Martinis they pressed the retreat severely. The ground favoured the tribesmen, who succeeded in out-flanking the 35th Sikhs. Their swordsmen and snipers frequently came to within 40 yards, and the Officers had to use their revolvers freely. There was also stone-throwing. The rear company was encumbered with the wounded. Here Lieutenant Hughes was killed and Lieutenant Cassels wounded. The enemy showed the greatest daring, and firing was maintained at under 100 yards for 15 minutes. As soon as the ground admitted, the charge was sounded, and the men responded well. Fixing bayonets they drove the tribesmen back up the hills. Some of the Buffs forming part of the same column under Lieutenant J. Hasler came up, and the enemy in retiring across the open suffered considerable loss from their fire. All this fighting was confined to Colonel Goldney's column. Colonel Vivian had found the villages allotted to him too strongly held to be attacked by so small a force and had returned to camp. Major Campbell's column had also avoided an action for the same reason, and after destroying some small hamlets had retired.

As soon as the enemy's resistance to Colonel Goldney's column was found to be vigorous, orders had been sent to the two other columns to concentrate, and reinforcements were ordered from the camp. Brigadier-General Jeffreys, who now arrived from the camp, ordered the Buffs again to occupy the village, to complete its destruction, and recover the bodies of the killed. Covered by the fire of the 8th Bengal Mountain Battery, the Buffs and the 35th Sikhs re-occupied the hill again, the tribesmen retiring and inflicting slight loss by sniping. At 2·30 the village was completely destroyed, and the force began marching back to camp again. The enemy once more attacked the columns, and the Buffs and Guides covered the retirement with great steadiness, but still the enemy, displaying a standard, advanced recklessly, and though suffering severe loss from carefully-aimed volleys, followed the troops to the camp, frequently firing at close range. Night had now come on, and the darkness was intensified by rain, but vivid lightning enabled the enemy to continue firing at the marching columns. The steadiness and endurance of the troops were admirable, and the camp was reached by the main body of the troops in perfect order at 8 o'clock.

Meanwhile, in addition to the main attack, the hills to the right of the enemy's position had been crowned by one strong company of the 35th Sikhs under Captain Ryder. This company was at 5 o'clock attacked by large numbers of Mamunds, and desperate fighting ensued. It was here that Captain Ryder and Lieutenant Gunning were wounded. To extricate these troops two companies of the Guides were detached from the main body, and in spite of severe fighting, darkness and rain, they were relieved and reached the camp safely. Their losses were, however, severe.

In the darkness and the pelting rain, which made it impossible at times for one company to hear or see anything of its nearest neighbour, four guns of No. 8 Mountain Battery and a half company of Sappers who had been covering the Guides's retreat found themselves separated from the main body, together with a few men of the Buffs. Brigadier-General Jeffreys, himself belated, and literally in the dark as to the exact whereabouts of the remainder of his brigade, joined these stragglers and assumed command. On reaching the village of Thana he decided to give up the idea of reaching camp that night, and halted the force, and they took up an entrenched position. The enemy, however, occupied half the village, and severe fighting at close quarters ensued. The guns fired case-shot through the walls, and eventually the enemy were expelled with the bayonet. Here Lieutenants Wynter and Watson were severely wounded, and the Brigadier himself had his head cut open by a fragment of rock. Captain Birch, R.A., had his left side cut by a bullet, and other Officers had bullets through their helmets. As soon as moonlight allowed, the cavalry, the 38th Dogras, and four companies of the 35th Sikhs proceeded from the camp and relieved the place. Our casualties for the day were :—British Officers—*killed :* Lieutenant V. Hughes, 35th Sikhs, and Lieutenant A. T. Crawford, Royal Artillery. *Wounded :* Lieutenant G. R. Cassels and Lieutenant O. G. Gunning, 35th Sikhs ; Captain W. I. Ryder, 1st Gurkhas (attached to the 35th Sikhs); Lieutenant F. A. Wynter, Royal Artillery ; Lieutenant T. C. Watson, Royal Engineers. *Slightly wounded :* Brigadier-General Jeffreys and Captain A. H. C. Birch, Royal Artillery. British soldiers—*killed,* 2 ; *dangerously wounded,* 1 ; *severely wounded,* 3 ; *slightly wounded,* 5 ; (all of the Buffs). Native soldiers—No. 8 Mountain Battery—*killed,* 6 ; *wounded,* 22. Guides—*killed,* 2 ; *wounded,* 1 Subadar, 2 Havildars, and 7 men. 35th Sikhs—*killed,* 22 ; *wounded,* 44. 11th Bengal Lancers—*wounded,* 2. Sappers and Miners—*killed,* 4 ; *wounded,* 15.

Another account of this action, which gave rise to much criticism, was published some time later. The following extract from it is worth adding :—

"The idea of the punitive operations in the early morning was it let loose nearly the whole brigade in the valley, to punish every village of importance in a single day, and then march back again to Inayat Kili. The brigade was already due in the Mohmand country to co-operate with General Elles's Division : its Commander and the troops composing it had the further prospect of Tirah before them ; and there was every inducement therefore to 'polish off' quickly the Mamunds who had been bold enough to fire into the camp below the Rambat Pass. To each Commandant was allotted a village, or group of villages, and he was directed to deal with it independently. Thus the Buffs, the 35th Sikhs, the 38th Dogras and the Guides Infantry, each six companies strong, moved off to accomplish their respective tasks : a detachment of the 11th Bengal Lancers, the Mountain guns and the Sappers being held ready for emergencies in case of any particularly strong opposition. The 38th Dogras on the right found the village of Damodolah far too strong to attack without artillery, and Colonel Vivian very sensibly returned to camp, instead of knocking the heads of his men against mud walls. On the left the Guides were successful in sweeping through some small hamlets, but had they pushed on to Agrah and Gat, they would probably have had to withdraw, as the 38th Dogras had done. Further up the valley the Buffs had disposed of one village also. It was in the centre that matters went wrong. The 35th Sikhs pushed on well into the hills at the far end of the valley, and as the further mistake was made of splitting the six companies into three parties, the Mamunds saw their chance and got to close quarters. Three companies which had begun to burn the village of Shahi Tangi were forced back, and they had to abandon the body of Lieutenant Hughes, who had been killed. Word was sent back for the Buffs and Guides to come up with all speed, and the 11th Bengal Lancers made a charge which, though it could not be driven home owing to broken ground, prevented the Sikhs from being surrounded. When the reinforcements arrived the Mamunds were driven back, and Lieutenant Hughes's body was recovered. Then came a long halt of some three hours, which enabled the enemy to collect in full strength; and when the retirement was eventually ordered, the tribesmen pursued their usual tactics with considerable success. Two companies of Sikhs, holding a hill over 2,000 feet high, were left to fight their way down alone: an order, it is said, was sent to them to retire, but it never reached Captain Ryder. There was some desperate fighting, and the Guides Infantry had to double back to save the Sikhs who were attacked by overwhelming numbers. It was here that the heavy losses occurred. The retirement down the Watelai Valley was weary work for the troops, for a thunderstorm came on, and as the enemy closed in, it became pitch dark. The guns, with a half company of Sappers and 15 men of the Buffs, got separated from their escort of four companies of the Sikhs, and in the thick darkness General Jeffreys found himself belated with this small party. The valley is intersected with ravines, and marching at night was no easy matter, as the Guides, who formed the rear-guard, discovered. The General eventually decided to take up a position under the walls of a village, and here for four or five hours the handful of British soldiers, gunners, and Sappers had to defend themselves against the enemy at very close quarters indeed. There were no means of sending off to camp for assistance, and it was not until the moon rose that the party were extricated, about an hour after midnight. The details of the fight under the village walls go to show that Officers and men behaved with the finest courage. Lieutenant Wynter fought his guns after he was wounded, until through faintness from loss of blood he could no longer give orders. Then a sepoy took him in his arms, and sat for hours shielding him with his own body against the enemy's fire. It was an heroic action, and the sepoy was severely wounded, while thus protecting his Officer. Another man coolly beat out with his coat the bundles of burning straw which the Mamunds threw from the house-tops to light up the ground and enable them to aim. The work was perilous in the extreme, but the sepoy went about it calmly, and repeatedly extinguished the flaming straw. A Sapper was sent out into the open to watch a door in the walls from which it was feared the enemy might rush: his figure was outlined clearly with every flash of lightning and he was repeatedly shot at, but he stuck to his post, calling out from time to time to show that all was well. Again, Major Worlledge, with the relief party from the camp, finding that he could not reach the spot whence the noise of firing came, sent out a sowar to open communication with General Jeffreys. This man passed safely through the tribesmen who were on the move across the valley, reached the village, only to get a volley from his own friends, delivered his message and carried back another to Major Worlledge. Other instances of devotion and gallantry could be given, but enough has been said to show that, as at Maizar, the Malakand, Chakdara, and the Samana* our troops acquitted themselves in splendid fashion."

General Jeffreys in his official despatch afterwards reported several conspicuous acts of gallantry during the fighting on the 16th September, and amongst them, as most remarkable, the behaviour of the Guides under Major Campbell, Captain Hodson and Lieutenant Codrington when they relieved the company of the 35th Sikhs which had got isolated, at which time Havildar Ali Gul of the Guides particularly distinguished himself. Captain Ryder and Lieutenant Gunning with the relieved company of the 35th Sikhs and Captain Cole with one squadron of the 11th Bengal Lancers did valuable service. Other Officers specially mentioned were Lieutenant-Colonel Bradshaw, 35th Sikhs, and Captain F. Duncan, 23rd Pioneers (distinguished himself when Lieutenant Hughes was killed), Captain Birch, R.A., and the men of No. 8 Bengal Mountain Battery, Lieutenant Watson, R.E. (wounded three times), Lieutenant J. M. C. Colvin of the Sappers, and Major Hamilton, D.A.A.-G.

In subsequently reporting the Mamund Valley action to Army Head-Quarters, Major-General Sir Bindon Blood, to whom General Jeffreys had reported events, entered into a full and detailed examination of all the facts. As this day's fighting has been much discussed and in some quarters severely criticised, we give in an appendix virtually

---

* Not yet related.

the whole of Sir Bindon Blood's despatches, these being the only official data available from which an opinion as to the tactics of the day can fairly be formed.

All was quiet in the camp at Inayat Kili on the night of the 17th September. At six the following morning, the available strength of the 2nd Brigade moved to attack the fortified village of Damodolah. The tribesmen appeared in considerable numbers, and firing began at 8-45. The 35th Sikhs crowned the spurs to the right of the village, and the 38th Dogras and the Battery occupied positions on the left, the Guides Infantry in the centre, and the Buffs in reserve. The village was carried and completely destroyed. The retirement was brilliantly executed by the Guides, and the enemy had no chance of rushing. The Buffs covered the homeward march of the brigade, inflicting loss on the tribesmen, who pursued. Much grain was captured. The casualties were:—35th Sikhs—*killed*, 1; *wounded*, 2. 38th Dogras—*killed*, 1; *wounded*, 2. Guides—*wounded*, 1. Firing ceased at 2-30.

Sunday, the 19th of September, was free from fighting, but some further punitive work was carried out, owing to the fact that the Mamunds, who had by this time sent in their *jirgahs*, nevertheless refused to comply with the terms imposed by General Jeffreys. This clan, which numbers only about 1,500 fighting men, was showing much determination, and though now suing for mercy, still refused to surrender its own rifles and those captured in the attack on September 16th. It was desirable, therefore, to demolish the fortifications of the villages in the centre of the Mamund Valley, and on the morning in question the force moved out against the village of Zagadirai, four or five miles from Inayat Kili, and destroyed it. No opposition was encountered, and later in the day *jirgahs* began to come in again. These *jirgahs* were informed by General Jeffreys that no proposals would be entertained unless their arms were surrendered. One day's grace was given to allow of this being made known. Much indignation was excited in the force by the news that the tribesmen had disinterred the bodies of the Mahomedan native soldiers killed in the recent fighting and had insulted their remains.

The following day (September 20th) Sir Bindon Blood, who had been kept well informed of events by means of the heliograph, was able to report from Nawagai to Army Head-Quarters that he had not found it necessary to reinforce General Jeffreys' Brigade, which had proved itself quite equal to dealing with the Mamunds, " in fact (he telegraphed), since Thursday night when the tribesmen inflicted such heavy losses upon the brigade, the operations in the Mamund Valley seem to have been completely successful."

Successful they had undoubtedly been, but hostilities were far from being over. At the very time when Sir Bindon Blood at Nawagai was telegraphing that the end of the fighting in the Watelai Valley was now in view, General Jeffreys' Brigade was obliged to march out to attack the fortified village of Zagai (once owned by Umra Khan). Sharp fighting ensued, chiefly with the Buffs on the right, and severe loss was inflicted upon the tribesmen. The village was taken and the retirement cleverly executed. Firing began at 8-50 A.M. and ceased at 12-30. A reconnaissance by a squadron of the 11th Bengal Lancers had revealed the fact that the village was strongly held. The Buffs were on the right, the 38th Dogras in the centre, the Guides Infantry on the left, and the 35th Sikhs in reserve. Firing began on the left at 8-50, and the guns came into action near the centre about 9-15. The Buffs, who had further to go, were engaged about 9-20. The enemy as usual retired, sniping; the village was occupied, and all the fortifications were destroyed. At 11 A.M. the retirement began, and immediately afterwards the tribesmen gathered on the flanks. On the left, the Guides Infantry were threatened by about 600 tribesmen displaying standards. These were dispersed by long range fire. On the right, the Buffs retired with admirable discipline, in spite of very sharp fire. Excellent practice was made with the Lee-Metfords; Lieutenant F. S. Reeves's section killed five men at one valley. The Dum-Dum bullet was most effective. Lieutenant R. E. Power was slightly wounded in the right arm, but after the wound was dressed he returned to his company. Lieutenant Keen was shot through the left arm and in the body. After the Buffs were clear of difficult ground, the line of the regiment lay across the open fields, and the enemy from cover fired with effect, several men being wounded. Firing ceased when the troops got clear, as the enemy did not dare to follow into the open. On the extreme left, considerable numbers of the enemy appeared. Captain F. H. Cole's squadron trotted forward, causing the tribesmen, ever in terror of cavalry, to bunch together. The Battery immediately exploded two shells with great effect, and this ended the action. The brunt of the fighting fell to the Buffs. The casualties were: two Officers wounded (Second-Lieutenant G. N. S. Keene, Unattached List, and Lieutenant R. E. Power of the

Buffs); British soldiers—*wounded:* Buffs, 9; Native troops—38th Dogras, 2. Total casualties, 13.

On the night of the 21st September, firing into camp took place, and several animals and one native orderly were wounded, and on the 22nd the important village of Dag was captured—together with great stores of grain—with the loss of one killed and two wounded.

In the 2nd Brigade alone the losses of a single week amounted to 14 British Officers and 153 men, besides nearly 150 transport animals, cavalry horses, and Officers' ponies. But General Jeffreys had now demonstrated the ability of his troops, when not divided into a number of weak parties, to sweep the valley from end to end.

General Jeffreys and his Brigade may now be left, settling accounts with the Mamunds, while the movements of General Wodehouse's Brigade with Sir Bindon Blood at Nawagai are brought up to date.

CHAPTER V.

WITH GENERAL WODEHOUSE'S BRIGADE.

WHILE General Jeffreys was countermarching his Brigade in order to deal with the aggressive Mamunds and Salarzai, the punishment of the Mohmands was steadily proceeding. Sir Bindon Blood was at Nawagai, and the Mohmand tribes to the south of this position had tendered their submission and agreed to surrender the arms demanded of them. The Hadda Mullah, however, was reported to have assembled a large gathering on the Bedmanai Pass, twelve miles from Nawagai, and it became evident after the arrival of this news that Sir Bindon Blood's position was by no means an easy one and might in certain contingencies become even critical. General Elles was still at or close to Shabkadr and could not therefore be looked to for prompt help, should help be required. The Hadda Mullah, with a large gathering, occupied a strong position in the Bedmanai Pass. The Mamund and Salarzai tracts were either in a blaze or at the combustion point. Between these two hostile forces lay Nawagai. The Khan, a man of great influence in those parts, might, by throwing his influence against the British have seriously increased the difficulties of the campaign. The pass of Nawagai would have been closed, and General Elles, arriving with his Brigade from Shabkadr, would have had to stand on the defensive or even to fall back without attacking the Mohmands at all. It is in fact easy to realise how serious the effects of such a development might have been.

Bold measures were necessary. Sir Bindon Blood decided to remain at Nawagai, to keep the Khan loyal and the pass clear at all costs. This action kept the tribesmen in two sections—the Mohmand on one side and the Mamunds on the other. It also paralysed the Khan, supposing his friendship were weak, though subsequent events proved his loyalty to be sincere. It maintained the communications. But it was not unattended with difficulty and danger.

Sir Bindon Blood considered himself strong enough to hold his position in spite of any attack that might be made, and he judged rightly. On Friday, September 17th, between 3 and 4 o'clock in the afternoon, some 800 tribesmen were seen near the mouth of the Bedmanai Pass.

The greater part of General Wodehouse's Brigade turned out, but the enemy remained among the ravines and only the cavalry could get near them. A few rounds were fired by dismounted men, and the Mountain Battery fired some shells. The force returned to camp in the evening. Evidently the Hadda Mullah was feeling his way.

At midnight, September 19th-20th, the Hadda Mullah, venturing out from his ravines, made a half-hearted attack upon General Blood's camp. Some 150 of the enemy, chiefly swordsmen, were in the first line, and about 1,000 in the second line. The first line crept up unperceived to within about 30 or 40 yards of the parapet held by the Queen's Regiment, and began firing, but being met by steady volleys, dispersed in a few minutes, after trying other faces of the camp in a half-hearted way. The tribesmen then turned their attention with much shouting to the picket held by the Khan of Nawagai's men on the low hills a mile to the west. After half-an-hour's sniping at this picket they made off. Our casualties were one man of the Queen's Regiment killed and one wounded. The enemy left no dead or wounded on the ground.

On the following night (September 20th-21st) another attack was made in force, the Hadda Mullah having been joined by the Saffi Mullahs and a contingent of Shinwaris from Afghan territory. The total strength was estimated at 3,000. Tactically the assault showed considerable skill, regular rushes being made, covered by rifle fire. It began about 9 P.M. and firing continued till 1 P.M. Constant charges were made from all directions more or less simultaneously. The troops on their part behaved with the utmost steadiness, and the fire discipline was perfect. The safety of the camp was never for a moment in doubt, though some of the tribesmen must have advanced to within ten yards of the parapet, as their bodies were afterwards found at that distance. The enemy must have suffered heavily, as they came under a cross-fire, and our men could see them plainly as they stood up. No. 1 British Mountain Battery fired four star shells very successfully. General Blood had been warned at 8 P.M. by the Political Officer that the attack was intended, so everything was ready when the enemy appeared. The Mountain Battery was of the greatest value, firing shrapnel as well as star shells. The casualties were :—In the British ranks, one man killed and four wounded ; in the Native ranks, fourteen wounded, most of these slightly. Brigadier-General Wodehouse was shot through the leg. Some horses and mules were shot. The enemy had breech-loading rifles, some of which were Lee-Metfords, as the bullets picked up in the camp showed.

General Blood moved out the troops next morning to find the enemy, but they had disappeared. He thereupon marched without further delay right on to Lokerai, where he knew, from heliographic signals, that he should meet General Elles, who had successfully carried out on his side the advance from Shabkadr.

On the night of the 21st September, after the meeting between Sir Bindon Blood and General Elles, there was considerable picket firing at individual tribesmen who endeavoured to approach the camp, also some sniping on the part of the enemy. Three star shells were fired. On the morning of the 22nd September the village of Das, west of Agrah, was attacked. The tribesmen, as usual, after the destruction of the village, followed and harassed the returning troops, and the following casualties occurred:—Guides Infantry—*killed*, 1; *dangerously wounded*, 1; 35th Sikhs—*slightly wounded*, 1. A squadron of the 11th Bengal Lancers protected the flank. The Guides executed the retirement with their customary skill and steadiness.

And now to trace briefly the less exciting movements of Major-General Elles's Division up to the time of his meeting Sir Bindon Blood's troops at Lokerai.

General Elles with his two Brigades under Brigadier-Generals Westmacott and Macgregor marched out from Shabkadr, as has been stated, early on the 15th September. Five miles out, the 20th Punjab Infantry, forming the advance-guard, were fired on. The Khorappa defile was found impassable for camels, and the General sent back orders for the 2nd Brigade to halt and camp, and left the 5th Company Bengal Sappers and the 28th Bombay Pioneers to improve the road. The six miles of very bad road were turned into one passable for camels by the evening of the 18th September, a very creditable piece of work for both Sappers and Pioneers, and General Elles continued his marched with a proportion of mule transport on September 15th to Galanai, 16 miles from Shabkadr.

On September 17th, news of General Jeffreys' fight at Rambat arrived. General Westmacott and the 1st Brigade, with the 20th Punjab Infantry, No. 3 Mountain Battery Royal Artillery, and two squadrons of the 13th Bengal Lancers, moved on six miles to Esuj Khel, three miles south of the Nahaki Pass. Plenty of forage was found in the valley between the top of Khorappa Jangi and Nahaki, but little supplies for the troops. Helio communication was established at Nahaki with General Sir Bindon Blood's force.

The Lower Mohmands, or Halimzais in the valley between Khorappa and Nahaki, accepted General Elles's terms, i.e., Rs.500, 300 *jezails* and 2,500 maunds of grain; all breach-loading rifles to be given up, and free forage to be provided for the force while in the district for seven days commencing September 19th. The 13th Bengal Lancers, after a reconnaissance towards Lokerai, reported very barren country beyond Nahaki with very little water. General Macgregor with the Oxford Light Infantry, the Patiala Regiment, and the Bombay Mountain Battery marched from Dand to Galani on September 19th.

The Saffi Mullah with 2,000 men was reported to be at Kung, 9 miles from Nahaki, and Major F. G. Atkinson with 100 men of the 13th Bengal Lancers, was sent to investigate the truth of the report. The Lancers were fired on from two sides, but they advanced in line, and the villagers fled. The Lancers held the village, and soon some villagers returned and spoke to Major Atkinson. He found two Sikh bunnias, who said they had bought up all the grain to sell to the *Sirkar*.

On the 21st September General Elles with General Westmacott arrived at Lokerai and met General Blood as already stated. General Macgregor had been left behind with two and a half battalions and two guns to hold a Nahaki Pass, which dominates the whole Mohmand country.

Having seen the completion of the first part of the plan of campaign Sir Bindon Blood left General Elles on September 23rd and rode down to Inayat Kili to see how the operations against the Mamunds were progressing. He had previously made over General Wodehouse's Brigade to General Elles, who united it with General Westmacott's Brigade for the purpose of making what was intended to be an overwhelming descent upon the Hadda Mullah's gathering reported to be still holding the Bedmanai Pass. Unfortunately General Wodehouse himself was not able to continue in command of his brigade being obliged, owing to the wound in his leg, to proceed by sick convoy to India. This was hard luck on a brave Officer, as much fighting had yet to take place. Colonel B. C. Graves of the 39th Garhwalis was given the command of the 3rd Brigade of the Malakand Field Force, with the temporary rank of Brigadier-General, and hereafter in the narrative of the Mohmand Campaign the brigade which has been known all along as General Wodehouse's Brigade will be styled General Graves's Brigade.

CHAPTER VI.

WITH GENERAL ELLES'S DIVISION.

On September 23rd, the day before Sir Bindon Blood left Nawagai to join Brigadier-General Jeffreys in the Mamund country, General Elles concentrated General Graves's Brigade and General Westmacott's Brigade at Kuz Chinarai, his camp being four miles north of the Bedmanai Pass, held by the Hadda Mullah and his supporters. The Mullah had outposts at the foot of the Pass, and our cavalry were fired upon when reconnoitring the position. Little parties of the enemy were also apparently prowling about the camp, as two followers were cut up and two wounded.

On the morning of the 24th September, the troops moved forward and, after some opposition, carried the Bedmanai Pass. The 20th Punjab Infantry, with Maxim detachments, particularly distinguished themselves in clearing the heights. The capture of the Pass, contrary to all expectation, proved easy of accomplishment, as only 500 of the enemy faced General Westmacott's Brigade, when it moved forward to the attack at 6-30 A.M. As to the actual assault, the 20th Punjab Infantry and the Maxim gun detachments led, and were opposed on every ridge, but the Maxim fire and the spirited manner in which the 20th Punjab Infantry moved forward were too much for the tribesmen. They were driven back until at last our troops crowned the peak 2,500 feet above the Pass. General Graves's Brigade was meanwhile moving in support of General Westmacott's up the centre, and guarding the right flank; but it was not actually engaged. Our casualties were only one sepoy killed and four wounded. No. 1 Mountain Battery, Royal Artillery, made excellent practice. The hills are most precipitous, making the performance of the infantry more creditable than would at first sight appear. General Graves's Brigade returned to Kuz Chinarai, General Westmacott's Brigade holding the villages round Bedmanai. Several forts and towers were destroyed.

This easy victory over the Hadda Mullah's forces was attributed to the previous want of success on their part in the night attack on General Blood's camp already described. They had made their real effort then, and failed, and when General Elles's two Brigades faced them they had very little heart for further fighting. The contingent of Afghan tribesmen also, who had been expected to help, no doubt considered it more advisable to retire across the frontier while their line of retreat was still open.

General Elles determined to advance from the Bedmanai Pass on to the much-talked-of Jarobi, where the Hadda Mullah had his head-quarters, uncertain whether that fanatical leader would be able to rally his men for another stand. The Afghan border is only a mile away, and once beyond this the Mullah and his followers would be safe, for British troops cannot cross the Durand line.

It is of no great importance to describe in detail how General Elles advanced from Bedmanai through the Bohai Valley breaking into the innermost seclusion of this hidden country, and sweeping away in the general destruction the very nest and hiding-place of the Hadda Mullah. As it turned out, the only spot bearing the name of Jarobi was a small glen, very picturesque to look at but quite devoid of mystery and significance. As for the often-mentioned "head-quarter buildings" of the Hadda Mullah, these were found to consist of nothing more than a few wretched mud huts. The troops had to pass through a difficult defile, but no real opposition was offered to their march. They, however, were fired at repeatedly by small parties of tribesmen, and some thirteen or fourteen casualties occurred during the advance. They returned to Bedmanai, having satisfactorily punished the various villages visited. The plan of operations had been admirably conceived and carried out. General Elles moved his force in two columns parallel with each other, sweeping the valley, thoroughly destroying all the forts, and punishing villages which declined to submit. Such opposition as was offered was easily broken down, and General Westmacott's Brigade pushed quite close up to the Durand boundary line. At Manzari Chena our troops were at the foot of the Sibala Pass, over which a road leads to Jellalabad. They skirted the range of hills which forms the boundary of Afghanistan in this direction, and worked southward, punishing the Khoda Khels, who would not accept the terms offered them. These operations must have convinced the Baizai, who had been hostile all through, that the force opposed to them was too strong to be faced. Their neighbours in the east, the Khwazai, submitted.

With regard to the punishment of Khoda Khels just mentioned, a few details may be given, as these villagers alone of all the others offered resistance. On September 26th, General Westmacott, with 4 guns of

No. 5 Bombay Mountain Battery, the 20th Punjab Infantry, 1st Gurkhas, a wing of the 28th Bombay Pioneers, half of No. 5 Company Bengal Sappers and the Devons' Maxim, joined by the Oxfords, who with four squadrons of the 13th Bengal Lancers had marched from Nahaki to Kung, started to destroy the forts and towers of the Khoda Khels, all in a sort of amphitheatre about two miles from camp. The advance-guard of the Gurkhas was met with a heavy fire from the villages and heights around, which were held for nearly a mile. The guns were immediately brought into action and soon cleared the villages, while four companies of Gurkhas on the left crowned the heights, their advance being covered by the guns and Maxims. This crowning of the heights was a difficult job, but smartly done. Meanwhile the Sappers thoroughly distroyed the forts and towers, and when this was completed the retirement was most deliberately carried out, covered by the guns and Maxims and the Oxfords. The casualties were : five Gurkhas wounded, Captain Knapp, commanding the guns, had his horse hit on coming into action. The Khwazai *jirgah* came in to General Westmacott during the fight so their forts and towers, which were to have been destroyed on the way back, were spared. The Khoda Khels were the best armed clan of the Mohmands, which no doubt explains why they refused to surrender their breech-loaders.

There was now no prospect of further fighting, as the Dawazai, Utmanzai and Khwazai had all made submission; and the troops were permitted to enjoy a well-earned rest. On September 28th, the Somersets, with the Maharaja of Patiala (who had accompanied General Elles from Shabkadr) returned to the Divisional Head-Quarters at Peshawar. His Highness had been treated all along like any other soldier and had shared all the hardships of service. He had faced everything in a true military spirit, taking the greatest interest in what was going on and showing the real Sikh keenness to see fighting. The Patiala Regiment, it may be added, was used under General Graves in chastising the Mittai and Sara Valley, and came into contact with the enemy.

The military part of this short but very successful expedition was now over, and the troops under General Elles moved back in separate columns to Peshawar, each force taking its own route. By the beginning of October the Mohmand expedition could fairly be spoken of as an event of the past

The effect of these short but completely successful operations had been very great. The utter rout and precipitate flight of the Hadda Mullah had made a deep impression on the tribes, who were paying up fines and surrendering arms in all directions. The campaign, conducted in an unexplored and mountainous country, with very bad roads, over difficult passes, and with a great scarcity of water—the enemy having breached the tanks, which are the chief sources of supply—had been virtually completed within a little more than three weeks of crossing the frontier. The rapid advance and attack on the Bedmanai Pass one day before it was expected, and at the moment when everything led the enemy to anticipate an attack on Mittai, and the subsequent sudden appearance of General Elles's force in Jarobi, the Mullah's stronghold, had utterly upset any organised resistance and prevented any further tribal combinations. The attacks on Shabkadr and other villages were now avenged and the tribes, if appearances go for anything will be quiet for many years to come, while the prestige of the British Government is completely re-established throughout the length and breadth of the Mohmand country. The Mohmand country was traversed in every direction for three weeks, the troops lived free upon the country, which was equivalent to a fine of four thousand rupees a day, seventy-two towers and forty forts were destroyed, and the troops penetrated to the farthest recesses of the mountain fastnesses deemed by the clansmen inaccessible to British arms: 800 swords and 100 guns, including breach-loaders and Enfields, were collected by the time the troops left the country, as well as fines aggregating thirteen thousand rupees in cash. A remarkable feature of the expedition was that after the demolition of the last Baizai forts the troops were in no way molested, and marched about the country in perfect peace and security, and not a single offence was committed on the line of communication. From these symptoms it is fair to conclude the Mohmands had taken to heart the lessons taught them. General Elles was fortunate in having as Chief Political Officer Mr. Merk, whose intimate knowledge of the people and country and great experience of frontier matters generally conduced not a little to the rapid progress and completion of the operations.

We have now to follow the adventures of Sir Bindon Blood with General Jeffreys' Brigade in the Mamund country.

CHAPTER VII.

FURTHER OPERATIONS AGAINST THE MAMUNDS.

It has been stated that on September 23rd, Sir Bindon Blood, after sending off General Elles with two brigades to capture the Bedmanai Pass, left Nawagai with his staff and divisional troops for Inayat Kili to see how the operations under General Jeffreys against the Mamunds were progressing. The situation at Inayat Kili at this period was somewhat peculiar, as for two reasons the 2nd Brigade was for the moment compelled to stand fast. In the first place it had lost a large number of transport mules, and in an undeveloped country of this kind the mobility of a large force must always depend on its pack animals. Secondly, the memorable fight of the 16th September, the attempt to clear the Watelai Valley in one day, had resulted in 150 wounded men being thrown on the field hospitals, and these could not now be carried nor could they be left behind, because deducting an adequate guard for them the rest of the brigade would not have been strong enough for the fighting which was to follow. Hence up to the time of Sir Bindon Blood's arrival on the scene with reinforcements only those villages within striking distance of the camp had been visited and the more remote villages of the valley remained untouched. Sir Bindon Blood's first step was to restore the mobility of the force. The wounded were sent to Panjkora where General Meiklejohn's Brigade was awaiting employment, and the transport animals killed were now replaced.

The last fight recorded in the previous chapter dealing with the Mahmund Campaign was the taking of the village of Dag on September 22nd. Early the following morning the brigade marched to visit the fortified village of Tangi, the inhabitants of which had been concerned in the recent fighting. The enemy appeared at first in small numbers, and the guns came into action at 8 o'clock. Firing continued until 11-45; the village was taken, the Guides first seizing the hills to the left. The 38th Dogras were in the centre, the 35th Sikhs on the right, and the Buffs in reserve. As usual, on the troops returning considerable numbers of tribesmen appeared, but not many cared to face our troops. A file of the Buffs now advanced from cover, and the Lee-Metford fire again checked the enemy. Our casualties were: the Buffs, Major R. S. H. Moody, slightly wounded; 38th Dogras, severely wounded, one. Lieutenant F. S. Reeves of the Buffs had a curious escape, the bullet striking his revolver and glancing thence through his case.

Here it may be mentioned that as the Mamunds live partly in Bajour and partly in Afghan territory, cultivating lands on either side of the frontier, they were always able during these punitive operations to retire in safety when hard pressed and then return again when our troops withdrew. They are notoriously turbulent, and the Afghan authorities have had much trouble with them since Asmar was occupied a few years ago. During the Chitral Expedition they caused us constant annoyance. They were among the tribesmen who opposed our troops in the advance beyond the Panjkora, and they were up in arms the whole time, the "sniping" into camp in the Jhandoul Valley being laid at their door. Again and again Sir Robert Low and Brigadier-General Waterfield wished to punish them but this step was forbidden from head-quarters. Our troops remained inactive for months, though the Mamund Valley lay only one march from Mandia; and the Field Force returned to India leaving the clan untouched. It would have been a simple matter to have sent a strong brigade to Inayat Kili and thence to have visited every village held by the tribesmen, for none are more then ten or twelve miles distant; but the Government would not sanction any punitive measures. The result was that the Mamunds, and their friends the Salarzai, believed that our troops were afraid to approach them; and thus, three years later, they were now harassing a force marching past the mouth of their valley and not intended to interfere with them in any way. That a grave disaster did not occur on the 16th September when General Jeffreys' Brigade weakened by division began reprisals, was due solely to the staunchness of our troops. However, the present punitive operations were going far to retrieve past omissions and already the Mamunds were beginning to send in their *jirgahs*. For a whole week after the capture of Dag and Tangi hostilities were stayed while negotiations with reference to the surrender of arms proceeded. Meanwhile, on September 25th, the Buffs marched off to Nowshera to join the Tirah Field Force and were relieved by the Royal West Kent Regiment from Panjkora. Their departure was much regretted, as in the recent fighting they had shown themselves worthy of the finest traditions of the British Infantry.

At this stage of affairs it did not seem to be advisable to hasten unduly the evacuation of the Mamund country. Apart from the fact that no arms had actually been surrendered, there were other and wider considerations to be seriously weighed. General Elles was about to return to Shabkadr, and it was doubtful in Sir Bindon Blood's view what course the Mohmands intended to pursue. True all the large Mohmand gatherings had been dispersed; the Bohai, Mittai and Suran Valleys, south-west of Nawagai, had been visited, and the Hadda Mullah chased into Afghan territory, while in the central parts of the Mohmand country our troops had effectually overawed the people. But there were probably some thousands of tribesmen just over the Afghan border who would return as General Elles's Brigades moved back to British territory. Nawagai might become their objective, as the Khan had cast in his lot with the British authorities. Inayat Kili is only one march from Nawagai, and General Blood would thus if required be able to extend a helping hand to the Khan until the excitement caused by the expedition had subsided. At the same time the reality of the submission of the Mamunds and the Salarzai would be assured.

On the 27th September Mr. Davis, Political Officer, in an interview with the Mamund *jirgah* found them determined not to give the 50 breech-loaders originally demanded as a punishment for their share in the attack on Chakdara, or the 22 Martinis captured from our troops on the 16th September. They admitted having taken part in the Chakdara attack without provocation, and coolly offered the excuse that all the world was doing *ghaza* and they went too. They further admitted going five miles from their valley to attack General Jeffreys' camp at Markanai on the 14th September. They stated that the rifles taken on the 16th September were in the hands of trans-frontier tribesmen from the Kunar Valley, who had shared in the fight, and that they could not be recovered. The *jirgah* flatly refused either to give up breech-loaders or surrender hostages, but offered a sum of money and a number of useless old matchlocks. Eventually they left to consult the tribesmen, promising to return. The promise was not kept, and on the 30th September, as no further reply had been received and as this amounted to a refusal of the Government terms, General Jeffreys, in the absence of Sir Bindon Blood who, anticipating a peaceful submission, had moved off with a small escort to Sarai, resumed punitive operations. All the villages in the centre of the valley were dealt with, and there was no opposition, the tribesmen declining to come into the open ground.

On the morning of the 1st October the brigade under General Jeffreys attacked the village of Agrah and very severe fighting ensued, resulting in the following casualties:—British Officers—*killed:* Lieutenant-Colonel O'Bryen, 31st Punjab Infantry, and Second-Lieutenant Browne Clayton, Royal West Kent Regiment; *severely wounded:* Lieutenant Isacke, Royal West Kent, and Lieutenant Peacock, 31st Punjab Infantry; *slightly wounded:* Captain N. Styles. British soldiers —Royal West Kent, *killed*, 3; *wounded*, 15. Native ranks—Guides Cavalry, *wounded*, 4; 31st Punjab Infantry, *killed*, 7; *wounded*, 15; 38th Dogras, *wounded*, 4. Total casualties: British Officers, 5; soldiers, 45. The enemy's losses were also heavy.

Some description of this severe action is called for. The Guides Cavalry reconnoitred the ground, and reported that the village was occupied and that the adjacent heights were strongly held. The enemy appeared in considerable numbers both on the hills where they displayed standards and among the scrub in broken ground to the left. The action was opened by the cavalry who at 8-20 A.M. were fired on from the scrub and hills. Dismounted fire was at once ordered by Lieutenant-Colonel Adams, and desultory skirmishing ensued. Meanwhile, the infantry were advancing, and at 9-15 A.M. the battery came into action shelling the enemy on the heights. The Guides Infantry then advanced to clear the hills to the left. The enemy, who occupied mortures and *sangars*, maintained a sharp fire, but on Major Campbell ordering the Guides to charge, the hills were splendidly carried. The Royal West Kent had now advanced in the centre and the 31st Punjab Infantry on the right, and very severe fighting ensued. The British Infantry cleared the village and attacked the tribesmen in the *sangars* behind it. Second-Lieutenant Clayton was killed by a volley at close range, and the enemy at once charged, causing a temporary check; but Major Western advanced with Lieutenant Jackson and one and-a-half companies of the Royal West Kent, and drove back the enemy and captured the *sangars* at the point of the bayonet. The losses had already been severe, and the 31st Punjab Infantry who had ascended the rocks on the right of the village, with a long spur on their flank occupied by the enemy, became exposed to a close and deadly cross-fire. It was here that Lieutenant-Colonel J. L. O'Bryen was killed. Moving swiftly from point to point he directed the fire and animated the spirit of the men, who were devoted to him. It was not long before the enemy's marksmen began to take aim at this prominent figure. But for a considerable period although bullets fell everywhere around him, he remained unhurt. At last however he was shot through the body and carried mortally wounded from the action. The fact that Colonel O'Bryen had been specially selected—while still a young man—to the command of a battalion, goes to show what a loss the army in India sustained by his death. Already he had passed through the drudgery of the lower ranks of the service and had reached a point when all the bigger prizes of the profession appeared in clear view. And though the death in action of a Colonel at the head of his regiment is perhaps the finest end that a soldier can hope for, everyone at the front deeply regretted the premature close of an honourable and brilliant military career. All the positions were held until the Sappers had completely destroyed the whole of the village. The return to camp was then ordered. The 38th Dogras under Lieutenant-Colonel Vivian now advanced to support the 31st Punjab Infantry on the right. The enemy, however, did not press the retirement as vigorously as usual, and the display of the cavalry prevented any advance into the open ground, but much firing was maintained from the hills with some effect. No. 7 British Mountain Battery fired sharpnel at close range and kept the nearest spurs clear. All firing ceased at 2-10 P.M., and the homeward march was not further molested, which was a tolerably sure sign that the enemy had suffered heavy losses. The Officers displayed great gallantry, most of the Royal West Kent having bullet holes in their clothes and helmets, and nearly all having strange escapes. The Guides Cavalry were of the greatest service during the action. They held a large force of the enemy in check on the left for five hours by dismounted fire and by threatening to charge whenever the tribesmen pressed heavily or advanced from the broken ground. No. 7 Battery Royal Artillery fired 140 sharpnel shells during the action, and when it was apparent that the Royal West Kent and 31st Punjab Infantry were severely engaged Major Fegan advanced his guns within 800 yards of the enemy and by constant fire kept many spurs clean. Though the guns came under sharp fire only one mule was killed. The want of more troops was severely felt ; three additional battalions could have been fully employed ; and only the great skill with which the Guides Cavalry on the left were handled checked the enemy's advance from that direction. The 31st Punjab Infantry also suffered from having no battalion on their right flank. The difficulty and danger of attacking fortified villages in broken ground and high crops are always great, and it should be remembered that after an adequate camp-guard and the details were deducted General Jeffreys' Brigade could only parade for fighting some 1,300 strong. Of this small number the loss in a fortnight of 245 was severe.

On the 2nd of October Sir Bindon Blood and Head-quarters with four guns of No. 8 Battery and four companies 26th Punjab Infantry arrived at Inayat Kili, the 10th Field Battery and the Highland Light Infantry following on behind ; and it was hoped that this formidable concentration of artillery would produce decisive effects. In his report to Army Head-Quarters Sir Bindon Blood telegraphed :—" I am crowding every man and gun on the decisive point and expect there will be an end of the Mamund business in a few days." He was right.

On the 3rd October at 6 o'clock in the morning, the 2nd Brigade with two batteries of artillery, under Brigadier-General Jeffreys, attacked the village of Badilai. Very little opposition was encountered until the return march of the troops commenced. Firing began at 8-45. The 31st Punjab Infantry cleared and occupied a spur on the right, while the West Kent moved against the village, and the 38th Dogras cleared the hills to the left, the Guides Infantry covering the left flank, on which the cavalry were also posted. The guns came into action at nine o'clock, shelling the village, which was captured and completely destroyed. Up to this time only two casualties had occurred, but as soon as the withdrawal of the troops began the enemy appeared in great numbers, as many as three thousand being roughly counted. Firing now became brisk and all the corps were involved, but the 31st Punjab Infantry were most severely pressed. The cavalry covered the retirement with great skill, but though the enemy showed much boldness, they did not advance into ground which rendered charging possible, and took refuge in *nullahs* whenever threatened. Firing ceased at 2-30, and the force reached camp safely. The whole affair was extremely successful, but the loss was not small. Sir Bindon Blood and the Head-quarters Staff watched the operations and reconnoitred the valley. The casualties were as follows :— Royal West Kent—*dangerously wounded*, 1 ; 31st Punjab Infantry—*killed*, 1 ; *wounded*, 5 ; Guides Infantry—*wounded*, 3 ; Guides Cavalry—*wounded*, 2 ; 39th Dogras—*killed*, 1 ; *wounded*, 3 ; total—*killed*, 2 ; *wounded*, 11. During the day General Meiklejohn and Staff arrived.

The Mamunds were now thoroughly broken. On the 6th of October 1,000 tribesmen from the Kunar Valley joined the enemy and expressed their intention of attacking the camp, but the Mamunds in terror of further reprisals dissuaded them from doing so and opened up negotiations for submission. Three or four days later ten rifles lost during the fight on the 16th September were brought in, and nine more were in the hands of the *jirgah* who now put out pickets to prevent trans-border men from sniping into the camp at night. The Mamunds had received a severe lesson. Details of their losses were not obtainable, but 272 men had been buried in the valley and the number of wounded must have been very large. The British casualties in the Mamund Valley since September 14th had been :—British Officers—*killed*, 6 ; *wounded*, 16 ; British rank and file—*killed*, 5 ; *wounded*, 43 ; Native ranks—*killed*, 50 ; *wounded*, 147 ; followers—*killed*, 1 ; *wounded*, 5 ; total 273, out of a force which never exceeded 1,360 fighting men. This shows how stubbornly the Mamunds fought. The Khans of Nawagai, Khar* and Jhar endeavoured to induce the Mamunds to comply unreservedly with the Government terms and eventually complete submission was secured. On the 12th of October the representatives of the Mamunds' *jirgah* arrived near camp and asked for an interview with Sir Bindon Blood. They sat under the trees near the village of Nawah Kili, and a durbar was arranged by Major Deane. Sir Bindon Blood and his staff arrived at 3 P.M. and received the *jirgah*, which promised to abstain from hostilities and to give no more trouble in future, also to turn Umra Khan's followers out of their country. They gave security for the two rifles still unsurrendered and declared that they wanted peace, having fought only because they feared annexation. Finally, all swore with uplifted hands to keep their promises, and were dismissed. The damage done to the valley amply settled all outstanding accounts, and our animals had lived free of cost for a month. There was no reason to doubt the sincerity of the Mamunds, for the ruins of their forts and villages in the Watelai Valley formed an object-lesson to which even the most turbulent of the tribe could not shut their eyes. Sir Bindon Blood and his two brigades under Generals Jeffreys and Meiklejohn now moved out of the Watelai Valley in the direction of Panjkora and from this point the Mamunds cease to figure in the frontier narrative. It is worth adding that No. 5 Company Queen's Own Sappers and Miners had the honor of sharing in the latter part of the operations in Bajour.

---

* In Bajour, as distinct from Khar near Malakand.

On his way back to the Malakand Sir Bindon Blood halted in the Salarzai Valley and easily forced the cowed tribesmen there to submit, 10 rifles and carbines and 139 guns being surrendered. In the same way the Shamazai section of the Utman Khels, who had shared in the Swat Valley rising, at once surrendered the arms demanded of them. On the 23rd October Sir Bindon Blood and General Jeffreys' Brigade arrived at Chakdara *en route* for the Malakand, and General Meiklejohn's Brigade followed the day after.

RAKZAI.

PART IV.

THE RISING OF THE AFRIDIS AND ORAKZAI.

PART IV.

THE RISING OF THE AFRĪDIS AND ORAKZAI.

CHAPTER I.

THE BREWING OF THE STORM.

ABOUT the middle of August, while Sir Bindon Blood was moving out from Chakdara to subjugate the Swat Valley, and while General Elles on the Mohmand border was awaiting permission to follow up his initial success against the Hadda Mullah's forces at Shabkadr, there came news of restlessness among the Orakzai, a tribe found in the hill country to the west of the Kohat district. A mullah had been trying to induce them to rise and attack our frontier posts, and had met with some success, though the tribesmen were urging that they had no representative leader to conduct the operations. The Orakzai country at that time was watched mainly from Fort Lockhart, our chief outpost on the Samana Range, a strong defensible position where six companies of the 36th Sikhs were stationed. A couple of days later another report came in that the restlessness was spreading westwards and that Parachinar, our last post in the Kurram Valley, was threatened by a large *lashkar*. As there seemed to be good foundation for both reports it was promptly decided to reinforce the Head-quarters garrison at Kohat (this post being the support of both Fort Lockhart and Parachinar) with the following troops :—The 9th Field Battery from Mian Mir, a wing of the Scots Fusiliers from Sialkote, the 18th Bengal Lancers from Rawalpindi, and the 15th Sikhs from Ferozepore. On inquiry it was ascertained that the mullah who was trying to brew mischief for us in this new direction was one Saiad Akbar, belonging to the Aka Khels, a poverty-stricken section of the Afridi tribe.

Further disquieting news was received shortly afterwards regarding the Afridis, who were said to have entered into a war alliance with the Orakzai tribe, the compact being that two simultaneous attacks should be delivered on British territory—one on our Kohat border, by the Orakzai; and the other on Jamrud and the mouth of the Khyber by the Afridis. The Aka Khel Mullah, Saiad Akbar, after sufficiently inflaming the Orakzai, had passed from their country to Tirah, the summer head-quarters of the Afridis. Apparently this fanatic was bent on doing in these two tracts of country what the "Mad Fakir" had done in Swat and what the Hadda Mullah was at that time doing in the country of the Mohmands.

The Orakzai are numerically a powerful tribe, mustering some 25,000 fighting men, and of no mean martial qualities. They hold the hills to the north-west of the Kohat district; the Afridi country lying to the north, while westward the Orakzai borders touch the Zaimukhts and extend to the foot of the Safed Koh Range. It is to the south that our own border faces them, and previous expeditions into the Miranzai Valley had been undertaken in order that the Samana Range might be held by a chain of posts, blocking the tribe from raiding into British territory. Since Fort Lockhart and its posts had been held the tribesmen had not ventured on any hostile demonstration, but they had been sullenly defiant and might now, while the whole frontier was in a ferment, be expected to give trouble if undeterred by the strengthening of the Kohat garrison. But no unanimity seemed probable. Of the six divisions of the tribe the Daulatzai and one sub-section of the Mahomed Khels were receiving allowances for keeping open the Kohat Pass, and these it was reasonably conjectured would in any event remain on their good behaviour. Moreover, the Orakzai are split up into two great factions, Samil and Gar, so that a general combination seemed difficult of attainment. The mass of the tribesmen are Sunis, but there are some Shiah sub-sections, and sectarian quarrels are not uncommon. Moreover as the whole tribe are a good deal dependent on the Kohat district for supplies, and especially for salt, it was believed that some sort of pressure could be brought to bear upon them; but it was nevertheless recognised as possible that they might listen to evil counsels and try conclusions with our troops.

The Afridis hold the country to the south and west of the Khyber, and their settlements touch the west of the Peshawar district. They are divided into eight clans, of which six, the Kuki, Malikdin, Kambar, Kamar and Zakka Khels and the Sipah are known collectively as the Khyber Afridis. The Aka Khels are found further to the south, beyond the right bank of the Bara River; while the Adam Khels hold the hills between the Peshawar and Kohat districts and are regarded as a separate community, their interests not being identical with those of the clans to the north-west. The whole tribe covers an area of about 900 square miles. In the summer months the majority of the Afridis move to Tirah, a high plateau inhabited chiefly by the Orakzai. The Rajgul and Maidan Valleys are studded with their mat huts during the hot weather, and their flocks and herds find good pasturage. The Kuki Khels always resort to Rajgul, while Maidan is left for the other clans. In the winter the whole population swarm down into the Bara and Bazar Valleys, and also into the low hills bordering the Jamrud plain. Tirah had never been visited by our troops, and was regarded as the Afridi stronghold. In the Afghan War of 1878—80 two expeditions were sent into the Bazar Valley, but it was not then considered expedient to enter the Rajgul and Maidan Valleys, as this would have involved the employment of at least 10,000 men. The Afridis muster in all some 26,000 or 27,000 fighting men, of whom about 6,000 belong to the Adam Khels, 4,500 to the Zakka Khels; and 4,000 each to the Kuki, Malikdin and Kambar Khels. The Kuki Khels under Amin Khan were the clan which had sent levies into the Khyber, and their standing feud against the Malikdin Khels as well as their professions of friendliness towards the Government of India prevented at least a portion of them joining in the contemplated rising. The Afridis are men of fine physique and grand fighting qualities, but their general character is of the worst. It is thus described by one authority: "Ruthless, cowardly, robbery, cold-blooded, treacherous murder, are to an Afridi the salt of life. Brought up from his earliest childhood amid scenes of appalling treachery and merciless revenge, nothing can change him; as he has lived, a shameless, cruel savage, so he dies. And it would seem that notwithstanding their long intercourse with the British, and that very large numbers are, or have been, in our service, and must have learned in some poor way what faith and mercy and justice are, yet the Afridi character is no better than it was in the days of his fathers." From such material as this, however, good soldiers have been made of the men enlisted in certain native regiments, and the trained Afridi fights with splendid *élan*. The blood feuds and quarrels between the various clans lead to much internal fighting, but any common menace to their country unites them. Already in the present instance they seemed to have sunk their differences and to have banded together in their hostile preparations against the British Government. They were posing as something more than religious fanatics. Their leaders had intimated to the authorities at Peshawar that certain concessions were desired from the Government of India. These were the withdrawal of all troops from the Swat Valley and the Samana Range, the rectification of the salt tax, and the rendition of all Afridi women living in British territory. Given these terms their fighting men would return to their homes.

For some days after the first rumours, Orakzai gatherings continued to be reported, but they were apparently waiting for the Afridis to move before carrying out their threatened attack on the Samana. Their attitude had caused some alarm among the friendly Turis of the lower Kurram, but reassuring news came presently from Parachinar. The garrison there was so confident of holding its own that one hundred men had been sent to reinforce the smaller post of Sadda held by 25 of the 3rd Punjab Cavalry as a link with Thall, which lies near the junction of the Kurram and Miranzai Valleys. The hostile tribesmen had gone to the length of cutting the telegraph wire, but messages were being sent through daily by sowars without hindrance. Apparently the tribes in the Kurram Valley, like the Orakzai of the Samana, were waiting in some doubt to see how matters developed in the Khyber direction.

Brigadier-General A. G. Yeatman-Biggs, then Commanding the Presidency District, was ordered up from Calcutta to take command of the troops at Kohat, and by the 22nd of August he was able to have a strong brigade ready to move out either to the Samana Range or to Kurram. No more striking instance of the want of union among the congeries of tribes on the North-West frontier had ever occurred than this vacillation of the Afridis and Orakzai. Instead of descending upon us swiftly and suddenly as the Swatis and the Mohmands had done, they were by their hesitancy giving us an opportunity to make better defensive preparations.

On the Peshawar side, owing to the intelligence that 10,000 Afridis were marching on the Khyber Pass from the Bozai Valley, Captain F. J. H. Barton, Assistant Political Officer at Landi Kotal, was withdrawn from that post, but the garrison remained in occupation. It was said that the Afridis, after capturing the Khyber Pass, meant to take Jamrud, our post at the Peshawar end of the pass. Jamrud was ordinarily held by detachments of native cavalry and infantry from Peshawar, while the Khyber Rifles, who were garrisoning the Khyber, had their head-quarters there. General Elles, who had not yet moved out from Peshawar against the Mohmands, now despatched No. 3 (British)

Mountain Battery from Peshawar to Jamrud Fort, together with strong detachments of British and native infantry and some cavalry. Mahomed Aslam Khan, Commandant of the Khyber Rifles, also concentrated four of his companies there. The remainder of the Khyber Rifles were distributed between the fortified *sarai* at Landi Kotal, the strong Fort at Ali Musjid, and the minor posts along the pass. These minor posts, it was already foreseen, might have to be given up if the Afridis should sweep down the Khyber, but Landi Kotal and Ali Musjid, if held with determination, could not, it was believed, be captured by any tribal force without artillery. The tactics of the Afridis would no doubt be to close the Khyber, and then appear in strength about the low hills which are found near the mouth of the pass. They were scarcely likely to venture far into the Jamrud plain, where they would lay themselves open to attack by cavalry, unless their numbers should indeed embolden them to make a demonstration against Jamrud Fort itself. Their raiding parties might also be expected to appear to the south, where Forts Bara and Mackeson, garrisoned by the Border Militia, guard our frontier between Jamrud and Kohat.

In a very short time General Elles had a column at Jamrud composed of "K" Battery, R. H. A., No. 3 (British) Mountain Battery, the 4th Dragoon Guards, a wing of the Gordon Highlanders, seven companies of the 1st Gurkhas, and a wing of the 26th Punjab Infantry. Bara Fort was held by detachments of native cavalry and infantry. By way of reserve there was the Shabkadr column, watching the Mohmand country, and a big garrison of 5,000 or 6,000 men in the Peshawar Cantonments.

On the 21st of August the Afridis really began to move, the Aka Khels, the Malikdin Khels, and the Zakka Khels having collected their fighting-men and started out from Tirah. Eventually six out of the eight clans into which the Afridis are divided joined in the hostile demonstration. Five of these, the Malikdin, Kambar, Kamar, Zakka Khels, and the Sipah have already been mentioned as forming with the Kuki Khels the Khyber Afridis: the sixth were the Aka Khels, south of the Bara River, to which the Mullah Saiad Akbar belonged. The Kuki Khels would not join, and their astute *malik*, Amin Khan, actually sent some of his followers to assist in the defence of Ali Musjid and Landi Kotal. The Adam Khels the last of the eight Afridi clans, holding the hills between Peshawar and Kohat, are in a sense a distinct community, and they were far-sighted enough to see that any temporary success secured by a raid would have to be dearly paid for in the long run. They are subsidised to maintain the road through the Kohat Pass and they declined to close the pass when urged to do so by the mullahs. Their *jirgah* went into Kohat when summoned, and the clan afterwards remained quiet. Some tribesmen bearing the name of Adam Khels did as a matter of fact join the Afridi *lashkar*, but these were a sub-section of quite a different clan inhabiting Tirah. This duplication of trans-frontier names is of frequent occurrence and is apt to be confusing.

In order to be on the safe-side, General Elles despatched a flying column of all three arms to Bara to watch for any hostile demonstration in that quarter, while the Jamrud column was kept even more on the alert than usual. The Commander-in-Chief, seeing the advisability of having a large force of cavalry in and about Peshawar, ordered up the 6th Bengal Cavalry from Rawalpindi, and these arrived at their destination on August 22nd. This gave General Elles 18 squadrons of cavalry in all, apparently quite enough to smash up a tribal force 10,000 strong if it should venture from the hills.

Information reached Peshawar about this time which shed a curious side-light upon the tribal risings on the frontier. It appeared that both the Hadda Mullah and the "Mad Fakir" wrote to Saiad Akbar, Aka Khel Mullah, urging him to incite the Afridis and Orakzai to take up arms against the British. Saiad Akbar hesitated at first to respond to the appeal, but eventually on the 13th August he managed to assemble a number of Afridi *maliks* in Musjid Bagh in Tirah the summer headquarters of the tribe. Here there was a great discussion as to the propriety of attacking British territory. The headmen were divided in opinion, many of them taking the sensible view that such an attack could not be successful and might bring reprisals upon the Afridis as a whole. Saiad Akbar then left for the Orakzai country, and here he succeeded in exciting the tribesmen to such an extent by working upon their fanaticism that they agreed to attack the Kohat border if the Afridis would move against the Khyber and Jamrud. The mullah hurried back to Tirah with this news and it was sufficient to excite the Aka Khels and Zakka Khels, who gathered their fighting-men at once. But, as has been seen, the delay in bringing about the tribal combination had given the Government of India ample time in which to reinforce the garrisons of Peshawar and Kohat, and it was now clear that the bellicose Afridis and Orakzai would shortly receive a severe lesson.

CHAPTER II.

THE CAPTURE OF THE KHYBER FORTS BY THE AFRIDIS.

AFTER twelve days of doubt as to the real intentions of the Afridis, the question was finally settled on the 23rd August by a sudden and overwhelming attack on Ali Musjid and on Fort Maude, the latter a small fort about three miles from Jamrud and just within the mouth of the Khyber Pass. The tribesmen had apparently advanced from the Bozai Valley by the Alachi route, which brought them into the pass quite close to Ali Musjid. This fort was held by a detachment of the Khyber Rifles and some Kuki Khel levies who, either because they mistakenly thought they could not possibly prevent it from falling into the hands of the enemy, or because they did not care to shoot down their own countrymen, abandoned it and retired to Jamrud; and the Afridis at once burned the building to the ground. Advancing further along the pass the raiders came upon Fort Maude, which though small was strongly built and well placed on an eminence overlooking the road. Its little garrison, some 40 or 50 of the Khyber Rifles, behaved staunchly, but could not save the situation, for the Khyber was now swarming with Afridis, whose line extended 1½ miles.

At three o'clock in the afternoon, the news reached Jamrud that Fort Maude was being attacked, and "K" Battery, with an escort consisting of the 4th Dragoon Guards and four companies of British infantry, was ordered out towards the mouth of the Khyber Pass with a view to render assistance if this should prove practicable. As the fort, however, was some distance up the pass itself, this force could not with safety move far into the hills, where it would have been liable to flank attacks. The battery eventually opened fire at 3,200 yards on a number of tribesmen who were sighted. These retired at once, but it was not found possible for the guns to proceed up the pass, and the would-be relieving force was obliged to return to Jamrud. At night Fort Maude was seen to be in flames. The post was one of no great importance in itself, but there was no telling how far its capture might encourage the Afridis to press forward.

Though the Afridis took Fort Maude they did not take the garrison. When "K" Battery with its escort came into action at 3,200 yards, it temporarily scared off the assailing horde, and the garrison, seeing the hopelessness of the position, took advantage of the brief but welcome diversion to withdraw in safety, joining the battery and returning with it to Jamrud. During that night Jamrud itself was sniped, but there were no casualties, and next morning all the enemy had disappeared.

There was a reason for the disappearance. An attack was to be made that day on Landi Kotal, the fortified *sarai* already mentioned, further up the Khyber. This attack began about noonday and the garrison, as a whole (for there were defections), offered a steady resistance, keeping the enemy outside during the afternoon and evening, and continuing to stand to the defence right through the night. Not until 10 o'clock the next morning—and then only by means of treachery on the part of certain Afridis within the stronghold—did the enemy get inside. As in the other instances, the building was set on fire, after which the raiders withdrew and soon afterwards dispersed quietly but exultingly to their homes.

Some of the details of the taking of Landi Kotal are interesting. The garrison of the *sarai* consisted of five Native Officers and 370 men of the Khyber Rifles, including 25 recruits and *munshis*. Of these 120 belonged to miscellaneous clans; thus 40 were Shilmani Mohmands, and a similar number were from the Peshawar Valley, while the rest were Adam Khels and men from the neighbourhood of the Kohat Pass. Of the remaining 250, 70 were Lawargai Shinwaris, within whose limits Landi Kotal lies, while 180 were true Afridis, their numbers being pretty equally divided among the Mullagoris, Zakka and Malikdin Khels. These 250 rifles formed the bulk of the garrison, and they seem to have behaved steadily enough on the 24th August, firing volleys at any groups of tribesmen who tried to approach the walls of the *sarai*. On the morning of the 25th a Shinwari jemadar named Jhawas Khan was wounded, and the Shinwari sepoys then concluded they had done sufficient fighting. They accordingly jumped down from the north wall of the *sarai* and bolted away to their villages. If we are to believe the story of some of the Khyber Rifles who afterwards came into Jamrud, the Afridi portion of the garrison were so disgusted with these deserters that a volley was fired upon them as they fled, three or four men being hit. A little later some Shinwaris and Zakka Khels among the attacking force managed to scale the wall on the north-east face near the Officers' bungalow, but they were promptly driven back. Then certain of the Afridis manning the wall began exchanging greetings the reverse of hostile with their fellow-tribesmen outside, and the sequel was that some traitors within opened the gate and the tribal mob poured in. It is not clear, and it probably never will be what exact proportion of the besieged gave friendly admittance to the besiegers and what proportion remained loyal to their salt. But there were undoubtedly many true-hearted soldiers among the garrison, as the protracted resistance would itself suffice to prove.

The Mullagori and Shilmani sepoys escaped over the wall with their rifles, while the Zakka and Malikdin Khel men took refuge under the flags of their clansmen in the attacking force, and joined in looting the post. The Adam Khel sepoys had joined the besieging *lashkar* at the very outset. Of the 40 Peshawaris, six were carried off as prisoners, while the remainder were allowed to escape after their rifles had been seized.

A Subadar who was killed just before the enemy effected an entrance into the *sarai*, and who conducted the defence, had two sons in the attacking force, and one son with him in the Khyber Rifles. The Subadar commanding the Mullagori company, when the enemy through treachery effected an entrance into the Fort, collected his company and fought his way through, losing several men in doing so. He then took his company through the Shilmani country, back to Jamrud, without the loss of a rifle.

When the Landi Kotal *sarai* had been looted and the quarters for the troops set on fire the Afridis began to break up, making for their homes in the Bazar Valley, and carrying their dead and wounded with them. This was done in spite of the protestations of the mullahs, who had organised the raid, and who wished to keep the *lashkar* together. There was apparently not enough fanaticism at work to induce the tribesmen to remain, and moreover they were running short of supplies. The most they were equal to was a promise to gather again on September 15th.

Coming now to consider the loss which the Khyber Rifles suffered throughout the whole raid upon the Khyber, Colonel Aslam Khan, their old commandant, who was acting as Political Officer in the Khyber, put it at 10 only, killed and wounded. The losses of the Afridi tribesmen were put at 34 at Fort Maude, 12 at Ali Musjid, and 200 at Landi Kotal.

It may be worth recalling here that in the agreement of 1881 between the Government of India and the Afridis the following paragraph was subscribed to by the headmen of the tribe : " We understand we are exclusively responsible for the future management of the Khyber, and that Government in no way shares in this responsibility, and this position we accept." Under the same agreement a corps of Thezailchis was raised among the tribes to garrison Ali Musjid and Landi Kotal, and this during the succeeding sixteen years had expanded into the corps of the Khyber Rifles, about 1,000 strong, the cost of which had been defrayed by the Government of India, the annual charge being roughly two lakhs. Yet another lakh yearly had been paid in tribal allowances. As an offset againt this the tolls levied on caravans had been collected by Government. The Afridis, therefore, in their raid not only attacked their fellow-clansmen enlisted in the Rifles, but broke the agreement which had been in force since 1881 and had worked till then without a hitch.

Before leaving the Khyber it has to be mentioned that one of the most serious results of the capture of Landi Kotal was that an immense quantity of ammunition fell into the hands of the enemy. When intelligence came in that 10,000 tribesmen were marching on the Khyber, Captain Barton, strong in the belief at the time that the pass would be held, sent up fifty thousand rounds to that place, and when he was peremptorily recalled by Sir Richard Udny he had of course to leave this reserve behind him. No effort was made by the authorities at Peshawar to secure the ammunition, though three days elapsed before the Afridis entered the pass.

CHAPTER III.

THE RISING OF THE ORAKZAI.

A FURTHER example of the extraordinary want of tactical combination among the frontier tribes was supplied by the inactivity of the Orakzai while their allies the Afridis were raiding the Khyber. The Orakzai, it will be remembered, had bound themselves by a compact with the Afridis to rise as soon as the latter made a demonstration, yet they waited until the Afridis had withdrawn from the Khyber and entirely dispersed before themselves commencing hostilities, thus losing a great opportunity. Now that the attention of our Peshawar and Kohat troops was no longer anxiously engaged, the Orakzai at last made a tardy advance upon our border and on the 26th of August imitated the Afridis by capturing the Ublan Pass. But their success was short-lived, for the very next day, as will presently be related, General Yeatman-Biggs recaptured the pass and completely routed the Orakzai *lashkar*.

The Ublan Pass, some six miles north-west of Kohat, lies on the boundary line separating the Bizoti section of the Orakzai from British territory. It was obviously a matter of very considerable importance, looked at from every point of view, that no disturbance should be allowed to ferment unchecked in the neighbourhood of a pass which overlooks the high-road of our communications to Kurram and is within so short a distance of a comparatively small cantonment like Kohat. Before narrating in detail the events which occurred during the recapture of this supposed impregnable position by the then small force under General Yeatman-Biggs, on the 27th August, it may be interesting to glance briefly at previous operations directed against the Bizotis. In March 1868, various offences against life and property committed by this section of the Daulatzai clan culminated in the occupation by them of the Ublan Kotal with a threat to attack the towers and village at the foot of the pass. Accordingly on the morning of the 11th March, a small force moved out from Kohat consisting of two guns of a light field battery and some 500 men of the 3rd and 6th Punjab Infantry. The position was assaulted and the enemy gradually driven back into a strong breastwork situated on the summit of a perpendicular crag on the right of the pass. Three attempts were made to storm this position, all of which failed, and the troops retired at sunset, having suffered the heavy loss of 11 killed and 44 wounded, including 1 Officer killed and 2 wounded. Again in the following year the pass was crossed secretly at night by a force sent out from Kohat. This movement being totally unexpected no resistance was encountered, and the force moved down to the village of Gora on the other side. Having destroyed this village the troops returned at once over the pass, closely followed by the enemy, who had by now taken the alarm and were up in arms. The losses on this occasion were 3 killed and 33 wounded, most of the casualties occurring on the way down from the summit of the pass, where the troops were exposed at every turn of the path to a galling fire from above. This short resumé of operations in the neighbourhood of the Ublan may suffice to show that the position is one of great natural strength, justifying the Bizotis to a certain extent in their boast that when properly defended it was impregnable. Let us now turn to actual events.

On the 25th August news was brought in from Mahomedzai, the fort which is situated near the foot of the pass, that some sniping had been going on at night and that the enemy had occupied the *sungars* which had been the scene of the defeat of our troops 29 years ago. The same day Major Bewicke-Copley, Intelligence Officer, and Captain Wake, Orderly Officer to General Yeatman-Biggs, rode out from Kohat and reconnoitred the ground. The next night our levy post was rushed by some Bizotis and Utman Khels,* and one man was killed, one havildar and one man wounded, and the remaining levies fled for refuge to Mahomedzai. At dusk on the 26th, Mahomedzai had been reinforced by one company of the 2nd Punjab Infantry under Captain Cooper.

At 4 A.M. on the 27th August a force consisting of one squadron 3rd Punjab Cavalry, six guns No. 9 Field Battery, two companies Royal Scots Fusiliers, and the 2nd Punjab Infantry moved out from Kohat to attack the pass. General Yeatman-Biggs arrived on the scene at daybreak and the guns took up a position near a tank on the plain at the foot of the pass, and opened fire at 2,200 yards. After some very pretty shooting, Major Wedderburn succeeded in almost completely silencing the enemy's frontal fire and also that on the crags to our left, but the latter afterwards broke out again during the advance. Dispositions were then made for the attack, the 2nd Punjab Infantry leading and the Royal Scots Fusiliers lying in reserve, with the squadron of the 3rd Punjab Cavalry as escort to the guns. The troops advanced up the centre of the pass, and when about half-way found themselves exposed to a galling and very accurate

---
* From a previous explanation it will be understood that this clan has no connection with the Utman Khels lying between Swat and Bajour.

fire, coming chiefly from the left flank, where a number of sharpshooters were concealed amongst some steep crags overlooking the pass. These crags were a serious difficulty during the whole progress of the engagement: they are perpendicular and quite inaccessible, and it is impossible either to scale or to outflank them. Here a number of the enemy remained concealed, keeping up a galling fire, and no counter-fire could dislodge them. About 8 A.M. the Kotal was gained—Lieutenant Elsmie, Adjutant of the 2nd Punjab Infantry, who had led his company most gallantly from first to last, being the first to arrive at the summit. The enemy did not wait to try conclusions at close quarters, but were seen rapidly retreating in a fairly compact body down the other side of the pass, where they crossed the Bara River and entered the village beyond. Volleys were fired after them, both from the main attack and also by the men of the 2nd Punjab Infantry on the right. Meanwhile the right attack had been having some sharp work: after fighting their way from ridge to ridge they gained the crest and swept the enemy before them, the two companies being well lead by Lieutenant Eales and Subadar Bhuta Ram respectively. The troops had to fight their way up a rocky and almost precipitous hill with little or no available cover, under a burning sun and exposed to a heavy fire. The heat indeed was terrible, and the European troops suffered a good deal, one man dying of heat-apoplexy. No water was procurable, and the ground was too bad to allow of mules being brought up. The casualties during the advance were: 1 sepoy, 2nd Punjab Infantry, killed, and Subadar Akhbar Khan and 10 sepoys, 2nd Punjab Infantry, wounded.

The retirement began about 10·30 A.M. and was carried out in *echelon*, the main body moving off first down the centre of the pass, followed in turn by the Royal Scots Fusiliers and the two companies of the 2nd Punjab Infantry who had originally advanced on the right. The enemy promptly followed up, and it was now that most of the casualties occurred. During all this time the snipers concealed among the crags on the left had maintained a galling fire, and they now kept moving down and harassing our rear-guard. About half-way down Captain Baird Smith and Lieutenant L. A. North, both of the Royal Scots Fusiliers, were severely wounded, the former in the ankle, and the latter in the stomach, the bullet by a fortunate chance running round under the ribs and coming out without having penetrated very deeply. Surgeons-Captain Beyts and Bamfield, A.M.S., rendered prompt and efficient aid to the wounded; the former with the aid of a sepoy carrying a wounded Officer for some distance down the hill under a heavy fire when the ground was too bad for *doolies* to be used. The retirement was well and steadily carried out, but the troops on reaching the foot of the pass were almost completely exhausted, 16 men of the Royal Scots Fusiliers having been knocked over by the sun. However tongas had been sent out from Kohat for these and the wounded, and after a short rest the remainder marched back to cantonments going well and strong. The total casualties were : 1 private, Royal Scots Fusiliers, and 1 sepoy, 2nd Punjab Infantry, killed; 2 Officers, Royal Scots Fusiliers, 2 Warrant Officers, 2nd Punjab Infantry, and 8 sepoys wounded, of whom two afterwards died. Several of the enemy were dressed in khaki and appeared to be old sepoys, both from the steadiness and accuracy of their fire and from the manner in which they at once distinguished the Officers. They were armed chiefly with Sniders.

While the action on the Ublan Pass was in progress other hostilities of less magnitude were occurring to the west, on the Samana Range. On the evening of the 20th August, pressing news having been received at Kohat from both the Kurram Valley and the Samana posts, a flying column started at 7 P.M. for Hangu, under the command of Colonel Richardson and consisting of the 18th Bengal Lancers, four guns No. 2 Derajat Mountain Battery, the 5th Punjab Infantry and one squadron 3rd Punjab Cavalry. The 26 miles were covered by 5 A.M. the following morning, and the force encamped at Hangu facing the Samana Range. Rumours of the enemy's movements and intentions being most conflicting, a reconnaissance was made by the cavalry the following day to Marai, about 7 miles from Hangu, and at the eastern end of the Khanki Valley in rear of the Samana; but without encountering any hostile force. The following days were spent in reconnaissance in various directions, but nothing definite could be ascertained regarding the enemy's position. Various dates were given for intended tribal attacks, Friday being the most likely day of the week, as the one most favoured by the Prophet. The mullahs were said to have given out that all Sikhs were to be wiped out, but special attention was to be paid to the 5th Punjab Infantry, this regiment being apparently singled out for tribal revenge owing to their occupation of the Samana for a year previously. On the 22nd August a convoy of ammunition to replenish Forts Lockhart and Gulistan was sent up to the Samana from Hangu under Colonel Jameson, the escort consisting of the 5th Punjab Infantry and 2 guns, and being accompanied by Colonel Richardson and his flying column. No opposition was met with, although it was ascertained afterwards that a thousand of the enemy had been watching the force the whole way, but had thought it more prudent not to attack. For the next few days nothing happened of much interest except that the usual rumours of an intended attack on the camp were more frequent than ever.

On the morning of the 27th August at 7 A.M., the troops at Hangu were aroused by three loud reports coming from the border police posts of Lakha just above Hangu on the Samana ridge. As this was the pre-arranged signal of distress, a column was at once ordered out, consisting of the 16th Sikhs and two guns, under Colonel Abbott. This column left at 9 A.M., and commenced the ascent up the graded road to Lakha. The enemy never appeared in large numbers, but contended themselves with firing from behind every possible bit of cover, and managed to enfilade the road so successfully that the infantry were forced to leave it when about half-way up and make a direct ascent up the khud. The ground was most difficult and steep, but the regiment went straight ahead, sweeping all opposition away and reaching the crest in a marvellously short time everything considered. The enemy melted away on the northern slopes of the Samana and also away to the east where they could find excellent cover. During this advance the 15th Sikhs lost one follower killed, one follower wounded and one sepoy wounded. Meanwhile a wing of the 5th Punjab Infantry had moved out from Hangu under Major F. P. L. White in support, and on reaching the crest this wing managed most successfully to keep the enemy in check, while Colonel Abbott with the 15th and his two guns moved further west to carry out the task assigned to him, viz., to relieve Lakha and bring away the garrison with their rifles and ammunition. This movement was followed up by small parties of the enemy incessantly : they did not, however, venture to anything like close quarters. Having relieved the Lakha Post, Colonel Abbott halted, after firing a few shells at the enemy dispersing down the northern slope of the Samana. Then hearing that the post of Saifaldara, still further to the west, was also hard pressed, Colonel Abbott pushed on as rapidly as possible, this movement being similarly covered by the 5th Punjab Infantry. Whilst all this was being done, the remainder of the 5th Punjab Infantry under Colonel Jameson had moved out from Hangu up to the foot of the hills, ready to cover Colonel Abbott's retirement. It was, however, found impossible to signal successfully so as to ascertain Colonel Abbott's intention, and eventually this wing, which was accompanied by Colonel Richardson and

Staff, moved along the foot of the hills to the Saifaldara road where it was thought Colonel Abbott would eventually descend. Great anxiety was for some time felt regarding his force, as heavy firing was continually heard and nothing could be seen of the force. At 7 P.M., however, the remaining wing was much relieved to see some guns about half-way down the Saifaldara road from the Samana, and this proved to be Colonel Abbott's force retiring covered by the first-mentioned wing of the 5th Punjab Infantry. The remaining wing now halted, and moved straight up the spurs covering the zig-zag road, for some thousand feet. The ascent was extremely difficult over huge volcanic jagged rocks with large crevices intervening, and the men were quite exhausted when they reached the last position to be held. Meanwhile it was getting quite dark, and the enemy grew bolder, yelling and firing as they came along down the rocky spurs and even venturing on the road. One small body of some 50 in attempting a kind of charge met with a severe check, six of them falling from a volley fired by the 5th Punjab Infantry. The retirement had now to be finally made, for when the zigzags had been passed the road debouched into a small basin behind the low hills, and then passed through the latter in a very narrow defile. When the last remaining companies reached this place, the enemy were still further emboldened and hovered all round, shouting and firing continuously. Still, fortunately, they did not charge home as they might and it was perhaps the darkness alone which prevented the regiment having a very bad time. As it was, three men were lost, two of whom however turned up during the night, the other being cut up. It was a great relief to reach the open country beyond. After forming up, the whole column moved off and reached the camp at Hangu, unmolested, by 11 P.M.; most of the troops having had no food and very little water for 14 hours.

The following night the troops were aroused by a tramp of feet in the distance and the familiar shouts of a *ghazi* rush. The men fell in quite quietly at their posts, and a few scattered shots were fired by the enemy, but nothing more occurred. That same night the Royal Irish and the 9th Field Battery arrived in camp from Kohat, which perhaps explained why the expected attack was not made.

There was now a fairly strong force concentrated at Hangu, ready to move anywhere at the shortest notice. At the same time there were persistent rumours that Hangu itself and the vicinity would shortly be attacked, and this prevented Colonel Richards's flying column from moving on to the Kurram Valley. A force was held in readiness to move out and assist Gulistan, but they helio'd that there was no urgency. On the night of the 29th August, just as the men were retiring for the night, fairly heavy and continuous firing began from the overlooking hills, several bullets falling in and about the camp one grazing a sepoy's puggari and one falling near the field hospital. The troops fell in, as usual, perfectly quietly and without the slightest confusion, and refrained from returning a single shot, and the enemy at last left the camp in peace. Transport, field hospitals, and other accessories had now been rapidly coming up, and the force received a useful addition in the Bombay Sappers and Miners.

Meanwhile news had been received that the border police post at Shinawari had been attacked and burnt, and that the Orakzai, emboldened by their success, had attacked and pillaged the adjacent villages of Kahi and Nariah, looting the Hindu bunniahs. The following morning the Field Battery and the 18th Bengal Lancers moved out to Shinawari, hoping to catch the enemy returning to the hills with their spoil. No sign however was seen of them, and the little force returned to camp on the evening of the 30th August much fatigued, having covered 40 miles. This movement was carried out under Colonel Mansel, 3rd Punjab Cavalry. That same evening it was noticed that several men were lurking about on the near hills above the camp, whence the firing had come, and some few were seen to make for a cave, evidently a refuge whence to safely snipe into camp. Accordingly one of the 12-pounders was trained on to the cave during daylight, and about 9 P.M. a shrapnel shell was fired into it. As may be easily imagined, no more sniping occurred, and five or six bodies were being buried the following day.

On the 31st August General Yeatman-Biggs with his Staff rode into Hangu from Kohat, bringing in news of the arrival of his brigade safely through the Kohat Pass. When about six miles from Hangu, the General's baggage was attacked by a small raiding party of the enemy. The driver was wounded, and Major Bewicke-Copley's servant was hit three times, without however being seriously hurt. The Major's baggage was riddled by bullets. Some of the baggage was carried off, but the escort to a large convoy then arriving, assisted by a small party sent out from Hangu, managed to recover everything and drive off the enemy.

The Maharajah of Kuch Behar joined General Yeatman-Biggs at Hangu on the 8th September. His Highness had volunteered for active service on four previous occasions, but this was the first time he had been allowed to proceed to the front.

CHAPTER IV.

THE RELIEF OF THE KURRAM VALLEY FORTS.

The night before the arrival of General Yeatman-Biggs, the 15th Sikhs, two mountain guns, two squadrons of the 18th Bengal Lancers and the Bombay Sappers and Miners, the whole under Colonel Abbott, moved out from Hangu towards Thal, serious news having been received that a general and simultaneous attack was intended on Thal and Sadda and various other points in the Kurram Valley. The column was followed at midday on the 1st September by the 5th Punjab Infantry, two other mountain guns, and two other squadrons, 18th Bengal Lancers, the whole being accompanied by Colonel Richardson, who had now been appointed to the command of all the troops composing the Kurram relieving force as well as of the troops already in the Kurram. This proved a most tiring march, for the troops had been on half rations for some time. The heat was terrific, the sun blazing down on the men's faces. The transport column, having been made up in a great hurry, consisted of carts, donkeys, bullocks, ekkas, besides the regulation camels and mules. Doaba was safely reached by the second half of the relieving column at about 11 P.M., but the rear-guard did not arrive until 2 A.M., having been fired into. Two of the snipers were captured and brought into Thal, where they were incarcerated. The troops bivouacked at Doaba inside a thorn zareba which a little while previously had been occupied by the 1st half of the column under Colonel Abbott.

It was ascertained that Captain Chesney of the 18th Bengal Lancers, who was with the 1st half of the column, after reconnoitring towards Shinawari had obtained a guide to show him a good camping ground at Doaba. This guide made a deliberate attempt to lead the cavalry into an ambush, for when nearing the large nullah which runs to the west of Doaba, it was seen to contain some 1,500 of the enemy, the ground moreover being unsuitable for cavalry work, and the enemy being in great strength. Captain Chesney dismounted some men and fired at the ambuscaders, retiring gradually so as to allow the 15th Sikhs to come up. He managed thus to kill three or four of the enemy, who disappeared in all directions on the approach of the 15th Sikhs and the battery. The guns completed their rout with a few well-directed shells, and the column marched into Doaba. The second night they were fired into heavily, good aim being taken at the mess table where the Officers were dining and where a lamp was burning, Colonel Abbott having a very narrow escape. Some companies were sent out, and a few volleys managed to keep the camp free from sniping for the rest of the night. Just before the arrival of the 2nd half of the column Colonel Abbott had left for Thal, intending to push on to Sadda in the Kurram Valley as soon as possible.

The camp of the 2nd half of the column was somewhat confused, and in the pitch darkness it was almost impossible to find one's way about the zareba, amid the jumble of transport animals. The troops were completely exhausted after their 23 miles in the heat, and had scarcely energy left to cook their food. At 6 A.M. the following morning, Colonel Richardson pushed on with the cavalry in the tracks of Colonel Abbott, to Thal, followed by the 5th Punjab Infantry and two guns under Colonel Jameson. This was again a very trying march, and the troops had comparatively little rest to prepare them for it. At 1 P.M., however, Thal was safely reached, and the march of 36 miles completed in 36 hours: no great record in itself but for the fact of the heat and want of food. The men, however, were rewarded here, for supplies were plentiful, and they could rest till the following morning. The cavalry meanwhile had had a small engagement. Whilst camping near Thal, some of the 18th Bengal Lancers had gone into the village, and the last of them, who, by the way, was a Sikh, was shot dead just as he entered. The alarm was quickly sounded, and the men, who were about to water their horses, mounted as they were, turned out and pursued some 20 or 30 armed men, who fled across the surrounding fields towards the hills, firing as they went. Six were killed and 14 taken prisoners, but unfortunately the man who had shot the sowar escaped. His property, however, was confiscated and destroyed, and the occurrence evidently had a good general effect on the people. Apparently that same night had been fixed upon for a big attack on Thal fort. The troops lined the ramparts all night, but the force was evidently too imposing for the enemy, and the following day the Kabul Khel Waziris, who were breeding this trouble, had dispersed. The march to Sadda was resumed in the same order on the 3rd September. Colonel Richardson pushing on with the cavalry in support of Colonel Abbott, and the remainder following a few hours later. Everything looked wonderfully peaceful and fertile all along the Kurram Valley.

Colonel Abbott's half of the column made Alizai on the morning of the 3rd September, and Sadda at 3-30 P.M. on the 4th, thus completing a very fine march under exceptionally difficult circumstances, the men being without tents. The 2nd half of the column halted at Manduri, 13 miles beyond Thal, marched the next day to Alizai, 9 miles, and reached Sadda on the 5th September at about 2 P.M., in pelting rain. The 3rd Gurkhas arrived shortly afterwards, whereupon the Kurram Valley Brigade under Colonel Richardson became complete, consisting of the 18th Bengal Lancers, No. 2 Derajat Mountain Battery (4 guns), one company Bombay Sappers and Miners, the 15th Sikhs, and the 5th Punjab Infantry.

No doubt when Colonel Abbott with the advance troops reached Sadda, after marching 49 miles in 40 hours, a little disappointment was felt at finding all quiet instead of a hardly-pressed garrison selling their lives dearly. But as a matter of fact the arrival of the troops was most opportune and probably saved the situation in the valley. A gathering of some 3,000 to 4,000 Orakzai was threatening Sadda village seriously, and the militia post at Balesh Khel still more closely, and their advance-guard of 500 men had actually committed themselves to an attack, the remainder waiting to see how things would go. So hard did the enemy press, that one mullah was killed at the very door of the fort. The moment the troops neared the place, however, the whole gathering melted as if by magic, and everything was now perfectly peaceful again. At Parachinar, beyond Sadda, the garrison could no doubt have held out against immense odds. Sadda, with its garrison of 50 Sikhs, 100 Kurram militia, and 300 or 400 Turis, would also have been a hard nut to crack. Yet the position was critical, especially in view of the scarcity of ammunition. Worse than all, the slightest advantage gained by the tribes would probably have doubled their numbers, and part of the Lower Kurram might also have risen, while the rest of the valley would have been given over to fire and sword. The political effect of such a reverse would have been serious. All this was saved by Colonel Abbott's promptness. Opening a telegram, as it afterwards transpired, from the Political Officer in the Karram Valley to the Commissioner (which was also addressed to the Officer commanding the troops on the road), he saw that troops were urgently required, and instead of waiting for orders determined to advance at once. Colonel Richardson arrived in time to approve of the plan. Meanwhile the troops, consisting of two guns No. 2 Derajat Mountain Battery, the 15th

Sikhs and half of No. 4 Company Bombay Sappers, had begun their trying march to Sadda. The heat, as already described, was intense by day while at night heavy rain added to the discomfort of the men. Owing to scarcity of mule transport only one blanket per man could be taken, and owing to the hostility of the villagers, supplies could scarcely be obtained. Once in the Kurram, however, the friendly Turis readily brought out supplies.

It has been said that the arrival of Colonel Richardson's flying column altered the situation in the Kurram Valley. That situation, so far as it had developed before the appearance of the relieving troops, may now be described at a little greater length. On the 29th of August it was reported that the Mussazai, Mamozai, and Alisherzai, three powerful sections of the Orakzai, had risen and determined to attack Sadda in force. The wire was working as far as Thal, but news was received that an important telegram, which should have been taken on from Thal to Hangu by sowars, had been brought back to Thal: the sowar carrying it, instead of finding a relief at the first police post, had found the post quite deserted. The mail had brought news of fighting on the Samana, and it seemed as if the disturbances on the Samana were spreading to the country between Thal and Hangu. As a matter of fact raiders were out in Upper Miranzai, and even Kurram villagers were turning against the garrisons. Under the circumstances, it seemed as if the Kurram Valley would be left to look after itself. The Sikh garrison of Sadda therefore was increased by 25 rifles and 200 Kurram militia were despatched under Captain Maconchy, District Staff Officer, to the village of Hassan Ali, 7 miles east of Sadda. His orders were to endeavour by making a show of strength to postpone the attack of the tribes as long as possible, and to help the neighbouring villages as far as possible, but not to engage any overwhelming force of the enemy; in the event of the tribes attacking in force, a retreat was to be made to the Kurmana River, 6 miles from Parachinar, where troops would be ready to cover the retirement. For the above purpose a movable column was organised, consisting of 20 sabres, 3rd Punjab Cavalry, two guns No. 2 Derajat Mountain Battery, 100 rifles 36th Sikhs and 300 rifles 1-5th Gurkha Rifles, the whole under the command of Major Vansittart, the Officer commanding the Kurram garrison. As little transport as possible accompanied the column, practically nothing but reserve ammunition and one day's cooked rations were carried on mules. On the 31st August Captain Maconchy reported that there had been slight firing during the night in the direction of Badama, a Mussazai village about 3 miles from Sadda; and that although the Mamozai and Alisherzai had gone off to the Samana, they had left 700 or 800 Mussazai threatening Sadda. A later report improved upon this by stating that 2,000 tribesmen were collected 5 miles from Sadda. Still graver news was received in the evening, when the Political Officer received a telegram saying that the advance of reinforcements had been postponed for the present. This, however, was capped at 10 P.M. by information arriving that 3,000 Afridis and Orakzai had now collected at Badama; that they had brought their women-folk and rations, and that they intended to make a combined attack on Sadda on the night of the 3rd September. The wire was still working as far as Thal, and a message asking for troops was sent off in the middle of the night. Almost immediately afterwards the line was broken up in three separate places, and damaged to such an extent that no attempt was made for the time being to repair it. On the morning of the 1st September the Intelligence Officer heard that the Afridis and Orakzai had been waiting for contingents to arrive from the Chamkannis and Alisherzai, amongst whom mullahs had been sent to stir up a feeling of fanaticism and hostility against the Government. But these two sections were disinclined to join the tribal gathering, so the Afridis had voted to attack without them. This they did the same night. About 2,000 men marched straight for Sadda, halting in the jungle about a mile off. The remainder proceeded to attack Balish Khel, an isolated militia post, about 3 miles from Sadda, which was built so as to enable raiders to be cut off, when returning to the hills. The Afridis apparently did not relish the idea of leaving this small post in their rear, and so determined to take it first, and then, uniting their forces, to attack Sadda. The firing began in broad daylight, and increased as twilight deepened into darkness, when a continuous fusillade was kept up on every side till midnight. The Balish Khel Post consists of a small tower with a courtyard on the south side, in which are the huts inhabited by the garrison, which amounted at the time of attack to 20 men of the Kurram militia, under a havildar. No doubt the Afridis expected to make short work of this mere handful of men. But the fire kept up from the ramparts was so severe that for a long time none of the attackers dared venture near the walls. About midnight ammunition began to run short; the Afridis crept up to the courtyard gate, and began to hew it to pieces with axes. This they soon succeeded in doing, but the fire from the tower still kept them, almost literally, at arm's length.

They tried, but failed to set the huts on fire. Matters were getting serious for the little garrison, and they made signals of distress by throwing up bundles of burning grass from the top of the tower. The enemy were now closing in, when help at last arrived from two directions. Fifty men (Malik Khels) arrived from Sadda, and charged right up to the fort walls, losing two of their number in doing so. The Afridis drew off, leaving two bodies in the gateway of the courtyard. Fifty Kurram militia also arrived from Hassan Ali, but they were just too late to get into touch with the enemy. Only one of our men in the fort was wounded. How many of the attackers were killed, it is impossible to say, but the Koran and standard of the mullah who led the attack were found on the ground in the morning, and blood stains were found here and there. The darkness of the night, however, and the good cover afforded by nullahs were a great advantage in favour of the attacking party. The Afridi havildar in command of Balish Khel had been called to by name, and asked to surrender; but he remained faithful to his salt, and replied to these overtures by volleys of Snider bullets. Both he and his men fought as well as men could, and the party of villagers from Sadda (only 50 strong) showed great pluck in going out to help the post, knowing as they did that the Afridis were attacking in force. It was lucky for them that they did not stumble in the darkness on the 2,000 men who were only waiting for the post to fall to advance and make an attack on Sadda. The 2nd September passed away quietly, so far as the tribes were concerned, except that some sowars were fired at close to Parachinar, when returning from patrol, about 11 P.M. But a passenger in the mail ekka brought in the pleasantly astonishing information that troops were on the road between Thal and Sadda, and that they would probably reach the latter place by the evening of the 3rd September. No official intimation of any move of troops had been received since the telegram came stating that the advance had been postponed; but next morning Mr. Hastings and Major Vansittart, who had proceeded to Sadda, got a letter saying that troops would arrive at Sadda by 6 P.M. The arrival of reinforcements was of course a still greater surprise to the Afridis than to the garrison; and instead of attempting a further attack the tribal gathering broke up.

The road into Sadda, on the 3rd and 4th September, presented a most extraordinary sight. On the 3rd, before the news of the advance of reinforcements had been confirmed by letter, bands upon bands of friendly Turis, horse and foot, could be seen making their way from

Upper Kurram to Sadda and other points likely to be attacked in Lower Kurram. The big attack was expected on the night of the 3rd September; all these men were going down to help to beat off the common enemy; they all gladly responded to the call of the Political Officer, and every village sent a contingent, just as they would have done in the old days, before we took over the safe custody of the valley. Many an old raider's heart must have beat quicker as he thought of the past, when he had ridden forth in just the same way on some foray far across the border. Breechloaders were very scarce, but two-thirds of the men had *jezails*, and all of them had the long Pathan knife stuck through their *kummerbunds*, while here and there was a revolver or pistol, the latter generally of native workmanship. To look at their merry faces, one would have imagined they were off to some wedding or other *tamasha* and not going to fight against odds for hearth and home. The Turi cavalry especially took things with evident lightness of heart. Here and there a grass *chupli* would be stuck up in the middle of the road, and the next minute it was to be seen at the end of a lance high in the air. The way they galloped along the hard high road was wonderful to see. The following day they were to be seen returning to their homes : the arrival of reinforcements in the very nick of time had made their presence no longer necessary in Lower Kurram. The Turis, the reader may be reminded, are Shiah Mahomedans ; whilst their tribal neighbours are almost without exception Sunnis, hence the division and inveterate animosity between the two.

But hostilities were not yet at an end in the Kurram Valley, despite the arrival at Sadda of Colonel Richardson's flying column ; indeed the very presence of so large a force in rear seemed to incite the now outflanked Orakzai tribes in the neighbourhood to renewed aggression. On the 16th September at 10-30 P.M., the Sadda camp was attacked from the direction of the Karmana defile. The advanced picket of the 5th Punjab Infantry was driven in by a sudden rush of the enemy, assisted by villagers living three miles east of Sadda. The retirement was admirably covered by the steady company volleys of the 5th Gurkhas, under Lieutenants Kitchen and Browne, and the section volleys of the 5th Punjab Infantry. The portion of the camp attacked was the east face, held partly by the wing of the 5th Gurkhas, under Major Vansittart, which had just arrived after a trying march from Parachinar, with two mountain guns, and partly by a wing of the 5th Punjab Infantry. The plan of the attack had evidently been carefully thought out, the force held by the Gurkhas being kept engaged by several hundred of the enemy, whilst the main attack was made on the south-east corner held by the 5th Punjab Infantry. Here the ground, especially that formerly held by the 5th Punjab Infantry picket, lent itself admirably to the tactics subsequently adopted by the enemy, who, finding the garrison on the alert, abandoned the idea of rushing the camp, and settled down to a musketry attack, pouring a steady and fairly well directed fire into the camp for about $2\frac{3}{4}$ hours, except for breaks of five minutes. The defence of the east face was valuably strengthened by a company of the 15th Sikhs, sent up by Colonel Abbott with admirable forethought. All the troops actively engaged were in position in the shortest possible time, and the first two steady and precise volleys of the gallant Gurkhas disabused the enemy's mind as to the possibility of effecting an entrance in that quarter, although their maintaining a position on broken ground 500 yards from the Gurkhas, coupled with the uncertain light, which concealed their numbers, prevented a counter-attack. Two companies of the 5th Punjab Infantry under Lieutenant A. G. Ames, and one company of the 15th Sikhs, the whole under Colonel Jameson's immediate command, consequently bore the main brunt of the enemy's attack. Colonel Richardson, commanding the flying column, and his Staff Officer, Captain Kennedy, were quickly on the spot, arranging for a reinforcement, and were assisted by Captain Eardley-Wilmot, and Lieutenants Rickets and Norman, of the 18th Bengal Lancers. The discipline of all ranks was excellent, and although the casualties amongst the horses and transport were heavy, the order that prevailed throughout the attack of three hours spoke highly for the arrangements of the column and for the quiet energy of all the British and Native Officers when exposed to a fire to which there was no opportunity of response. The enemy was estimated at 2,000 strong; their casualties were unknown, but from a visit to Badhura village it was apparent that large numbers were wounded, the dead having already been buried. Our total casualties were: 1 man killed, 5 wounded, and 5 followers wounded ; 2 horses killed and 9 wounded ; 3 mules killed and 2 wounded ; 2 camels killed and 5 wounded.

A week later the Chamkanni tribe, of about 1,700 fighting men, in north Kurram, joined the ranks of the enemy ; a fact of no great importance except so far as it illustrated the unusual extent to which excitement on the border had now spread, for according to Bellew's *Races of Afghanistan* the Chamkannis are "a quiet, inoffensive and industrious people, and distinguished by the non-existence among them of feudal fights and highway robberies."

CHAPTER V.

TRIBAL ATTACK ON OUR SAMANA FORTS—SARAGHERI AND GULISTAN.

On September 10th, information reached General Yeatman-Biggs on the Samana that a combined Orakzai and Afridi *lashkar* had begun to move down the Khanki Valley. A reconnaissance confirmed the news, as several thousand men were seen marching eastwards. It was surmised that Shahu Khel was their first objective, and that the large village of Ibrahimzai on the Kohat-Hangu road might also be threatened. Shahu Khel is only three miles north of Ibrahimzai, which again is five miles east of Hangu. General Yeatman-Biggs accordingly set his column in motion, and marched along the Samana ridge towards Lakha and Shahu Khel in order to intercept the enemy and cover Ibrahimzai. The column consisted of a detachment of the Royal Irish Regiment, the 1st Battalions of the 2nd and 3rd Gurkhas and the 2nd Punjab Infantry. The enemy, who came in touch with the rear of the column at dusk, numbered from 3,000 to 4,000, all Sheikhan, Mishti and Mala Khel clans of the Orakzai, carrying 11 standards. They attacked the rear-guard, consisting of a half battalion of the 3rd Gurkhas and five companies of the 2nd Gurkhas, about 4 miles from the bivouac by Gogra Hill. The rear-guard kept the enemy in check by steady volleys, in spite of rushes made up to 20 yards from the muzzles, and escorted all the mule transport in safety. The *sarwans* left the camels and bolted, with one exception, and the camels threw off their loads and wandered off the road, several being hit by bullets. Two companies of the 2nd Punjab Infantry, under Lieutenant Elsmie, accompanied by Captain Scudamore, Deputy Assistant Quartermaster-General, went out and covered the retirement of the Gurkhas very smartly. Of the enemy Yar Muhamed, a leading Chief of the Sheikhan, five lesser chiefs of the Mala Khel, and 25 others were killed, and a very large number of wounded were carried off. Our casualties were 4 men killed and 9 wounded. Captain J. G. Robinson, 2nd Gurkhas, was slightly wounded. The bodies of our killed were recovered the next morning by Colonel Lawrence's column.

Having checked the enemy's advance, General Yeatman-Biggs was obliged, owing to the want of water, to return to Hangu, where his column halted on the 12th and 13th September, ready to move out again in any direction should the enemy reappear.

As for the Orakzai, finding they were blocked on the east of the Samana they turned their attention to the small posts on the range itself, a *lashkar* moving up from Khorappa so as to place itself between Forts Lockhart and Gulistan.*

After repeated assaults, the tribesmen succeeded in capturing on the 12th September, under circumstances that will long be remembered, the small post of Saragheri on the road between the two forts. The garrison, which consisted of only 21 men of the 36th Sikhs, made a gallant defence, holding out from 9 o'clock in the morning till 4·30 in the afternoon against odds which from the first were clearly overwhelming. Two determined assaults were brilliantly repulsed, but at the third rush the enemy succeeded in breaking down the door, and when the plucky Sikhs manning the walls rushed down from their posts to defend the doorway the swarming tribesmen scaled the walls and all was over. But not a sepoy even then thought of surrendering while life remained, and eventually the whole of the gallant defenders fell victims to their heroism. One stout-hearted soldier in the guardroom killed twenty of the enemy without hurt to himself, and lost his life by refusing to budge when the Afridis, unable to get at him, finally set the room on fire. The signaller, as brave as the rest, coolly kept up communication with Fort Lockhart up till the very last moment. The entire garrison in fact behaved with splendid courage, and there is perhaps no more touching instance of inflexible devotion to duty than this in the whole narrative of frontier fighting. The details of the fight will never be known, for not a soldier came out of Saragheri alive, but if the story could be told it would beyond doubt be one of the most thrilling that Sikh valour has ever furnished. The facts related here came mainly from the enemy, and may not be absolutely correct, but at all events no more reliable account of the fall of Saragheri will ever be obtainable.

A fund was subsequently opened by the *Pioneer* with the object of benefitting the widows and families of the 21 fallen Sikhs and of erecting some suitable monument in the Punjab to perpetuate the memory of the defence of Saragheri. Before the end of the year over Rs.20,000 had been subscribed.

It has been mentioned that the signaller at Saragheri kept up communication with Fort Lockhart while the Afridis were storming the walls. On the receipt of the news of the attack, the garrison at Fort

---
* Otherwise known as Cavagnari.

Lockhart attempted a diversion by sending out 100 rifles, but this little force was threatened on its right flank and forced to fall back.

The capture of Saragheri and the slaughter of its brave little garrison served to direct attention some time later to the system under which small posts are held along the frontier. "Some of them," wrote the *Pioneer* in an indignant article, "are certain death-traps in case of attack by large bodies of tribesmen, and in the interests of those who have to defend them something should be done to give the garrisons some chance of holding out until help can reach them. In more than one instance we read of wooden-doors having been forced open: is there any good reason why those doors should not be so placed as to be out of the reach of any one who has not a scaling ladder? Cannot thick sheet-iron be substituted for wood? All along the borderland and in Afghanistan are towers which might well be taken as patterns for our very small posts. The lower portions of these are of rocks and stones; the door is 10 or 15 feet above the ground; and access to the tower is gained by a ladder which is pushed up when there is an alarm of an enemy approaching. At Saragheri, and at Sadda also, the doors seem to have been flush with the ground, and the tribesmen could thus get at them with pickaxes, and, in the case of Saragheri, force an entrance. The fact seems to be that our smaller posts are built for occupation by levies, and the men ordinarily occupying them can generally arrange to make terms with their assailants and so escape with their lives. But when war breaks out and there is a great rush of hostile bodies across our frontier, some of the posts have to be taken over by regular troops and held at all costs. They are hastily provisioned, a scanty supply of water is given to the garrison, and only in the matter of abundant ammunition are our sepoys made happy. They cheerfully face the danger into which they are thus thrust and they die fighting to the last. There must be something very wrong in a system which thus makes the fate of a small party of soldiers a foregone conclusion. We are told that it was essential to hold Saragheri in order to maintain communication by signalling between Forts Lockhart and Gulistan. If that were so the little post should have been originally made so strong that it could hold out for at least three or four days."

The opinion may also be quoted here of an Officer who inspected what was left of Saragheri after it had been re-captured by our troops.* He declared that the post was situated in a hopeless place and that an attacking force could get up all round, under cover, quite close to the

---

* The re-capture of Saragheri has yet to be related.

walls. To have defended it successfully 100 men at least would have been required, and the door should have been bullet-proof. The 21 Sikhs had no chance of holding their own. The discovery was also made that the bastions of all the forts on the Samana have a "dead corner," so that if a few men can manage to creep up undiscovered they can dig away at the walls in perfect safety from rifle-fire. This was what actually happened at Saragheri.

On the 12th of September, at the time that Saragheri was attacked, Fort Gulistan was closely invested by a large Orakzai *lashkar*. On the fall of Saragheri, at about 4 P.M., the investment of Gulistan became a regular attack, the enemy there being joined by a considerable part of the force which had been at Saragheri. During the night of the 12th-13th, the enemy, who were in great force behind Picket Hill, about 350 yards from the western end of the hornwork, pushed their advanced parties close up to the hornwork, especially on the west and north. On the morning of the 13th September, the situation was decidedly serious; in addition to the force attacking Fort Gulistan all communication was cut off by *lashkars* of the enemy holding Saragheri heights, the Gogra heights and the Samana Suk. The most advanced post of the enemy, with several standards, was within 20 yards of the south-west corner of the hornwork, under cover of banks improved by *sangars* erected during the dark night. The enemy, elated by their success at Saragheri, were very bold, and it was feared that they might, as they had done at Saragheri, breach the fort wall at the dead angle of a bastion. Under these circumstances Major Des Vœux approved of the suggestion of Colour-Havildar Kala Singh, 36th Sikhs, who volunteered to take his section and attempt to drive the enemy out of their advanced post. The responsibility was very great : on the one hand, should the sortie be successful, the moral effect would be very great, both in dispiriting the enemy and in raising the spirits of the garrison; on the other hand failure would mean something very nearly akin to disaster ; and in any case it was certain that the small garrison, originally numbering 166 of all ranks, but already much reduced by casualties, would suffer still greater losses at a time when a single man could ill be spared.

Havildar Kala Singh's section numbered only 16 men in addition to their gallant leader, but they were men indeed. The enemy at the immediate point to be attacked numbered at least 200. The little party, with bayonets fixed, crept out of the south-east gateway and along the south wall of the hornwork; then when within 20 yards or so of the enemy made a rush. They were met with such a fire that they could not get up to the enemy; but though sadly reduced they had no thought of retreat, but lay down at a distance of only six paces from the enemy's *sangar* and returned the fire. At this juncture Colour-Havildar Sunder Singh and 12 men posted in the hornwork at the nearest point to the *sangar*, without waiting for orders and of their own initiative, scrambled over the wall and joined Kala Singh's section; and the combined party then charged the enemy, killed and wounded a great number, drove the remainder out and captured three of their standards, which they brought back to the fort amidst ringing cheers from their comrades. It was then discovered that two wounded men had been left behind. Three sepoys, two of whom had taken part in the sortie, at once of their own initiative again got over the wall and brought the two wounded men in.

During the sortie a hot fire was kept up from every effective rifle in the fort and hornwork, and thanks partly to this the casualties were not greater, though 12 of the first party and four of the second were wounded and several afterwards died.

The effect of the sortie was great, the garrison were in the highest spirits, whilst, it is said, the three sections of the Mamuzai represented by the three standards captured, returned to their homes, and Fort Gulistan saw them no more.*

Havildar Kala Singh was so seriously wounded that he died shortly afterwards. The so-called hornwork at Fort Gulistan, is an enclosure about 80 yards long by 30 broad, having the fort on one side and being surrounded by a wall of loose stones—a mere *sangar*—on the other three sides. This wall had been temporarily improved in places by logs of firewood, and atta bags and kerosine tins filled with earth and stones, to give a little head cover to the defenders.

Major Des Vœux now got through a letter for help to Fort Lockhart on the pretence of asking leave to surrender, the Afridis having offered to spare the lives of British Officers if all the forts were given up. By evening the enemy closed all round, and kept up a heavy fire. There were several casualties among the Officers and men, who had now been at their posts for 30 hours continuously. The enemy kept up the fire all night again, but at 7 P.M. the garrison saw a field battery in the Miranzai Valley firing on the enemy, and were much

---
* Till here the story of the seige of Gulistan is given in the exact words of Colonel Haughton's official report.

encouraged. All the next day and right through the night—the third night of the attack—the fatigued garrison were forced to stand to the defence, but at 8 o'clock on the morning of the 15th September they again heard firing in the distance, indicating the approach of help from Hangu, and felt cheered, though the enemy now closed in more fiercely than ever. At noon the tribal force then occupying the captured Saragheri post was shelled out by General Yeatman-Biggs's relieving force and soon afterwards Gulistan itself was rescued and the enemy completely driven off. The strength of the Gulistan garrison was as follows:—Major C. H. Des Vœux, Commanding; Lieutenant H. R. E. Pratt, Surgeon-Captain C. B. Pratt, and 165 rifles, 36th Sikhs; besides Mrs. Des Vœux, four children and two nurses. The Major had conducted the defence with untiring courage and cheerfulness, and was well backed up by Lieutenant Pratt. The Medical Officer, assisted by Miss McGrath (Mrs. Des Vœux's nurse) attended and nursed the wounded under continuous heavy fire; Miss Teresa McGrath's heroism was spoken of by Major Des Vœux in the warmest terms. The total loss was: 2 killed, 8 dangerously wounded, 8 seriously and 24 slightly wounded, of whom 7 did not report themselves wounded till the fort was relieved. There is no doubt that this fort, as well as the small posts of Sangar and Dhar, would have fallen but for the timely arrival of the relieving column. The following is an extract from a private letter, dated 18th September, received in Australia, from Major Des Vœux, and published in the *Queenslander:*—" My men here fought like tigers, but we lost heavily—44 out of 166, killed, wounded, and missing. Things were very serious indeed, but my men pulled me through. The enemy were all round, within twenty yards, well under cover and firing like mad. I ordered a sortie at 8 A.M. on the 13th, as the enemy were getting too close, and it was carried out with the most splendid gallantry, and we captured three standards. Teresa (Miss McGrath) surpassed herself attending to the sick and wounded. Her name has gone forward for reward and I hope she will get it. She will certainly get the medal, and probably an order. I have recommended thirty of my men for the Order of Merit (The Indian Victoria Cross). . . . A good many of my poor wounded are dead or dying; the rest have been sent to Fort Lockhart. I had 10,000 tribesmen all round me for three days, and we held out: they could have taken the fort easily if they had had the pluck. We killed and wounded 200 of the enemy." It afterwards transpired that Mrs. Des Vœux, who gave birth to a daughter during the fighting, had done noble service previously in attending to the wounded.

We have now to relate how it came about that General Yeatman-Biggs's relieving column arrived on the scene at such an opportune moment. It is necessary to go back to the 10th September, when General Yeatman-Biggs, hearing of the advance of the Orakzai and Afridi *lashkar*, had marched his column along the Samana ridge and after some rear-guard fighting had driven the enemy back up the Khanki Valley. It will be remembered that the absence of water on the Samana had compelled the General to hurry back with all speed to Hungu, and it was while he was making this return march that we left him, in order to follow the further movements of the enemy. From this point the Special Correspondent of the *Pioneer* at Hangu may be allowed to take up the narrative :—

"At 3-30 P.M. (he wrote) just as we had started on our return to Hangu, we received news by helio that the greater part of the *lashkar* we had been hunting had doubled on its tracks, and was at that moment investing the posts we had left the day before; Saragheri and Gulistan being hard pressed. There was not a drop of water to drink nearer than Hangu, and to fight our way back in the dark without it was, in view of the condition of men and animals, a physical impossibility. Very reluctantly the General, not daring to leave Hangu unprotected, followed the convoy, and we toiled painfully down the path, much harassed by the tribesmen, and at 6-30 P.M. arrived in camp dead beat. All next day we rested as well as we could, after receiving the news of the fall of Saragheri, which reached us that evening, haunted by the fear that we should be too late to relieve Gulistan, which, be it remembered, contained English women and children. As a diversion, five squadrons and four field guns were sent off under Major Middleton, 3rd Bengal Cavalry, to get as near as possible under Gulistan and do what they could. As it turned out, this was a good deal, for though their fire at that range could not be very effective, their appearance not only greatly cheered the beleagured garrison, but misled the enemy by suggesting to them that our advance would be made by Doaba. This they showed by breaking up the roads and planting *sangars* against us.

"At midnight the relieving force started from Hangu, carrying only great coats, waterproof sheets, blankets and one day's provisions, with every *pakhal* we could muster. The whole force was concentrated at Lakha by 4-30 A.M., and at daybreak we advanced to Gogra Hill. As we anticipated, the enemy, though taken by surprise, soon took possession of an ideal position on the hill with advanced posts at Tsalai, with 11 standards and about 4,000 men. They opened a hot and fairly accurate fire on our advance, but the guns which were brought up quickly into the front line soon produced an effect, and the 3rd Gurkhas, supported by the 2nd Gurkhas, stormed the hill. The enemy's retreat was pounded by the guns and long-range fire of the Royal Irish, and Colonel Haughton on the west, hurrying down from Lockhart Fort with all of the 36th Sikhs and signallers and sick of the Royal Irish that could be spared, materially quickened their pace.

"Our force rapidly pushed on for Fort Lockhart, passing on its way the little post of Sangar, besieged for the last 24 hours; its garrison of 41 men of the 36th Sikhs, were drawn up, as we passed, proudly displaying a standard they had captured in a smart little sortie the night before. On we pushed to Fort Lockhart, and the General, mounting the Fort tower, could see Saragheri Hill on which the captured post stood, covered with masses of the enemy. At last we believed in the oft-reported 'thousands' of the *lashkar*, for there must have been at the lowest computation 8,000 tribesmen in battle array. Still there was no news of Fort Gulistan, so the General ordering up the guns, soon had the hill so swept by shrapnel that on the advance of the infantry not a soul was found. It was a thousand pities, for had we but known it, Gulistan was safe for some hours yet, and had we but had the time we might have inflicted heavy loss on an enemy whose line of retreat would have been open to our fire. However, so far as we knew, no time was to be lost, so limbering up we pushed on another two miles, and there, on the opposite hill, stood Gulistan Fort still bravely holding out. The slopes above and beyond were literally packed with swarms of the enemy, now warned by the sound of our guns that the time for their departure was at hand. At the sight of our skirmishers on the skyline every man of the beleaguered garrison who could stand, wounded or whole, sprang to the parapets and opened a heavy fire on the now wavering foe. Our guns hurried up and, unlimbering, poured in their shrapnel, while the infantry, racing down the steep hillside, did their best with long-range volleys to persuade some at least of the tribesmen to stay behind. The guns under Captain Parker made beautiful practice, even at extreme ranges, across the wide valley, searching out and dispersing every group we could see and putting shell after shell into a village where the tribesmen had imagined themselves at least secure.

"Saragheri was a piteous sight; the fort, which only two days before we had deemed impregnable unless reduced by want of ammunition, water or food, was almost levelled to the ground, while the bodies of its gallant garrison lay stripped and horribly mutilated amid the ruins of the post they had so bravely held. The whole attack had been clearly visible to the garrisons at Gulistan and Lockhart, who were however powerless to render effective aid. After the second assault on Saragheri two of the enemy had been left behind in a dead angle of the Flanking Tower. These, working with some instrument, had speedily removed a stone and then mass after mass of masonry fell. Soon a practicable breach was made, and in less time than it takes to write all was over. Hundreds swarmed in through the breach and over the walls. The little garrison, 21 rifles only in all, before the fight began, retreated to their sleeping quarters and fought it out grimly to the bitter end.* Tales have come from the very enemy, how one man in the guard-room slew 20 before they burnt him inside, and how one wounded man on his *charpoy* shot down four before they could gain admittance. Their comrades looked on silently as we drew out corpse after corpse, but there will be, I ween, a bitter day of retribution to come. Sikhs and Gurkhas have now seen their mutilated dead.

"However, Fort Gulistan was safe, and with lightened hearts, some of us pushed on. By 2 P.M., we were within its walls. Blackened with gunpowder, worn out with 36 hours of continuous toil and stress, many bandaged and blood-stained, the garrison still presented a brave front. Drawn up at the gate were the survivors of the sortie with the three standards they had captured. Out of the original garrison of 165 rifles two had been killed, 8 dangerously and some, I fear, mortally wounded ; 8 severely and 24 slightly wounded. Of these latter, 9 did not report themselves wounded till relief had come. Major Des Vœux, who had his anxieties doubly intensified by the presence of his family, had been the life and soul of the defence, guarding against every danger and showing a fine example of cheerfulness and steadfastness to all. Lieutenant Pratt, an Officer of a year's standing had ably seconded him, though suffering from dysentery : Surgeon-Captain Pratt had untiringly tended the wounded under heavy fire, helped by Miss Teresa McGrath, Mrs. Des Vœux's maid, who amid the flying bullets could be seen here bathing a wounded sepoy's head and there tying up another's arm till the doctor could come. Last, but not least, every sepoy of this gallant band did his duty, and at times almost more than his duty, in a way worthy of the proud name of Sikh. The state of

---

* This account, it will be noticed, differs slightly in detail from what may be called the enemy's version of the affair, already given.

the fort may be better imagined than described. Bearing in mind the number of dead and wounded in that small space and the impossibility of any but the most primitive conservancy arrangements, it is due only to the wonderful purity of this mountain air that the place was in any way endurable."

Leaving the fort with two mountain guns and the 2nd Punjab Infantry to guard it, the main column returned to Fort Lockhart and there bivouacked, having marched since midnight 24 miles without food and come into action three times. From "friendly" Rabia Khels it was afterwards ascertained that the losses of the enemy, all told, during these several operations, exceeded 400, including some 180 killed in the taking of Saragheri. The next day General Yeatman-Biggs visited Gulistan and issued a stirring Force Order extolling the heroic defence of these two posts and promising to forward the names of the most distinguished for valour. Major Des Vœux presented to him his Officers and, last but not least, Miss McGrath, and he then visited the wounded, many of whom wore ghastly signs of what they had gone through, and gave orders for the remedying of the most obvious defects of the post.

For the time being hostilities had ceased, but there was every prospect of this kind of desultory fighting being resumed. The difficulty which General Yeatman-Biggs had to face was one not easily overcome. Each time his troops advanced on to the Samana Range the tribesmen at once drew off into the Khanki Valley, and then began marching eastwards so as to threaten our border north-east of Hangu. But it was impossible for any large body of troops to remain on the range for more than two days at a time, as the water-supply was limited and the springs only yielded a certain quantity. This quantity was ample for the normal garrison of six companies of infantry, but not for a whole brigade with followers and transport animals. Hence the marching and countermarching that had to be done. If the Orakzai had only advanced well beyond the Samana there would have been some chance of punishing them severely, but large as their numbers were they were not bold enough to do this. The operations therefore became a game of hide and seek, with the advantage on the side of the Orakzai that they could move rapidly from point to point, as they were not incommoded by any transport train and each man carried his own supplies. Our forts were strong enough to resist any ordinary attack, but they could not be left to be beleaguered for days together.

After the fighting of the 15th September, culminating in the relief of Gulistan, the tribal gatherings on the Samana disappeared, and the Afridi *lashkar*, separating itself from its Orakzai allies, returned dispirited to Tirah. The Orakzai villages in the neighbourhood of the Samana forts were completely abandoned, the enemy betaking themselves with all their cattle into temporary security up the Khanki Valley. A reconnaissance along this valley as far as Khorappa showed that all was quiet, and advantage was taken by General Yeatman-Biggs of the suspension of hostilities to improve the very defective water-supply of the Samana by digging fresh tanks, and to repair the roads and the telegraph lines. On the 18th of September a representative *jirgah* of the Aka Khels came in professing their loyalty and pleading that they were in fear of the more powerful clans of the Afridis. They received orders regarding the making of a road through their country, and departed promising compliance.

Several plans for assuming the offensive against the Orakzai were now considered, but the time was not deemed ripe for any general advance into the Khanki Valley. The plan most favoured was to move four regiments with mountain guns down to Khorappa, where water was plentiful, and take up a strong position within a mile or so of the Khanki River. This movement, it was thought, would cover the front of the Samana, and would at the same time permit of the Sappers and working parties improving the two routes from Shinawari, which any punitive force advancing into the Afridi country later on would have to follow. The Orakzai would then hesitate to move down the Khanki Valley, as their rear would be threatened. In order, however, to guard against possible raids east of the Samana, more troops were sent to Kohat, so as to permit of a flying column operating in the neighbourhood of Ibrahimzai and Hangu: the Northamptonshire Regiment and the 2nd Battalion 2nd Gurkhas were railed from Rawalpindi to Kushalgarh, whence they marched to Kohat

CHAPTER VI.

THE TIRAH PUNITIVE EXPEDITION.

EARLY in September the Government of India announced their determination to institute punitive operations on an extensive scale against both the Afridis and the Orakzai : the campaign to be under the supreme control of Lieutenant-General Sir William Lockhart, Commanding the Forces in the Punjab and Commander-in-Chief-Elect of the Army in India. Sir William Lockhart was then at Home, but he left Brindisi on the 3rd September at almost a day's notice, accompanied by Major-General Lord Methuen, who desired to have an opportunity of seeing how a big frontier expedition is carried out.

We publish at the end of this volume full details of the composition and staff of the Tirah Field Force, as finally selected after several necessary revisions. As will be seen, it was a magnificent force, and indeed was quite correctly described as "the flower of our Army in India." It comprised, firstly and most importantly, two divisions, each consisting of two brigades and divisional troops, the whole forming what was officially styled the "Main Column." This column was to be under Sir William Lockhart's personal direction, being charged with the foremost task of advancing over the Samana into the heart of the Orakzai and Afridi country and sweeping away all opposition *en route*. The column as a whole was composed of eight regiments of British Infantry and twelve regiments of Native Infantry, with six Mountain Batteries, one regiment of Native Cavalry and five companies of Sappers. Three subsidiary columns were also formed, one to move from Peshawar into the Bara Valley, another to stand ready for action in the Kurram Valley, and the third a reserve brigade made up of four regiments of infantry and the Jodhpur Lancers placed at Rawalpindi. The following corps constituted the several columns of the Tirah Field Force :—

MAIN COLUMN.

First Division. — Commanding : Brigadier-General W. P. Symons, C.B., (Commanding one of the Tochi Valley Brigades), with the local rank of Major-General.

1st Brigade.—Commanding :* Brigadier-General R. C. Hart, V.C., C.B., (Commanding Belgaum District). Troops : 2nd Derbyshire Regiment, 1st Devonshire Regiment, 2nd Battalion 1st Gurkhas, 30th Punjab Infantry.

2nd Brigade.—Commanding : Brigadier-General A. Gaselee, C.B., (Commanding Cawnpore Station). Troop : 2nd Yorkshire Regiment, 1st Royal West Surrey Regiment, 2nd Battalion 4th Gurkhas, 3rd Sikhs.

Divisional Troops.—No. 1 (British), No. 2 (Derajat), No. 1 (Kohat) Mountain Batteries, two squadrons 18th Bengal Lancers, 28th Bombay Pioneers, Nos. 3 and 4 Companies Bombay Sappers, Nabha Imperial Service Infantry, Maler Kotla Imperial Service Sappers.

2nd Division.—Commanding : Major-General A. G. Yeatman-Biggs, C.B., (then Commanding the troops already on the Samana).

3rd Brigade.—Commanding : Colonel F. J. Kempster, D.S.O., (Assistant Adjutant-General, Madras Command) with the temporary rank of Brigadier-General. Troops : 1st Gordon Highlanders, 1st Dorsetshire Regiment, 1st Battalion 2nd Gurkhas, 15th Sikhs.

4th Brigade.—Commanding : Brigadier-General R. Westmacott, C.B., D.S.O., (Commanding Nagpur District). Troops : 2nd King's Own Scottish Borderers, 1st Northamptonshire Regiment, 1st Battalion 3rd Gurkhas, 36th Sikhs.

Divisional Troops.—Nos. 8 and 9 (British) and No. 5 (Bombay) Mountain Batteries, Machine gun, 16th Lancers, two squadrons 18th Bengal Lancers, 21st Madras Pioneers, No. 4 Company Madras Sappers, Jhind Imperial Service Infantry, Sirmur Imperial Service Sappers.

Line of Communication.—Commanding : Lieutenant-General Sir A. Power Palmer, K.C.B., (Commanding Punjab Frontier Force). Troops : No. 1 (Kashmir) Mountain Battery, 22nd Punjab Infantry, 2nd Battalion 2nd Gurkhas, 39th Garhwal Rifles, 2nd Punjab Infantry, 3rd Bengal Cavalry, No. 1 Company (Bengal) Sappers.

PESHAWAR COLUMN.

Commanding : Brigadier-General A. G. Hammond, C.B., D.S.O., (Commanding Rawalpindi Station). Troops : 2nd Royal Inniskilling

---

* The command of this brigade was originally given to Colonel Ian Hamilton, V.C., D.S.O., Deputy Quartermaster-General in India, but he had the misfortune to be thrown from his horse before the fighting had begun and his injuries placed him *hors de combat*.

Fusiliers, 2nd Oxfordshire Light Infantry, 9th Gurkhas, 34th Pioneers, 45th Sikhs, 57th Field Battery, R.A., No. 3 British Mountain Battery, 9th Bengal Lancers, No. 5 Company Bengal Sappers.

KURRAM MOVABLE COLUMN.

Commanding: Colonel W. Hill (Assistant Adjutant-General for Musketry). Troops: 12th Bengal Infantry, Kapurthala Imperial Service Infantry, four guns 3rd Field Battery, R.A., 6th Bengal, Cavalry, one Regiment Central India Horse.

RAWALPINDI RESERVE BRIGADE.

Commanding: Colonel C. R. Macgregor, D.S.O., (Commanding 42nd Gurkhas and officiating in command of Fyzabad Station), with temporary rank of Brigadier-General. Troops: 2nd King's Own Yorkshire Light Infantry, 1st Duke of Cornwall's Light Infantry, 27th Bombay Light Infantry, 2nd Regiment Hyderabad Contingent, Jodhpur Imperial Service Lancers.

The approximate strength of the Field Force, including the Reserve Brigade, was as follows: British Officers, 1,010; Native Officers, 491; hospital assistants, 197; British troops, 10,182: native troops, 22,123; grand total, 34,203. Excluding the Reserve Brigade the total was just under 31,040, with 18,250 followers, 966 ordnance mules, 13,000 pack mules and 2,200 camels. The strength of the 1st Division was about 9,460; 2nd Division, 9,268; Line of Communication troops, 5,000; Peshawar Column, 4,500; Kurram Movable Column, 2,600; Rawalpindi Reserve Brigade, 3,200. The British infantry regiments were shown as having each 29 Officers and 103 rank and file: the native infantry regiments each 9 British Officers and 16 Native Officers and 721 rank and file.

Major-General Sir Bindon Blood and Brigadier-Generals Jeffreys and Meiklejohn were to have been given commands, the former of a Division and the two latter of Brigades, in the Tirah Field Force, but this arrangement was prevented owing to the necessity of retaining a full Division at and beyond the Malakand to watch Nawagai and Bajour, the Mamunds being then still in arms.

A question arose at this juncture whether it would be quite wise to strain the loyalty of the Afridi sepoys in the Indian Army by employing them against their kinsfolk in the forthcoming Tirah Expedition; and while the point was still being publicly discussed, a Government Order was issued on the 7th of October, which set the question at rest. The order read as follows:—

"The Government of India lived at peace with the Afridi tribe, and made an agreement with them under which British forts in the Khyber were entrusted to their care. Allowances were paid to the tribe, and arms issued, so that they might be strong in the alliance of friendship with the Government of India and have the means of forcing turbulent persons to keep the peace. Without any provocation the Afridis, in conjunction with other tribes, have broken their alliance with the British Government, and have attacked and destroyed forts which their tribe had engaged to guard. Further, they have waged war against our garrisons on the Samana and elsewhere, killing some of the soldiers in the British service and causing great loss of property. The British Government, confident in its power, cannot sit down quietly under such defiance and outrages, and has been forced by the wanton acts of the Afridis themselves to inflict punishment on them in their own country, and to send a force into Tirah to exact reparation for what has lately taken place. The Afridi soldiers in the service of the Government have given proofs of their loyalty, devotion and courage on many a hard-fought field, and the value of their services has been fully appreciated by the Government of India. After a most careful consideration of the circumstances connected with the Tirah Expedition, the Government have decided to show consideration to those Afridi soldiers who wish to be loyal to their engagements, and to excuse them from service in the campaign which the Government has been forced to wage against their fellow tribesmen. On these grounds alone it has been determined that Afridi soldiers who are serving in regiments detailed for service on the Peshawar-Kohat border, are not to be employed near the Tirah frontier at the present time, but their services will be utilised elsewhere. The necessary orders to this effect will at once issue. As far as possible care will be taken that no property belonging to the Afridi soldiers in the service of the Government who have not taken part in the raids on British territory is either confiscated or destroyed during the time our troops are engaged in Orakzai or Afridi territory."

The Afridi soldiers in the ranks of the native army had done such splendid service that every effort was made to spare them any reproach in communicating the foregoing Order to regiments composed in whole or part of Pathans. At the same time the fact that desertions had occurred, not only on the Kohat-Peshawar border but further afield, showed that the action of the Government was quite justified. As to the number of trans-frontier tribesmen enlisted in infantry battalions it may be interesting to state here that these numbered about 4,000 in all, of whom 1,907 were Afridis, 309 Orakzai, 283 Bunerwals, and 232 Ghilzai; while Bajouris, Duranis, Swatis, Shinwaris, Hazaras, and Mohmands mustered less than 200 each; and Waziris, Utman Khels, and other clans contributed between them only a total of 226.

Sir Richard Udny received orders to accompany the Tirah Field Force as Civil Political Officer, but to General Sir William Lockhart was committed the supreme political as well as military control of the expedition. Colonel R. Waburton, C.S.I., who had recently retired from the political charge of the Khyber, and whose knowledge of the Afridis and their country is probably unrivalled, was also asked by the Government to return temporarily to the scene of his former labours, and to accompany the expedition. Mr. Lorimer, Mr. King, Mr. Donald and Mr. Blakeway, were appointed Assistant Political Officers with the force.

There was a good deal of survey work to be done during the operations in Afridi land, for no European had been in the country since Captain L. H. E. Tucker, in 1872, made a hurried trip *viâ* the Bara Valley to the eastern portion of the plateau. Colonel Sir T. H Holdich, R.E., was given charge of the survey parties, the Departmental Officers with him being Major Bythell and Captain C. L. Robertson. Sir Pertab Singh was permitted to join General Lockhart's Staff as Aide-de-camp.

Sir William Lockhart arrived at Simla on the 20th September, and after visiting Rawalpindi and Murree, reached Kohat on the 5th October, accompanied by his Chief of Staff, Brigadier-General W. G. Nicholson, C.B., and Lord Methuen. He had the great advantage of being able to bring to bear on the task before him not only exceptional ability but exceptional knowledge; for the Miranzai Campaigns of 1891 and 1892 had made the Samana Range and the Khanki Valley familiar ground to him. It was quite expected that the Afridis would give our troops plenty of fighting, particularly as a mischievous notice in Urdu had been circulated among them by their mullahs stating that a war of extermination was to be waged against them. To counteract as far as possible the effects of this false announcement and to present the Tirah Expedition in its true light in the eyes of the whole of the north-west border, Sir William Lockhart issued the following proclamation to the Afridis and Orakzai preparatory to advancing against them:—

"In the year 1881 the Afridis of the Khyber Pass entered into treaty engagements with the British Government, undertaking, in consideration of certain allowances, to maintain order throughout the Pass, to deal with offences on the road, to furnish levies for the above purposes, and to abstain from committing outrages in British territory. Up to the month of August 1897, these engagements have been, on the whole, faithfully observed, but during that and the succeeding month the Afridis have broken their engagements, attacked, plundered and burnt the posts in the Khyber Pass, which were garrisoned by the levies furnished for the purpose by the Afridis themselves, and have joined the Orakzai in an attack on British posts and villages on the Kohat border. For these offences all tribal and service allowances hitherto granted by the British Government to the Afridis and Orakzai are declared to be forfeit, and entirely at the disposal of the British Government to withhold or to renew, wholly or in part, as they may think fit. The British Government has also determined to despatch a force under my command to march through the country of the Orakzai and the Afridis, and to announce from the heart of their country the final terms of the British Government. This advance is made to mark the fact that these tribes took part in the attacks above mentioned, and that the British Government have power to advance if and when they choose. The Government have neither the intention nor the wish to inflict unnecessary damage on the tribes, provided they immediately make submission and reparation. The terms and conditions on which such submission will be accepted will be announced to the *jirgahs* of the tribes when I have arrived in Tirah, and I am authorised to enforce the fulfilment of these terms and conditions, and of any further terms and conditions which opposition by any tribe, or section or individuals thereof, may render it necessary to impose. It is therefore notified that all who wish to live in peace with the *Sirkar* and desire to possess their own country and to see it no more in the power of and occupied by the *Sirkar*, should assist to the utmost of their abilities in the work of enforcing compliance with my orders and with the said terms and conditions, by which means they will save the tribes from the further punishment which any opposition to the advance of the British troops will infallibly bring upon them, and the tribal country from further occupation."

Some time afterwards the Mussazai clan in the Kurram Valley sent back to Fort Lockhart the copy of the Government proclamation which had been sent to them, and on the back of it they had scribbled their views. They had four grievances: one was that the British Government had occupied the Khyber; another that the salt tax was too high (their desire being to buy four maunds for a rupee); the third was a protest against the occupation of the Samana Range; the fourth also related to this subject, their complaint apparently being that our forts prevented free passage over the range. The Kham Khel Chamkannis replied to Sir William Lockhart's proclamation, saying that they had no option but to fight, as they were under the orders of the Fakir of Swat and the Hadda and Aka Khel Mullahs. The proclamation also drew forth a reply from another clan of the Orakzai, the Daulatzai, near Kohat. They alleged they had serious grievances against the Government in the matter of the salt tax, while they complained that unfaithful wives who leave their husbands and take refuge in British territory, were no longer surrendered, as was the case formerly.

Before proceeding to describe the advance of the Tirah Field Force it is necessary to make a digression in order to explain at some length the attitude of the Amir of Afghanistan towards the frontier risings and the relations which came into evidence between His Highness and the fanatical tribes then in arms against us.

CHAPTER VII.

THE ATTITUDE OF THE AMIR.

WHEN, on enquiries being made regarding the Mohmand attack on Shabkadr on August 7th, it was ascertained that the Hadda Mullah had with him on that occasion a considerable number of men who were subjects of the Amir, hailing from Eastern Afghanistan, public attention became directed to the policy of our ally of Kabul with reference to the hostile frontier tribes generally, and the Government of India were not slow to recognise the extreme importance of this factor in planning operations. Various rumours was circulated connecting Abdur Rahman more or less intimately with the earlier rising in Swat, and when, afterwards, the Afridis captured the Khyber, there was some who thought they perceived the hand of the Durani Chief in this new outbreak also. To clear the air, a strong expression of the Governor-General's opinion regarding General Ghulam Hyder's relations with the Hadda Mullah and the part taken by Afghans from Jellalabad district in the Mohmand disturbance, was forwarded to the Amir, together with an admonition that something more than a mere formal disclaimer of responsibility was expected from him. The response to this communication was satisfactory enough, especially as His Highness had forestalled it by previously despatching a *firman* to Jellalabad forbidding his subjects to engage in hostilities on the border. The reply to the Governor-General was couched in very explicit terms. The Amir denied that any Afghan soldiers had shared in the Mohmand fighting, and at the same time solemnly and personally engaged on behalf of the Sipah Salar and the regular army that no such hostility should ever be committed by them. As regards non-military Afghan subjects, he alleged that if any of them had joined the Mohmands at all they must have done so secretly, for they would not dare to take up arms openly for fear of him. He attributed all the border disturbances to the action of the mullahs, especially the Hadda Mullah, who he said had in former years excited risings against the *gadi* of Kabul, and he denounced their conduct.

The Amir had certainly known in years gone by what it was to be plagued by fanatical mullahs, but he had made short work of these when they became dangerous to his authority. His sincerity in disapproving of the present tribal risings was shown by the careful manner in which he arranged for the forwarding of his reply to the Viceroy. So anxious was he that his answer should be safely delivered at its destination that he took the precaution of sending a duplicate *viâ* Kandahar. His postal runners always use the Shilman route to Peshawar in preference to the Khyber route, but knowing that the Mohmand country was disturbed, His Highness sent mounted messengers from Kabul through Ghazni and Kandahar. The duplicate letter reached New Chaman towards the end of August, whence it was forwarded to the Governor-General's Agent at Quetta.

About the same time the British Agent in Kabul reported that the Amir read in public *durbar* on the 17th August the Viceroy's letter which called upon His Highness to restrain his subjects from taking part in the frontier disturbances. His Highness solemnly swore that he had always maintained friendly relations with the British Government, and had never induced his subjects or sepoys to take hostile action against the British. The Amir also read the draft of his reply to the *durbar*, which was very largely attended, as it was held on the anniversary of his assumption of the title of *Zia-ul-Millat wa ud-din*.

A few days after this *durbar* the British Agent addressed a letter to His Highness on the subject of rumours which had reached him that people from Laghman and other places in Afghanistan were still joining the Hadda Mullah, and that supplies were being sent from Lalpura for the support of the Mullah's gathering. The Amir at once replied in an autograph letter, reminding the Agent of what had taken place at the *durbar*, and adding that though the Mullah's disciples had helped the Mullah secretly they certainly had not done so openly because of their fear of His Highness. The Amir also informed the British Agent that he had issued instructions to all officials in Ningrahar, and they were now secretly keeping a watch; that he would as far as possible watch the disciples of the Hadda Mullah in Afghanistan; and that the Governor of Laghman had recently attacked and dispersed a gathering of 500 men collected by one of the Mullah's disciples who were about to proceed from Laghman to join the Mullah. The Governor had also arrested 40 of them, and was taking steps to capture the leader of the gathering, who had escaped. This last statement was quite true, and it was also true that some Sangu Khel Shinwaris, who had collected near Pesh Bolak and who probably intended making for the Khyber at the invitation of the Mullah Saiad Akbar, had been dispersed by Afghan cavalry. Further, under orders from Kabul, the Afghan troops were withdrawn from the outlying posts because of the possibility that they might be tempted to slip away temporarily to join some tribal gathering. At the same time the Amir issued orders that no bodies of armed tribesmen fleeing before the Government of India's troops in any of the operations about to be undertaken, should be allowed to enter Afghanistan. In return for Abdur Rahman's frankness the Government of India were no less open with him and in further correspondence informed His Highness that the expedition against the Mohmands had been undertaken principally to punish the Hadda Mullah and his gathering and to disperse all who opposed our troops, and that there was no intention of remaining in the country.

After the attack on the Khyber and the subsequent spontaneous dispersion of the Afridi force, the mullahs, in order to induce the tribesmen to renew hostilities played the bold game of pretending that the Amir was at their back, and even paraded mule loads of ammunition which they asserted had been sent from Afghanistan, but which had actually been captured from the Khyber Rifles at Ali Musjid and Lundi Kotal. As a matter of fact they knew very well that the Amir, so far from sympathising with the Afridis in their rising, was extremely angry with them for having closed the Khyber, as this caused heavy loss to him owing to the stoppage of the caravan trade, besides preventing a consignment of arms and stores imported by him from Europe being sent up from Peshawar.

About the middle of September the Afridis began to realise the danger which menaced them, as definite preparations for invading Tirah had by that time been begun. They held a big *jirgah* and decided to send a deputation to Kabul to ask the Amir to help them in the coming struggle. The members of this deputation got as far as Jellalabad, where they were stopped by the local Afghan officials and turned back, in obedience to orders received from Kabul. A request was preferred for ammunition but this was refused. Thereafter, to remove all possible doubt the Amir caused to be posted in Kabul a public reply to the Afridi deputations. The notification, which was dated September 23rd, was as follows :—

"The Afridis of Tirah have sent me now eighteen of their men, consisting of Maliks, Ulama and Elders, each sect sending a separate petition and asking for help. In accordance with my orders they were detained in Jellalabad, their petitions were sent to me and I have refused them. I have written and sent them replies to their petitions to

Jellalabad, that they may receive them and go back. The particulars of their petitions are as follows :—

"'The British Government have been from olden times gradually encroaching upon our country, and even upon Afghan territory, and they have erected forts at various spots and places. We complained of this to the Afghan Government on numerous occasions, but Your Highness paid no attention to our complaints. Therefore, being helpless and having regard to Islam and our constancy in religion, we have, under the guidance of God, opened the door of *jehad* in the face of the said Government, and we have severed our connection with them in every way. We have plundered and destroyed five forts on the Samana above Hangu, one fort at Shinawari at the foot of the Samana in British territory, one fort at the Ublan Pass near Kohat, one *thana* at Tora Wadi, a second *thana* at Kahi, one *thana* at Ghalo China, one *thana* at Shams-ud-din, one *thana* at Chardi, one *thana* at Kar Killa near Khatak, one *thana* at Namak, one *thana* at Narai Ab and the Hindu bazaar at Narai Ab. There are three big forts on the top of the said mountain which have not been taken yet. By the grace of God we will destroy and burn these also. All the people of Tirah have taken up their position on the top of the mountain; and at its base, from Kohat to Rud-i-Kurman in the district of Kurram, the frontier of the Orakzai runs, and the tribesmen have been making *jehad* from time to time within their respective limits. We will never consent to tender our allegiance to the British Government and become their subjects. We will never give up the reins of authority of our country to the hands of the Government. On the contrary, we are willing to tender our allegiance to the Government of the King of Islam. It is incumbent on the Government of Islam not only to look after our interests and to consider our position, but that of the whole of Afghanistan. We therefore send these eighteen persons from among our Maliks, Ulama and Elders, with our petitions to Your Highness' presence. We are at present engaged in a *jehad* on the Samana Range, and we request that Your Highness will be pleased to do what is for our good and benefit ; and by the grace of God we will act up to Your Highness' instructions, because we leave the conduct and management of our affairs in the hands of Your Highness in every respect. We have used our endeavours with our tribesmen to do service to Your Highness. This is the time to gain the object of Your Highness. All the Moslems are now at the disposal of Your Highness in the shape of regular troops, artillery and money. If the British prove victorious they will ruin the Moslems. The services to be done on this side may be left to us Your Highness. We hope that after the perusal of our petition Your Highness will favour us with a reply. Dated 7th Rabi-us-Sani, 1315.'

"I have perused your petitions, all of which were founded on one object. I now write to you in reply that it is eighteen years since I came to Kabul, and you know yourselves that I went to Rawalpindi by the Khyber route. In consideration of my friendship with the British Government I had gone to their country as their guest, and on my way I found many of your tribesmen on both sides of the Pass who made *salaams* to me. If what you now state is true why did you not tell me at that time about the matter, so that I might have conferred with His Excellency the Viceroy about it? Some years after this, when the boundary was being laid down, Sir Mortimer Durand passed through the Khyber and came to Kabul. All the frontier tribesmen knew of this and saw the Mission with their own eyes. Why did not then your Mullahs, Maliks and Elders come to me when Sir Mortimer Durand came with authority to settle the boundary, so that I could have discussed the matter with him? At that time you all remained silent, and silence indicates consent I do not know on what account a breach has now taken place between you and the English. Now, after you have fought with them and displeased them you inform me.

"I have entered into an alliance with the British Government in regard to matters of State, and up to the present time no breach of the agreement has occurred from the side of the British, notwithstanding that they are Christians. We are Moslems and followers of the religion of the Prophet and also of the four Khalifas of the Prophet. How can we then commit a breach of an agreement? What do you say about the verse in the *Koran*—' Fulfil your promise: to fulfil a promise is the first duty of a Moslem. God, on the day when the first promise was taken, asked all the creatures whether he was their God or not. They said: Yes, you are our God and our Creator. Therefore on the day of the resurrection the first question will be about the observance of agreements. Infidels and Moslems will thus be distinguished by this test.' You will thus see that the matter of the agreement is of great importance. I will never, without cause or occasion, swerve from an agreement, because the English up to the present time have in no way departed from the line of boundary laid down in the map they have agreed upon with me. Then why should I do so? To do so will be far from justice. I cannot at the instance of a few self-interested persons bring ignominy on myself and my people.

"What you have done with your own hands you must now carry on your own necks. I have nothing to do with you. You are the best judge of your affairs. Now that you have got into trouble—(*literally*, spoiled the matter)—you want me to help you. You have allowed the time when matters might have been ameliorated to slip by. Now I cannot say or do anything. I have sent back from Jellalabad the Maliks you had deputed to me. I gave them each a *lungi* and Rs.10 for their road expenses, and I did not trouble them to come to Kabul."

The Amir also issued in Eastern Afghanistan a proclamation by way of warning to Afghans. It began:—

"This proclamation is from Amir Zia-ull Millat wa ud-din"—(*i.e.*, Light of Union and Faith). Let it be known to the learned men of Afghanistan, whether in the Amir's territory or the hill tracts, that I have come to know of your circumstances by your petitions as well as through my informants, and am fully aware that you talk in your houses and meetings that I (the Amir) have sold you to the British Government for money, and that in these days when fighting is going on between you and the British Government I have held myself aloof and am sitting in ease and comfort. Under these circumstances I think it advisable to explain to you all the facts in detail, and mention the intent and purport of your talk."

His Highness then proceeded to explain at length the policy of the British Government towards Afghanistan in Shere Ali's time. "Shere Ali," he said, "was a fool, and his son, Yakub, also a fool; the former for intriguing with Russia, the latter for making himself responsible for Major Cavagnari's safety when he himself had not much control over the Afghan troops and tribesmen." He pointed out that the English had never any intention of annexing Afghanistan in those days, but wished only to avenge Major Cavagnari's murder and find a ruler in the place of Yakub Khan. He (Abdur Rahman) recognised these things and satisfied himself that the British Government only wished to defend Afghanistan from any enemy that might arise. He explained how he had had to exercise full authority, as he had failed to make the Afghan people wise and moral. Turning then to the tribesmen he showed how they "tendered their allegiance to the British Government, accepted the allowances, made agreements, and then, without any cause, raised disturbances and rebellion at the instance of a fakir whose parentage is not even known to the King of Islam." As they did not consult him when they raised the revolt, they were not justified in throwing the blame upon him. They had frequently declared to the British Government that they were independent of the Amir, and had set themselves up as kings. That being so, they should settle their affairs themselves.

He added:—" Why do you call these disturbances *jehad* or *ghaza?* The time will come for *jehad*, and, when it does come, it will be announced to you. If you behave yourselves courageously on that occasion, I shall be glad to call you religious leaders. But the first condition of a *jehad* is the co-operation of the King of Islam. It is curious that the King is on friendly terms with the English and yet you are making a fuss about *jehad*. It appears that you yourselves are independent kings, and do not require a king over you. A similar instance occurred in France thirty years ago, when the people there revolted against their king, dethroned him and sent him to London, where he died. I will never interfere with you in religious matters, nor prevent you from prosecuting your own object provided these be in accordance with the principles of religion; but the present disturbances have nothing to do with religion, because all Mussalmans and most of the Khans and tribesmen are taking sides with the English and helping them. When you yourselves are rendering them assistance how can I be to blame ?"—(It should here be noted that the proclamation, though issued late in September, was dated August 13th, that is to say, before the Afridi soldiers fighting on the British side had been withdrawn from the front.)—After noticing that the tribesmen in talking among themselves, were ascribing the rising as due to the British occupation of Chitral and Swat, the Amir said :—" I tell you that in taking possession of Chitral the object of the British Government is not to assess revenue, or tax them. Their only desire is to increase the population of the country and strengthen their own position, so that it may serve as a barrier against any future invasion by Russia. They have remitted the revenue of villages in Swat of which they have taken actual possession."

His Highness concluded :—" In short, I have nothing to do with your affairs, and no concern with you because I have no trust in you. Do not be led to think that, like Shere Ali, I am such a fool as to annoy and offend others for your sake. Your real object is to make me fight with the British Government, and if I were to do such a foolish thing, I am sure you would assume the position of simple spectators."

In the foregoing proclamation there was an echo of the Amir's former utterances so far as the unruly and troublesome character of his people was concerned. In his letters to the Indian Government in 1880-81 when he had just become Amir, he frequently referred to his difficulties in dealing with his subjects. Thus he wrote: "The people of Afghanistan are of such a nature that they step beyond the bounds of subjection and aspire to the position of rulers." And again: "The ignorance of evil-minded persons, the unwisdom of the principal persons in Afghanistan, and the short-sightedness of this nation, are manifest. They incite the people to tumult and commotion, and drive them out of the path of humanity. A wise man is unwise in their sight. They lead people astray, and for the sake of a trifling gain they prefer disorder and tumult. For their own selfish ends they wish to see the whole world desolate and ruined. From their ignorance they do not know and see what would tend to their lasting comfort." In other letters he abused his unruly subjects in unmeasured terms, and appealed to the Government to give him rifles and ammunition in order that his regular army might be equal to keeping the peace.

After this nothing further was heard of the Amir in connection with the frontier operations, and it may be said at once that throughout the remainder of the fighting the Amir adhered honourably to the attitude he had taken up. Nothing further remains to be said therefore on this head except a word about the Sipah Salar. Beyond all reasonable doubt General Ghulam Hyder continued secretly to urge the Orakzai and Afridis to remain in arms, but his action was clearly contrary to the line of policy taken by his master, and the Sipah Salar would no doubt have been called to account had he not been in a position to defy the Amir owing to his influence over the troops and tribesmen in the Jellalabad district.

CHAPTER VIII.

CROSSING THE SAMANA—THE CAPTURE AND ABANDONMENT OF DARGAI.

By the beginning of October the concentration of the troops composing the Tirah Field Force was in full swing, and the tribesmen now began to realise to the full the meaning of the preparations menacing them. An urgent *jirgah* of the Orakzai and Afridis was held at Bagh, in Tirah, at which it was decided that unless an arrangement could be made with the Government of India to include all sections of the two main tribes in an amnesty, attacks should be made concurrently on the Kurram, the Samana and Jamrud. The Chamkannis, Zaimukhts and Alisherzai of the Kurram country were not represented at the *jirgah*, but the Tirah Alisherzai attended. An oath was taken on the *Koran* that if any individual tribe or section should come to an understanding with the Government that did not include all the others, that clan should be publicly anathematised as enemies of Islam. All the same the Khanki Valley Orakzai, who had been giving us so much trouble on the Samana, became considerably less pugnacious, and before very long all of them were asking to be allowed to make their submission, promising to surrender all loot and Government rifles. The Mishtis also made humble *salaams* and offered our troops a free passage through their territory. But at this late stage the tribes had too much to answer for: no reply was returned to their overtures, General Yeatman-Biggs especially declining to treat with the enemy while they still had raiding parties out on the Samana harassing our outposts. But the Kohat Pass tribesmen had behaved well, and they now continued impassive, causing us no annoyance during the march of the several brigades from Khushalgarh to join Sir William Lockhart. The Adam Khels on the one hand and the Jowakis on the other refused to obey the exhortations of the Mullah Saiad Akbar to join in the so-called *jehad*, and carefully refrained from molesting the advancing columns. The last march into Kohat, through the pass, was indeed sufficiently trying without the addition of hostilities; as no proper road existed, and there was only a rough pebbly track, about 19 miles long from Aimal Chabutra, the last halting-place before Kohat.

On the 10th October Brigadier-General Hart's column arrived at Kohat; next day Brigadier-General Kempster's column marched in;

and the day after that Brigadier-General Westmacott's column emerged from the long pass. From Kohat the troops marched to Shinawari, where they stood with their faces to the north ready to march upon the Samana as soon as the Sappers and Pioneers should have prepared the way.

On the 7th October a *jirgah* was held at Kandi Mishti in the Khanki Valley of the irresolute Mishtis, Sheikans, Abkhels and Mulla Khels who had come across the Sampagha Pass for the purpose. The Abkhels upbraided the Mishtis for having given in to the *Sirkar*, and the Mishtis denied this, but admitted they did not want to fight. A bigger *jirgah* of the Orakzai tribes was held on the 10th October at which it was decided to hold the Sampagha Pass against General Lockhart's advance.

On the 19th of the month the Mullah Saiad Akbar again issued his war orders, in which something like a tactical disposition of his available forces was apparent. Thus the Kuki and Zakka Khels of the Bazar and Khyber districts were to hold Ali Musjid road ; the Zakka Khels of the Bara Valley, the Sipah, Kamar, Aka and the Usturi Khels were given the Bara route ; while the Kambar, Malikdin, Zakka and Adam Khels of the Maidan were to co-operate with the Orakzai in defending the Tirah passes facing the Samana Range. The clans were also to give mutual aid whenever necessity might arise. It was thus plain that Sir William Lockhart's advance would be opposed at the Sampagha and other passes leading into the Rajgul and Maidan Valleys. The Sampagha Pass, it may be explained, leads direct from the Khanki Valley, and the approach to it is fairly easy. The late Colonel Mason reconnoitred almost to the top of the pass during the Miranzai Expeditions of 1891, so that our troops would march over ground which have been mapped out to a certain extent and would present no great difficulties. The pass can be turned on either flank, and it was clear that many thousands of tribesmen would be required to hold it even for a short time against the force which Sir William Lockhart would be able to bring to bear when once he had concentrated his two divisions in the Khanki Valley. The Sampagha is almost due north of our line of forts on the Samana, and it was apparently intended to form the left of the enemy's line of defence, the right resting on the Arhanga Pass, seven or eight miles away. This latter pass again was said to be an easy one for pack-animals, but it had never been reconnoitred. Once our troops crossed it the southern valleys of Tirah, the summer quarters of the Afridis, would lie beneath them, and almost immediately Sir William Lockhart would be in the heart of the tribal country, if all went well; for the distances to be traversed from the Khanki Valley are short, the ranges of hills guarding Tirah on the south being within one march from the left bank of the Khanki River.

To follow the actual operations. On the 11th October a working party on the Chagru Kotal road over the Samana consisting of Pioneers, Sappers and 1,000 Punjab coolies was fired on by the enemy, of whom very large numbers were disclosed near the village of Dargai. Fortunately General Yeatman-Biggs, who had gone down a spur from Gulistan in force that morning on a reconnaissance, was close at hand, and he quickly brought his guns to bear on the assailants who thereupon retired, and the force returned to Fort Lockhart that evening with no casualties. Reports were afterwards brought in that the losses of the tribesmen in this little brush were very heavy. One of the surest tests of the success of an action was whether the troops were followed up during the return to camp, and in this instance the rear-guards were left quite unmolested, which went to prove that the enemy were for the nonce thoroughly beaten off.

On the 12th of October a covering party of a half-battalion of the 15th Sikhs and the Jhind Infantry on the north side of the Kotal was fired on and compelled to withdraw by a force of Gar Orakzai who pressed the retirement vigorously. No. 2 Derajat Mountain Battery however successfully covered the withdrawal, and the only casualties were one Jhind sepoy severely and one slightly wounded. After this the enemy continued almost daily to annoy our working parties on the Chagru Kotal road, the completion of which was essential to a rapid advance of the expeditionary force.

Finally on the 17th October Sir William Lockhart issued orders for the forward movement, as follows:—"On the 20th October the 3rd Brigade, under Brigadier-General Kempster, with No. 8 Mountain Battery Royal Artillery, No. 5 Bombay Mountain Battery, the machine gun detachment and signallers of the 16th Lancers, one squadron and head-quarters of the 18th Bengal Lancers, the 21st Madras Pioneers, No. 4 Company Madras Sappers, the Sirmur Sappers, and Gurkha scouts will advance on Khorappa in the Khanki Valley under General Yeatman-Biggs; and on the 21st October a column, under Colonel Claytor, composed of the Northampton Regiment, the 36th Sikhs and No. 9 Mountain Battery Royal Artillery, will move from Samana to the Talai spur, to protect the right flank of the 3rd Brigade moving in the Chagru Valley. The troops named above, under General Yeatman-Biggs, will stand fast at Khorappa, and improve the road above and below that place, Colonel Chaytor's column advancing from Talai to Khorappa; and on the same day the remainder of the 2nd Division, i.e., the 4th Brigade and remaining Divisional troops, under Brigadier-General Westmacott, will advance from Shinawari to Khorappa, as also a wing of the Line of Communication troops for the permanent garrison of Khorappa. On the 22nd October the 2nd Division will cross the Khanki River and move to Khangirbar and entrench for the night, and the 1st Division will march from Shinawari to Khorappa. On the 23rd October the 2nd Division will advance to the vicinity of Ghandaki and entrench for the night, and the 1st Division advance to Khangirbar. A wing of the Line of Communication troops will advance from Shinawari to Khorappa on the same date, as permanent garrison. General Yeatman-Biggs accompanies the 3rd Brigade on the 25th."

It has been mentioned that the working party on the Chagru Kotal road had been repeatedly interfered with by parties of tribesmen coming from the direction of Dargai, a village on the Samana Range west of Chagru Kotal. It was now determined to punish these tribes, and it was arranged that Sir Power Palmer, who commanded all the troops on the Line of Communications, should for this purpose have the troops of the 2nd Division temporarily under his orders to co-operate with the troops he already had at Shinawari. It is necessary here to attempt to explain, though it is difficult to do so clearly, the military geography of the ground which was destined to be the *venue* of the most important action fought during the whole campaign. The village of Dargai lies on the northern side of a plateau; and from this plateau a very steep and narrow spur, gradually growing less steep, runs down to a village on Chagru Kotal. This village is situated on a narrow neck or saddle from which the road runs south to Shinawari, 6 miles distant, and in a more or less northerly direction into the Khanki Valley to Khorappa. This saddle, though narrow, is a long one, and at the other end, after the road falls into the Chagru Valley, on the northern side, is another village called Mama Khan. From Mama Khan to Dargai a very steep, stony and narrow mountain track runs up the spur to Dargai ridge, mostly on the northern side of the spur and well under view and fire from the tribesmen holding the crest of the plateau, which on the Chagru Kotal side is almost precipitous and shelves gently away on the western or further side.

South of the Dargai plateau a very high and broken spur trends circuitously down towards Shinawari, the summit of this spur commanding the Dargai ridge and plateau.

The general idea of the operations ordered by Sir William Lockhart was that Brigadier-General Kempster's Brigade and some of the Divisional troops of the 2nd Division, and also the 3rd Sikhs of the 1st Division, 2nd Brigade, the whole under the command of Sir Power Palmer, should start at 4 A.M., ascend this long spur and appear on the right flank and rear of the Dargai position. This position had been artificially strengthened by *sangars* or stoneworks, and to take it in front by the one narrow path approaching it would have been an almost impossible task if it had been strongly and resolutely held. If, on the other hand, a frontal attack by another column from the direction of Chagru Kotal and Mama Khan under the command of Brigadier-Genearl Westmacott were threatened and made strongly demonstrative, there was every chance that the enemy's attention might be distracted and General Kempster's Brigade allowed to execute its advance to some extent unperceived, and cut in on the tribesmen either in flank or when retreating. Presumably it was intended that the frontal attack should, if it was to be merely demonstrative, at all events wait for the flank attack to develope, but so difficult was the country which Brigadier-General Kempster's Brigade advancing to make this turning movement had to traverse, that at 12 noon, though the column had started at 4 A.M., there were no signs of it apparent from the Samana Suk, whence Sir William Lockhart and his Staff were watching the operations. Nor indeed is this to be wondered at, for the crest of the hill along which General Kempster had to advance was a series of precipitous spurs, to crown which was almost an impossibility, and many baggage animals carrying ammunition were lost owing to their falling over the cliff. So razor-like in shape were the crests of these hills that it was quite impossible for even a mountain battery to come into action. As very few of the enemy were in evidence about the Dargai ridge, Brigadier-General Westmacott (commanding the column which was to create the diversion in front for the benefit of General Kempster) decided on making his attack without waiting for Brigadier-General Kempster's flank attack to develope. Brigadier-General Westmacott had under his orders two mountain batteries, No. 9 Mountain Battery Royal Artillery (Major Rowdy) and No. 5 Bombay Mountain Battery under

Captain de Butts, also the King's Own Scottish Borderers, the Northampton Regiment and the 1-3rd Gurkha Rifles. The remaining regiment of Brigadier-General Westmacott's Brigade, the 36th Sikhs (who had recently come prominently under notice for their gallant defence of Fort Gulistan under Major DesVœux and their equally gallant though unsuccessful defence of Fort Saragheri) were retained for the day at Fort Lockhart, for the contingency might arise that Fort Lockhart itself would be attacked if all the garrison except the half-battalion 2-2nd Gurkhas were withdrawn. For this reason then the 36th Sikhs were not able either on the 18th or again on the 20th to take part in the operations against Dargai. Thus with three battalions and two Mountain Batteries Royal Artillery at his disposal the task lay before General Westmacott of capturing the Dargai ridge, with the possible, but in these precipitous regions far from certain, assistance of the flanking column commanded by General Kempster.

About 9 A.M. the two mountain batteries opened fire on the Dargai ridge and on the point more especially where the precipitous path is seen to cross the ridge, at a range of about 1,800 yards; whilst the infantry, with the exception of two companies Northampton Regiment, who remained as escort to the guns, pressed forward to the village of Mama Khan. The enemy meanwhile appeared in small numbers gradually increasing from the direction of Dargai village, and fired a few shots at 9-30 on the infantry now in and behind Mama Khan village. The infantry, covered by the ground and avoiding the path which lay on the enemy's side of the spur, advanced slowly along the precipitous hillside, the 1-3rd Gurkhas leading, the King's Own Scottish Borderers in second line, and the six companies Northampton Regiment in third line, till they reached a saddle with a few fir trees on it about halfway between Mama Khan and Dargai, and in advancing beyond which they must come under the enemy's fire. About 11 A.M. the infantry opened fire from here, and the guns, which had temporarily ceased fire, joined in again. Thence the Gurkhas, led by their Colonel forty yards ahead of everybody else, advanced by rushes from one coign of vantage to another, covered from the rear by infantry fire and forming up wherever any dead ground gave them breathing time for a fresh advance. The King's Own Scottish Borderers meanwhile, in the second line, were rapidly decreasing the distance between themselves and the Gurkhas and straining every nerve to reach the summit simultaneously. The 800 yards start the Gurkhas had, however, was not, on such ground and with soldiers so accustomed to hill warfare as the Gurkhas, easily regained ; and before they could quite catch them up the leading Gurkha company, 1-3rd Gurkhas, with Lieutenant Beynon, District Staff Officer, at their head, revolver in hand, were seen to be rapidly ascending in single file the rough staircase (rather than path) leading up over the crest, while the remainder of the regiment and the King's Own Scottish Borderers followed close behind. This Indian file assault was magnificently carried out, and although as a matter of fact the enemy offered little or no resistance at the last moment, they *might* for all the troops below knew have been assembled in large numbers behind the crest, and as soon as the artillery fire ceased, which it would necessarily do as the infantry approached the crest, they *might* have poured in such a fire as to render any approach in single file an absolute impossibility. But no such fear daunted the Gurkhas and the position was gallantly carried. Dargai village was soon in flames, and its fortifications destroyed, and the Narik Suk hill, which dominates the Dargai village and ridge, crowned. It was about 12 noon when the Dargai crest was crowned; and the enemy, not awaiting the assault, had just begun to clear off when Brigadier-General Kempster's Column with Sir Power Palmer, was seen slowly advancing with enormous difficulty. The losses sustained by General Westmacott's Column in the direct attack were 2 killed and 14 wounded in the 1-3rd Gurkhas, and 1 killed and 5 wounded in the King's Own Scottish Borderers.

So difficult was the country over which General Kempster's force had had to advance, that it had been found necessary to send back to Shinawari every mule and retain only *dhooly*-bearers and stretchers. General Kempster's Column joined General Westmacott's Column on Dargai height about 3-10 P.M., having had in the meantime to beat off an attack of several thousands of the enemy. The advance in the face of this opposition was splendidly carried out, and undoubtedly it was this turning movement which, though hidden by intervening heights from the view of General Westmacott, nevertheless made the way easy for the charge of his 3rd Gurkhas, the enemy having lost heart as General Kempster swept slowly but irresistibly onwards. This turning movement in the teeth of a powerful foe moreover was so cleverly executed that only two or three casualties (among the 1-2nd Gurkhas) occurred throughout the whole march to Dargai. But General Kempster's force had more work cut out for it before the day was over.

Just as he began to make arrangements for returning to Shinawari *via* Chagru Kotal, the retreating enemy receved reinforcements of about 8,000 Afridis from the Khanki Valley and thereupon halted and faced about. The return to Shinawari *via* Chagru Kotal in the face of such overwhelming numbers, with darkness growing rapidly, was a most difficult and dangerous operation: but so well conceived were General Kempster's dispostions, so admirable the manner in which the troops, both British and native, carried them out, and so great the assistance afforded by the mountain artillery both from Chagru Kotal and the Samana Suk, that the enemy did not dare to press an attack home, and after Chagru Kotal the return to Shinawari was practically unmolested. But unfortunately during the preceding stage in the retirement—in coming down the hill between Dargai and Chagru Kotal—the losses, with the enemy swarming on the heights above, were considerable: the Gordons had Major R. D. Jennings-Bramly killed and Lieutenant M. L. Pears and 14 men wounded, while the 15th Sikhs had 3 killed and 11 wounded. These two corps were covering the retirement and hence their heavy losses. The 3rd Sikhs had also 1 wounded and the 1-2nd Gurkhas 1 killed and 4 wounded. But, on the other hand, as already stated, the enemy had been so severely punished that they had not the courage to attempt to follow up the column when General Kemspter, following the lead of General Westmacott, marched back to Head-quarters, and not a shot was fired on the rear-guard, even in response to a farewell volley from the troops.

As the abandonment of Dargai, after it had once been captured, has been severely commented upon by some military critics, it is as well to give here, for what they may be worth, the reasons suggested why Sir Power Palmer did not deem it advisable to retain possession of the position. Very large numbers of Afridis, attracted by the sound of the firing, were hurrying up from the Khanki Valley; added to which the troops were without water, without food and without warm clothes, and must have suffered severely if they had bivouacked for the night unfed and unprotected on the inclement heights. But seeing that to abandon the position meant that it would have to be taken all over again two days later when the main advance of the expeditionary force was to take place, it was certainly very unfortunate that when captured on the 18th October it could not be retained. It is but fair however to quote, even at the risk of repetition, the words of the

Pioneer's Special Correspondent at Dargai :—"Great as the tactical and strategical advantage of such a retention would have been, clothing, firewood and supplies for tired troops at a height of over 6,000 feet are an absolute necessity, and if this was true in regard to the European troops, it applied with still greater force to the sepoys." Retirement then on Shinawari *ard* the Chagru Kotal was ordered, and the bravely-won heights of Dargai were abandoned for the time to the enemy who, though thoroughly beaten, were clever enough to perceive what a splendid stroke it would be to return at once to the occupation of this really impregnable position in stronger force than ever, and so re-impose upon our troops the heavy task of once again scaling those awful slopes in the face of a deadly hailstorm of bullets.

CHAPTER IX.

THE RE-CAPTURE OF DARGAI—GALLANTRY OF THE GORDONS.

On the 20th October General Yeatman-Biggs was instructed afresh by Sir William Lockhart to advance with the 2nd Division, consisting of the 3rd Brigade under Brigadier-General Kempster and the 4th Brigade under Brigadier-General Westmacott, *viâ* Chagru Kotal to Khorappa, in the Khanki Valley. It was in the execution of this order that the memorable capture of the Dargai heights was carried out for the second time. In the calm and critical reflection which has succeeded the first outbursts of enthusiasm at this fine feat of arms, it has been questioned by some military men whether there was any real necessity to take Dargai at all; or at least whether the tactical disadvantage of allowing the enemy to remain in occupation of the crest could possibly have led to such a sad crop of casualties as the Gordon Highlanders, the Dorsetshires, the 2nd Gurkhas and the 3rd Sikhs suffered in attacking an all but impregnable position.* The road from Shinawari (Sir William Lockhart's advance base in the Miranzai Valley) to Khorappa on the Khanki River runs through the valley of Chagru Kotal, and this valley is "absolutely dominated" (as some contend) or "overlooked from a distance" (as others prefer to describe it) on the west by the Dargai ridge and the Narik Suk. The musketry range so far as tribal molestation was concerned was certainly a very long one, varying from about 3,000 up to about 1,000 yards, and the argument which has been raised is that with a well-posted flank defence on the Samana Suk no mere musketry fire at such a range upon troops marching heedless of it through the valley below could have been so destructive as the point blank volleys which the enemy poured out at distances up to 300 yards when Dargai crest was assaulted.

It will be remembered that when Dargai was captured, two days previously, the frontal attack by General Westmacott's Brigade had been more or less combined with a turning movement by General Kempster's Brigade; but on the present occasion only a frontal attack from Chagru Kotal was made, and that along almost the identical route which General Westmacott had followed. Consequently the tribesmen holding the ridge were enabled, though fortunately they did not know

---

* Sir William Lockhart's own opinion on this point will be found expressed in his Despatches, published as an Appendix.

it, to give all their attention to this one slope which owing to the ruggedness of the ground could not be properly ascended in regular formation by assaulting parties, but had to be scrambled over as the assailants best could. In the result the action was the severest ever fought on the north-west frontier since the Ambela Campaign, nearly 200 Officers and men being either killed or wounded within six hours.*

Serious as the casualties were, they might have been still heavier if the whole of the enemy had concentrated their undivided attention on the holding of Dargai from the Chagru Kotal side. But by a very fortunate circumstance it so happened that they had been led to apprehend a repetition of Sir Power Palmer's tactics of the 18th October, and under this belief felt obliged to make preparations for a flank attack, thus weakening their powers of resistance against the frontal attack—the only attack actually delivered. Major Bewicke-Copley and Mr. Donald, Political Officer, had told some pretended friendlies, who were really the enemy's spies, as a dead secret that an attack on the right flank of Dargai village formed a certian part of General Yeatman-Biggs's plan of operations, and this of course ensured the " secret " being carried to the tribal forces crowning Dargai. It was evident all through the subsequent fighting that such a turning movement was seriously apprehended, as large numbers of the foe were visible from the Samana Suk awaiting attack far away on the right flank, where two days previously General Kempster's Brigade had appeared; and this division of forces greatly lightened the otherwise almost impossible task of taking the crest direct from Chagru Kotal. The tribesmen, however, were in a fine fighting mood and full of valour, for they had misconstrued the abandonment of Dargai after its capture on the 18th of October: frontier men habitually regard any movement which is not in the nature of a direct advance as an acknowledgment of defeat. They had additional reason to be plucky, for their aggregate strength on this occasion was computed at 20,000, and they were almost entirely protected from our guns by rocks, which indeed was the reason why the position could not be captured otherwise than by a hand-to-hand assault.

General Yeatman-Biggs marched out of Shinawari at 4-30 A.M. on the 20th October, and on finding the enemy in strength on Dargai ridge, gave Brigadier-General Kempster the simple but weighty order to

---

* It will be seen from the Official Despatches published at the end of this Volume that Sir William Lockhart criticises unfavourably the tactics adopted by General Yeatman-Biggs, and moreover affirms that they were not in accordance with his expressed wishes.

"take the position." General Kempster at once attacked the ridge with the 1st Battalion 2nd Gurkhas in advance, the Dorsetshire Regiment in support, the Derbyshire Regiment (from the First Division) in reserve, and the Gordon Highlanders with the maxim guns in rear. It was not originally intended that the Gordons should take a leading part in the assault, and the task at first allotted to them was to assist the assaulting party by long-range volleys from Mama Khan. Further support was accorded to the advance by No. 8 Mountain Battery at 1,800 yards, by the Northamptonshire Regiment, by No. 9 Mountain Battery well posted on the Samana Suk, and by No. 1 Kohat Mountain Battery and the 3rd Sikhs (from the First Division).

At 9-30 A.M. the enemy opened fire from the ridge, and at 10 A.M. our guns responded, continuing at work almost incessantly up to 2 P.M. The guns on the Samana Suk had the exact range, which was 3,300 yards, and their shells were repeatedly seen bursting just over the Dargai crest. At 10-30 A.M. the infantry opened fire, and a few minutes later the leading wing of the 1st Battalion 2nd Gurkhas succeeded in reaching a wooded spur half-way between Mama Khan and Dargai. Beyond this the enemy's fire was most deadly, and further advance was impossible until the artillery could inflict greater damage upon the enemy and shake their position. Attached to the 2nd Gurkhas and keeping pace with the foremost companies were Lieutenant Tillard and his scouts of the 1st Battalion 3rd Gurkhas, and these men played a prominent part at this stage. The upward route beyond the wooded spur sheltering the advanced wing of the 2nd Gurkhas ran across a bare slope about 100 yards in extent, on which the watchful enemy was prepared to direct an all-exterminating fire at about 300 yards range. Nothing daunted, however, Lieutenant Tillard and his scouts and the left wing of the 2nd Gurkhas, led by Lieutenant-Colonel Travers, Captain Norie (Adjutant) and Captains Macintyre and Bower (attached) dashed out from shelter and made a desperate rush across the exposed slope for the next bit of cover. Every rifle from the crest above was promptly aimed at the daring band and 30 men fell dead or wounded, their bodies of course having to be left on the ground. Not to be outdone, the right wing of the 2nd Gurkhas followed suit shortly afterwards, and it was here that Major Judge, was shot dead. The Gurkhas were now protected by cover again; but for additional troops to reinforce them, now that the enemy realised that the advance over what was with stern truth termed the "death-zone" had seriously begun, was doubly difficult and was for long vainly attempted, both by the Dorsetshires and the Derbyshires. Captain W. R. Arnold of the Dorsetshires was seen by the Gurkhas in front suddenly to spring up, and calling out heroically "Come on 'E' Company!" he fell, dangerously wounded. Lieutenant Hewitt of the same regiment, undismayed by the slaughter he had witnessed, led a whole company forward and every man dropped in his tracks dead or wounded, he alone of the whole company getting across to cover, his elbow being just grazed by a bullet. Occasionally after that single men from both the Derbyshires and the Dorsetshires still ran the terrible gauntlet; but for either regiment to advance in a body for the purpose of helping the 2nd Gurkhas to deliver the final assault was an impossiblity until the guns had played with better effect on the position, and until further strong reinforcements were available. Meanwhile the situation was becoming serious. For more than two hours onlookers below and from the adjacent heights anxiously contemplated the probability of a retirement, and all that such an event would mean; and the later the hour grew the more urgent it became to bring the action to a speedy end by a successful *coup de main.*

It was then that the Gordon Highlanders and the 3rd Sikhs were ordered up, and it was arranged that for three minutes before they advanced over the exposed slope every gun—there were 24 in all—should pour a hot fire on to the ridge. At the proper signal a terrible fusillade was thundered out by the artillery, and when the mighty roar had subsided the Commandant of the Gordon Highlanders, Colonel H. H. Mathias, turning with a glowing face to his regiment, addressed to them in an impassioned voice, a speech that has since been echoed and re-echoed throughout the length and breadth of the British Empire, a speech that thrilled every man who heard it:—" The General says the position must be taken at all costs. THE GORDON HIGHLANDERS WILL TAKE IT!" Cheering wildly, and with the pipers lustily playing the slogan, the brave Highlanders, hesitating not a single moment, dashed forward *en masse* across the fatal slope, led with splendid energy by the Colonel, the Adjutant and the Sergeant-Major at the head of the regiment, and Major Downman at the head of the leading company. A single example will suffice to show how terribly deadly was the enemy's fire. Lieutenant Dingwall of the Gordons was hit on his revolver, the impact knocking him down. Springing to his feet again he was hit on his ammunition pouch, the blow exploding the cartridges inside. A third bullet immediately afterwards went through his coat, and the next moment he was twice hit on the knee. Lieutenant Lamont was shot dead, Major Macbean was dangerously wounded, and Major Donovan was twice hit on the helmet. Two pipers were killed and three others wounded. One hero, Piper Findlater, was knocked over by a Dum Dum bullet which shattered the bone of his leg, yet he sat up on the ground and played on until a second bullet came and he could play no longer. For this fine exhibition of pluck the piper was subsequently awarded the Victoria Cross.

At 3 P.M. the Gordons had gained a sheltered position at the foot of the last cliff, and after recovering themselves were ready to combine with the 2nd Gurkhas in climbing the precipitous path ahead for the purpose of delivering the final assault. Led by their Officers and again loudly cheering, the two regiments, with the few daring soldiers of the Derbyshire and Dorsetshire Regiments who had managed to get across the exposed slope, advanced indiscriminately in a procession: the narrow path or saddle admitted of no other order. But the moral effect of the earlier advance across the death-zone had been too much for the enemy, whose fire had already begun to slacken, and when at 3-10 P.M. this final assault was made the beaten tribesmen would not face the onrushing procession, but turned tail and fled precipitately down the hill. For six hours the enemy had offered a most stubborn resistance, during the latter half of the time *ambiguo Marte*, and the relief at this sudden and brilliant termination was intense. But great as is the honor due to the Gordon Highlanders and the 2nd Gurkhas, it has to be said in fairness to the other assaulting troops that until a few minutes before the Gordon Highlanders' advance the enemy's position had not yet been sufficiently shaken by artillery fire. Moreover, at the precise moment when the Gordons rushed forward an overwhelming volley of shells was poured on to the Dargai crest by the guns, which to some extent must have interfered with the enemy's fire. The personal gallantry of Colonel Mathias was subsequently rewarded by the bestowal of the Victoria Cross.

The casualty list was a sadly heavy one, the number of killed and wounded amounting altogether to 200, *e.g.*, four Officers and 34 men killed, and five Officers and 157 men wounded. The Officers killed were Captain C. B. Judge, 2nd Gurkhas; Lieutenant A. Lamont, Gordon Highlanders; and Captain W. E. C. Smith, Derbyshire Regiment. The

Officers wounded were: Captain J. G. Robinson, 2nd Gurkhas (dangerously)[*]; Captain H. T. Arnold, Dorsetshire Regiment; Major F. Macbean and Lieutenant K. Dingwall, Gordon Highlanders; and Lieutenant G. E. White, 3rd Sikhs (all seriously); Colonel H. H. Mathias, Captain H. P. Uniacke, Lieutenant M. F. M. Meiklejohn, and Lieutenant G. S. G. Crawford, Gordon Highlanders (all slightly). The distribution of the casualties among the non-commissioned officers and men was as follows:—
Dorsetshire Regiment, 8 killed, 38 wounded; Gordon Highlanders, 2 killed and 35 wounded; Derbyshire Regiment, 4 killed and 8 wounded; 2nd Gurkhas, 16 killed and 49 wounded; 3rd Sikhs, 2 killed and 16 wounded; 3rd Gurkhas, 2 killed and 9 wounded.

It may be mentioned here that the late Captain Charles Bellew Judge, of the 2nd (Prince of Wales's Own) Gurkha Regiment, was formerly attached to the Leinster Regiment and was appointed to the Indian Staff Corps in 1881. He was Brigade Transport Officer in the expedition against the Hazaras in 1888, being present at the battle of Kotkai, and for his gallantry on that occasion was mentioned in despatches. He also served in the Manipur Expedition of 1891. The late Captain William Edward Clifton Smith, of the Derbyshire Regiment, entered the army in 1889. He joined the 1st Battalion, and on his return from employment with the Royal Niger Company was posted to the 2nd Battalion which had already been in India since 1882. The late Lieutenant Alexander Lamont, of the Gordons, was born in 1872, and after being educated at Eton joined the Gordons three years and a half ago. He was the second son of Mr. James Lamont of Knockdow, Argyllshire, D. L., and formerly M. P. for the County of Bute. He came of a warlike race, many of his ancestors falling by land and sea, at Seringapatam, Trafalgar, and Waterloo. Major Forbes Macbean, who was wounded, served with the 92nd through the Afghan War of 1879-80, and participated in Lord Roberts's march to Kandahar. He also took part in the Boer War of 1881. Lieutenant Kenneth Dingwall (wounded) joined the 92nd in 1891, and served with the Chitral Relief Force in 1895, and was among the storming party who took the Malakand Pass in that year. He received a medal and clasp for his services.

As for the enemy they were completely driven from the hills, and retired in confusion down to the Khanki River, thus leaving the road through the Chagru Kotal open for the further advance to Khorappa.

---

[*] Died three days later.

But it was too late in the day for the 2nd Division with its baggage train to move forward, and General Yeatman-Biggs bivouacked for the night on the captured position.

The next morning the Division marched on to Khorappa unopposed together with the Northamptons, the 36th Sikhs and No. 9 Mountain Battery Royal Artillery, and pitched camp about a mile short of the Khanki River.

CHAPTER X.

LIFTING THE PURDAH FROM TIRAH.

AFTER the re-capture of Dargai on the 20th October Sir William Lockhart lost no time in pushing forward, his aim being to give the Afridis and Orakzai no breathing time. Accordingly on the morning following the action, the 2nd Division continued its march across Chagru Kotal in the direction of Khorappa. The King's Own Scottish Borderers, the Dorsetshires and the Jhind Infantry were left behind at Dargai and about the *kotal* in case of any further hostile demonstration from the west. Sir William Lockhart himself, with the troops remaining on the Samana, followed the 2nd Division down to Khorappa, there to establish his head-quarters within gunshot of the Khanki River, across which the main body of the enemy had retired.

On the night of the 21st October the new camp at Khorappa was fired into from across the river by about 8,000 of the enemy, carrying 15 standards; but a few rounds from the guns put an end to the fusillade, which was rather fortunate as there had not yet been time enough to prepare proper cover. On the night of 22nd there was more firing into camp, and again on the 23rd to a smaller extent, but the damage was principally among animals. The 25th was a very bad night. Firing into camp began about 5 P.M., and continued more or less without intermission till 10 P.M. Bullets were whistling everywhere, and there were some extraordinary escapes, but unfortunately also a great many casualties. The 1st Division had sent a foraging party out that morning, and though they obtained a good deal of forage, the enemy lined the heights above them as they returned, and some thirteen casualties occurred. Later in the evening there were some 24 sniping casualties among the 1st Division, and 10 among the 2nd Division. Captain F. F. Badcock (District Staff Officer, 5th Gurkhas), Field Intelligence Officer, was hit on the left elbow while sitting at dinner and his arm had unfortunately to be amputated. Curiously enough, Captain Badcock was wounded on the same arm at the storming of Nilt Fort in the Hunza Nagar Expedition where he showed great gallantry in leading a party of the 5th Gurkhas after the gate of the fort had been blown in by Captain Aylmer. Lieutenant Croker (Munster Fusiliers), Orderly Officer to Brigadier-General Kempster, was hit on the right shoulder, also when at dinner, but not seriously injured. Sir William Lockhart himself had a narrow escape, for barely had some grain bags been placed round his tent as a protection, when two bullets whizzed through the canvas and were buried in the grain. On the morning of the 26th October a British soldier and six followers were found cut to pieces a few hundred yards from the camp. They were so slashed about as to be quite unrecognisable, but it was presumed they had been detained till late on the Chagru Kotal road and had tried to get into camp after dark. The approximate number of troops in camp was:—British 6,400, natives 11,200, followers 17,000, and the animals numbered 24,000.

Tribal attention was plainly concentrated now on the defence of the Sampagha Pass, for contrary to expectation no attacks had been made on the long Line of Communication from Kohat to Shinawari, there had been no hostile demonstration in the direction of the Kurram Valley, while on the Peshawar frontier General Hammond's Column had not seen any great gathering beyond Bara. The Khyber also lay neglected, and the Zakka Khel, who had been told off by the Afridi leaders to watch the road from Jamrud to Ali Musjid, had not apparently mustered in force. The flower of the Afridi fighting men were assembled with the Orakzai to defend Tirah against the main attack, and small contingents only could be spared to guard the Bara and Bazar Valleys against possible flank attacks.

On the evening of the 27th October the order was issued for a further advance from Khorappa, and a very welcome order it was, for everyone was tired of the long wait at that place, and the camp, with its thousands of men and animals was not so salubrious a spot as to invite a longer stay. The water-supply was particularly bad: the only procurable water ran through a number of paddy-fields—through what in fact sooner or later promised to be a snipe *jheel*—and was muddy and dirty in consequence. But so great had been the difficulties of transport along the road from Shinawari to Khorappa, that it was only on the 27th that the Commissariat godowns were able to supply the indents for three days' reserve rations for men and two days' for followers.

The move on the 28th was only a short one, some four miles or less, to a place called Ghandaki, higher up the Khanki Valley and in the direction of the Sampagha Pass. To ensure that this move should not be molested from the right flank, the Northampton Regiment and 36th

Sikhs, under Colonel Chatyor, commanding the former regiment, were sent to seize a high hill overlooking the route and the new camp, on the top of which large numbers of the enemy had been visible the day before and on previous days, and from which doubtless many men had descended towards dusk to fire into the huge camp. Colonel Chaytor's two regiments moved off at 5 A.M. and found the hill unoccupied. The sudden start had very probably surprised the enemy, for there was every indication that the hill had been recently occupied, and the column as it moved up was fired into from an adjoining eminence. A reconnaissance was made later in the day to the foot of the Sampagha Pass itself. The enemy were seen in large numbers on the summit of the range and also on the spurs of the hills to the east and west. Colonel Sage, commanding the 1st Gurkhas, was severely wounded during the reconnaissance, but there were no other casualties.

The troops were now in a position to deliver their attack upon the Sampagha, and only awaited daybreak. The Afridis and Orakzai had naturally a strong position, and their favourite method of defence, fighting behind stone breast-works with a line of retreat open, was once again adopted. They evidently feared a turning movement, and their disposition was mainly designed to guard against this as much as possible. Hence they had *sangared* the spurs to the right and left, so as to avoid being outflanked at the beginning of the action, in which case the pass would have become untenable. The real plan of attack was, however, very different from anything the enemy expected, and consisted in the 2nd Brigade (General Gaselee's) followed by the 4th Brigade (General Westmacott's) with the 3rd Brigade (General Kempster's) behind it making a direct attack; while the 1st Brigade (General Hart's) sent one battalion to cover the right flank, and another battalion to cover the left flank. The 3rd and remaining battalion of General Hart's Brigade seized a hill opposite the pass as an artillery position, acted as escort to the guns, and held itself in readiness to support either of the two battalions on the flanks which might require assistance. The remaining battalion of this brigade (the 30th Punjab Infantry) was at Dargai.

The 1st Brigade, followed by the artillery of the 1st and 2nd Divisions, left camp at 5 A.M. on the 29th September and was followed by the other brigades at short intervals. The hill destined for the first artillery position was seized without opposition by the Derbyshire Regiment of Brigadier-General Hart's Brigade, while the Devonshire

Regiment worked their way up by a village called Nazeno, guarding the right flank, and the 2-1st Gurkhas on the left flank made for Kandi Mishti. The two regiments on the flanks had very difficult ground to work over, and though they thoroughly accomplished the protection of the flanks of the main column, they necessarily took but little part in whatever fighting there was. A portion of the artillery—the whole six batteries of which were commanded by Brigadier-General Spragge—came into action about 7·30 A.M., when the three batteries of the 1st Division under Lieutenant-Colonel Duthy, fired on a large *sangar* covering the road to the pass, and very effectually shelled it, while, as there was neither sufficient room nor objective for the other three batteries under Lieutenant-Colonel Purdy, they remained in temporary reserve. The 2nd Brigade meanwhile began its advance in line of regiments: the 3rd Sikhs on the right, the Yorkshire Regiment on the right centre, the Queen's on the left centre, and the 2-4th Gurkhas on the left flank of all. All these regiments had very precipitous ground to work over, and perhaps some regiments encountered greater difficulty than others, but the Queen's (commanded by Major Hanford-Flood who, despite a wound in the arm received early in the advance, persisted in going on) were the first to crown the crest. The two regiments on the right of the line, *viz.*, the 3rd Sikhs and the Yorkshire Regiment, were then sent off to crown a hill on the right of the pass, from which some of the enemy were firing; while of the other two regiments the Queen's remained about the summit of the pass (which was taken about 9·45), and the 3-4th Gurkhas pressed up a hill to the left. This advance of the 2nd Brigade of General Symon's Division had been well prepared by the artillery. Brigadier-General Spragge, as soon as he saw that the 2nd Brigade were advancing against the hill on which the large *sangar* was situated, and which formed a sort of "advanced post" to the enemy's position, at once sent on his other brigade of division of artillery, under Lieutenant-Colonel Purdy, for the preparation of the infantry assault already described. This brigade division of artillery made beautiful practice against the main ridge, which the 2nd Brigade was assaulting. Although owing to the steep reverse slopes on which the enemy could shelter themselves, no great number of casualties resulted from the artillery fire, the physical effect of the guns in the actual destruction of *sangars*, and the moral effect in that the enemy were prevented from lining the crest to oppose the infantry advance, were both undoubtedly great, and here, as at Dargai, very greatly facilitated the infantry advance and diminished the infantry losses. As the 2nd

Brigade was seen to be nearing the crest of the main position, Brigadier-General Spragge sent forward No. 5 Bombay Mountain Battery to the top of the pass to assist in finally clearing the *sangars*. In rounding a corner in order to get this battery into action Captain De Butts was killed: he was struck by a bullet in the stomach, and death was almost instantaneous. Captain De Butts was a very well known mountain battery officer; he commanded the same battery in the late Suakim Expedition, and was invalided home from there very ill indeed. He made however a wonderful recovery, and had only lately rejoined his battery. Two guns of this battery under Lieutenant Edlmann managed to get into position near the top of the pass, and did excellent service, whilst two guns of No. 9 Mountain Battery Royal Artillery, which had also been pushed on came into action at the highest point of the road and managed to shell the last *sangar* held by the enemy at a range of 900 yards. The 3rd Sikhs and the Yorkshire Regiment, when they reached the top of the pass, were sent off, as already stated, to a hill on the right, commanding a road over the pass; and the trained scouts of the 3rd and 5th Gurkhas, supported by two companies of the Queen's, worked up a spur between the Yorkshire Regiment and the 3rd Sikhs, and "contained" or held back a large number of the enemy who were trying to get down to the pass. The 4th Brigade (Brigadier-General Westmacott's) had meanwhile been supporting the 2nd Brigade, and arrived on the crest, and the 36th Sikhs, assisted by long-range volleys from the King's Own Scottish Borderers and by the very accurate fire of two guns of No. 1 Mountain Battery Royal Artillery, crowned the crest. The losses in the 2nd Brigade in the taking of the Sampagha Pass were 1 killed and 14 wounded, of which the Queen's lost 1 killed and 7 wounded. The total casualties in the whole force were about 24. The enemy on the whole had really offered but little resistance, and whatever casualties they had, the killed and wounded were successfully removed. The 3rd Brigade (Brigadier-General Kempster's) had pressed along hard after the 2nd Brigade, but despite all efforts arrived too late to take any part in the action, and was now sent on almost immediately down into the Mastura Valley. No sooner had the troops reached the top of the pass than fires were seen at many of the villages down in the valley below on the road to the Arhanga Pass : the enemy, with a view to hindering the advance by creating difficulties of food supply, had fired the stock of fodder at many of the villages. So precipitate was their retreat, however, that the destruction of the fodder was far from successfully accomplished, and very ample quantities remained. The Afridis, except the Kuki Khels, did not assist at all in the defence of the Sampagha Pass; either because they deemed the attack on their own country so imminent that they could spare no time to assist their allies, or because they had quarrelled with the Orakzai as to the disposition of the force in the pass.

The same evening, after the capture of the pass, both divisions of the Tirah Field Force moved down into the Mastura Valley where the Orakzai in times of peace have their permanent head-quarters. Unfortunately the baggage of the troops, even great-coats and blankets, could not follow them in all cases the same day, and many corps were without these and had to spend a bitterly cold night, and in the case of the Dorset Regiment and the Gordon Highlanders, not only without any warm clothing but with nothing to eat except what they had carried with them in their havresacks. Of course to pass two divisions with their obligatory mules even, i.e., without anything in the shape of tents and heavier articles of equipment along a bad mountain track on the same day on which an action had been fought in the morning (thus delaying the start of the baggage) was an obvious impossibility; and the corps who were without their baggage were doubtless prepared for that eventuality. The two divisions remained the next day (the 30th) at the Mastura Camp. The Mastura is a fine wide valley, with numerous homesteads of solidly built two or three storied houses, with good outhouses, and with the usual towers and walled enclosures. All this day the baggage began to slowly trickle in from the Sampagha Pass, where the block on the narrow road was enormous; and in the evening the block being hopeless for that day, orders were issued postponing the further advance of the troops and the attack on the Arhanga Pass until the next day.

The Arhanga Pass leads direct from the Mastura Valley into Maidan the summer home of the Afridis. The order of advance was: 4th, 3rd, 2nd and 1st Brigades in the sequence named, beginning at 6 A.M.; all baggage animals, except pakhal mules, following in rear of the clounm. Mr. Donald, the Political Officer with the 2nd Division, who has a most intimate knowledge of these tribesmen and their ways, predicted the night before the attack that not more than about 500 men would hold the pass, and his prediction proved absolutely correct. The enemy were very few indeed in number, and offered little if any resistance. The 4th Brigade threw forward a regiment, the King's Own Scottish Borderers, and seized a conical hill some 1,200 yards from the centre of the pass, and on to this hill Brigadier-General Spragge brought to play the three batteries of the 2nd Division, under Lieutenant-Colonel Purdy. The 3rd Brigade (Brigadier-General Kempster's) then made a demonstrative movement to the left; while the 2nd Brigade (Brigadier-General Gaselee's), accompanied by General Symons, made a flank attack on the right with a view to seizing a hill commanding the pass from the east. The order of advance of this brigade—which practically took the position by itself, so weak was the resistance—was that the Yorkshire Regiment, with the trained scouts of the 3rd and 5th Gurkhas on their right, and the 2-4th Gurkhas were in first line, with the 3rd Sikhs in the second line and the Queen's in the third line. There was a great race up the hillside between the Yorkshire Regiment and the 2-4th Gurkhas; the Yorkshire Regiment just winning on the post. The enemy fired very few shots, and the total casualties were only five; amongst whom was Captain Searle of the 36th Sikhs, wounded by a stray shot as his regiment was supporting the King's Own Scottish Borderers in the 4th Brigade.

After the Arhanga Pass had been crossed the valleys of Maidan and Rajgul in Tirah, the summer quarters of the Afridis, lay before Sir William Lockhart, and these he now proceeded to enter, having lifted the *purdah* from Tirah in four days from the time of leaving Khorappa in the Khanki Valley. The ease with which the Afridis had been ousted from positions vaunted as virtually impregnable, was the more gratifying, as the experience at the Chagru Kotal had been thought by some to foreshadow stubborn resistance throughout the campaign. Their impotence to bar the advance of such a force as the Government of India had sent against them, was now probably as clear to the tribesmen as to anybody else; and the only question was whether they would frankly accept at once the terms soon to be announced by Sir William Lockhart, or attempt to partially preserve their military prestige among the frontier tribes by avoiding a regular action and maintaining a guerilla warfare. The latter course they well knew could only bring severe punishment upon their country; but as there were at least 30,000 tribesmen in arms, the more fiery of the tribal leaders could not be expected to see the necessity of submitting on the spot without striking a further blow.

We may take advantage of the long delay which once again occurred at Maidan in bringing up stores from the Samana base, in order to take a view of the country in which Sir William Lockhart had now established himself. Tirah or Maidan Valley, which the two divisions of the Tirah Field Force reached on the night of the 31st October, lies in a wide basin surrounded by steep hills, crowned in places on the north side with fir trees, but there are no forests of trees either in the valley or on the hills. The valley is quite open, with large areas of fairly flat ground with deep *nullahs* between them; the whole valley is well cultivated and very fertile. There were numerous homesteads rather than villages everywhere: these homesteads generally consisted of a tower and two or three double or three storied houses surrounded by smaller buildings and outhouses and with many walnut, peach, apricot, cherry and other trees round them. They were full of grain and fodder, though in some cases the fodder had been burnt before the troops arrived. But the numerous fowls, bowls of *ata*, honey, walnuts and other comestibles found in the houses showed that the rapid advance of our troops had rather taken the Afridis by surprise. The water-supply was good; the nights were not so cold as in the Mastura Valley, just traversed, and the whole situation of the troops was greatly improved, from the point of view of camp comfort. Autumn was well advanced, but it was easy to see that in the spring or summer the country must be very beautiful. In the hot weather the central valley is no doubt densely populated; the banks of the stream were found to be honeycombed with cave-dwellings. It was difficulty to ascertain how many Afridis stay during the winter in Maidan, probably not more than one-fifth of its summer inhabitants. In a warm winter, or if troubles were apprehended towards Peshawar, no doubt more would remain. Regarded geographically, Tirah is thus described in *Records of Frontier Expeditions* (Paget and Mason):—"Maidan is a circular valley or basin, about ten miles in diameter, surrounded by forest-covered mountains rising from 8,000 to 9,000 feet. The valley is well drained by three or four large watercourses: that to the west, where the Malikdin Khel hamlets stand, is known as the Shilober, which name is also applied to the entire stream after the others have joined it, *viz.*, the Sherdara, occupied by the Zakka Khels from the east: the Manakass, occupied by some families of the Jowaki and Ashu Khel sections of the Adam Khels; and the Kahudara, occupied by the Kambar Khels. These converge from the Shilober Toi, which, leaving Maidan, enters a narrow rocky gorge three miles long commanded by heights rising one thousand feet above it on either side. After emerging from this defile, the torrent flows through open country for two or three miles, then joins the Rajgul stream at Dwatoi, after which the united stream receives the name of the Bara

River." Beyond Maidan lies the Rajgul Valley, of which we read:—
"Its length is about ten miles and the breadth of the open country lying on either side of the central stream about four to five miles where widest, its elevation being probably over 5,000 feet. Rajgul is inhabited by Kuki Khel Afridis, and their hamlets lie near the stream in the centre of the valley. Temporary sheds are erected by the shepherds among the pine forests which clothe the surrounding mountains. On the south Rajgul is separated from Maidan by a steep, rocky, well-wooded spur, 8,000 to 9,000 feet in elevation."

While reserve supplies were being slowly pushed forward from Khorappa, through difficult country overrun with daring Afridi skirmishers, at the tedious rate of about two days' supplies in twenty-four hours, there was for a long time no occurrence in Tirah to give to the expedition the outward semblance of activity. The road from the Arhanga Pass to the Tirah Valley was at first very stony and precipitous, but the Bombay Sappers and Miners rapidly improved it; and once down into the valley the path or paths were quite easy, and in time the whole road from Khorappa was made practicable for camels. The ordinary baggage moved through the Arhanga Pass more quickly than it had done over the Sampagha Pass, and every British regiment got their great-coats and blankets on the night of the 31st October, that is, the night of the arrival of the troops. Part of the baggage belonging to the 15th Sikhs, however, was caught by the enemy in the narrow defile on the Maidan side of the pass after dark: the tribesmen fired from the heights above, the mule *drabies* bolted, the escort of the 15th Sikhs with great presence of mind closed round the ammunition mules and effectively protected them, but some 71 Jeypore ponies and some 200 kits were carried off. Three drivers were shot dead in the dark, and two wounded.

The next morning, November 1st, Bagh, the place where the great tribal *jirgahs* are usually held, was reconnoitred. The enemy fired on the reconnoitring party but were driven off by a few shells. Captain MacLaren, King's Own Scottish Borderers, was slightly wounded, and the 1-3rd Gurkhas lost one sepoy killed and two severely and one slightly wounded. The Afridis were seen at 1 P.M. coming down in considerable numbers from the hills to the east of the camp with bullocks to carry off fodder and goods; and the 2nd Brigade, with the Derajat Mountain Battery, moved out to stop their operations, returning to camp at 5 P.M. Lieutenant E. G. Caffin, Yorkshire Regiment, was severely wounded in this affair. A picket of the 36th Sikhs moving out to their post at 6 P.M. were attacked, but they drove off the enemy: one sepoy was wounded. The transport from the Arhanga Pass coming into camp about 7 P.M. was also attacked, and hand-to-hand fighting ensued; and our casualties were:—2nd Royal West Surrey—*killed* 3; *wounded* 4; Northamptons—*wounded* 1; transport followers—*wounded* 3; Jeypore Transport Train *killed* 1; *wounded* 3. Some baggage was lost.

The main body of the Afridis seemed chiefly concerned in getting their families and flocks into a place of safety. For the moment the upper part of the Bara Valley lay open to them, and although this could only be a temporary refuge it was the best they had to turn to without entering Afghanistan in unwelcome numbers. Excluding the Adam Khels and a part of the Kuki Khels, who had not risen, there were probably not less than 20,000 Afridis bearing arms; counting old men, women and children, the whole Afridi population at the lowest estimate must number 50,000; winter was drawing near; and Sir William Lockhart, who was playing a driving game, hoped by properly combining the movements of his main column in Maidan with the movements of the Peshawar Column then at Bara Fort to make the position of the tribe one that must compel complete submission. It was considered quite unlikely that a huge tribal exodus into eastern Afghanistan would take place, though doubtless many separate families would flee towards this the only safe line of retreat left open. The conclusion generally drawn was that the Afridis would rally their scattered forces in the Bara Valley and would then be driven eastward, the scene of the operations gradually shifting nearer to the Peshawar frontier so as to play into the hands of the Peshawar Column which would advance from Bara for the purpose. There was a possible escape for the Afridis from the Bara Valley into the Bazar Valley which runs north of and parallel to it; indeed already the Bokar Pass connecting the two valleys was thronged with the families and flocks of the Zakka Khels, the Aka Khels and the Kambar Khels. But this evasion at the best could only prolong the chase, and it was thought that the warlike Afridis, after having been driven all the way from Chagru Kotal to Khorappa, from Khorappa to the Sampagha and Arhanga Passes, and thence through Tirah into the Bara Valley would at last make an all-decisive stand.

For the moment the Afridis alone were engrossing attention, but as may be well supposed the Orakzai were not dropping out of the plan of campaign, as heavy scores had yet to be settled with the beseigers of

Gulistan and Saragheri. A reconnaissance in force was ordered down the Mastura Valley, which runs south of the Bara Valley to discover what opposition the Orakzai were preparing to offer, and it was intended later on to look up the Khanki Valley also, still further south. But operations in these two directions could be deliberately undertaken by Sir Power Palmer with the strong body of troops forming the Line of Communication, at a later stage, after the base of Sir William Lockhart's main column had been transferred from Kohat (*viâ* Shinawari and Khorappa) to Peshawar.

(185)

CHAPTER XI.

GUERILLA WARFARE—A HEAVY CASUALTY LIST.

Having removed their families to places beyond the immediate reach of our troops, the Afridis now began to grow extremely bold, and on the 5th November they attacked the convoy with the head-quarter staff baggage from Khorappa as it was approaching the Arhanga Pass. They also attacked a foraging party from the 2nd Division, killing a Jamadar and one man of the 15th Sikhs and wounding five others severely, besides carrying off about 40 mules. The same night there was heavy firing for three hours into Maidan Camp. Lieutenant C. L. Giffard of the Northamptonshire Regiment was shot dead and Captain E. L. Sullivan of the 36th Sikhs was severely wounded while walking about in the mess tent. Two nights later, Captain E. Y. Watson, Commissariat Officer, 4th Brigade, was shot through the head by a stray bullet and died almost immediately. On the 7th November, a Sunday, while the 2nd Brigade were at church parade, a bullet was fired into the assembly and nearly brought the service to an abrupt conclusion, as it only just missed the chaplain. Every tent and sleeping place in camp was now provided with shelter from bullets, either by excavation or by making stone and mud walls, and the messes were similarly protected. The 2nd Brigade went out foraging on the 8th, and owing to the precautions taken by Brigadier-General Gaselee, the enemy were kept at a distance and there was only one casualty, in the 2-4th Gurkhas. Large quantities of grain were seized and much more had to be left behind. On the 9th November the 4th Brigade destroyed many of the towers and fortified posts of the Zakka Khels, this tribe having defiantly refused to send in a *jirgah*, and having moreover been mainly responsible for the heavy firing night after night into camp. Desultory brushes with the enemy continued to occur while the Tirah Field Force remained at Maidan awaiting the completion of its reserve supplies, but they led to nothing of moment.

One unfortunate event which occurred in the Kurram Valley at this period cannot be left unnoticed here, though it had no immediate connection with anything then taking place in Tirah. Colonel Hill, Commanding the Kurram movable column, taking advantage of the suspension of hostilities in the neighbourhood of Sadda, made a reconnaissance up the Karmana defile, which, though very successful in itself, was incidentally marred by a heavy and quite unnecessary loss of life. The reconnaissance, which was made in force, took place on the 6th November, and a good survey was made of a portion of the Massuzai country. The defile is seven miles long, and, according to all appearances, could be held by a thousand tribesmen with proper defensive preparations against almost any attacking force, as the river bed is commanded from both sides within easy rifle range throughout. The enemy, however, were on this occasion completely surprised, and did not even hold a stockade across the defile. About six miles from Sadda the road was found passable for cavalry, and the Central India Horse went through in force and reached the village of Esor at 11 o'clock. Here a lance belonging to a Duffadar of the 3rd Bengal Cavalry, killed near camp in September was discovered, and also a quantity of arms, gunpowder and grain. The arms were confiscated, but nothing was destroyed. The retirement began at 1 P.M., when the enemy collected in considerable force. The 5th Gurkhas, as rear-guard, proceeded a mile down the defile without trouble, but here a stoppage occurred owing to some delay in getting in a picket of the Kapurthala Infantry from the heights above the right bank of the river. The Gurkhas were detained an hour, and the enemy meanwhile advanced in strength with standards flying. A few casualties occurred, the Gurkhas losing one killed, one severely and two slightly wounded, the Kapurthala Infantry one slightly wounded, and the Kurram Militia one dangerously and one slightly wounded. The enemy on their part lost heavily, and though the ground was suited for the peculiar following-up tactics of the Pathan, they gradually fell back discomfited, the last five miles into camp being covered without a shot being fired. The Maxims and long-range volleys of the Royal Scots Fusiliers were very effective. So far the reconnaissance, which had been conducted in a very able manner, had apparently been a complete success, and what was very important it had served to reveal the true state of this shorter route from the Kurram to the Khanki Valley. But, unknown to everybody except the unfortunate troops concerned, a sad disaster had befallen the Kapurthala picket already referred to. The picket consisted of thirty-five Sikhs under a Subadar, and their position on the heights above the right bank of the river had apparently been chosen as it overlooked not only the road along the river bed but also the Gao defile which joins the Karmana defile at Jani Kot. When the picket was first signalled to withdraw and join the main body, the message was acknowledged; but unfortunately the withdrawal was not begun forthwith, though the route by which the picket had ascended was a perfectly safe one, as none of the enemy were near it, having in fact begun to retire up the defile. What was worse, the delay made in executing the order of withdrawal entirely escaped attention, and indeed it was eventually reported to Colonel Hill that all units of his column were present. Thereafter the march of the column to Sudda was resumed, and the five miles home were covered in ignorance of the absence of the picket. Stranger still, "all present" was again reported to the Officer Commanding the Force in camp the next morning, and it was actually not until late in the day that Colonel Hill was informed that a Subadar and thirty-five men of the Kapurthala Infantry were " missing." Search parties were sent out, but no trace of the party could be found, and all too late it was discovered that only a few members of it had actually rejoined the column when it started back from Jani Kot. What really happened to the ill-fated picket was only discovered later. The Subadar in command had apparently watched the running fight in the Karmana defile with the closest attention, and conceived the idea of sharing in it. The sepoys were equally keen, and it is perhaps not to be wondered at that a body of brave men, whose discipline is not of the hard-and-fast kind which obtains in our own regiments, should have become excited when they saw an action taking place only a couple of miles or so away in which they had no prospect of participating. When the signal to retire was received, the last hope of the picket of even a chance skirmish disappeared. Very reluctantly they began to descend. The route by which they had ascended was taken at first, but after it had been followed for some distance the Subadar and the more impetuous spirits decided to disobey the order signalled to them and to move down the ridge in a direction which would bring them into the defile at a point considerably higher up than Jani Kot. The signallers and five men went on in the original direction and reached the main column in safety. So far as could be made out the Subadar's party soon got into very broken ground, among cliffs and *nul als*, and eventually dropped into a narrow and difficult ravine. If they had been able to follow this to its junction with the Karmana defile they would have come out above the Gurkha rear-guard, and would even then have been in a highly dangerous position. But as they moved down the ravine they discovered that the way was barred, the jungle being on fire. Finding themselves trapped they endeavoured to retrace their steps and were observed by some of the tribesmen. The *lashkar* thereupon halted in its retirement, and the enemy turning back swarmed about the *nullah*, effectually cutting off all retreat. As heavy firing might have attracted the attention of the main body of the troops, the Massuzai and Chamkannis contented themselves by sitting on guard, and it was not until the moon rose that they made their attack, rolling stones into the ravine and shooting down the whole party. Deplorable as the result must be held to be, there could be little doubt that it was directly due to over-eagerness on the part of the little band of men and their leader to give a good account of themselves. They were brave to a fault, and they paid the penalty which sometimes attaches to rashness in the face of an enemy. After this affair, the attitude of the tribesmen east of Sadda became more hostile than ever, and the Massuzai were reinforced by all the Chamkanni clans. But no actual fighting ensued, and we may once again leave the Kurram Valley, to follow events in Maidan.

On the 9th November, by way of preparing for an early forward movement, Sir William Lockhart ordered a reconnaissance in force from Maidan to the Saran Pass, which leads into the Bara and Bazar Valleys through the Sipah Afridis' country; and again the day's operations though in themselves entirely successful, were marred incidentally by an unlooked-for disaster. The force which made the reconnaissance to Saran Sar was a mixed brigade under the command of Brigadier-General Westmacott. Sir William Lockhart followed the column to the Saran Sar but returned in advance of it and had reached camp some two hours before the disaster in question occurred. The regiments forming the mixed brigade were the Northamptons, the Dorsets, the 15th Sikhs and the 36th Sikhs. After the crest of the Saran Sar had been crowned the troops started back with all speed, hoping to cover the five miles to camp before sunset. All went well until within about a mile of the camp; no sign of the enemy being visible. It was then dusk, and one company of the Northamptons, while marching alone down a *nullah*, were ambuscaded by a party of tribesmen. The enemy would seem to have been lying close up to the route taken, and their fire at short range was terribly effective, as the regiment had 49 casualties, including three British Officers. The three other regiments were only slightly engaged during the retirement; their losses being 3 killed and 15 wounded. The list of casualties for the day was as follows: British Officers—*killed:* Lieutenant J. T. Waddell and 2nd-Lieutenant A. H. Macintyre, Northamptonshire Regiment; *wounded:* Lieutenants G. A. Trent (Northamptonshire Regiment), O P. S. Ingham and A. A. Mercer (Dorsetshire Regiment). Native Officer—*wounded;*—one Subadar, 15th Sikhs. Rank and file: Northamptonshire Regiment—17 killed and 29 wounded; Dorsetshire Regiment—2 killed and 6 wounded; 15 Sikhs 1 killed and 3 wounded; 36th Sikhs—3 wounded. Total of all ranks—*killed,* 22; *wounded,* 45. The ambuscade must either have been most carefully planned, or, as seemed more likely, the attacking party were lying concealed on the lookout for stragglers from camp, when they became aware of the regiment moving down the ravine, and decided to pour in a few rapid volleys at close quarters before a counter-attack could be made. The tribesmen chiefly concerned in the attack were again the Zakka Khels, amidst whose villages in Maidan the Tirah Field Force was then encamped.

It was not very plain at first how the Northamptons came to find themselves alone in a *nullah* cut off from their main body; and the later details never entirely cleared up this point. The facts which ultimately came to light are these. In clearing the way for the reconnaissance, in the first instance, a commanding position was captured by the Northamptons, who as advance-guard enveloped the west flank of the ridge which the enemy occupied. The position was taken at 11 A.M. with only 5 casualties. Sir William Lockhart and staff arrived about 1·30 P.M. and at 2·15 the retirement was ordered. Here the casualties began in earnest: for the enemy, following their favourite tactics of withholding their attack until the withdrawal of our troops, emerged suddenly from the woods, and the Northamptons who now formed the rear-guard had 1 man killed and 11 wounded in quite a short time. The removal of the wounded became increasingly difficult, and the ground was too precipitous for stretchers. The 36th Sikhs were sent back up the hill to assist the Northamptons, who were seen to be seriously encumbered by their numerous killed and wounded, and the foot of the hill was only reached at 5 P.M. Up to this point the Northamptons, though having many casualties, had merely suffered the ordinary fortunes of rear-guard fighting. But being now belated, and anxious (as one version suggested) to make up for lost time, they took a short cut which, as it chanced, lay through a *nullah* ambuscaded by the enemy, feeling secure from further molestation by reason of their nearness to camp. The march through the *nullah,* under a deadly shower of bullets, was conducted with wonderful coolness. Though powerless to retort upon the concealed enemy, and losing strength at every step, the unlucky band stuck bravely to their wounded. When camp was at last reached at 8 p.m. Lieutenant Macintyre, a Sergeant and eleven men of the regiment were reported missing, and were all found killed next morning. Sir William Lockhart at once ordered a military court of enquiry to be held regarding this very unfortunate affair, and after evidence had been recorded the papers were sent up to Army Head-Quarters.

Two days later the 2nd Brigade under General Gaselee, with two mountain guns and one company of Sappers, paid a second visit to Saran Sar to complete the survey, bring in forage and destroy the fortifications of such Zakka Khel villages as could be reached. This was all accomplished satisfactorily and without any serious misadventure; the defences of about 40 villages being destroyed. Our casualties were: Second-Lieutenant Wright, 2nd Queen's, slightly wounded; one man of the 2nd Queen's killed, and one sepoy of the 1-3rd Gurkhas slightly wounded. The enemy's loss was considerable, being at least 12 killed and 30 wounded by rifle fire, while the artillery fire was also effective.

While all this guerilla fighting was in progress the Political Officers under Sir William Lockhart were endeavouring to arrange for the submission of the tribesmen. Letters were sent out to all the sections of the Afridis and Orakzai, intimating that if they would send in their *jirgahs* and promise submission, the terms of the Government would be made known to them. The Orakzai *jirgahs* came in promptly and were informed that they would be required to make a formal declaration of submission to the Government, to restore all rifles and Government property *looted*, to surrender 500 of their own rifles, to pay a fine of Rs 30,000 and to give hostages for the fulfilment of such terms as were not required to be carried out forthwith. They were further informed that compensation for damage done to their buildings would be taken into consideration later on, when the relations of the Government with the border tribes would be re-arranged. A fortnight's grace was allowed them to comply with these terms, and the different clans departed severally to consider their courses. Before leaving, the *jirgahs* asked that the Government should apportion the fine among the various sections of the tribe, but after consultation with the Political Officers Sir William Lockhart decided that the entire demand should be divided equally between the Gar and Samil factions and that these should make all further internal distribution themselves without assistance from the Government. As for the Afridis, most of their *jirgahs* also came in, some at once and others at intervals, to hear what terms the Government intended to impose, but two Afridi clans refused to come in or to hear any terms at all, and defied the Government to "come on." These were the Zakka Khels and the Aka Khels. To the Afridi *jirgahs* which did come in Sir William Lockhart returned a stern answer, declining to listen to anything they had to say or to declare any terms to them until the two recalcitrant clans of their tribe had come in also, and warning them that unless submission were voluntarily and quickly made it would be vigorously enforced. The Zakka Khels, who alone of all the Afridi clans were really responsible for keeping hostilities so vigorously alive, have their settlements in the Bazar Valley and Khyber tracts during the winter, and move to Maidan and the upper part of the Bara Valley during the summer, and are the most powerful of all the Afridi clans, mustering 4,500 fighting men, mostly well armed. They are notoriously bloodthirsty and treacherous, and are dreaded even by their fellow tribesmen. It was they who had planned and mainly carried out the attack on the Khyber posts, and in all the tribal councils during the past few weeks they alone had formed the irreconcilable war party. The Aka Khels are found during the winter to the south-west of Peshawar, near Akhor. Their fighting strength is 1,800 men, and their poverty prevents their possessing many breechloaders. In the summer they migrate to the Waran Valley, which lies due north of the Mastura Valley, within striking distance of the place where Sir William Lockhart's force then lay. By nature the Aka Khels are not a very bloodthirsty clan, but in this instance they were dragged in the wake of the Zakka Khels, and the fact that the Mullah Saiad Akbar belonged to the clan no doubt prompted them still more strongly to hold out a while for the sake of their *izzat*. The appearance of a brigade in the Waran Valley, where the Aka Khels were then strongly mustered, was therefore one of the first measures called for, and Brigadier-General Kempster was instructed to carry out this manoeuvre forthwith.

At daybreak on the 13th November General Kempster's Brigade with No. 8 Mountain Battery Royal Artillery and No. 5 Bombay Mountain Battery, the 36th Sikhs and some companies of Sappers started out for the Waran Valley by the Seri Kandao Pass. Contrary to expectation the troops entered the valley practically without any opposition either during their advance or later in the day; the camp was not fired into during the night; forage was obtained in large quantities and without opposition, both on the 13th and 14th, and all appeared quiet. Some very interesting letters were found in Saiad Akbar's house—which was visited and destroyed during the reconnaissance—amongst them one from the Hadda Mullah, written in July or August. It said that the Turks had completely defeated the Greeks, that the English had been turned out of Egypt and deprived of the use of the Suez Canal, that the Mohmands had defeated us, that our power in India was on the wane, and that now was the time to rise against us, as English troops could not stand campaigning in the hot weather. On the 15th November the force moved out to make a further reconnaissance towards the junction of the Waran and Mastura Valleys so as to have this point accurately fixed in the survey of Tirah which was being made under the general superintendence of Colonel Sir Thomas Holdich. Although the Aka Khels on the previous two days had shown no active hostility to the free movement of our troops, due military precautions had been taken throughout, and the wisdom of this cautiousness was well exemplified on the 15th. No sooner had the advanced guard got beyond the limits of the camp, than a British flag of truce sent out in the direction of some Aka Khels, who were seen coming out of their houses, rifles in hand, was fired on by Zakka Khel tribesmen posted on an adjoining height, a Gurkha Havildar being killed, and a sepoy wounded. The reconnaissance was pushed forward, the tribesmen keeping up a continuous fire, more especially on the return of the troops to camp. The casualties during this day were 1 killed and 6 wounded; 2 of the latter being Gordon Highlanders, who were shot as they were going to their picket post at dusk. It appeared later on, from information received by Colonel Warburton, who accompanied General Kempster, that the Zakka Khels had entered the Waran Valley during the night of the 14th November and had tried to incite the Aka Khels to fight, in the hope that General Kempster would retaliate by wholesale destruction of villages, and so drive the Aka Khels into the ranks of the irreconcilables. The Aka Khels, however, held aloof on the 15th, and consequently no damage was done to their houses, in spite of the shots fired by Zakka Khels.

Orders had been sent to Brigadier-General Kempster to return to Maidan on the 16th, Sir William Lockhart's intention being that the first move from Maidan—to Bagh—should begin on the 17th with the 2nd Brigade and the Divisional troops of the 1st Divison. Brigadier-General Kempster accordingly issued orders to the effect that the baggage with sufficient escort was to move soon after daybreak; and the road over the pass and for a great way on each side had been so improved by the exertions of No. 4 Bombay and No. 4 Madras Sappers that nearly all the baggage was safely in camp at Maidan by 3 P.M.

But as soon as the retirement of the troops began, the enemy, both Zakka Khels and Aka Khels, pressed boldly forward, and there ensued one of the severest rear-guard actions of the whole campaign. To describe in the exact order of occurrence all that took place is to incur some risk of confusing the narrative, for several bodies of troops, isolated from the main body, met with independent adventures in different parts of the field and during different stages of the general action. But the following extended account of the fighting, while faithful enough in detail, will perhaps be found as little involved as any that could well be prepared of such an affair.

At the outset the enemy were held back by the 1-2nd Gurkhas, admirably handled by Lieutenant-Colonel Travers, to whom two companies of the Dorsets afforded great assistance. The 36th Sikhs had been sent on to hold the pass for a time, and were eventually relieved by the 15th Sikhs; the two companies of the Dorsets and the 1-2nd Gurkhas retiring over the pass, covered by the 15th Sikhs, who had parties out holding heights on each side of the pass. The 36th Sikhs had orders when relieved by the 15th Sikhs to take up a position further down the road and nearer Maidan, and to hold various positions on the high ground above the road, so as to cover the retirement of the 15th Sikhs. The Gurkhas had some very heavy fighting before they reached the pass—which they did not cross till 3 P.M. or later—for the enemy's marksmanship was as usual excellent, and 3 men were killed and 5 wounded, despite the cleverness of the Gurkhas in availing themselves of cover. Surgeon-Captain Selby, I.M.S., attached to the 1-2nd Gurkhas, showed great courage in tending the wounded under fire, a perilous duty unflinchingly performed. Lieutenant Wylie, a most popular Officer with all who knew him, who had only very lately been transferred for duty from the 2nd Battalion of his regiment at Samana to the 1st Battalion with the Main Column, was shot through the head by a stray bullet, Captain MacIntyre of his regiment carrying his dead comrade's body himself till a litter could be obtained. The Gurkhas, once they had crossed over the pass, met with no further casualties till they reached camp. But the 15th Sikhs, who had covered the Gurkhas' retirement and who were now in rear of every other regiment, had a far more stirring adventure awaiting them. As they began to draw in their pickets from the heights above the pass, the enemy pressed forward anew in great numbers, and many losses were suffered before Colonel Abbott assembled most of his men (he had only five weak companies) on the *sungars* on the spur preparatory to a retirement further down the hill. The enemy had by this time collected in a wood within about 40 yards of the main *sungar*, and while Captain Lewarne was taking a company of the 15th Sikhs down from a post they had been occupying to a position further down the hill, a large number of swordsmen charged after him. Captain Lewarne very coolly halted and fronted the company, fixed bayonets, and waited before opening fire till the swordsmen were within 40 paces. At the same time a second party, under Lieutenant Vivian, perceiving the enemy's manœuvre, dashed gallantly up to Captain Lewarne to aid him in checking it. On this occasion the Afridi losses were undoubted, for the charging tribesmen melted away before the Sikh fire, and the company reached the point it was making for without further molestation. The fire on the main body of the 15th Sikhs with Colonel Abbott in the large *sungar* west of the wood was very heavy indeed; and at length Colonel Abbott deemed it advisable to apprise Brigadier-General Kempster by signal that his retirement was being greatly delayed by the presence of wounded Sikhs in the *sungar* whom it would be extremely difficult to carry away under a heavy fire. Brigadier-General Kempster at once issued orders for two companies of the Dorsets and five companies of the 36th Sikhs to return towards the 15th Sikhs and assist the retirement. Lieutenant-Colonel Haughton, Commanding the 36th Sikhs, was at that time riding with one of his companies nearest the pass, while Captain Custance was in command of another company of the 36th Sikhs holding a hill further away to the right. Before receiving General Kempster's order Colonel Haughton, as soon as he was informed of the difficulty in which the 15th Sikhs were immersed, at once, and of his own initiative, started away with the single company near him, and left Major Des Vœux, his second-in-command, to bring on the remaining three companies and the two companies of the Dorset Regiment. Captain Custance with his isolated company however was the first to reinforce Colonel Abbott, the time being then about 4-15 P.M. The enemy were firing with very great precision from the wood, and to show one's head above the *sungars* was to risk having a bullet through it. Colonel Abbott had already been wounded by a shot from a jhezail, apparently loaded with pieces of telegraph wire, which struck him in the face, inflicting a serious though happily not a dangerous wound. Captain Custance, while reconnoitring for a good position for his company, received two bullets through the helmet and was then shot through the thigh, and both he and Colonel Abbott were being carried down the hill in stretchers when Colonel Haughton arrived on the scene. Major Des Vœux, before following his Colonel, had awaited the arrival of three other very weak companies of the 36th Sikhs, and with these he had also brought a company of the Dorset Regiment under Captain Hammond, with Lieutenant Cowie and Lieutenant Crooke, Suffolk Regiment (attached to the Dorsets for duty), as his subalterns. Soon afterwards Lieutenant Hales, East Yorkshire Regiment (attached to the Dorsets), also came up with half a company. In making his way to reinforce Colonel Haughton Major Des Vœux decided to take the company of the Dorset Regiment under Captain Hammond on with him, and to leave the other half-company, of which Lieutenant Crooke was in command, to hold a house close by above the road, Lieutenant Hales also remaining on the spot with his half-company. The object in leaving a company of the Dorset Regiment to hold the houses was to give a *point d'appui* for the troops in rear further up the pass. Major Des Vœux then hurried on with the remaining companies of the 36th Sikhs to catch up Lieutenant-Colonel Haughton, so that eventually the latter had near him—though not all concentrated in the same place, but in different positions on the spur west of the wood—10 companies Sikhs and half-company Dorsets. It should be remarked here that although for the sake of simplicity the narrative is forced to speak of "companies" they were only companies in name, or the nucleus of companies. The half company under Captain Hammond, Dorset Regiment, for instance, had only 16 men, and the Sikh companies, especially those of the 15th Sikhs, only numbered from 20 to 30 men each, so that in all probability Lieutenant-Colonel Haughton had not more than 200 men in all under his command, especially after he had sent on the wounded ahead. As a matter of fact, most of the regiments in General Kempster's Brigade were very short of men at that time, for this brigade had borne the brunt of the losses, and many men had been invalided. Moreover, there were men absent on baggage duty and employed in conveying the wounded back to camp. Lieutenant-Colonel Haughton's force was at this stage in two portions, the greater part holding the *sungar* close to the wood and a smaller part a *sungar* further down the spur. Soon after Colonel Haughton's arrival the fire from the wood, which had hitherto been intense, began to slacken. Apparently this was due to the tribesmen leaving the wood and working round by the north to try and cut in on the line of retreat further down the hill. In any case, as the fire had begun to slacken and it was rapidly getting dark, and as the wounded had all been sent on and the *sungars* held were untenable for the night, Colonel Haughton ordered a gradual retirement.

The party in the westernmost *sungar* covered the retirement of the other party from the *sungar* nearest the wood, and the march was made to the foot of the hill without further loss. Here in the darkness the troops were reformed, each Officer calling to a certain company to rally round him, and search had to be made for a path, as it was considered advisable to remain on the spur on high ground rather than follow the real road down the *nullah*. At this moment a heavy fire was opened on the force from in front, in flank, and in rear. To have continued the march under this fire would have involved heavy loss and possibly disaster. To have remained stationary would have been to submit helplessly to being shot down. In this critical situation Colonel Haughton did not for a moment lose his presence of mind. He observed, as well as it was possible in the darkness, that the fire came principally from some houses about 300 yards distant, and with splendid decision he ordered the troops to fix bayonets and turn the enemy out of the houses. Equally decisive was the response of the troops. The Dorsets with a cheer, and the Sikhs shouting their war-cry, advanced up the cultivated terraces against the houses, which by the way had been set on fire that morning, the mud walls only remaining. The enemy replied with defiant shouts, and waited till their assailants were within 10 paces before opening a very heavy fire. Luckily, and probably owing to the ground being in steps, the Afridi fire was too high, and only one man of the 15th Sikhs, a Subadar, was hit and badly wounded. Of three principal houses the 15th Sikhs occupied the northernmost house, the Dorsets the centre, and the 36th Sikhs under Colonel Haughton the southern house. Lieutenant Munn, the Adjutant of the 36th Sikhs, ran one tribesman through with his sword on reaching the plateau or spur on which the houses stood : and a few others were shot. But there was now great danger of the separated parties firing on one another, and the "cease fire" was accordingly sounded. The 15th Sikhs and the Dorsets then moved down to the building held by Colonel Haughton. All the buildings were still too hot, after having been burnt, to allow of their being entered, and the troops were placed in a sort of semi-circle with the main building behind them. There were no materials for making barricades and *sungars*, and before the troops could be got into position and lie flat on the ground a very heavy fire was poured in on them, killing Captain Lewarne, 15th Sikhs, wounding Lieutenant Munn, 36th Sikhs, and killing 3 sepoys and wounding 5 others. After this a desultory fire was kept up by the tribesmen outside till the moon began to rise.

Meanwhile Major Des Vœux with his small force found himself cut off from his Colonel. In the attack on the villages he had taken two companies and selected for assault a house further to the south. Captain Hammond, temporarily separated from his own company in the darkness, accompanied him. When the house had been seized, it was found to be untenable and a move was made to another house. This building, though it had been burnt, had cooled down, and the party of about two weak companies at once set to work to make a breastwork with clods of burnt earth and pieces of timber. Major Des Vœux was not attacked in force, though the enemy hovered round for hours, shouting that they would serve the defenders as they had served the defenders of Saragheri, and even throwing stones over the walls of burnt houses behind. Communication was established with Colonel Haughton's force by whistle, and the sentry had orders to fire an occasional shot to show the enemy our troops were on the alert and not short of ammunition. The night was miserably cold, especially for Colonel Haughton's men, as they had not even a house to go into, and neither party had great-coats or blankets. Colonel Haughton himself went out and reconnoitred under a heavy fire before daybreak, and finding that there was no very intricate ground between himself and Major Des Vœux, started off to join him, the wounded being carried on charpoys found in the houses. The enemy fired, but the dim light did not admit of accurate aim, and the retirement was well covered by Lieutenant Cowie with the Dorsets. When the whole force had been concentrated a move was made towards camp, and the troops sent out by General Kempster to relieve Colonel Haughton were met about 8 A.M. Thus ended one of the most exciting rear-guard actions in the whole Tirah Campaign. But one painful episode remains to be related.

It had fared very badly with the two half-companies of the Dorsets left behind by Major Des Vœux on the pass the previous night to cover the intended retirement of Colonel Haughton's little force, especially with the half-company under Lieutenant Crooke. At the outset the two half-companies, some 35 to 40 men in all, with Lieutenants Crooke and Hales, occupied a house and some *sungars*, a strong position, a little above the road. It will be remembered that Lieutenant Crooke had been told by Major Des Vœux that he was to hold on to the houses whatever might happen in order to cover the retirement of the Sikhs from the pass. It was dark, and men were heard moving down the road in the *nullah* below. These were challenged and it is said they replied they were Sikhs. This point will probably never be cleared up for both

Lieutenant Crooke and Lieutenant Hales are dead, and the men and possibly also the Non-Commissioned Officers, who all come from Madras cantonments are unacquainted with Hindustani, and the fact of the challenging is not clearly established. In any case, Lieutenant Crooke, a very capable Officer and of great experience, believed that the men below him were the 15th and 36th Sikhs, and in that erroneous belief he probably gave the order to retire—his half-company on one side of the spur nearest the *nullah*, the other half-company further away. As a matter of fact the men whom he had challenged were Afridis, and they came on Lieutenant Crooke's half-company, killing him and 9 men and wounding 7 others. Private Vickery of this half-company, who had previously distinguished himself by trying to save a wounded man under a heavy fire at Dargai was one of the wounded. He was shot through the foot and was then attacked by three swordsmen. He shot the first, bayonetted the second, losing his bayonet in the man's body, and then clubbing his rifle knocked the third man's brains out. Finally he returned to camp bringing with him a wounded comrade. Lieutenant Crooke's half-company, which suffered so severely, belonged to Captain Hammond's company of the Dorset Regiment which had afforded such great assistance to the Northampton Regiment on the 9th October, by helping to cover their retirement, and, assisted by the 36th Sikhs, to carry in their wounded.

A few words remain to be said about the main body of Brigadier-General Kempster's force. These troops had held on as long as possible to the foot of the hill the previous evening in the hopes of being able to cover the retirement of the 15th and 36th Sikhs and the two half-companies of the Dorset Regiment; but as darkness came on, and it was impossible, for the artillery especially, to see to fire, Brigadier-General Kempster ordered the retirement to be continued, and camp was reached about 8 P.M. Arrangements were at once made for a force to be sent out at daybreak towards the pass. All through the night single men of the Dorset Regiment, a great many of them wounded, straggled into camp, but the half-company which Lieutenant Hales had commanded was brought intact by the Sergeant. The bodies of Lieutenants Crooke and Hales and nine men were found close together in a *nullah*, and the funeral of the two Officers and nine men took place on the evening of the 17th November in one part of the camp, while Captain Lewarne and Lieutenant Wylie were buried together in another part. It was a sad ending to what had otherwise been a very successful expedition, but one and all who spent the night in the captured houses were unanimous on one point—however much their testimony on main points owing to the darkness was in conflict—that Lieutenant-Colonel Haughton's coolness, excellent tactical arrangements, and presence of mind, from the moment he arrived with his small reinforcements at the pass till the relieving troops were met next day, completely outmatched the enemy and prevented what might under the leadership of a less cool and able commander have been an actual disaster. As it was, every man of the Dorsets, 15th or 36th Sikhs, who took part in the bayonet charge on the houses, had good reason to be proud of his performance.

Our casualty list for the whole affair was a long one, and included 4 Officers killed and 3 wounded; the total for all ranks being 33 killed and 36 wounded. The full return is as follows:—Dorsets—*killed:* Lieutenant G. D. Crooke (Suffolk Regiment), Lieutenant Hales (East Yorkshire), both attached to the Dorsets, and 10 men; *wounded:* 8 men. 15th Sikhs—*killed:* Captain Lewarne and 10 men ; *wounded:* Colonel Abbott (slightly) and 13 men. 36th Sikhs—*killed :* 6 men; *wounded:* Captain Custance, Lieutenant Munn and 7 men. 2nd Gurkhas—*killed:* Lieutenant Wylie and 3 men ; *wounded :* 4 men. No. 5 Bombay Mountain Battery—*wounded :* one man.

CHAPTER XII.

THE PLAN OF CAMPAIGN FURTHER DEVELOPED.

On the 18th of November Sir William Lockhart was at last able to make a move from Maidan, and he turned his face to the north-east in the direction of Bagh. There were several reasons why it was considered desirable to move from Maidan: the troops had exhausted nearly all the grain and forage in the vicinity of the camp; a move to Bagh threatened other sections of the Afridi tribe, notably the Malikdin and Kuki Khels (for from Bagh a path exists into the Rajgul Valley by following the Shaloba stream to Dwatoi); and the moral effect of our troops encamping round Bagh which bears a somewhat sacred character, would also have a wholesome effect in convincing the enemy generally of our power to move and encamp anywhere. Part of the 1st Division (Major-General Symons') began the move on the 18th November, the force consisting of the 2nd Brigade and the Divisional troops. The distance to Bagh from Maidan is about 3 miles, and the attitude of the tribesmen as the troops advanced on Bagh was at first undecided, as they were seemingly under the impression that the movement was in connection with either foraging or reconnaissance, and that it would be followed by the usual retirement to Maidan in the evening. As soon, however, as it was perceived that the intention of General Symons was to camp at Bagh the enemy's resistance became very strong, and some portion of the troops were under fire for nearly eleven hours, *i.e.*, from about 7 A.M. to 6 P.M., the enemy firing from the surrounding heights in three-quarters of a circle. The fire was particularly heavy from a hill north-west of the camp; and this eminence had to be heavily shelled by the artillery and then attacked by the Queen's and the 3rd Sikhs before the force could occupy it. The assaulting troops having captured it, Captain Parker's Battery, No. 2 Derajat, came into action on the hill and made excellent practice against scattered parties of tribesmen on surrounding hills; but so bold were the enemy that a certain number crept up to within 500 yards of the battery, and the Battery Officers had some very narrow escapes. Captain Parker was shot through the clothes without the bullet hurting him; one subaltern had his ear grazed by another bullet and another had the knot of his sword shot away. To the west and north-west of the camp the enemy were holding some towers and houses and were keeping up a very galling fire, and they had to be dislodged from their positions by single companies of the Yorkshire Regiment, who were most gallantly led,—notably so by 2nd-Lieutenant Edwards, who with a section of 13 men advanced and turned the enemy out of a house on his front in the most gallant manner, losing the Colour-Sergeant of the company and one man. The total losses incurred before the enemy could be expelled from all the positions they had been holding and pickets placed on such of them as it was deemed desirable to hold for the night, were 5 men killed and 22 wounded. Undaunted by temporary reverses, the enemy as soon as darkness came on crept in between the picket posts and opened a most galling fire, and at one time a concerted volley was fired straight at Major-General Symons' head-quarters, the bullets fortunately all being too high. So excellently had the troops entrenched themselves that there were no casualties from this night firing, though some animals were hit. The Gurkha scouts of the 5th Gurkhas did excellent service during the 18th November, killing several of the enemy and many more were seen being carried away wounded.

On the 19th the troops under Major-General Symons were employed in still further fortifying the picket posts. All the spare animals were sent back to Camp Maidan to assist in removing some 10,000 maunds of stores belonging to the 4th Advanced Depôt at Maidan, and so excellent was the work done by the Commissariat and Transport Officers at Maidan that the whole of these stores were removed to Bagh by 12 noon on the 20th. On the 19th, too, the 4th Brigade, with most of the Divisional troops of the 2nd Division, Major-General Yeatman-Biggs, and Divisional Staff, accompanied by Sir William Lockhart with the Head-quarter Staff, moved to Bagh, leaving Brigadier-General Kempster's Brigade and some of the Divisional troops behind to cover the removal of the 4th Advanced Depôt stores to Bagh and to follow on when all was clear. There was a good deal of firing into camp at Bagh on the 19th, but Camp Maidan was left completely alone by the enemy, though every preparation had been made by Brigadier-General Kempster to meet an attack. The temperature at Camp Bagh, although the ground lies at a lower altitude than Camp Maidan, was considerably colder, for the minimum temperature on the 19th was 21° and the maximum 113°, and after that date the cold greatly increased in severity so much so that on the night of the 29th 21° of frost were recorded.

On the 20th November at about 10 o'clock in the morning the Zakka Khels made a determined effort to cut off the tail of a convoy proceeding up towards the Arhanga Pass. No. 4 Company Madras Sappers were working not very far from the scene of the occurrence, and Major Kelly, Commanding the Royal Engineers, 2nd Division, directed the company to cease work and move off to the scene of attack. So promptly did the company act under Captain Wright's command that the enemy were driven up the valley towards the Arhanga Pass, where, as good luck would have it, a half-battalion Gordon Highlanders under Major Downman were posted. Two companies of this regiment, moving separately, hurried down two spurs lying on either side of the ravine, and the enemy were thus caught between two fires, their losses being estimated at something like 40. Unfortunately a sowar of the 12th Bengal Cavalry who was with the convoy, and four *drabies* had been killed before the Madras Sappers could arrive to their assistance. The same day a great number of towers and fortified houses, from the neighbourhood of which foraging parties had been fired on and from which sniping into camp had taken place, were destroyed, and this and the further destruction of towers and fortified posts south of the camp next day, had a most salutary effect, for there was little or no night firing afterwards and foraging parties were practically unmolested.

On the 21st November Brigadier-General Kempster's Brigade with the remainder of the troops of the 2nd Division, moved to Camp Bagh. As the last of the 3rd Brigade troops marched off from Camp Maidan, the enemy, who had been watching the movement from neighbouring hills, swooped down on the site of the old camp, running hither and thither in the hope apparently of finding something of value left behind, but they were doomed to disappointment, and a few shells from some guns in the rear-guard, within range of which they had incautiously ventured, troubled them considerably, whereafter the march of the 3rd Brigade was practically unmolested. Meanwhile the 2nd Brigade, Brigadier-General Gaselee's, had moved out from Bagh very early that morning and had set fire to some 60 or 70 towers and loopholed houses south of Camp Bagh.

There being no definite prospect of the Zakka Khels making submission the terms of the Government were now at last announced to four Afridi *jirgahs* which had been in camp awaiting the declaration for about a fortnight. These terms were: the surrender of all stolen property, a fine of Rs.50,000, and the handing in of 800 breech-loading rifles. The four *jirgahs* in attendance represented the Malikdin, Adam, Kambar and Aka Khels: to the other tribes proclamations announcing the terms were sent out by the Political Officers.

On the 22nd November a most adventurous and, as it proved, successful reconnaissance was made to Dwatoi or Diva Toi (*signifying* two rivers), at the junction of the Rajgul and Shaloba streams. Brigadier-General Westmacott commanded the force, which Sir William Lockhart, Brigadier-General Nicholson, and some of the Officers of the head-quarter staff accompanied. The column was composed of the King's Own Scottish Borderers, the Yorkshire Regiment, the 36th Sikhs, the 1-2nd and 1-3rd Gurkhas, the 28th Bombay Pioneers, two companies of Sappers, (No. 4 Madras and No. 4 Bombay) and two batteries. The route taken was a difficult one, and goes for the most part along the bed of the Shaloba stream, through a deep and narrow gorge; the track crossing and recrossing the stream, which is knee deep in places. Wet to the waists as they were, and with no food beyond what they carried in their havresacks, the troops spent a most trying night out in the bitter cold at Dwatoi without even their blankets and great-coats: Sir William Lockhart himself had no great-coat or bedding that night. Although the tribesmen on either side of the pass were held off as far as was possible by the Yorkshire Regiment on the right flank and the 1-2nd Gurkhas on the left flank, the enemy were nevertheless able by occupying subsidiary spurs from the main line of hills on both sides to keep up a well aimed fire on the troops and animals moving along the ravine below, and they also sniped a good deal at the pickets placed round the camp at night, the total casualties on the 22nd being 2 killed and 15 wounded. Of these casualties, two were Officers, one being Lieutenant Jones of the Yorkshire Regiment, killed, and 2nd-Lieutenant Watson of the same regiment, dangerously wounded. It appeared that as the Yorkshire Regiment were moving along the crest of the hills on the right flank of the line of march, Lieutenant Jones saw a few men on a spur below firing at the troops in the ravine and took three men with him to try and turn them out. The enemy were so well concealed, however, that although he approached very near indeed to where they were thought to be, their exact whereabouts could not be discovered: and Lieutenant Jones then most courageously, leaving his men where they were, went off by himself to try and get round the enemy's flank. Even this manœuvre did not avail him, and he shouted to one of his men to come round to him : but before the man reached him he was seen to jump on to a rock and empty his revolver, and then fall back wounded. He had succeeded in unearthing the foe, but his daring cost him his life. A section of his company hurried down to his assistance and 2nd-Lieutenant Watson, who commanded, under a heavy fire proceeded to get the wounded Officer into a stretcher, divesting himself of his coat to serve as a pillow. By the time this was done Lieutenant Watson himself was most dangerously wounded. The bullet broke a rib, having entered his left side and come out between the shoulders; fortunately without actually hitting any vital part. A Lance-Corporal with him was shot dead. These however were the only casualties in the Yorkshire Regiment that day; though the regiment met with a good deal of opposition. The completion of the reconnaissance without further loss on the 22nd and the equal success of the return journey on the 24th were undoubtedly due to the skilful manner in which the troops were handled and to the facility with which the men had adapted themselves to the peculiar conditions demanded in warfare against skilled marksmen and skirmishers like the Afridis. The Yorkshire Regiment, which left camp before daybreak on the 22nd, had such extremely difficult ground to traverse that their baggage mules could not accompany them, and their baggage had to be conveyed up to them by hand on the 23rd, by which time they had been 36 hours without great-coats, blankets or food other than that which they had brought in their havresacks. The 1-2nd Gurkhas performed equally good service on the left flank with that rendered by the Yorkshire Regiment on the right, and had three men wounded. The ground they had to traverse was also very difficult, and instead of there being one continuous crest on which they could move smoothly along, the range of hills is broken up into a series of knolls with deep ravines between them, so that the Gurkhas were continually ascending and descending over very rugged ground. A curious incident occurred during this portion of the march. As the Gurkhas were advancing on the 22nd November the leading scouts shot an Afridi who was trying to drive off some cattle, and when the man's body was found a little Afridi baby was discovered by his side. It devolved on the Mess President of the regiment, who computed the baby's age to be 18 months, to arrange for its nourishment and nursing. For the former essential he provided from the scanty mess stores some Swiss milk, and for the latter a Kohati follower was found who, being next door in blood to an Afridi, was promoted to the post of nurse. The question of the disposal of the baby on the 24th, when the return journey to Bagh was to be made, became rather embarrassing and the Mess President decided to restore the infant to its kinsfolk. Accordingly, as the house was being passed where this curious capture was made, the baby was deposited on the threshold in full view of the Afridis who as usual were pressing on the retirement.

As has been said, the Main Column effected a most successful retirement to Bagh from Dwatoi on the 24th November, the brunt of covering which fell on the 36th Sikhs was admirably performed. The enemy at first pressed on the retirement strongly, and so boldly at one juncture that they actually essayed to cut in between a company of the 36th Sikhs and drive off some hospital ponies which were being kept back to carry any slightly wounded men. Another company of the 36th Sikhs, however, charged down on these adventurous spirits, who as a result had several killed and five or six of their fire-arms captured. The column moving along the ravine were all back in camp before dusk; having suffered losses to the extent of 17, of which the 36th Sikhs had 2 killed and 13 wounded, including Captain Venour, 5th Punjab Infantry, attached to the 36th Sikhs, slightly wounded. Owing to the very late arrival of the baggage on the 23rd a thorough reconnaissance of Rajgul Valley and the entrance to the Bara Valley could not be made, but enough of it was seen to show that the route from Dwatoi onwards through the Bara Valley is considerably easier than that from Bagh to Dwatoi. Thus ended what under the circumstances was pronounced one of the most successful reconnaissances yet carried out in Afridi-land. It is worth mentioning here that when the 3rd Brigade left Maidan on the 21st November, the 15th Sikhs had been obliged under orders from Sir William Lockhart to part company with the brigade and march back to the advance base at Shinawari. Before their departure Sir William Lockhart issued a most complimentary order in regard to this gallant corps, stating that it was only because the regiment was reduced by wounds and disease that he had decided to send it back to the Line of Communication. He further said that the regiment had nobly upheld the grand traditions of the Sikhs and of the 15th Sikhs in particular. The place of the regiment in the 3rd Brigade was taken by the 2nd Punjab Infantry.

Now that Rajgul Valley had been invaded it could fairly be said that the whole of Tirah had been overrun by our troops, who moreover had steadily applied themselves for many days to destroying the villages and fortified enclosures of the obstinate Zakka Khels. There was now apparently no further object to be gained by remaining in Tirah and wintering in the cold uplands, as the tribesmen, with their homesteads in ruins and their supplies eaten up, would of necessity move down to the Bara and Bazar Valleys, even if not driven thither by the troops. In fact many of them had already left Tirah, and those who remained in Rajgul were probably regretting they did not make their escape before our troops appeared at Dwatoi. The time had consequently come for changing the base of operations from Shinawari to Peshawar, and this transfer was begun forthwith by removing all heavy baggage back to Shinawari. The troops being then more lightly equipped were enabled to operate with greater freedom, while the milder climate in the Bara Valley would permit of their bivouacking without serious hardship. General Hammond's column also made ready to move at short notice.

But before Sir William Lockhart began this movement in concert with the Peshawar Column, it was desirable first of all to settle up accounts in the Kurram Valley, or at all events to make quite sure that Colonel Hill, Commanding the Kurram Movable Column, was master of the situation in that quarter. Captain Ross-Keppel, Political Officer in the Kurram, had a few days previously sent out the following declaration of terms to the Khanki Khel Chamkannis :—To pay a fine of Rs.1,000, to surrender 30 breech-loading rifles, and to restore all Government property looted. On the 19th November the Chamkannis sent in their reply, deliberately rejecting the Government terms, and defying Colonel Hill to enforce them. On learning of this, Sir William Lockhart promptly ordered an advance into the Chamkanni and Massuzai country, by way of the Lozaka Pass, the movement to be made in concert with an advance of the Kurram Column up the Kharmana defile. Owing however to the more important operations undertaken in the neighbourhood of Bagh, as already described, it was not until the 26th November that the 2nd Brigade of the Tirah Field Force was free to start for the Lozaka Pass. On the 27th November Sir William Lockhart himself, with more troops and accompanied by Brigadier-General Nicholson, Chief of the Staff, followed the 2nd Brigade into Kurram. The whole column was placed under the immediate command of Brigadier-General Gaselee, and consisted of the West Surrey, the 3rd Sikhs, the 2-4th Gurkhas, the 28th Bombay Pioneers, No. 1 Kohat Mountain Battery, No. 5 Bombay Mountain Battery and No. 3 and No. 4 Companies Bombay Sappers. The troops following behind with Sir William Lockhart were No. 2 Derajat Mountain Battery, the Yorkshire Regiment, the 1-2nd Gurkhas and the half battalion Scots Fusiliers. Brigadier-General Gaselee met with no serious opposition when he crossed the Lozaka Pass on the 28th November. The enemy occupied a *sungar* at the top of a hill on the line of advance, and a company of the Queen's Regiment under Lieutenant Engledue speedily dislodged them, losing only one man killed. The other casualties were seven sepoys wounded. After the neighbouring villages had been destroyed by way of reprisal, the advance was continued, and on the morning of December 1st Sir William Lockhart and Colonel Hill met at Lowarimela, about a mile east of Esor (the scene of the unfortunate reconnaissance which three weeks previously had ended in the disaster to the Kapurthala picket). There was at this period much sniping into camp at night time, and on the 29th November Sir Pratab Singh, Extra Aide-de-camp to Sir William Lockhart, was wounded in the hand. Sir William Lockhart, in reporting the incident to Army Head-Quarters, remarked:—" He (Sir Pratab Singh) had his hand bound up by his servant and said nothing on the subject. This plucky behaviour on Sir Pratab Singh's part is only what might be expected of a man of his race and soldierly instincts."

After the meeting of the two columns at Lowarimela the Kurram Column under Colonel Hill marched towards Thabi, the chief village of the Khanki Khel Chamkannis with orders to burn and destroy all villages on the way. The force was divided into two columns: No. 1 Column under Colonel Money, Central India Horse, consisting of the 2-4th Gurkhas, a half-company of the Bombay Sappers and Miners, No. 1 Kohat Mountain Battery, 150 carbines of the Central India Horse, dismounted, and one field troop Central India Horse; and No. 2 Column under Colonel Gordon, consisting of the 6th Bengal Cavalry and the 12th Bengal Infantry, 2 Maxim guns, the Scots Fusiliers, 150 carbines of the 6th Bengal Cavalry dismounted, the Kapurthala Infantry, and the 1-5th Gurkhas. The 1-5th and 2-4th Gurkha scouts covered the advance of both columns on the left flank. No. 1 Column advanced upon Thabi from the south and No. 2 Column from the west. The latter arrived at some outlying hamlets about one mile south and west of Thabi at 9-50 A.M., and the advanced guard came under the fire of some sharpshooters occupying the hills beyond; but the two Maxim guns took up an excellent position in some scrub jungle on a knoll and kept the enemy's fire under. The Engineer party with a strong escort then proceeded to burn and destroy the hamlets. Signalling communication was now established with No. 1 Column, and orders were sent by Colonel Hill, who was with that column to proceed right up the defile to Thabi and join hands with him; he being then within one mile of and overlooking Thabi. Colonel Gordon at once issued orders for the 1-5th Gurkhas to proceed, followed by the Maxim guns, the 6th Bengal Cavalry, the Kapurthala Infantry and the 12th Bengal Infantry. The defile was very narrow, in some places not more than 50 yards across, with precipitous cliffs on either hand rising to 800 or 1,000 feet above the bed of the river. On debouching from the defile at Thabi the head of the column turned to the south to join Colonel Money, whereupon the enemy, following their invariable plan, appeared on the high ground over the ravine and commenced a heavy fire. The 1-5th Gurkhas and the 6th Bengal Cavalry at once extended to cover the withdrawal of the remainder of the force through the ravine, and while this was being done Lieutenant Richmond Battye of the 6th Bengal Cavalry was killed. A little later the two companies of the 1-5th Gurkhas and the 6th Bengal Cavalry, after debouching from the defile, came under a trying fire from the enemy's sharpshooters on the opposite hill. The enemy had excellent cover among trees with the additional advantage of being posted above the Gurkhas and the cavalry, who were on the edges of rice terraces which formed the side of the slope up which they had to retire to join Colonel Money's Column. It was during this period and among these troops that most of the casualties of the day occurred. On the rear of the column reaching Colonel Hill the 6th Bengal Cavalry and 1-5th Gurkhas retired without further molestation, their return march being covered by the Gurkhas (scouts and 2-4th) together with the mountain battery of No. 1 Column, and they arrived back in camp at Lowarimela about 7-30 P.M. During the general retirement the total casualties of No. 2 Column had been—*killed :* Lieutenant R. M. Battye, 6th Bengal Cavalry, 2 sepoys 1-5th Gurkhas, 3 sepoys 12th Bengal Infantry, and 1 sepoy Kapurthala Infantry; *severely wounded :* Lieutenant Villiers Stuart, 1-5th Gurkhas, also *wounded*, 1 Native Officer and 5 sowars 6th Bengal Cavalry, 2 sepoys 1-5th Gurkhas, 3 sepoys 12th Bengal Infantry, 2 sepoys Kapurthala Infantry ; and 1 follower killed. With reference to the death of Lieutenant Battye, the *Pioneer* wrote :—" It is now almost a tradition with the Battyes that all shall die on the battlefield; but one may nevertheless regret the death so early in life of yet another of this gallant family. Richmond Battye was a young Officer of only eight years' service, eager, active, alert and conscientious in the discharge of his duties, of a sound understanding and full of a generous enthusiasm for his profession. He had acted as correspondent of the *Pioneer* with the Kurram Column for some time back, and his letters and telegrams gave abundant evidence of the interest he took in his work."

While Colonel Hill was engaged in punishing the Chamkannis, General Gaselee had the less troublesome task of moving against the Massuzai. This clan made their submission at once, and as they readily paid up 67 breech-loaders, including 4 of the Kapurthala Infantry rifles captured on the 7th November, and nearly all their share of the Orakzai fine, their villages for the most part were spared.

It is worth adding here that the Chamkannis do not really belong either to the Afridi or the Orakzai tribe. They are a distinct race and but little is known as to their origin. Mr. Oliver in *Across the Border* refers to the more powerful mountaineers on the upper slopes of the Safed Koh and then goes on to say: "The petty settlement of Chamkannis, dropped in amongst them, deserves a passing word of notice—a people described by Bellew as originating in a heretical sect of Persian Islamites, driven out of their own country by constant persecution on account of their peculiar religious ceremonies and immoral proceedings. One of the stories against them is not altogether without a savour of the 'Love-feast' of more modern sects in England; and consisted in putting out the lights at a stage of the religious performances in which both sexes joined indiscriminately. The Persians called it *chiragh-kush* (lamp-extinguisher) and the Pathans *or-mur* (fire-extinguisher); but the Chamkannis have turned over a new leaf and become orthodox Mahomedans." According to Scott, it is supposed that the Chamkannis held most of the best land in the Kharmana Valley, but were pushed back by the Massuzai Orakzai into the wilder and colder tracts to the west. The Massuzai, in fact, claim proprietary rights over the whole Kharmana basin, 200 square miles in area; but neither the Chamkannis nor the Shaonkanris, a pastoral race in the upper part of the district, ordinarily have any dealings with them. During the disturbances on the Kohat-Kurram border Chamkannis and Massuzai had made common cause against the British Government, though Chikkai—the "Umra Khan" of the district—had remained loyal to his promise not to take part in hostilities and had kept together a following sufficiently great to prevent his enemies from molesting him.

Unlike the Massuzai the Chamkannis were not yet conquered; the operations of the 1st December, just described, having only served to increase their ire. Accordingly, by way of further chastisement, Sir William Lockhart sent Colonel Hill to Thabi again on the 2nd December, and the enemy turned out in great force to oppose him, but were beaten off at the point of the bayonet. The column on this occasion consisted of a wing of the Queen's, the Kohat Mountain Battery, a wing of the 3rd Sikhs, the 2-4th Gurkhas, 200 men of the 5th Gurkhas, and Gurkha scouts. The work of destruction was this time completely carried out in the face of strong opposition, the heights overlooking Thabi on the west having first to be stormed by the Gurkha scouts led by Captain Lucas. Many of the enemy were killed and wounded, some 30 bodies being left behind. Our casualties were : Major Vansittart, 5th Gurkhas, slightly wounded ; *killed :* 2 men of the 5th Gurkhas; *wounded :* 2 men of the 3rd Sikhs.

The power of the Chamkannis, such as it was, having by this second operation been thoroughly broken, Sir William Lockhart was able to leave Colonel Hill in secure command of the Kurram country and turn his own attention once again to the Tirah Afridis. In returning with his column to the main body of his troops in the Maidan Valley he did not follow the direct route over the Lozaka Pass by which he had moved into the Kurram Valley, but struck out south-east, entering the Khanki and Mastura Valleys at their upper extremities and sweeping through the principal settlements of the Orakzai. No opposition was encountered. The Orakzai were completely cowed and hastened to comply with all the terms previously imposed upon them, delivering up to Mr. Donald, the Political Officer, 317 rifles and 22,250 Government rupees. Sir William Lockhart, having thus fully accomplished his object in making the detour, returned to Maidan by way of the Chingakh Pass and reached Bagh on the 6th December.

CHAPTER XIII.

THE PLAN OF CAMPAIGN COMPLETED.

WITHOUT any further delay the combined movement into the Bara Valley of the Main Column in Maidan and the Peshawar Column at Bara was now begun, the village of Barkai being the common objective, where the two columns were to join hands. Sir William Lockhart's Column did not make the march *en masse;* the 2nd Division under General Yeatman-Biggs with the Divisional troops and staff being taken by Sir William Lockhart himself through the Rajgul Valley *viâ* Dwatoi, while the 1st Division under General Symons, after being further divided, proceeded in two brigades, the one under Brigadier-General Hart through the Waran Valley and the other under Brigadier-General Gaselee through the Mastura Valley.

It will be convenient to follow first the march through Rajgul of General Yeatman-Biggs's Division with Sir William Lockhart—a march which has been severely criticised. The tactical difficulties besetting the route from Bagh to Dwatoi had been in a great measure removed by the fact that the Malikdin Khels, who had partially complied with our terms, had been told that their houses, which are large and solid and amply stocked with grain and forage, would be spared if our progress down the valley was unopposed, and who therefore not only kept the peace themselves, but probably prevented other hill men from breaking it. Their neutrality was a most important factor, for although of course no military precautions were neglected by either column, nothing could have prevented large losses of men and animals had the Malikdin Khels been resolutely hostile. As regards the road itself, Major Kelly, R.E., with the 28th Bombay Pioneers, No. 4 Company Madras and one company Bombay Sappers had been at work on it; and by the time the 3rd Brigade marched forward on the 8th December, the track, though still difficult, had been greatly improved, and in the result out of the transport of the whole 2nd Division only 15 animals were lost on the road; though the number of dead ponies and mules which had fallen into the bed of the stream from the rocks above during the reconnaissance made by General Westmacott's Column to Dwatoi on the 22nd November, offered striking evidence of what the difficulty of the road had been before the Sappers and Pioneers got to work on it.

The head-quarters of the 4th Brigade (General Westmacott's), which left Bagh at daybreak on the 7th December, arrived at Dwatoi about 11 A.M. The 3rd Gurkhas had exceptionally heavy work all day, and some of them were on picket duty the same night and were employed again on the 8th December, so that a proportion of them were on duty for nearly 36 hours. There was some slight opposition when the leading troops reached Dwatoi, which was easily brushed aside, the total casualties that day being 2 killed and 2 wounded; but the pickets guarding the heights round the camp were fired at during the night of the 7th December and attempts were made to rush them, the brunt of the attacks being borne by the King's Own Scottish Borderers. On the 8th December No. 5 Bombay Mountain Battery Royal Artillery, about 100 rifles of the 36th Sikhs, and about the same number of the 3rd Gurkhas and the 5th Gurkha scouts were employed to seize a hill held by the enemy whence the pickets had been fired on and commanding the entrance to Rajgul Valley. This hill was taken in gallant style by the infantry: Lieutenant West with the Gurkhas and Lieutenant Van Someren with the 36th Sikhs distinguishing themselves by their gallant behaviour and skilful leading. The enemy was very quickly dislodged with a loss on our side of 1 killed and 4 wounded; the enemy suffering considerably.

The 3rd Brigade (General Kempster's) began its march from Bagh on the 8th December about 7-30 A.M., and hardly had the last troops begun to evacuate the camp at Bagh when unarmed men of the Malikdin Khels with women and children, and showing every sign of being famine-stricken, rushed into the camp with the hope of picking up food and grain, a rather forlorn expectation. The 3rd Brigade commissariat godowns had marched on ahead with the 4th Brigade the previous day; but had halted about half-way to Dwatoi, and the advance of the remainder of Brigadier-General Kempster's Brigade was much delayed in consequence; so much so that when night fell the head of the brigade had only covered about four miles and had then to halt for the night. The rear portion of the brigade, comprising two field hospitals, was on the march from 8 A.M. to 9 P.M., and then could only advance about three miles, so great was the congestion of traffic on the narrow path ahead ; and the last baggage did not get into camp, about three miles from Bagh, till very nearly 11 P.M. The day was cold and raw, without any sun till about 2 P.M. and then only fitful gleams broke the gloom; and the long standing about, with feet wet and cold from fording and re-fording the icy stream was very trying to the men, much more so than if they had been on the march throughout. The 3rd Brigade resumed its march fairly early next day (the 9th), the last of the troops reaching camp about 4 P.M. There were no casualties in the 3rd Brigade either on the 8th or 9th December.

On the 9th December some troops, mainly of the 4th Brigade (Brigadier-General Westmacott's), viz., two companies of the Royal Scots Fusiliers, the 3rd Gurkhas, the scouts of the 5th Gurkhas, two companies of the 2nd Punjab Infantry, four companies of the 28th Bombay Pioneers, two companies King's Own Scottish Borderers, two companies 36th Sikhs, No. 8 Mountain Battery Royal Artillery and No. 5 Bombay Mountain Battery, all under the command of Brigadier-General Westmacott, accompanied by Sir William Lockhart, moved up the Rajgul Valley and destroyed all the houses in the centre of the valley, some 60 in number, inflicting considerable loss on the enemy. This destruction of villages had been provoked by the renewed hostility of the Kuki Khels, who inhabit the Rajgul Valley. This clan had apparently abandoned their intention of submitting the moment the troops appeared at their door, for they had opposed the advance even at Dwatoi and of course resisted still more strongly any further progress up their valley. So admirably, however, were the troops handled by Brigadier-General Westmacott, that the casualties numbered only four: while on the other hand immense damage was done to the Kuki Khel property.

On the 10th December the movement down the Bara Valley began. The 4th Brigade with Divisional Staff and Sir William Lockhart marched first, followed by Brigadier-General Kempster's Brigade some two hours later. The 4th Brigade marched about eight miles that day to a camp at Shundana, and Brigadier-General Kempster's Brigade marched about five miles to a camp near Karana. The day was miserably cold, without sun, and the stream, which was very chilly, had to be constantly forded and re-forded. The enemy began to fire from long ranges the moment the troops prepared to move off, shooting one man of the Royal Scots Fusiliers dead in the ranks as the company was falling in on the camping ground. The Bara Valley at its upper end is wide and the going was easy, for no rain had fallen, and movements across the cultivated country and dry rice-fields were quite practicable. The casualties in Brigadier-General Westmacott's Brigade that day numbered seven, and in the 3rd Brigade five; not including Lieutenant F. Fowke, of the

Dorsets, severely wounded on picket duty in the evening. About 9 P.M. that night a cold drizzling rain began to fall and occasioned great discomfort to those who were sleeping on the ground, and who had not dug trenches. The rain in fact came as a most unpleasant and uncomfortable surprise: it had threatened so long that the soldiers had begun to think it would not really come after all.

It had been intended that the 3rd Brigade should start early next day (the 11th) at 7-30 A.M., catch up the 4th Brigade, and that the whole division should continue the march united. But the next morning was very dark indeed, the followers were benumbed with cold, rain was still falling steadily, and the ground was deep in mud. All these circumstances unfortunately delayed the start, and moreover there was no company of Sappers and Miners with General Kempster's Brigade, besides which the means of getting down from the camping ground, which was on high ground, to the river-bed below, were very inadequate, and so slippery were the descents that animals were falling about on all sides, and it was nearly 11 A.M., before the last animals were drawn off the hill. To add to all these troubles, the 4th Brigade for reasons which have yet to transpire, did not picket the heights on the flanks of the 3rd Brigade, as the latter had expected them to do, and in consequence these heights had to be captured and crowned by troops of the 3rd Brigade which greatly delayed the advance. The enemy pressed the rear-guard and flanks of the baggage from the first, the mist which prevailed enabling them to creep close up unobserved; the ground except in the stony bed of stream was heavy and yielding and quite unlike that traversed the previous day, and the cold and wet combined with the constant fording of the stream seemed to deprive the mule-drivers and followers of their senses and to leave them with one idea only, *viz.*, to press along as fast as possible, quite regardless of how their animals or their loads were getting on, and to escape the enemy's bullets constantly flying over their heads. Some extraordinary scenes ensued. Brigadier-General Kempster called several halts in order to close up the transport and rear-guard, and to send out fresh troops to guard the flanks of the line of march; and every endeavour was made to keep the transport in the river-bed and to prevent the mule-drivers taking short cuts across country and so getting entangled in heavy ground or in deep-water channels. The moment, however, the head of the column moved on, the wave of transport swept on after it like a pent-up stream suddenly released, spreading out sometimes to a front of half a mile or more; every man pushing blindly forward, all anxious to avoid fording the river, in places knee-deep, and all acting on the principle of "each man for himself and the devil take the hindmost." Twenty times the number of Transport Officers present could not have controlled this seething mass: it was an indescribable jumble, sometimes all jostled together on a front of 100 yards and sometimes all spread out to a width of over 800 yards. Those who took short cuts across country, despite every endeavour on the part of the Transport Officers to stop them, seemed to be gaining ground at first, and others madly followed them; so that everywhere were animals either bogged, or slipped up in ditches with their loads under them; or with the chain broken between them and the leading animal : while the *drabi*, all unconscious or reckless of everything else, provided he had only the leading animal of his three following him, pressed on blindly. Where soldiers, British or native, were with the animals, the situation was of course different, and the *drabi* could then be stopped, though usually only by main force ; but whatever baggage had no special escort or guard with it ran very little chance of reaching the next camp intact. Where the going was fairly easy, and the transport was on a broad front, it moved at a most extraordinary pace, certainly not less than four miles an hour ; so eager presumably were the drivers to get in to the next camp and settle down to a fire, for the rain was still falling incessantly, and every follower must have been wet to the skin. About 5 P.M. the head of the main column of General Kempster's Brigade arrived in sight of the 4th Brigade Camp; and he had the option of either going on and joining that brigade or halting where he was for the night. As the other camp, however, seemed near and as the mass of his transport was reported close up, Brigadier-General Kempster decided to push on. This had the disadvantage that it still further lengthened an already very long march; but, on the other hand, the 3rd Brigade had now been following the 4th Brigade for four days in succession and fighting a continuous rear-guard action during the last two days, and if General Kempster could now overhaul General Westmacott the order of march might be reversed, the flanking and picket duties would be lessened and the men enabled to get more rest. Whether or not these were the reasons which actually influenced Brigadier-General Kempster's decision, the fact remains that the order was given to press on and gain the 4th Brigade Camp, an order very welcome to the leading troops, but hopelessly impossible to those in rear. The additional march was easily accomplished by the troops of the advance-guard and main column of the 3rd Brigade, most of whom arrived in camp just before dusk; but the transport and rear-guard had still to come. Darkness now came on rapidly, the rain continued, the road to camp was difficult to see, and many of the *drabis* stupidly made a bee-line for the lights of the camp. Those *drabis* who took this rash course were leading most of the animals and loads which eventually got lost; for the ground, which was easy at the start, was afterwards intersected with deep water-courses nearer the camp, and an animal once involved was not to be easily extricated. Many drivers deserted their animals, and many followers disappeared into houses in search of wood, &c.; while some *kahars* either broached a keg of rum or found one already broached and got hopelessly drunk: three of those who got to camp dying from the effects of intoxication, and others lying about helpless in the camp. Heavy firing could be heard just outside camp; and between 7 and 8 P.M. a party of Gordon Highlanders with Surgeon-Major Beevor, who had been escorting and carrying some wounded whom the *dhoolie* bearers had deserted, arrived in camp. So fatigued were the men who were carrying their wounded comrades, that Surgeon-Major Beevor himself had helped to carry one man's stretcher, or rather the bottom of the *dhoolie* used as a stretcher. At that moment several of the enemy had crept up in the dark to within 20 yards and fired at the party; and heavy firing had continued for some minutes, but fortunately no damage was done, and the gallant Medical Officer, who had lent such valuable moral and physical assistance, brought all the wounded up to his hospital without further hurt. Major Downman, Gordon Highlanders, who was the senior Officer with the last portion of the rear-guard, (consisting of one company of the Dorset Regiment, one company of the Gordons, half a company of the 2nd Punjab Infantry, and about three companies of the 1-2nd Gurkhas,) as he was retiring and while still some two miles from camp, came upon a large number of transport animals entangled in ditches with their drivers benumbed with cold. Meanwhile the enemy began to press closely on the rear and flanks. To go on to camp unless the animals were left where they were was impossible, and Major Downman with presence of mind and judgment decided on seizing some houses and holding them for the night. Once in those houses the enemy's attacks were very easily repulsed, and shelter was gained from the ever falling rain, which continued till 9 P.M. that night, and then to everyone's intense relief finally stopped.

To contemplate a resumption of the march early next day from Sher Khel, where most of the troops of the 2nd Division were now encamped, as had been previously intended, was clearly out of the question so far as the 3rd Brigade were concerned, since 400 men were still some three miles behind on rear-guard duty and probably encumbered with wounded, many animals and followers were missing, and many followers were lying about like logs hopelessly drunk. At an early hour Brigadier-General Kempster went out with two battalions and a battery to help to bring in Major Downman's troops, on whom the enemy had made continual attacks at daybreak, killing one and wounding three of the Gordons in a single volley. The troops came in by 11 A.M. without further losses. The casualties in the 3rd Brigade on the 11th and the early morning of the 12th amounted altogether to between 30 and 40: and included Captain Norie, 1-2nd Gurkhas, very severely wounded (his arm was afterwards amputated); Lieutenant Williams, Hampshire Regiment, Transport Officer, severely wounded; and 4 men killed and 11 wounded in the Gordons, and 2 killed and 9 wounded in the 1-2nd Gurkhas. Between 100 and 150 transport animals with their loads were missing, besides many followers, and one unit alone had lost as many as 50 animals. No. 24 British Field Hospital, under Surgeon-Lieutenant-Colonel Bourke, only lost three animals altogether, despite the fact that a unit like this has a much fewer number of Non-Commissioned Officers and men in proportion to the animals than any other unit. The Medical Officer in charge of this hospital had taken extraordinary pains to make in efficient; and not only did the wounded under all circumstances receive every attention and constant food and care, but the disciplinary and transport arrangements were equally excellent—due to the fact that Surgeon-Lieutenant-Colonel Bourke personally superintended everything. Surgeon-Major Beevor, previously referred to in connection with his gallant conduct in helping to carry the wounded men on the night of the 11th, was attached to this hospital. He had come out to India for a year from England, where he was one of the Medical Officers attached to the Brigade of Guards, in order to experiment with the Röntgen rays, and the help he was able to render to his brother Medicial Officers and the benefits he conferred on wounded men were enormous. All day on the 12th December Surgeon-Major Beevor and Surgeon-Captain Marder, the third Medical Officer with this hospital, were dressing the wounded, for no sooner had one case been dealt with than another was brought in.

On the morning of the 12th December the sun shone out brightly again, and seldom has its warmth been more appreciated. Everywhere wet clothes and blankets were spread out to dry; and soldiers, British and native, basked in the genial rays. There had been no such day of sunshine since the 2nd December, but though the sun was warm, there was a very cold wind. All the afternoon and evening there was continual firing into camp, and some followers and animals were hit, one Afridi with a Lee-Metford rifle being particularly aggressive.

On the 13th December the march from Sher Khel was resumed, the idea being to move rather more than half-way to Barkai. The Sappers had greatly improved the roads out of camp, and the 3rd Brigade moved off at 7-30 A.M.; the 4th Brigade, Brigadier-General Westmacott's bringing up the rear. On this occasion, unlike the march of the 10th and 11th December, the front brigade performed the task of picketing the heights on the flanks of the rear brigade, and thus greatly facilitated the progress of the latter. The leading brigade met with practically no opposition, but the 4th Brigade had perhaps the heaviest rear-guard fighting that had hitherto occurred in the campaign, not even excluding the operations related in the preceding chapter. The enemy began to fire before the troops had left camp, and five animals in the King's Own Scottish Borderers were killed whilst loading up; and an equal number in the 3rd Gurkhas. The latter regiment acted as rear-guard at first, the King's Own Scottish Borderers being on one flank and the 36th Sikhs on the other; whilst the half-battalion Royal Scots Fusiliers moved behind the last of the baggage. Brigadier-General Westmacott personally superintended the fighting all through the day, remaining always with the rearmost troops, and the ultimate success of the day was largely due to this. The enemy showed great boldness and followed across the river; but the King's Own Scottish Borderers and the 3rd Gurkhas were lining the banks above; and the Afridis came under a heavy cross fire while in the water, and also under the fire of a machine gun, and their losses were very heavy. The road is along the bed of the river for about three miles, to a place called Gali Khel, and then leaves the stream up a very steep ascent on the left bank and passes through undulating country covered with scrub jungle; with very high hills on the left flank, which were ably crowned and held by flanking detachments from Brigadier-General Kempster's Brigade. The enemy's intention in crossing the river was evidently to try and get at the left flank of the baggage. An attempt had been made to keep the 3rd Brigade and 4th Brigade baggage separate; a whole regiment being behind the 3rd Brigade baggage at starting and a half-battalion at the head of the 4th Brigade. All this was in vain, however, for the river-bed was very wide, and the heavy firing in rear made the mule-drivers press on regardless of consequences, regiments, roads or even mules. One driver actually tried to take his mules over a high stone wall; the leading mule scrambled over, the other two hung back, the coupling chain broke, but the mule-driver went on with the one mule, probably thankful enough that he had a stone wall between himself and the flying bullets. About 4 P.M. the head of the 3rd Brigade halted and encamped, having marched some seven or eight miles; and as the 4th Brigade were hotly engaged and could not make such a long march, the Divisional Staff tried to stop the 4th Brigade baggage travelling beyond a camp two miles further back; but much of it came into the 3rd Brigade camp near Sher Kamar. The 4th Brigade hospital baggage especially had got far to the front; and when dusk fell all the hospitals in the division, or what could be collected of them, had congregated together. The followers had largely absented themselves; men an followers, though all warned before starting to carry full water bottles, as no water might be obtainable, had in many cases neglected to take this precaution and no water was obtainable; and even *pakkal* mules in some cases came in empty.

To return to the 4th Brigade. The enemy continued to press very heavily after the river-bed had been left, and casualties were frequent; each casualty taking away several men from the fighting line, for from the 12th December till the arrival at Barkai, *kahars* and *dhohlie*-bearers had to be almost entirely replaced by fighting men, and especially so on the 14th December. The force at General Westmacott's disposal was becoming much reduced, and he had towards dusk only some 200 of the Northampton Regiment and about 150 each of the King's Own Scottish Borderers, the 36th Sikhs, the 3rd Gurkhas and the Royal Scots Fusiliers. Seeing how far the 4th Brigade Camp was, he decided to halt for the night on a convenient ridge, and hardly had he halted than the enemy made a rush. Bayonets were fixed and the rush repelled with loss, but Lieutenant West of the 3rd Gurkhas was shot dead, and many casualties occurred. The enemy continued firing on the pickets till about 9 P.M., and the troops had no water beyond the little remaining in their bottles; their kits were on ahead and they had the prospect of continued fighting next day. The losses during this memorable day were about 70; and in addition to Lieutenant West, killed, Captain Bateman-Champain of the same regiment was slightly wounded, and Captain Short, Royal Scots Fusiliers, and Lieutenant Sellar, King's Own Scottish Borderers, were severely wounded. The wounded from the previous day had a most trying time, but all—Captain Norie with his amputated arm conspicuously—bore their sufferings most patiently.

The march to Barkai was resumed and completed next day, the wounded in both brigades being carried almost entirely by their comrades, and the head of the 3rd Brigade was soon in contact with the advanced troops of General Hammond's Column which had already arrived at Barkai from Bara. All the 3rd Brigade got into camp in good time; but the 4th Brigade had continuous fighting till they were out of the scrub jungle, and they got into their camp just before dusk, with a further loss of about 10. From the time the brigade left Camp Sher Khel on December 13th, and despite the enemy's constant endeavours to get round the flanks and attack the baggage, there was practically no loss at all of baggage or animals; and the general opinion seemed to be that the troops had been most admirably handled by Brigadier-General Westmacott during the two days' continuous rear-guard fighting. A rest was now ordered and never had troops better deserved it than those of the 3rd and 4th Brigades; and though the division had lost 166 between Bagh and Swai Kot, they had the satisfaction of knowing that in the last few days at any rate the enemy's losses had much exceeded their own.

Having seen the completion of the march of the 2nd Division, under General Yeatman-Biggs, through the Rajgul and Bara Valleys to Barkai, we have now to follow the less chequered progress of the 1st Division under General Symons, through the Mastura and Waran Valley, to the same objective. The whole division marched down the Mastura River as far as Hissar without meeting with any opposition, the 1st Brigade under Brigadier-General Hart being in front and the 2nd Brigade under Brigadier-General Gaselee following at a distance of a day's march. On the 10th December extremely successful operations were carried out in the Waran Valley against the Aka Khel Afridis by way of reprisals for their recent attack on General Kempster's rear-guard (described in the previous chapter). On a reconnaissance made by Captain E. W. S. K. Maconchy, 4th Sikhs, orders were issued on the evening of the 9th for the 1st Brigade and Divisional troops to cross the range between the Mastura and Waran Valley early next morning. The Aka Khels were completely surprised, and the whole of the towers and walled houses in the Waran Valley for a length of three miles were burnt or blown up. General Hart commanded the troops in the valley so skilfully that the enemy had no chance. Major-General Symons and Staff assisted for four and-a-half hours in passing the troops over the hills, and then watched the proceedings from the heights. The Mullah Saiad Akbar's towers and village were levelled to the ground; the damage to these buildings previously inflicted by General Kempster, having all been repaired. The Afridis were bold and fired a great deal, but were prevented from closing at any point. The troops in retirement passed through each other, and the successive lines prevented the enemy approaching within effective range. During the day the Zakka Khels from the west joined the Aka Khels, and used Lee-Metford rifles. The troops were all back in their new camp by 7 P.M. It had been an arduous day, and extra rations and rum were issued to all. The two mountain batteries were particularly well handled, and their accurate fire was most effective. Our casualties were one Havildar of the Nabha Imperial Service Infantry killed, and two privates of the Derbyshire Regiment, one Bengal Sapper, one sepoy of the Nabha Infantry, and one transport driver wounded. The Nabha Regiment were greatly delighted at having been in action for the first time. The regiment was well handled by Captain Cox, and by its Commandant Sirdar Sher Singh, who was a lion under fire.

Later in the day the 1st Brigade, commanded by Brigadier-General Hart, and the Divisional troops of the 1st Division, all under the command of General Symons, marched right up to the southern end of the Sapri Pass, where a halt was called for the night. The Sapri Pass leading from the Mastura to the Bara Valley is a defile of 11 miles in length which had never been crossed by any European and was quite unknown. The path the whole way through was "commanded" in such a manner as to require but a few of the enemy to make the passage of a force very difficult and dangerous, if not impossible. Fortunately the enemy failed to take advantage of the position. After a reconnaissance all the companies of Sappers and Miners with the division and a regiment of Pioneers were set to work on the path, as without this preparation the passage, though it looked fairly easy from a distance, could never have been made by the baggage transport. For the first two miles of the glen the ascent, was gradual enough and the track a wide, well-worn one;

but the last half mile up to the top was extremely difficult. Boulders of rock had to be blasted and a zigzag road made to the top, which was about 900 feet above the camp on the Mastura River. The hills were beautifully wooded throughout on the south side, principally with the evergreen holly ilex. But the thick weather during the day's halt at Mastura did not permit of survey operations. The troops started before daybreak on the 11th December, and when at dawn the clouds lifted, the view down the pass showing the snow-covered heights between the steep, dark wooded slopes was very fine indeed. The descent for a short distance from the top of the pass on the north side was easy, but soon the gorge became more contracted and rocky; and the advance had to be delayed from time to time to allow of the Sapper companies in front blasting the rocks to clear a path for laden mules. The drop in elevation from the top of the pass to Sapri itself was about 2,390 feet. With a mass of transport animals carrying supplies for the force, the long line stretched along the entire road from end to end, a distance of 11 miles, and it was 5 P.M. before the last of the force was able to make a start. The rear-guard of the 30th Punjab Infantry had to bivouac on the top of the pass, and the transport that could be passed along down the descent was collected and parked at Khwaja Khidda, the first place where there was water and a little open space. General Hart had bonfires lit at short intervals the whole way down the road, wood luckily being plentiful, and by the light of these fires the animals were passed along during the dark hours of the night. This was the most curious feature of the crossing, and was perhaps unique in the passage of any military force through a long defile and over a difficult mountain range. From Khwaja Khidda, the path continued down the rocky bed of a mountain stream, and here and there the way for mules had again to be made by blasting and clearing a passage over difficult places. General Symons with half of the force having reached Sapri by nightfall encamped there for the night, while Brigadier-General Hart with such troops as could not get beyond Khwaja Khidda when darkness fell bivouacked there, the remainder of his force coming on by the light of the fires, or bivouacking where they were. The bivouac at Khwaja Khidda was fired into during the night and a man of the Derbyshire wounded, and the rifle of another smashed. In the morning when the march through the defile was continued, some of the enemy fired into the line of transport wending its way down and a mule was killed. There were also two casualties among the followers. Under the circumstances it was remarkable that more damage was not done. At Sapri the troops had to camp in rice-fields sodden with the rain, these being the only spaces where it was possible to get level ground to camp on. Luckily Sapri is at a much lower level than the camp at the Mastura end of the pass, and the temperature proportionately warmer. The defile the whole way down was most picturesque.

On the morning of the 12th December General Symons continued his march with the troops that had reached Sapri the previous evening, Brigadier-General Hart following with those that had remained in the pass. The road from Sapri, after passing some fields, ran through a very narrow rocky gorge. Rocks had again to be blasted by the Sappers, who, to the front as usual on this march, had begun this work on arrival the previous evening. After crossing a stream, the track ascended on to higher ground to the left, and passing round some low spurs brought the troops along a level and easy road to the new camp ground near Swai Kot just beyond Barkai. The march was a short one, about four miles, and at the end of it General Symons joined hands with Brigadier-General Hammond. Brigadier-General Hart with the remainder of the 1st Brigade arrived the same evening, the rear-guard arriving about 10 P.M. General Symons had reason to congratulate himself and his Division at the very successful crossing of his large and hampered force over one of the most difficult passes in the whole trans-frontier country.

On arrival at Mamani, General Symons received orders to proceed at once to Bara. This sudden move was one of necessity. The 2nd Division with Sir William Lockhart had not yet appeared on the scene, but it was expected to arrive next day, and with General Hammond's force it would have been difficult to feed more than the three brigades which, besides General Symons's Division, would then be collected at a place where supplies had to be brought from India. Shortly after these orders were received it was brought to notice that the march of the 1st Division down the road would block the path by which a single file of mules brought up the daily convoy with supplies. On this General Symons made inquiries regarding a road reported to be used by the Afridis. A reconnoitring party was sent out, and the Sappers and Miners were set to work to make the path down and up the steep banks of the Mastura River passable for mules. The Sappers began operations very early next morning, long before dawn, by the light of the moon; and later in the morning, half the 1st Brigade and Divisional troops were started on a new and unknown road, prepared to pass the night in bivouac if unable to get through in the day. By the assistance of the Sappers and Pioneers, however, the difficult part of the road was passed. The path became easier and finally led out on to the plain that extends down to Bara. General Symons thus had the satisfaction on arrival at Ilam Gudr, only two and-a-half miles from Bara, of being able to telegraph that he had practically discovered a new road from Bara to Mamanai and had made it as fit for camels as was the road which General Hammond had followed over the Gandao Pass.

It now only remains for us, in connection with the general concentration at Barkai, to dispose of the Peshawar Column which, under General Hammond, had marched in from Bara; and before this not very eventful movement is alluded to a brief retrospect of the doings of the Peshawar Column from the time it was constituted may be conveniently introduced. The constant fighting in Tirah had so completely absorbed public attention that the very existence of a brigade at Peshawar had been almost forgotten. As a matter of fact nothing had occurred to direct more than passing attention to this force, as the task originally assigned to the column had been to play a waiting game on Sir William Lockhart's Main Column in Tirah and in the meantime to prevent local raids on the Peshawar border. But the long stay at Peshawar and Bara, though necessarily uneventful in the absence of concerted hostilities, proved to be no picnic for the troops. The British Cavalry with General Hammond in particular had a most trying time, not so much from sniping by straggling tribesmen—though they did not escape this experience and its attendant losses—as from the feverish climate of the Peshawar Valley during autumn. In the two squadrons of the 11th Hussars every Officer, and all the rank-and-file with four exceptions only, had suffered from fever. Some men had been unlucky enough to have three or four attacks, and the squadrons on arriving at Barkai were still thoroughly fever-stricken. The medical returns for the 4th Dragoon Guards were nearly as bad as those of the 11th Hussars. In fact even the unfortunate division in the Tochi had not fared much worse in this respect than had the Peshawar Column. But in addition to much sickness the column had also to report at least one regrettable episode in connection with the work of reconnoitring: due to the fact that the tribesmen, though careful not to expose themselves, were always very alert and allowed no opportunity to pass by of displaying their deadly marksmanship. On Sunday, October 10th, a troop under Captain F. T. Jones of the 4th Dragoon Guards was sent to reconnoitre the Bara Valley, and Captain

Jones, leaving his troop at the mouth of the Samghakhi, trotted through the pass with his advance party, consisting of Corporal Walton, one trooper and a mounted Khyber Rifle. As they reached the end a party of the enemy fired a volley at about 30 yards distance, killing on the spot Captain Jones, Corporal Walton and two horses. The enemy bolted before the troop could get a single shot at them. Information was immediately sent in to Colonel Sulivan, Commanding at Jamrud, who ordered out two guns of "K" Battery Royal Horse Artillery under Lieutenant Nairn, one squadron of the 4th Dragoon Guards under Captain Sellar, two companies of the Sussex Regiment under Major Donne, and two companies of the Khyber Rifles under Captain Barton; the whole being commanded by Major Littledale, 4th Dragoon Guards. Although this force searched the whole of the neighbouring valley and the adjacent hills, they could find no sign of the enemy, and eventually returned to camp about 2 P.M. The two bodies were brought in by Sergeant Clarke and his party. Captain Jones was hit in two places and Corporal Walton in four. It is scarcely worth while to recount other unfortunate incidents of a less serious nature, but it will be easily credited from what has already been said that the troops were highly delighted when at last the order came for them to move up the Bara Valley and they were thus given a possible chance of getting into action. As for General Hammond's march to Barkai, owing to the entire absence of opposition, there were no incidents calling for mention except those connected with the difficulty of getting the baggage through the valley, —a purely physical difficulty not enhanced as in the case of General Yeatman-Biggs's Division, by fierce hostilities. On the 15th December the column, after regretfully learning that, owing to the flight of the enemy, no employment could be found for them in the Bara Valley, returned from Barkai to Jamrud, pending a new projected movement, this time up the Bazar Valley into which the tribesmen had apparently retreated.

We left Sir William Lockhart with General Yeatman-Biggs's Division on the last stage of his eventful march to Barkai, but as in the case of General Symons's Division and General Hammond's Column the stay of the troops at Barkai Camp was a short one, for the Bara Valley was by this time clear of large bodies of the enemy, besides which the poverty of the surrounding country and its inability to support a large force, with the consequent necessity of running daily convoys with supplies from Bara, rendered it inexpedient to establish a winter camp in this inhospitable region. Accordingly a move was made for British territory, and by the 17th December the division found itself comfortably ensconced at Bara, where there were already gathered the whole remainder of the Tirah Field Force as well as the Peshawar Column.

Thus the original plan of campaign was at an end, and the whole of the Tirah Field Force was back in British territory with its task—the task of subjugating the Orakzai and Afridis—only partially accomplished. Without a doubt the Orakzai had been brought to their knees but the more warlike of the Afridi clans like the Zakka Khel were as fiercely defiant as ever.

It unfortunately happened at this period that General Yeatman-Biggs, who had been in ill-health for some weeks past, but who had nevertheless courageously persisted in carrying on the whole of his difficult and responsible duties, was at last obliged, owing to increasing weakness, to give up the struggle and to relinquish the Command of the 2nd Division of the Tirah Field Force. The Commander-in-Chief had arranged that the gallant General should return to Calcutta and resume the less exacting Command of the Presidency District, but by this time he was already too ill to move back, and after travelling as far as Peshawar he completely broke down and had to call a halt. It proved to be "the long halt." Day by day as he lay at Peshawar his condition grew worse until it became first critical and then hopeless, and on the 4th January the late Commander of the 2nd Division of the Tirah Field Force breathed his last. Those around him understood then for the first time how much he had suffered from broken health all along, and how for many weeks his indomitable spirit had triumphed over the frailty of his body. The following General Order was issued in Calcutta, January 10th :—" The Commander-in-Chief has it in command from the Viceroy and Governor-General in India to express to the Army His Excellency's deep regret at the loss which it has sustained in the death of Major-General Arthur Godolphin Yeatman-Biggs, C.B., and his high appreciation of the services rendered to the State by that Officer. The record of General Yeatman-Biggs's services covers a period of 37 years, during which he was employed in the following campaigns and military expeditions :—The operations against the Taeping rebels in China, 1862; the South African War, 1879, during which he commanded one of the parties sent in pursuit of Ketchawayo, and subsequently served as Staff Officer of the Lydenburg Column against Sekukuni; the Egyptian Campaign of 1882. In August, 1897, General Yeatman-Biggs was entrusted with the command of the troops in the Kohat and Kurram Valleys, then threatened by a formidable combination of the Afridi and Orakzai tribes, and he conducted the operations on the Ublan Pass, as well as those on the Samana, which ended with the defeat of the tribesmen and the relief of Gulistan. On the formation of the Tirah Expeditionary Force he was appointed to the Command of the 2nd Division, which he held until a few days before his death. The Commander-in-Chief shares the regret which will be felt by the Army at the premature death of this gallant and distinguished Officer."

Sir Power Palmer, who had hitherto commanded the Line of Communication, was appointed to succeed General Yeatman-Biggs in the Command of the 2nd Division, Tirah Field Force. The vacant post of Commandant of the Line of Communication was not filled up, as owing to the change of base from Shinawari to Peshawar it had now become an easy and simple matter for each General of Division to manage his own transport and supply. The Gwalior and Jeypore transport trains, which throughout the Tirah Campaign had been of the greatest service continued in use.

Orders were now issued for the breaking up of the Reserve Brigade at Rawalpindi, commanded by Brigadier-General Macgregor; as the necessity or supposed necessity for maintaining it no longer existed. The brigade consisted of the Duke of Cornwall's Light Infantry, the Yorkshire Light Infantry, the 1st Baluch Battalion, the 2nd Infantry (Hyderabad Contingent) and the Jodhpur Imperial Service Lancers; but of these the Baluchis had already been despatched to Mombasa, while the Hyderabad Contingent Infantry had gone to Peshawar. The Duke of Cornwall's Light Infantry was now ordered to join General Kempster's Brigade, (relieving the Dorsets,) and the Yorkshire Light Infantry was sent to General Westmacott's Brigade (relieving the Northamptons).

CHAPTER XIV.

THE RE-OCCUPATION OF THE KHYBER AND THE EXPEDITION INTO THE BAZAR VALLEY.

It was now decided to re-occupy the Khyber Pass, and for this purpose General Symons's Division and General Hammond's Column were ordered to concentrate at Jamrud. No great tribal rising in the Khyber was expected, and, in any case, once Ali Musjid was seized, the Zakka Khels, who alone of all the Afridi clans seriously menaced the pass, would not presumably be able to do much mischief. In concert with this manœuvre the new plan of campaign also included the despatch of a punitive force into the Bazar Valley, the winter quarters of the Zakka Khels.

On the 17th December the Peshawar Column marched into Jamrud, followed by General Hart's Brigade (with General Symons) the same day and by General Gaselee's Brigade the next day. At this period, for no avoidable fault of its own, the Devonshire Regiment was recalled from the front, and General Symons issued a Divisional Order in which he said: "In losing the 1st Battalion Devonshire Regiment from the 1st Division the Major-General Commanding desires to record his great appreciation of the good services throughout the campaign of this particularly efficient battalion. It is returning to cantonments solely on the recommendation of the Medical Officers, and on account of the scanty numbers to which it has now been reduced owing to fever and sickness previously contracted in the Peshawar Valley. It has been a great pleasure to Major-General Symons to have this extremely well-behaved and good fighting West Country Regiment in his Command."

The morning after his arrival at Jamrud, December 18th, General Hammond, with an escort of a few troops and two companies of the Khyber Rifles under Captain Barton, and accompanied by Colonel Aslam Khan, Political Officer in the Khyber, visited Fort Maude. Not a soul was seen in the pass, and Ali Musjid, of which a good view was obtained at a distance of about three miles, appeared to be deserted. The road through the pass was in very good condition. The telegraph posts, with one or two exceptions, were standing, but with no wire attached. Fort Maude itself and other fortified posts nearer Jamrud had been dismantled and burnt, and the walls in some cases breached.

This reconnaissance being entirely favourable, preparations were made for the advance upon the Khyber, and on the 22nd December the Peshawar Column received orders to march out next morning. The advanced guard started about 7 A.M. and proceeded in road formation as far as Fort Maude, up to which point the hills on the flanks had been previously crowned by Captain Barton's Khyber Rifles. After leaving Fort Maude the 9th Gurkhas, who acted as advanced guard to the column, took up the duty of sending out flanking parties and occupied all important points right up to Ali Musjid. About two miles beyond Fort Maude the village of Lala Cheena was passed on the left, lying peacefully in the sunshine in its riverside position, but deserted by its inhabitants. A short way further on the advanced guard entered the true gorge of the Khyber, which commences at Ali Musjid; and passing below the isolated conical hill on which the Fort stands, halted. A company of the 9th Gurkhas was sent up to occupy the Fort till the arrival of the 45th Sikhs, who were on rear-guard, and the Staff Officers proceeded to lay out the camp on the low spurs and the flat round bordering the river on the east of the Fort. Not a man was seen nor a shot fired the whole day. Once the camp was marked out, the units soon got their tents up, and the ordinary routine of camp life was once more in full swing.

Considerable damage had been done to Fort Ali Musjid, but the outer walls were not so seriously damaged as had appeared at first sight: the breaches in the front wall as seen from below being those made in the original wall, which had never been rebuilt, by our guns in 1878. Inside, however, everything was dismantled, all the woodwork burnt, all the roofs fallen in, and nothing left standing but blackened crumbling walls. In one room the concrete floor had been picked up to uncover an old well-shaped excavation, which had, previous to our occupation of the Khyber, been used as a magazine. It had been covered in by us because a child had accidentally fallen in and been killed, but the wily Afridi, evidently thinking it was likely to contain something of value had gone for it at once, only to find it empty. Besides the Fort, there are circular blockhouses on the commanding points near at hand; these are entered from the outside by a ladder, which leads on to a platform raised some four feet from the level of the ground, and the walls are loopholed at a convenient height above the platform. These blockhouses had also been dismantled and the doors and platforms burnt, so that the pickets sent up to occupy them found the loopholes out of all reach, and had to bivouac outside.

On the 24th December the 1st and 2nd Brigades arrived at Ali Musjid from Jamrud, and went into camp on the low ground about Lala Cheena. This was a busy day for the Peshawar Column: there were parties out in four different directions. A wing of the Inniskillings went out to crown the heights for the incoming brigades; a wing of the Oxfords went out to form a covering party to the 34th Pioneers who were engaged in opening out the roads that the two brigades were to take next morning; a party of 100 a men from each regiment with the Sappers and Miners went out to blow up the Lala Cheena towers and bring in wood and forage; and a fourth party of two companies of the 9th Gurkhas went out with Captain Barton to reconnoitre the hills on the right of the road to the Alachi Pass, with a view to finding a way by which General Hammond's Column could move next day, so as to cover the right flank of the 1st Brigade in its projected advance into the Bazar Valley.

On Christmas Day, the 1st and 2nd Brigades commenced their punitive expedition into the Bazar Valley—the 2nd Brigade, on the left, went by the Chura Kandao Pass, and the 1st Brigade, on the right, by the Alachi Pass. Sir William Lockhart accompanied the 2nd Brigade. A force from the Peshawar Column, consisting of a wing of the Oxfords, four guns No. 3 Mountain Battery Royal Artillery, five companies Sappers and Miners, four companies of the 9th Gurkhas and the 45th Sikhs, held the hills on the right and guarded that flank for them as far as the pass. The 45th Sikhs found some 30 men on the extreme right and drove them off, but not without loss, for one man was mortally wounded, and two others were severely and one slightly wounded. General Hammond himself pushed on to the pass with the Sappers and Miners and blew up the towers of Alachi village. A few shots were fired here, but without inflicting any damage. Meanwhile the 1st Brigade had hardly got two miles from camp; it was then 4 P.M., the transport ahead was badly blocked, and the troops were obliged to spend a cheerless Christmas night in the hills, cold and exposed.

After seeing the 1st Division well started on its way to the Bazar Valley, General Hammond marched his column on December 26th to Landi Kotal, a distance of 10 miles, which he covered without meeting any opposition. As at Ali Musjid, the whole place had been dismantled inside. Walls had been left standing, but every bit of woodwork had been removed or burnt. The house of Captain Barton, late Political Officer in the Khyber, was a wreck; all his property, much of it very valuable, had of course been removed, and everything portable had been carried off. The caravan *serai* and the blockhouse had been treated in a similar manner, nothing but bare walls being left. In subsequently destroying villages the column came across many small bits of Captain Barton's property, such as books, letters, and stray articles of furniture, but nothing of value was recovered, except his tum-tum, which was found in a *nullah*, placed there no doubt by the original thief, who wished to avoid recognition. Empty ammunition boxes were also found, but practically all the Khyber villages were empty; household goods, cattle, agricultural implements and such like having been taken away to unknown fastnesses in the high hills, or hidden in caves.

When the Peshawar Column first arrived at Landi Kotal the attitude of the Khyber Zakka Khels was uncertain. They had been offered terms, which were that they should pay up half the rifles taken by them in the late attack on the Forts, in addition to the half of those demanded as a fine (154 rifles) and should give hostages for the payment of the other half, and that they should pay the sum of nine thousand rupees as a money fine; and they had been given till the 28th December to accept or refuse our terms. The Shinwaris had at once accepted the terms offered them and were therefore not to be reckoned with, and Captain Barton took advantage of their compliance to make them picket the hills to the north of camp and safeguard it by day and night from that direction, and also to picket daily the high ridge under which the road runs through the Saddu Khel country. Pending the final reply from the Zakka Khels, General Hammond set forth on the 27th December with the 57th Field Battery Royal Artillery, four guns No. 3 Mountain Battery Royal Artillery and the 9th Gurkhas, to reconnoitre the Bori Pass, which runs between the Khyber and the Bazar Valley and from which General Symons's Division was expected to emerge on its return from the Bazar Valley. This movement necessitated passing close to the Saddu Khel villages, and the *maliks* sent word that they did not want to fight, but if the troops approached their villages, they had 400 men there and would resist. General Hammond's only reply was to send back for first reserve ammunition, to deploy the Gurkhas into line, and bring up the field battery. Two companies of the Gurkhas were then extended and sent round to flank the villages, commanding heights were occupied and the force advanced through the villages and up the pass unmolested. The road to the pass runs through a defile in the hills, at first fairly open, but the valley soon contracts and is flanked by high, craggy, isolated peaks so placed as to render it impossible to efficiently command the flanks. At a distance of about three miles from the pass the valley still further contracts, and the path runs through a gorge about one hundred and fifty yards in length, so narrow as to be impassable for a laden mule, and between precipitous rocks about 100 feet high. The route is in fact impracticable, nor can it be improved.

The next day, December 28th, was wet and cold, and the troops did not move out. The tribes had not come in, but on the contrary had added to their list of offences by shooting a sepoy of the 9th Gurkhas during the night, close outside the entrenchments, and by carrying off about five miles of telegraph wire and breaking down the posts. On the 29th, therefore, the force moved out, partly to forage, partly to punish the tribes for their presumption, and partly to guard outgoing and incoming convoys; and operations of this nature continued to form the regular programme of work for many days afterwards. Every day villages were destroyed, and more forage seized, but not without loss, for the Zakka Khels were well armed and were good shots, with an accurate knowledge of the country, and of the range of every prominent object. They sniped at the troops almost incessantly and also destroyed the telegraph lines with such persistence that all attempts at repairs had to be given up for the time being.

On the 30th December the Oxfordshire Regiment, who were out on convoy duty, met with a serious misadventure. After seeing the *dak* through and completing the day's work, four companies of the Oxfords, who were crowning the furthest heights towards Ali Musjid and had to form the rear-guard to the retirement, became seriously engaged with the enemy. About 5-30 P.M. General Hammond at the camp at Landi Kotal received a report that the rear-guard was hard pressed and in need of reinforcements. The troops in camp were at once spread out smartly and hurried to the scene of action. The 34th Pioneers were sent to occupy the villages on the right, and General Hammond with the remainder pushed on, occupying points on the flanks as he advanced. He found the Oxfords, as well as 20 men of the Inniskillings and one company of the 9th Gurkhas (who had been left on flanking heights to co-operate with the retirement) holding three villages. All firing had ceased, and under cover of the reinforcements which he had brought General Hammond withdrew the Oxfords and the Gurkhas from the villages, retiring off the hills. It appeared that the Oxfords when first attacked had taken cover in a deep *nullah* which proved to be also exposed to the enemy's fire. The *dhoolie*-bearers thereupon bolted, and as it was found impossible to get away the killed and wounded it became necessary to occupy the villages till reinforcements arrived from Landi Kotal. The casualties in the Oxfordshire Regiment were :—*killed :* one Sergeant, one Lance-Corporal, and one private ; *wounded :* Lieutenant-Colonel F. H. Plowden, Commanding; *severely wounded :* Captain C. Parr, Lieutenant R. C. R. Owen, Sergeant-Major Dempsay ; *mortally wounded :* four Sergeants and six privates. Not only were the dead and wounded carried safely back to camp, but all rifles, ammunition and accoutrements were brought in, so that nothing fell into the hands of the enemy.

On New Year's Day most of the troops were again employed in blowing up towers and in foraging. The Zakka Khels, awakening at last to the daily seizure of their *bhoosa*, took the extreme measure of setting fire to the *bhoosa* stocks, and after this date little or no forage was found in any of the villages. The same day General Hammond, covered by a wing of the Inniskillings and Oxfords, went up the Tsera Nullah to examine some caves nightly occupied by the enemy. Household goods were found in the caves, and while the troops were engaged in clearing the caves and destroying the goods some shots were fired at General Hammond and the group of Officers standing with him. Several bullets fell quite close, and one hit Lieutenant H. D. Hammond, R.A., General Hammond's Orderly Officer. Some shots were also fired at the troops when retiring. The day's casualties were :—*wounded :* Lieutenant Hammond ; *severely wounded :* one Sergeant, Royal Inniskilling Fusiliers, one sepoy, 34th Pioneers, and one follower.

It had been intended to surprise the villagers on the morning of the 3rd January; 200 of the 9th Gurkhas were to start out into the hills early and get into position over the Bori Pass by daylight while the rest of the troops demonstrated over the villages at the mouth of the pass. The effect would have been to drive the enemy up the pass, whence the Gurkhas would have driven them back, and further loss would have been inflicted on any line of retreat they might have taken. The Gurkhas started at 4 A.M., but the weather was so inclement with rain, sleet and snow, that the whole movement was countermanded. Later the same day Major Hickman of the 34th Pioneers, who was in command of a picket party guarding the road between Ali Musjid and Landi Kotal, was shot through the heart by a stray bullet fired from a distance of 800 yards.

On January 5th a foraging party went out as usual but failed to find any sign of the enemy, and not a single shot was fired, the tribesmen having apparently crossed over the hills into the Bazar Valley. The blowing up of their villages was a far greater loss to the Khyber Zakka Khels than to those of the Bara and Bazar Valleys, for the Khyber men stay in the pass all the year round, do not migrate, and have no other homes except caves in the hills. They must have been suffering considerable distress, for it was now very cold, the thermometer at night time registering 13 degrees of frost.

The story of the re-occupation of the Khyber is now complete, and in leaving the Peshawar Column in possession of Landi Kotal and Ali Musjid it has only to be mentioned that from this date the "Peshawar Column" nominally ceased to exist, the force under General Hammond till then so styled being re-named the "5th Brigade of the Tirah Field Force."

We now return to General Symons's Division, which we left in the Khyber at the mouth of two passes leading into the Bazar Valley, prepared to strike another blow at the Zakka Khels and their villages of refuge. Before the advance was continued the Imperial Service Troops with the Division, who throughout the Tirah Campaign had acquitted themselves with very great credit, received orders to return to their respective States, as their work was over; and General Symons in parting with them issued the following complimentary order:—"The General Officer Commanding the 1st Division, desires to record his appreciation of the good services and soldier-like demeanour of these corps. Their discipline and good behaviour have been beyond reproach, and quite equal throughout the campaign to that of the best of our native troops. General Symons in the name of the whole Division begs to thank them for their incessant and hard work, always cheerfully performed. The Major-General's especial approbation is due to Commandant Sardar Sher Singh, Commanding the Nabha Regiment, and to Commandant Sardar Meter Khan, Commanding the Maler Kotla Sappers. These Officers have displayed zeal, intelligence, and good qualities of command. The 1st Division will miss their services, and they all leave with congratulations and good wishes."

It was a great disappointment to the troops under General Symons not to find the enemy in force in the Bazar Valley, as the men of the 1st Division were anxious to avenge the recent losses of the 2nd Division during the march from Dwatoi to Barkai. The Zakka Khels had the whole of the upper part of the Bara Valley once again open to them, and they discreetly left Bazar to the care of small bodies of men. Cheena is the only village of importance in the valley, and the enemy did not consider it worth while fighting for. Their cave-dwellings along the Bazar River could not be destroyed. During this little expedition the troops were for the most part admirably handled; but the Alachi route proved difficult, and a battalion of infantry with commissariat stores had to be left all night on the pass : fortunately it was not attacked. General Gaselee's Brigade alone went as far as Cheena, which was destroyed, while General Hart's Brigade halted at Burg ready for action in case the Zakka Khels should show themselves in great strength. The tribesmen however never numbered more than 200 men in any one spot. On the 27th General Hart remained at Burg, whilst part of his force went on to the Bazar Valley to meet Sir William Lockhart, and to picket the left bank so as to assist in protecting General Gaselee's Column returning from Cheena. The rear-guard of the 2nd Brigade was followed up as usual, but when the Afridis met the pickets of the 1st Brigade they transferred their attention to the latter. The Royal Sussex Regiment, who were on this picket duty, were engaged warmly for $2\frac{1}{2}$ hours, and when they retired on Burg the enemy followed them close into camp. The regiment lost 3 killed and 3 wounded. Lieutenant St. de V. A. Julius was also slightly wounded. A private in the Royal Sussex behaved with great gallantry. He was shot through the leg and severely wounded, but after this he helped a wounded comrade away, and assisted in carrying the *dhoolie* all the way back to the camp. He then went to his company's bivouac to get some food and then to the hospital to have his wound dressed.

On the morning of the 28th December at a quarter to five o'clock General Hart started in the darkness and rain to surprise and surround the Karamna villages as it was reported that the tribesmen had returned. All the villages were surrounded before daylight, but the Zakka Khels had been too sharp and had flown. The subsequent withdrawal of the force from Burg up a steep ravine was an extremely difficult operation. The pickets on the hill tops reported the enemy in force on the south of the camp; and the rear-guard, consisting of the Royal Sussex and the 21st Madras Pioneers, the latter in the rear, were heavily engaged for several hours. The great difficulty was to get the pickets down safely: there were ten of them all pinnacled on the steep rocky hills, and Colonel

C. H. W. Cafe, who commanded the rear-guard, managed the operation admirably. The more distant pickets were brought down and passed up the ravine, and the others followed in their turn. The Afridis followed closely and persistently, and approached within 100 yards of the Madras Pioneers, thus giving our men a much better chance than usual, and many were seen to fall. Our losses were two men of the Royal Sussex severely wounded, one sepoy of the 21st Madras Pioneers killed, four severely and one slightly wounded. All the valuable towers in Burg and Karamna were blown up, and in carrying out this duty a distressing accident occurred whereby Lieutenant C. R. Tonge, R.E., and a sapper of No. 4 Company Bombay Sappers, were accidentally killed. One of the charges under a tower exploded, and Lieutenant Tonge, thinking that the other fuse had failed, went up to the tower, when the second charge went off.

On the 29th December the 1st Brigade under Brigadier-General Hart, accompanied by General Symons, returned to Ali Musjid. The withdrawal was closely and boldly followed by the Afridis, who in places got quite near, being much aided by clouds on the hills. They followed the rear-guard for six miles, and shot well. Our casualties were: six men of the Derbyshire Regiment severely wounded, and three other men slightly wounded; one rifleman of the 2-1st Gurkhas dangerously wounded. Several of the casualties occurred in withdrawing the pickets from the hills round Karamna Camp. They were all eventually passed through the strong rear-guard placed in position at the exit of the camp. The baggage was all sent on ahead and the operation of the withdrawal was skilfully executed, the troops supporting each other admirably. Brigadier-General Hart himself came in with the last company. The transport did very well; not one load being lost. General Gaselee's Brigade marched by another route to Jamrud. They also had 12 or 13 casualties *en route*.

The next few weeks were uneventful, and towards the end of January it seemed as if the efforts of the Political Officers were likely to be crowned with success. Even the Zakka Khels were known to be debating for the first time whether it would not be wiser to come to terms, than risk another invasion in the spring. The news, therefore, which reached India on the 30th January that out troops had met with a serious reverse was wholly unexpected. As it afterwards emerged, the operations which led up to this unfortunate business had been carefully planned beforehand and every effort had been made to keep the proposed movement of troops secret. News had been received that the Afridis had driven their cattle and camels to graze on the Kajurai Plain, which is due east of Fort Bara and is enclosed on the northern, western and southern sides by spurs which run down from the main range of hills separating the Bara and Bazar Valleys. It was accordingly resolved to capture the Afridi herds and herdsmen. For this purpose four columns, one from each brigade, were formed, and ordered to move concentrically so as to cut off the tribesmen's line of retreat westwards. The points from which the columns moved on the morning of the 29th January were Ali Musjid, Jamrud, Bara Fort and Mamani. General Symons reported that the Ali Musjid and Jamrud Columns had seen nothing of the enemy, though they had marched over twenty miles. The Bara Column which presumably moved straight across the Kajurai Plain, had also nothing of interest to report. The column, however, further to the west, drawn from General Westmacott's Brigade, and consisting of the King's Own Yorkshire Light Infantry, four companies of the 36th Sikhs and two guns of No. 5 Bombay Mountain Battery, with Colonel Seppings of the King's Own Yorkshire Light Infantry in command had a very different experience. Little opposition was experienced in the advance, but when the retirement began through a narrow defile known as the Shin Kamar Pass the enemy appeared in considerable numbers and pressed hard upon the small column. It was the old story of a small force completely at the mercy of skilful marksmen securely planted on both sides of a narrow gorge. Too few in numbers to clear the hills, their only course was to retire as best they could, though men were dropped in their tracks at every step and the column was every moment becoming more and more hampered with the wounded. Fortunately it was found possible to send a message to General Westmacott, who turned out with 200 of the King's Own Scottish Borderers, 100 Gurkhas and two guns. He found the little column retiring in good order, but very slowly. Promptly grasping the situation he brought his guns into action from the hills at the mouth of the gorge on the enemy's left, and turned the direction of the retirement through his troops. When the whole had passed through he retired slowly, reaching camp at 7-30 P.M., and being the last man himself to get in. Even as it was our losses were extremely heavy, and our dead had to be left on the field. The casualty list comprised : British Officers— *killed :* Lieutenant-Colonel Haughton, Lieutenent Turing, 36th Sikhs ; Lieutenants Walker, Dowdall and Hughes, King's Own Yorkshire Light Infantry ; *wounded :* Major Earle, Captian Marrable and Lieutenant

Hall of the King's Own Yorkshire Light Infantry. The rank and file of the Yorkshires also suffered heavily, losing 22 killed and 17 wounded; the 36th Sikhs lost 3 men killed. On the 31st January General Westmacott advanced again to the Shin Kamar Pass for the purpose of bringing in the dead, and 22 bodies were recovered. His force consisted of 400 of the Gordon Highlanders, 300 Sikhs, 300 2nd Gurkhas, 400 3rd Gurkhas, 250 King's Own Yorkshire Light Infantry, 400 King's Own Scottish Borderers, and No. 8 Mountain Battery Royal Artillery. Little opposition was made to the advance, the few casualties taking place as the force retired. One gunner was killed, one gunner and one man of the King's Own Yorkshire Light Infantry, one Gurkha, and one *bhisti* were wounded. Surgeon-Captain M. Dick and Lieutenant Browne, 30th Sikhs, were slightly wounded.

So ended what was certainly one of the most unfortunate episodes of the campaign. The loss of the Colonel of the 36th Sikhs in particular was deeply regretted throughout the army. On more than one occasion since the operations against the Afridis began, Colonel Haughton's quick resolve, magnificent courage, and inspiring leadership had saved a critical situation, and he was idolised by every soldier in his regiment.

PART V.
TO MINOR EXPEDITIONS.

PART V.

TWO MINOR EXPEDITIONS.

CHAPTER I.

THE UTMAN KHEL EXPEDITION.

WHILE in the early part of November Sir William Lockhart was engaged in punishing the Afridis in the Maidan Valley, the Malakand Field Force, which under Sir Bindon Blood had co-operated with General Elles's Force in subjugating the Mohmands and the Mamunds, was enjoying a well-earned rest and awaiting fresh employment. After the health of the force had been thoroughly recruited, it was thought desirable in the absence of any other work to give some portion of the two brigades a ten days' promenade through the Utman Khel country, west of the Malakand. The Utma Khels had informally expressed their willingness to comply, as far as possible, with the terms imposed upon them by Major Deane, and the troops visiting their villages were not likely to meet with resistance. A certain number of rifles and other arms had to be collected, and the mere presence of a strong brigade would, it was rightly expected, prove sufficient to remind the tribesmen of their obligations. Preparations for the expedition were accordingly begun at Jalala in the Peshawar District, and the Guides Cavalry and Infantry were ordered to rejoin the Malakand Field Force. Sir Bindon Blood's plan was to detach a strong brigade to visit the Utman Khels, and yet have a sufficient force left to keep a close watch upon the still suspected Buner border.

The Utman Khels are not an important tribe, as their fighting strength is put at only 1,200 or 1,500 men, but they have been notorious evildoers on the frontier for many years past. Years ago they attacked the gangs of labourers employed on the Swat River Canal and cut up a number of unarmed coolies, an offence for which they were never thoroughly punished. They shared in the attack on the Malakand, but withdrew in haste when the relieving force arrived. The northern section of the clan living beyond the Panjkora were dealt with by Major Deane, Political Officer, after the operations in the Mamund Valley; and it was the southern sections that had now to be visited. They had hesitated for weeks, thinking, perhaps that all military operations were at an end; but the instant Sir Bindon Blood's troops started, their *jirgah* hastened to make formal submission. Their object was, of course, to prevent our troops entering their country; but it was important that the Totai Valley and the passes leading into it from the Swat Valley, Dargai and the Peshawar District should be thoroughly explored.

Colonel A. J. F. Reid was given the command of the expeditionary force, with the temporary rank of Brigadier-General, and the force itself consisted of the following troops :—The Buffs, No. 8 Mountain Battery, one squadron 10th Bengal Lancers, the 21st Punjab Infantry, the 35th Sikhs, No. 5 Company Queen's Own Sappers and Miners, "C" and "D" Sections No. 1 British Field Hospital, "A" and "B" Sections No. 35 Native Field Hospital, and No. 50 Native Field Hospital. The following Officers were appointed to the staff of the column :—Commanding, Brigadier-General Reid ; Deputy Assistant Adjutant-General, Captain A. B. Dunsterville, East Surrey Regiment ; Deputy Assistant Quarter-Master-General, Major L. Herbert, Central India Horse; Orderly Officer, Lieutenant H. A. Vallings, 29th Punjab Infantry; Extra Orderly Officer, Lieutenant W. S. Fraser, 19th Bengal Lancers; Field Engineer, Captain H. J. Sherwood, Royal Engineers ; Intelligence Officer, Lieutenant A. C. M. Waterfield, 11th Bengal Lancers ; Commissariat Officer, Captain A. R. Burlton, Staff Corps ; Transport Officer, Lieutenant R. S. Weston, Manchester Regiment ; Provost-Marshal, Lieutenant H. E. Cotterill, Royal West Surrey Regiment ; Signalling Officer, Lieutenant W. H. Trevor, The Buffs ; Senior Medical Officer, Surgeon-Lieutenant-Colonel P. F. O'Connor, Indian Medical Service ; and Senior Veterinary Officer, Veterinary-Lieutenant G. M. Williams, Army Veterinary Department. Co-operating with General Reid was a small force consisting of the 16th Bengal Infantry and one section of No. 51 Native Field Hospital, under the command of Lieutenant-Colonel A. Montanaro.

The expedition started out from Jalala on November 22nd, its destination being the Totai Valley, about three marches distant. Harainkot was reached on the 24th, and the Utman Khel *jirgahs* which had mustered at Kot, were so anxious to prevent their country being entered by the troops that, as already stated, they sent word on ahead that they were prepared to make submission. General Hill's reply was that he would meet the *jirgah* at Kot in the Totai Valley. To Kot he accordingly marched that day, crossing over the Bhar Pass *en route*. The road over the pass, although it had been considerably improved the day before by No. 5 Company Queen's Own Sappers and Miners and by working parties from all corps, proved very difficult for laden camels. The baggage, however, was all got over with the loss of a few camels, and reached the camp late in the evening. Shortly after passing Bhar on the west side of the pass the valley widens considerably, and is very green and full of cultivation. The villagers of Lower Totai showed an unmistakable wish to be friendly. *Jirgahs* from Lower and Upper Totai and Agrah met General Reid on arrival at Kot, and were told what the Government terms were, namely,—(1) The surrender of 300 guns and all breech-loaders; (2) survey of the country; (3) formal submission to the Political Agent at Malakand; (4) forage for the force; and (5) road-making as required—an important matter, as the column had 600 camels in its carriage equipment. All the clans accepted the terms unconditionally, except the Agrah *jirgah*, who, as they showed some hesitancy, were told that the force would exact compliance with the terms at Agrah. The force halted on November 25th at Kot in order that the two routes to Agrah might be reconnoitred. That over the Khels Pass was found impracticable for camels, and it was decided to use the route *viâ* Silipatai which, however, also required much work to make it passable. Bargolai was seen to be in a wide cultivated plain among the hills, and the reconnaissance was made to within two miles of Agrah Pass. Groups of people were seen here and there, but no shot was fired.

At 8 o'clock on the morning of the 26th November the force left Kot and marched to Silipatai, about five miles, the road following the bed of the stream in a deep gorge the whole way. It was necessary to cover the march of the column by parties on the hillsides marching parallel to the column. Progress was necessarily slow, but the rear-guard reached the camp at 2 P.M. without any mishap. No. 5 Company Sappers and Miners, covered by the 21st Punjab Infantry, proceeded towards Bargolai and made the road passable for camels up to 1½ miles from that place. The reconnaissances from this point to Bargolai proved the road to be quite practicable for the remainder of the way. The villagers of Dheri, Silipatai and Bargolai were very submissive, bringing in supplies. Groups of men were seen on the Agrah Pass and the surrounding hills, and were said to be the Agrah *jirgah* who had come to their boundary to tender their submission to General Reid at that place. The force bivouacked at night on terraced hillsides near Bedani village half a mile south-east of Silipatai. The surrounding villages were warned that the penalty for any sniping into camp would be exacted from them and they crowned all the heights in the neighbourhood with pickets.

Next day, November 27th, the force marched from Silipatai to Bargolai, the road having been made passable for camels by the Queen's Own Sappers and Miners. Bargolai is at the extremity of the long narrow gorge that leads from Kot, about eight miles long, and the column bivouacked in a pear-shaped valley with a considerable amount of cultivation, hills rising to three or four thousand feet all around. A reconnaissance up the Agrah Pass showed the road to be impassable for camels, and only fair for mules.

On the 28th November General Reid with 500 rifles of the 21st Punjab Infantry, 250 of the Buffs, 250 of the 35th Sikhs, four guns of No. 8 Bengal Mountain Battery, and half of No. 5 Company Queen's Own Sappers and Miners as a flying column, with mule transport only, marched from Bargolai over the Agrah Pass and bivouacked on a low spur in the centre of the valley which gives the pass its name. No opposition was met with, the grain and fodder demanded were brought in at once and the rifles were surrendered the next day. The valley or rather group of valleys were all under cultivation, the wheat crops being a few inches high. About 2 o'clock in the afternoon of the 28th the advanced pickets reported the presence of a gathering of about 500 men carrying a few standards on the right bank of the Swat River, about five miles away. They appeared to be Shamozai, but they showed no signs of intending to cross the river. There are rope bridges over the river at this point, but crossing is a slow operation and to get back hurriedly is impossible, so the (supposed) Shamozai contented themselves with watching General Reid's movements. The night of the 28th passed quietly, and next morning a reconnaissance under Lieutenant-Colonel Faithfull went out to the Inzari Pass, which was visible about three miles off.

The reconnaissance under Colonel Faithfull to the Inzari Pass showed the road over the pass to be a very fair one, and quite passable for mules. The ascent for the last 200 yards is very steep. The reconnaissance pushed beyond the pass enabling the Government Surveyor to complete his sketch to the point reached from the Malakand side in August last. The view from the top of Inzari was magnificent. The hill drops almost perpendicularly to where the Panjkora and Swat Rivers join, and in the distance the snow peaks of the Lowari Range were visible. General Reid accompanied the reconnaissance in person, and the party returned at 5 P.M. By this time all the arms demanded had been surrendered, and the district having made complete submission orders were issued for the force to return to Bargolai next day. The night passed quietly, and the Flying Column left Agrah at 8 A.M., all being in Bargolai Camp by 11-30. The remainig arms required from Bargolai having been surrendered, the force took its departure from Bargolai on the 1st December and marched to Kot.

As the Kanawari *jirgah*, which had been granted leave to meet General Reid on his arrival, had not come in and had not sent in the arms required of them, it was decided to visit their villages and enforce submission. The villages lie high up in the hills to the west of the site of General Reid's Camp and about 3,000 feet above it. The road was very bad and very steep and progress was slow. About half-way up, the representatives of the villages were met hurrying down to General Reid with all that was required of them in the way of weapons, but as they had neglected to attend at the prescribed time the force continued its march on the villages and the arms were accepted there. One of the principal *maliks*, however, having refused to appear or tender any submission, the fortifications of his dwelling were destroyed. A survey was made of the heights overlooking the Panjkora River and the force then returned to camp, arriving at 4-30 P.M., having been out 11 hours.

The Utman Khel Expedition was now at an end, its object having been fully accomplished without the necessity of any fighting; and the column under General Hill broke up. In his despatches to the Adjutant-General in India Sir Bindon Blood wrote:—" You will observe that the objects in view of which the operations reported on were undertaken, were fully and expeditiously attained, and that no hitch or *contretemps* of any sort occurred. I venture to think that much credit is due to Colonel Reid for the perfect manner in which he arranged and carried out the movement of his force and overcame the conisderable physical difficulties which he encountered; and I fully endorse the favourable remarks he makes regarding his troops and staff. I would further express an opinion that Lieutenant-Colonel Montanaro also carried out what he had to do with tact and judgment; and I have the honour accordingly to recommend both these Officers, together with all who served under them, to the favourable notice of His Excellency the Commander-in-Chief. In making the necessary preliminary arrangements for the operations under reference, I was much assisted by information and advice received from Mr. Merk, Civil Service, the Commissioner of Peshawar, from Major Deane, C.S.I., the Political Agent at the Malakand, from Mr. C. Bunbury, Civil Service, Deputy Commissioner of Peshawar, and also from Mr. Stuart Waterfield, Punjab Police, who was specially appointed Assistant Political Officer for the operations."

CHAPTER II.

THE EXPEDITION AGAINST THE BUNERWALS.

AFTER the return at the end of December of the Tirah Field Force to British territory, the Government turned their attention to the Bunerwals with whom a long outstanding account had to be settled. The tribesmen of Buner had shown an extreme spirit of hostility during the attack on the Malakand in July and again at Landaki when Sir Bindon Blood's Force was advancing into Upper Swat. An ultimatum was now sent to the tribe calling upon them to comply with the following terms within a week :—(1) A representative *jirgah* to make complete submission at Mardan ; (2) the restoration of all Government property ; (3) the surrender of 600 guns, including 60 Enfield rifles stolen on the Rustam border ; and (4) the payment of fine of a Rs.11,500. The following terms were simultaneously announced to the Chamlawals, who inhabit the small valley south-east of Buner : the surrender of 100 guns, a fine of Rs.1,500 and the handing in of 100 swords and standards from Koga and Nawagai.* The terms for the Gaduns, who live south-east of the Chamlawals, were not for the moment announced, but like their neighbours the Khudu Khel, they were expected to voluntarily make submission. The Chamlawals and Gaduns, like the Bunerwals, had both sent contingents to fight at Malakand and in the Swat Valley.

Formal notice was given that in the event of non-compliance with the Government's terms a column commanded by Sir Bindon Blood would be sent to invade Buner and exact submission by force of arms. The troops selected for the expedition were :—1st Brigade (General Meiklejohn's), the Royal West Kent Regiment, the Highland Light Infantry and the 20th and 31st Punjab Infantry ; 2nd Brigade (General Jeffreys's), the East Kent, the Guides Infantry, and the 16th and 21st Punjab Infantry ; Divisional troops : four squadrons of Cavalry, 10th Field Battery, Nos. 7 and 8 Mountain Batteries, No. 5 Company Queen's Own Sappers and Miners and No. 4 Company Bengal Sappers and Miners.

---

*This village has to be distinguished from the place of the same name in Bajour.

The following staff was appointed:—Commanding, Sir Bindon Blood; Aide-de-Camp, Lord Fincastle; Orderly Officer, Lieutenant W. S. Fraser, 19th Bengal Lancers; Assistant Adjutant-General, Major H. H. Burney, Gordon Highlanders; Assistant Quarter-Master-General, Lieutenant-Colonel A. Masters, Central India Horse; Deputy Assistant Quarter-Master-General, Intelligence Department, Captain F. W. S. Stanton, R.A.; Superintendent, Army Signalling, Captain E. V. O. Hewitt, Royal West Kent Regiment; Chief Commissariat Officer, Major H. Wharry; Brigade Transport Officer, Captain C. G. R. Thackwell; Assistant to Chief Commissariat Officer, Captain R. C. Lye, 23rd Pioneers; Assistant to Brigade Transport Officer, Lieutenant E. F. Macnaghten, 16th Lancers; Principal Medical Officer, Surgeon-Colonel J. C. G. Carmichael; Senior Veterinary Officer, Veterinary-Captain H. T. W. Mann; Commanding Royal Artillery, Colonel W. Aitken; Adjutant, Royal Artillery, Captain H Rouse; Commanding Royal Engineers, Colonel W. Peacocke; Adjutant, Royal Engineers, Captain H. G. Sherwood; Field Engineers, Major E. Blunt and M. C. Barton; Chaplain, Rev. L. Klugh; Survey Officer, Captain C. L. Robertson, Royal Engineers; Superintendent of Telegraphs, Lieutenant W. Robertson, Royal Engineers; Field Intelligence Officers, Captain J. K. Tod, 7th Bengal Cavalry, and Lieutenant A. C. M. Waterfield, 11th Bengal Lancers; Commissariat Officer, Advanced Depôt, Captain W. E. F. Burlton, S.C.; Transport Officer, Lieutenant R. S. Weston, Manchester Regiment; Brigade Commissariat Officer of the Rustam Column, Lieutenant E. G. Vaughan; Ordnance Officer, Captain L. G. Watkins, Royal Artillery; Section Commandant, Captain C. E. Belli-Bivar, 7th Bombay Lancers. The Field Postal Staff consisted of Mr. H. C. Sheridan (Senior Postal Superintendent), Mr. A. D. Appleby, and Mr. M. N. Cama. Mr. Sheridan, by the way, had acted in a similar capacity with the Malakand Field Force and the Mohmand Field Force. In the former he had been assisted by Mr. Appleby and Mr. G. M. Nicholl; and in the latter by Mr. C. J. Stowell and Mr. Nicholl.

1st Brigade: Commanding, Brigadier-General W. H. Meiklejohn; Orderly Officer, Lieutenant C. R. Gaunt, 4th Dragoon Guards; Deputy Assistant Adjutant-General, Major E. A. P. Hobday; Deputy Assistant Quarter-Master-General, Captain G F. H. Dillon; Assistant Superintendent, Army Signalling, Lieutenant J. W. O'Dowda, Royal West Kent Regiment; Provost Marshal, 2nd-Lieutenant S. Morton, 24th Punjab Infantry; Brigade Commissariat Officer, Captain C. H. Beville; Brigade

Transport Officer, Captain J. M. Camilleri ; Regimental Commissariat and Transport Officer, Lieutenant J. Duncan, Royal Scots Fusiliers ; Veterinary-Lieutenant W. A. Macdougall, Army Veterinary Department.

2nd Brigade : Commanding, Brigadier-General P. D. Jeffreys; Orderly Officer, Lieutenant J. Byron ; Deputy Assistant Adjutant-General, Captain A. B. Dunsterville ; Deputy Assistant Quarter-Master-General, Major H. C. Powell, 2-1st Gurkhas ; Assistant Superintendent, Army Signalling, Lieutenant W. H. Trevor, East Kent Regiment ; Provost Marshal, Captain W. E. Banbury, 25th Madras Infantry ; Brigade Commissariat Officer, Captain G. A. Hawkins ; Brigade Transport Officer, Captain D. Baker, 2nd Bombay Grenadiers ; Regimental Commissariat and Transport Officer, Lieutenant G.C. Brooke, Border Regiment ; Veterinary Officer, Veterinary-Lieutenant G. M. Williams, Army Veterinary Department.

It was not at all easy to predict what course the Bunerwals would adopt. There were those who believed that as their Swati neighbours had submitted the men of Buner also would give in, seeing that they could not well arrange for a great tribal combination : but others argued that, like the Swatis when the Chitral Expedition began, they would make one stand in the passes for their name's sake and thereafter open negotiations. The military authorities were fully prepared for either contingency. The pass by which it was decided to enter Buner in the event of the tribesmen withholding submission is known as the Tangi or Tangao ; it is immediately beyond Sanghao where Sir Bindon Blood, on receiving the order to advance, concentrated his two brigades in readiness. The receipt of the Government's ultimatum by the Bunerwals was followed by a summons from the Buner *jirgah* to the tribesmen to watch the passes and be prepared to defend them ; the Shaszai sections being detailed to the Tangao Pass, the Malizai sections to the Malendir and the Chamlawals and Hindustani fanatics to the Ambela Pass. The Upper Swatis and Yusufzai sections north of Buner refused to join the Bunerwals. These defensive arrangements having been made, a reply was sent in to the Deputy Commissioner of Mardan intimating that the Bunerwals had decided not to comply with the Government's terms.

The concentration of the force at Sanghao was completed on the 6th January, and at once Sir Bindon Blood in person, accompanied by the Brigadiers and the Officers Commanding the regiments, went out to examine the Tangao Pass and decide on the plan of attack. The enemy were seen in large numbers crowning the crest of the hills on the north of the gorge leading to the pass, and on the top of the pass itself, which is about 3,800 feet above sea level. As the camp was at an elevation of about 2,000 feet the rise to the pass was about 1,800 feet, accomplished in about one mile of road, the hills on both sides of the gorge being very steep.

The Sappers and Miners, covered by the 20th Punjab Infantry, were busy all day improving the entrance to the gorge, whilst the Buners were energetically but ineffectually loosening large rocks from the crest of the hills in the hope of crushing the working parties beneath. About 30 standards were visible on the hill top and the enemy were estimated at about 1,000, mostly Salarzai, who received the reconnaissance by firing a few guns at intervals at long ranges. After the Sappers had knocked off work it was still very uncertain whether the mules would be able to get over the pass next day after the fight, but 500 coolies were engaged to carry up actual necessities for the troops should it be impossible to get the mules up.

The assault on the Tangao Pass was successfully delivered on the 7th January. The dispositions for the attack were as follows:—20th Punjab Infantry to execute a turning movement, scaling the hill to the north of the camp some one and-a-half miles from the pass; the Royal West Kent, the Highland Light Infantry, and the 21st Punjab Infantry, followed by the 16th Bengal Infantry, to make the frontal attack; the 10th Field Battery on a low spur at the mouth of the gorge, and two mountain batteries on an eminence to the south of it. The Buffs and the 3rd Bombay Light Infantry escorted the guns and the former extended a long way up the high hills to the south, being overlooked by high impassable cliffs. The 20th Punjab Infantry left camp about 8 A.M., the batteries and escort a little later, and the remainder of the troops at 8-30. The 10th Field Battery opened at 9 A.M., and throughout the day fired some 480 rounds at ranges from 2,200 to 2,600 yards. No. 8 Bengal Mountain Battery opened at 9 A.M., and No. 7 British Mountain Battery at 10-15. A large numbers of standards, about 28, lined the crest, but few of the enemy were visible at any time. The Mountain Battery ranges were 1,650 yards to 2,050. The frontal attack was sent forward about 12 noon, about which time the 20th Punjab Infantry were heard heavily engaged with the enemy. The latter appeared to have few guns, but kept up a hot fire with what they had.

When the frontal attack got somewhat up the steep slopes, the enemy also tried rolling stones down on the advancing troops, but ineffectually. The shooting of the guns was remarkably accurate, and prevented the enemy from collecting. A party of five Buners started for a *ghazi* rush, but only one kept it up and he was quickly shot. About 1·30 the 20th Punjab Infantry had surmounted the high peak, capturing some standards, and began to descend along the crest to the pass under a dropping fire. Shortly after this all the standards were one by one carried away from the crest, and the opposition practically ceased. The crest was crowned by 2 o'clock. One man of the Highland Light Infantry was dangerously wounded. The operations throughout were conducted with great skill and were materially assisted by the long-range volleys of the Buffs, who were firing from 1,100 to 1,400 yards. The Political Officer's report on the operations stated that the tribal gathering on the Tangao Pass consisted of Salarzai, Asherzai and Gadizai, numbering in all about 2,000; and that their losses for the day amounted to about 20 killed and 60 wounded.

After the capture of the pass Sir Bindon Blood went up to the top and found the road very difficult for mules. These animals, which had been loaded about 11 A.M. and had been pushed forward some way up the gorge, were therefore sent back to the camp, but the blankets and great-coats for the troops had followed them on coolies. The descent from the pass on the other side was found to be sudden and steep. The valley to the village of Kingargali is from 400 to 800 yards wide, and the village lies on the border of a level and well-cultivated plain about 2,500 yards from the top of the pass. The two companies of Sappers were at work on the road until dark, and bivouacked there for the night.

Meanwhile the 1st Brigade went on and occupied the village of Kingargali, reaching it about 3·30 P.M. The village was found deserted, but with plenty of grain and fodder in it. A quiet night was passed, there being no sniping. Next day more work was done on the road, and some 250 mules were passed up with rations for the brigade at Kingargali, but the road was still difficult in parts and very trying to aden mules, being steep and narrow.

While Sir Bindon Blood was carrying out the main advance from Sangao a small column acting under his instructions and consisting of the Guides Infantry, the 31st Punjab Infantry, three squadrons of the 10th Bengal Lancers, and a party of Sappers, the whole under the immediate command of Colonel Adams, V.C., marched out from Rustam partly to reconnoitre the Rustam passes into Buner and partly to distract the attention of the Bunerwals from Sir Bindon Blood's advance and divide their forces. On the 6th January Colonel Adams began work by sending three reconnoitring parties towards the Pirsai, Malandri and Ambela Passes. All three parties reported that the passes were held, and at Pirsai the enemy fired on the cavalry. The infantry of the column left Rustam at 4 P.M. on the 6th January, bivouacking near Pirsai village. The night was cold and frosty. At daybreak on the 7th the infantry left Pirsai, the Guides Infantry covering the advance of the 31st Punjab Infantry; and the enemy bolted after a slight resistance. They were evidently quite taken by surprise, and had not time to collect contingents from Malandri Pass, where Hindustani fanatics guarded the road. The cavalry followed at noon. After arrival on the Pirsai Pass Colonel McRae with six companies of the Guides and four companies of the 31st Punjab Infantry pushed on to the village of Chowbanda on the Buner side. There was no opposition, and all the inhabitants had fled. Colonel Adams, Guides Cavalry, reconnoitred four miles on to the village of Kai, and the cavalry after crossing the pass tried to effect a junction with the main body of the Buner force under Sir Bindon Blood, but as it was nearly dusk Colonel Adams decided to return and bivouac with the infantry. Next day the column joined hands with the main body.

The Salarzai and Asherzai sections of the Bunerwals now hurriedly sent in their *jirgahs* to Sir Bindon Blood's camp and were clearly reduced to a very submissive mood. A few days later other clans followed suit, and by the middle of January the object of the expedition was completely accomplished without any further fighting. The power of the Bunerwals, like that of the Swatis, the Mohmands and the Bajouris, was, for the time being at least, thoroughly broken, their fighting prestige destroyed, their strongest defences shown to be futile, their arms taken away, and their country explored.

[THE END.]

APPENDICES.

APPENDIX I.

THE REWARDS FOR MAIZAR.

The following rewards to the native troops engaged on the Maizar action were notified in the *Gazette of India* :—

Subadar Narayan Singh, 1st Sikhs, is admitted to the 2nd class of the Order of British India with the title of Bahadur.

The admissions to the 3rd class of the Order of Merit are as follows :—

Havildar Nihal Singh commanded his sub-section with great coolness, firing blank cartridges when the supply of shell was exhausted, so as to induce the enemy to think the gun was still in action, and helped to carry the carriage back to the relief line.

Naick Shara Ali kept his gun in action under great difficulties. The gun and carriage twice turned over backwards, and twice the lanyard broke, but he continued to load and fire after getting a spare lanyard from Havildar Nihal Singh.

Salutri Kewal helped to carry Captain J. F. Browne, R.A., out of action, and dressed his wound, under a heavy fire.

Driver Havildar Rur Singh carried the body of Lieutenant F. A. Cruickshank, R.A., out of action, and gave great assistance in sending the wounded to the rear and saddling up the mules under fire.

Gunner Jawala Singh helped to carry the carriage of No. 3 Sub-division to the relief line, and then returned to help in carrying Lieutenant Cruickshank's body.

Gunner Diwan Singh, after finishing his duties in limbering up, picked up Gunner Chet Singh, who was lying stunned, and carried him out of action.

1st Sikh Infantry.

Havildar Maha Singh, Sepoy Tara Singh, Sepoy (Lance-Naick) Jalandhar. These three men brought Colonel Bunny, when mortally wounded, out of action under a very heavy fire.

Havildar Mahomed Baksh, Sepoy (Lance-Naick) Khoja Mahomed, Sepoy Isar Singh, Sepoy Habibulah. These four men carried Surgeon-Captain Cassidy out of action under a heavy fire. Sepoy Khoja Mahomed was also subsequently very prominent in the firing line, and Sepoy Isar Singh helped to bring away the reserve ammunition under a heavy fire.

Naick Lachman Singh was in charge of the reserve ammunition which was stacked in the valley when the firing commenced. Though under heavy fire he remained by the boxes, opening two, ready for issue, and subsequently helped to carry the reserve ammunition away.

Sepoy Sheo Singh helped to bring away the reserve ammunition, returning twice under a heavy fire, each time bringing away a box. He was subsequently twice wounded.

The action of these men in bringing away the reserve ammunition enabled fire to be kept up throughout the retirement, and probable was the means of enabling the escort to secure its retreat.

Sepoy (Lance-Naick) Shah Sowar helped to carry Captain J. F. Browne, R.A., out of action when wounded, and kept off some Waziris, who came close up, by his steady firing. He then again helped to carry Captain Browne when the enemy fell back.

Sepoy (Lance-Naick) Sundar Singh helped to bring Lieutenant Higginson out of action, when wounded, under a heavy fire, and remained with him the rest of the day, taking him back from the entrance of the lane to the kotal under a heavy fire.

1st Punjab Infantry.

Bugler Bela Singh assisted in saving and distributing the reserve ammunition, and was also one of the defenders of the garden wall, where he fought bravely with a rifle he had taken from one of the killed.

Sepoy (Lance-Naick) Ishar Singh behaved with great gallantry at the garden wall, where he bayoneted two men, and much encouraged his men by his example and tenacity, only retiring when actually ordered to do so.

Sepoy Allayar Khan carried Lieutenant Seton-Browne, when wounded, to the kotal, where the second stand was made.

Naick Assa Singh helped Lieutenant Seton-Browne during the subsequent retirement, though they were hard pressed by the enemy and under heavy fire. Without his aid Lieutenant Seton-Browne could not have played the part he did in the conduct of the retirement.

Sepoy Nurdad shot down several of the enemy at very close quarters, and subsequently led a gallant counter-charge against them, repulsing them, but being himself very severely wounded.

The Governor-General in Council is also pleased to notify that had the undermentioned non-commissioned officers and men survived, the distinction of the 3rd class of the Order of Merit would have been conferred upon them in consideration of their conspicuous gallantry and heroic devotion to duty on the occasion referred to. Their widows are admitted to the pension of the 3rd class of the Order of Merit, with effect from the date of their death.

No. 6 (Bombay) Mountain Battery.

Havildar Umardin and Lance-Naick Utam Chand.

1st Sikh Infantry.

Lance-Naicks—Atr Singh, Kesar Singh, and Achar Singh. Sepoys—Shankar Khan, Mahomed Khan, and Roshan Khan.

1st Punjab Infantry.

Naick Bur Singh, Lance-Naick Khanaya Singh, Sepoy Indar Singh.

The promotion to the 2nd class of the Order of Merit is also sanctioned of Havildar (now Jemadar) Hussain Shah, 1st Sikh Infantry, for conspicuous gallantry on the same occasion, in having helped to carry Surgeon-Captain Cassidy out of action under a heavy fire.

The Governor-General in Council is further pleased to sanction the admission to the 3rd class of the Order of Merit of Langri (Cook) Jhanda Singh, 1st Sikh Infantry, for conspicuous gallantry on the same occasion, in having, when Lance-Naick Atr Singh was killed, run out and brought in the box of ammunition the Naick was carrying when he met his death.

APPENDIX II.

THE TOCHI FIELD FORCE.

THE following General Order gives the exact details of the above Force :—

The Governor-General in Council sanctions the despatch of a force, as detailed below, to exact reparation for the treacherous and unprovoked attack on the escort of the Political Officer, Tochi, on the 10th June 1897. The force will be styled the Tochi Field Force:

Formation of Force.—The force will be composed as follows :—

1st *Brigade.*

2nd Battalion Argyll and Sutherland Highlanders.
1st Regiment of Sikh Infantry, Punjab Frontier Force.
1st Regiment of Punjab Infantry, Punjab Frontier Force.
33rd (Punjabi-Mahomedan) Regiment of Bengal Infantry.
Squadron, 1st Regiment of Punjab Cavalry, Punjab Frontier Force.
6 Guns, No. 3 (Peshawar) Mountain Battery, Punjab Frontier Force.
No. 2 Company, Bengal Sappers and Miners.
2 Sections, No. 2 British Field Hospital.
No. 28 Native Field Hospital.
2 Sections, No. 29 Native Field Hospital.

2nd *Brigade.*

3rd Battalion, The Rifle Brigade.
14th Sikh (The Ferozepore) Regiment of Bengal Infantry.
6th Regiment of Bengal (Light) Infantry.
25th (Punjab) Regiment of Bengal Infantry.
1 Squadron, 1st Regiment of Punjab Cavalry, Punjab Frontier Force.
4 Guns, No. 6 (Bombay) Mountain Battery.
2 Sections, No. 2 British Field Hospital.
No. 30 Native Field Hospital.
2 Sections, No. 29 Native Field Hospital.

C and D Sections, No. 32 Native Field Hospital, are detailed for the Line of Communications, and Section No. 1, Field Veterinary Hospital, for the Base.

Commands and Staff.—The following Officers are detailed for the staff of the force :—

General Officer Commanding the Force.	Major-General G. Corrie Bird, C.B.
Aide-de-Camp ...	... Captain H. M. Twynam, East Lancashire Regiment.
Orderly Officer ..	... Captain S. W. Scarse-Dickens, H.L.I.
Assistant Adjutant-General	... Major J. Wilcocks, D.S.O., Leinster Regiment.
Assistant Quarter-Master-General	... Brevet-Lieutenant-Colonel J. E. Nixon, 18th Bengal Lancers.

Deputy Assistant Quarter-Master-General (Intelligence).	Major G. V. Kemball, R.A.
Field Intelligence Officer	... Lieutenant G. K. Cockerill, 28th Punjab Infantry.
Superintendent, Army Signalling	... Captain G. W. Rawlins, 12th Bengal Cavalry.
Principal Medical Officer ...	... Surgeon-Colonel R. H. Carew, D.S.O., A.M.S.
Field Engineer	... Major T. Digby, R.E.
Assistant Field Engineer ...	... Captain A. L. Schreiber, R.E.
Assistant Field Engineer ...	... Lieutenant W. D. Waghorn, R.E.
Field Paymaster	... Captain P. G. Shewell, Military Accounts Department.
Ordnance Officer	... Major C. H. L. F. Wilson, R.A.
Chief Commissariat Officer	... Major G. Wingate, Assistant Commissary-General.
Assistant to Chief Commissariat Officer.	Lieutenant J. L. Rose, 2nd Battalion, 1st Gurkhas.
Divisional Transport Officer	... Captain H. James, Assistant Commissary-General.
Assistant to Divisional Transport Officer.	Lieutenant E. C. Hagg, 18th Hussars.
Inspecting Veterinary Officer	... Veterinary-Major G. T. R. Rayment, A.V.D.
Survey Officer	... Lieutenant F. W. Pirrie, I.S.C.
Provost-Marshal	... Captain P. Malcolm, 2nd Battalion, 4th Gurkhas.

1st Brigade Staff.

Commanding	... Colonel C. C. Egerton, C.B., D.S.O., A.-D.-C. with the temporary rank of Brigadier-General.
Orderly Officer	... Captain A. Grant, 2nd Battalion, 4th Gurkhas.
Deputy Assistant Adjutant-General	... Captain H. P. Watkis, 31st Punjab Infantry.
Deputy Assistant Quarter-Master-General.	Brevet-Major F. Wintour, Royal West Kent Regiment.
Brigade Commissariat Officer	... Lieutenant E. C. R. Annesly, Deputy Assistant Commissary-General.
Brigade Transport Officer	... Captain M. S. Welby, 18th Hussars.
Regimental, Commissariat and Transport Officers.	Lieutenant H. W. R. Senior, 20th Punjab Infantry. Lieutenant T. S. Cox, 11th Bengal Lancers. Lieutenant J. Muscroft, 2nd Battalion, 1st Gurkhas.
Veterinary Officer	... Veterinary-Lieutenant F. W. Hunt, A.V.D.

2nd Brigade Staff.

Commanding	... Brigadier-General W. P. Symons, C.B.
Orderly Officer	... Captain A. G. Dallas, 16th Lancers.
Deputy Assistant Adjutant-General	... Captain J. McN. Walter, Devonshire Regiment.
Deputy Assistant Quarter-Master-General.	Major H. M. Grover, 2nd Punjab Cavalry.
Brigade Commissariat Officer	... Lieutenant E. A. R. Howell, Deputy Assistant Commissary-General.

Brigade Transport Officer	...	Captain P. W. D. Brockman, 5th Bengal Infantry.
Regimental, Commissariat and Transport Officers.		Lieutenant N. J. H. Powell, 23rd Bengal Infantry (Pioneers). Lieutenant P. H. Cunningham, 1st Bombay Infantry (Grenadiers). Lieutenant G. E. Tuson, 16th Lancers.
Veterinary Officer	... ...	Veterinary-Lieutenant C. B. M. Harris, A.V.D.

APPENDIX III.

THE TOCHI VALLEY DESPATCHES.

THE following is extracted from the *Gazette of India* :—

The Governor-General in Council is pleased to direct the publication of a letter from the Adjutant-General submitting a despatch from Major-General Bird, Commanding the Tochi Field Force, describing the operations of that force from June to November last. The Field Force has, under Major-General Bird, fully carried out the objects of the expedition, and the Governor-General in Council, in concurrence with the Commander-in-Chief, desires to express his high appreciation of the discipline, resolution, and patient endurance displayed by all ranks under the severe trials to which they have been exposed.

The Adjutant-General in his letter says :—The force has accomplished the object for which it was detailed, and the tribesmen have submitted to the terms imposed by the Government of India. Although practically unopposed by the enemy the duties devolving on the troops have been of an unusually trying nature, owing to the unhealthiness of the climate. Amidst much sickness, which has resulted in a heavy death-roll, the good discipline, endurance, and soldierly qualities of all ranks have been most marked, and are, in the opinion of the Commander-in-Chief, deserving of high commendation. His Excellency would draw attention to the excellent work which the Medical Department is reported to have performed during the operations, and to the good service rendered by the other departments of the force, and by the Officers whose names are mentioned in the despatch. I am desired to add that the Commander-in-Chief considers that much credit is due to Major-General Bird for the manner in which he has conducted the operations committed to his charge.

Major-General Corrie-Bird, in the course of his despatch, says :—On 30th October the 3rd Battalion Rifle Brigade, which had been in this Valley four months, left Bannu for India. This fine corps had been the victim of an epidemic of dysentery and enteric fever, and had lost three Officers and 75 non-commissioned officers and men, besides a very large percentage of Officers and men invalided or left behind in the field hospitals. I cannot bear too high testimony to the discipline which cheerfully endured, and the pluck which combated the scourge during a long and trying season, and the battalion carried away with it the regrets of the whole force at the losses they had sustained. The losses by disease have, I regret to say, been very heavy. Three British Officers and over 100 British soldiers have died from sickness, besides 50 native soldiers and many followers. Great numbers have been invalided or are still in hospital. The troops notwithstanding these trials have worked cheerfully, and done their duty splendidly, and I thoroughly endorse the high opinion formed of them by the General Officers Commanding the Brigades, and would here place on record my high appreciation of their discipline and soldierly qualities.

I submit for the favourable consideration of the Commander-in-Chief the names of the following Officers :—Lieutenant-Colonel J. E. Nixon, Assistant Quartermaster-General ; Major Wilcocks, D. S. O., Leinster Regiment, Assistant Adjutant-General ; Lieutenant-Colonel Wingate, Chief Commissariat Officer ; Captain H. James, Captain Clements and Major Williamson, Surgeon-Colonel Carew, Surgeon-Lieutenant-Colonel Simmonds, Surgeon-Major

Hudson, Surgeon-Captain Mamby, Major Kemball, Deputy Assistant Quartermaster-General, Intelligence Branch; Major Digby, Commanding Royal Engineers; Captain Malcolm, 4th Gurkhas, Provost-Marshal; Captain Rawlins, 12th Bengal Cavalry, Superintendent, Army Signalling; Lieutenant Cockerill, 28th Punjab Infantry, Field Intelligence Officer. The Officers of the Personal Staff:—Captain Twynam, Captain Scarse-Dickens, Highland Light Infantry, and Lieutenant Talbot, Royal Horse Artillery; Brigadier-General Symons, Brigadier-General Egerton, Colonel the Hon. M. Curzon, Rifle Brigade; Lieutenant-Colonel Hogge, 33rd Punjab Infantry; Lieutenant-Colonel Coats, 25th Punjab Infantry, and Major Pollock, 1st Sikhs.

Of the Officers specially brought to notice by the General Officers Commanding the Brigades, the following are mentioned :—Major Wintour, Deputy Assistant Quartermaster-General; Captain Watkis, Deputy Assistant Adjutant-General; Major Grover, Deputy Assistant Quartermaster-General; Captain Walter, Devonshire Regiment; Lieutenant-Colonel Cunninghame, 1st Punjab Cavalry, Road Commandant.

Major-General Bird adds :—I desire to record my recognition of the assistance afforded me by Major G. T. Younghusband, who has been Chief Political Officer of the expedition throughout. I trust his services may receieve a suitable recognition. My thanks are also due to the other Civil Officers, Mr. Lorrimer and Mr. Kettlewell. For the good work done by the Telegraph Department, I would record my special thanks. A new line was constructed from Bannu to Datta Khel most expeditiously by Lieutenant Green, Royal Engineers. I would commend the work done by the Postal Department under Mr. Van Someren.

APPENDIX IV.

THE MALAKAND AND SWAT VALLEY DESPATCHES.

We take the following extracts from the despatches which appeared in the *Gazette of India* :—

No. 727-F.—Field Operations—Malakand, dated Simla, 15th September 1897.

From Major-General G. de C. MORTON, c.b., *Adjutant-General in India, to the Secretary to the Government of India, Military Department.*

I have the honour, by direction of the Commander-in-Chief, to forward, for the information of the Government of India, the accompanying report from Brigadier-General W. H. Meiklejohn, C.B., C.M.G., giving details of what occurred at the Malakand from the 26th July to the 1st August 1897, on which latter date Major-General Sir B. Blood, K.C.B., took over command of the Malakand Field Force.

2. The Commander-in-Chief desires to draw attention to the success with which the first sudden attack of the tribesmen was promptly met and repulsed, while he considers that the subsequent arrangements made to hold the position reflect great credit on Brigadier-General Meiklejohn and the force under his command.

3. Sir George White wishes to express his entire concurrence with the remarks of Brigadier-General Meiklejohn as regards the admirable behaviour of the troops during the defence of the Malakand. For five consecutive nights large numbers of the enemy, led on by their Mullahs, and strongly imbued with a spirit of fanaticism, attacked the position with determination, during which time the troops had no rest or sleep. Each successive attack was met and repulsed with steadiness and success.

4. The incident mentioned when an advanced post in the line of defence was held by a party of a native officer and 25 men of the 31st Punjab Infantry cannot pass unnoticed. The small party detailed for this duty gallantly maintained their position for $6\frac{1}{2}$ hours, and resisted what is described as a most determined attack, until at length the Serai they were holding was set on fire and rendered untenable. Out of the party of 26 men detailed for the duty, 19 were either killed or wounded, which in itself testifies to the gallant stand they made.

5. His Excellency also wishes to express his admiration of the manner in which the Corps of Guides marched at very short notice from Mardan, a distance of 32 miles. Despite the intense heat they had gone through, the corps arrived in such a soldier-like condition that, on reaching the Malakand, the Infantry of the Guides at once took up the position allotted to them in the line of defence, and were under arms and fighting throughout the same and ensuing nights. Nor can Sir George White omit a reference to the march of the 35th Sikhs and the 37th Dogras, under Colonel Reid, which regiments proceeded to reinforce the Malakand Brigade as rapidly as possible. The march was carried

out under the most trying conditions and in exceptionally sultry weather, but all ranks pushed on to reinforce their comrades, notwithstanding that they left 18 of their number dead from heat apoplexy *en route*, a loss which His Excellency deeply deplores.

Sir George White has also heard with the deepest regret of the death of Lieutenant-Colonel J. Lamb, 24th Punjab Infantry, Major W. W. Taylor, 45th Sikhs, Lieutenant L. Manley and the non-commissioned officers and men mentioned in the report.

In conclusion, the Commander-in-Chief desires to recommend to the favourable consideration of the Government of India Brigadier-General W. H. Meiklejohn and the Officers mentioned by him in his report.

Brigadier General Meiklejohn, in a despatch, deals with the attacks from July 26th to August 1st. He says:—

Of the behaviour of the troops of all ranks, I cannot speak too highly. The courage with which they have faced overwhelming odds night after night, the endurance with which they have stood and fought with next to no sleep for five days and five nights, has been beyond all praise. The trial has been a very severe one, and I trust that His Excellency will agree that they have come out of it honourably.

All have done well, but I should like to bring before His Excellency for favourable consideration the following names of Officers and men:—

24th Punjab Infantry.

Lieutenant-Colonel J. Lamb, on the first alarm being sounded on the night of the 26th July, took prompt action in reinforcing the outpost line held by his regiment, and later was of great assistance in directing the defence of the central enclosure till he was severely wounded.

Captain H. F. Holland showed great courage in assisting to drive a number of the enemy out of the central enclosure and was severely wounded in doing so.

I would specially wish to mention Lieutenant S. H. Climo, who commanded the 24th Punjab Infantry after Lieutenant-Colonel Lamb and Captain Holland had been wounded. This Officer has shown soldierly qualities and ability of the highest order. He has commanded the regiment with dash and enterprise and shown a spirit and example which have been followed by all ranks. I trust His Excellency will be pleased to favourably notice Lieutenant Climo, who has proved himself an Officer who will do well in any position and is well worthy of promotion.

Lieutenant A. K. Rawlins has behaved well all through. I would recommend him to His Excellency for the plucky way in which he went to the fort on the night of the 26th July to bring down reinforcements, and again for the dash he showed in leading his men on the 27th and 28th, of which Lieutenant Climo speaks most highly.

Lieutenant E. W. Costello, 22nd Punjab Infantry, temporarily attached to the 24th Punjab Infantry, has behaved exceedingly well, and is the subject of a separate recommendation.

31st Punjab Infantry.

Major M. I. Gibbs commanded the regiment in the absence of Major O'Bryen with skill and in every way to my satisfaction.

Lieutenant H. B. Ford, Acting Adjutant, 31st Punjab Infantry, rendered valuable assistance in helping to bring in a wounded sepoy during the withdrawal from North Camp. He also behaved with courage in resisting an attack of the enemy on the night of the 28th when he was severely wounded.

Surgeon-Lieutenant J. Hugo, attached to 31st Punjab Infantry, rendered valuable service on the night of the 28th in saving Lieutenant H. B. Ford from bleeding to death. Lieutenant Ford was wounded and a branch of an artery was cut. There were no means of securing the artery, and Surgeon-Lieutenant Hugo for two hours stopped the bleeding by compressing the artery with his fingers. Had he not had the strength to do so, Lieutenant Ford must have died. Early in the morning thinking that the enemy had effected an entrance into Camp, Surgeon-Lieutenant J. Hugo picked up Lieutenant Ford with one arm, and, still holding the artery with the fingers of the other hand, carried him to a place of safety.

45th Rattray's Sikhs.

Colonel H. Sawyer was away on leave when hostilities broke out, but he returned on the 29th and took over command of the regiment from Lieutenant-Colonel McRae, and from that time rendered me every assistance.

I would specially bring to the notice of His Excellency the Commander-in-Chief the name of Lieutenant-Colonel H. N. McRae, who commanded the regiment on the 26th, 27th and 28th. His prompt action in seizing the gorge at the top of the Buddhist Road on the night of the 26th and the gallant way in which he held it undoubtedly saved the camp from being rushed on that side. For this, and for the able way in which he commanded the regiment during the first three days of the fighting, I would commend him to His Excellency's favourable consideration.

Also Lieutenant R. M. Barff, Officiating Adjutant of the regiment, who, Lieutenant-Colonel McRae reports, behaved with great courage and rendered him valuable assistance.

The Guides.

I also wish to bring the name of Lieutenant-Colonel R. B. Adams of the Guides to His Excellency's notice. The prompt way in which the corps mobilised and their grand march reflect great credit on him and the corps. Since arrival at the Malakand on the 27th July and till the morning of the 1st August, Lieutenant-Colonel Adams was in command of the Lower Camp, i.e., that occupied by central and left position, and in the execution of this command, and the arrangements he made for improving the defences he gave me every satisfaction. I have also to express my appreciation of the way in which he conducted the cavalry reconnaissance on the 1st August on which occasion his horse was shot under him.

Great credit is due to Lieutenant P. C. Eliott-Lockhart, who was in command of the Guides Infantry, for bringing up the regiment from Mardan to Malakand in such good condition after their trying march.

Captain G. M. Baldwin, D.S.O., behaved with great courage and coolness during the reconnaissance of the 1st August, and though severely wounded by a sword cut on the head, he remained on the ground and continued to lead his men.

Lieutenant H. L. S. Maclean also behaved with courage, and displayed an excellent example on the night of the 28th July, when he was severely wounded.

11th Bengal Lancers.

Major S. B. Beatson commanded the Squadron, 11th Bengal Lancers, which arrived at Malakand on the 29th, and led them with great skill and dash on the occasion of the reconnaissance on the 1st August.

No. 8 Bengal Mountain Battery.

Lieutenant F. A. Wynter was the only Officer with No. 8 Bengal Mountain Battery from the 26th till the 30th July, and he commanded it during that time, when all the severest of the fighting was going on, with great ability, and has proved himself a good soldier. I should like especially to mention him for His Excellency's consideration. The Battery did excellent work all through.

No. 5 Company, Queen's Own Madras Sappers and Miners.

Lieutenant A. R. Winsloe, R.E., commanded the company from the 7th July till the 1st August to my entire satisfaction. His services in strengthening the defences were invaluable.

Lieutenant F. W. Watling, R.E., was in command of the company in the absence of Captain Johnson on the 26th, and commanded it well until he was wounded in gallantly trying to resist a charge of the enemy. After Lieutenant Watling was wounded the command for the remainder of the night of the 26th and till Lieutenant Winsloe returned on the 27th devolved on Lieutenant E. N. Manley, R.E. He performed his duties with great credit, and afterwards was of great assistance, by his zeal and his exertions, to Lieutenant Winsloe.

Medical Staff.

Brigade-Surgeon-Lieutenant-Colonel F. A. Smyth was most zealous and performed his duties to my satisfaction. He volunteered to perform the duties of Provost-Marshal, and did so for a short time during the illness of Lieutenant H. E. Cotterill.

The arrangements made by Surgeon-Major S. Hassan, Senior Medical Officer, 38th Native Field Hospital, and the indefatigable attention and care with which he devoted himself to the wounded deserve great praise. The list of casualties is large, and Surgeon-Major Hassan has been untiring in his exertions for their relief. I hope His Excellency will think fit to consider his services favourably.

Surgeon-Captain T. A. O. Langston, 38th Native Field Hospital, rendered valuable assistance in attending to the wounded under a heavy fire on the night of the 26th and each following night, and behaved with courage and devotion in carrying out his duties under very exceptional circumstances.

Surgeon-Lieutenant W. Corr has worked night and day in the hospitals in trying to alleviate the sufferings of the wounded, and has most ably and efficiently aided Surgeon-Major Hassan.

Brigade Staff.

Major L. Herbert, my Deputy Assistant Adjutant and Quarter-Master-General, was of the greatest assistance to me by the zeal and energy with which he performed his duties from the moment the news of the approach of the enemy was received till he was severely wounded while standing next to me in the enclosure of the Sappers and Miners' Camp on the night of the 26th. Since being wounded, he has carried on all his office duties on his bed. I would wish to commend his gallant conduct for the favourable consideration of the Commander-in-Chief.

Although Major H. A. Deane is in no way under my authority, I feel I am under a great obligation to him for the valuable assistance he rendered me with his advice and for volunteering to put himself at my disposal with the object of carrying on the active duties of Deputy Assistant Adjutant-General when Major Herbert was wounded. He was indefatigable in assisting me in every way he could, and I am anxious to put on record my grateful appreciation of the services he rendered me.

The above list of names may appear to be somewhat long; but I would point out that the fighting was almost constant for a week, and was of such a close nature as to demand incessant exertion from every Officer in the force and to elicit constant acts of courage and gallant example which cannot be overlooked.

I would not like to close this despatch without paying a tribute to the memory of a fine soldier and charming companion whose death the whole force deplores.

Major W. W. Taylor had behaved with the greatest gallantry and dash in meeting the enemy's first charge with Lieutenant-Colonel McRae, and had he lived he would undoubtedly have distinguished himself in his career. His loss is a heavy one to his regiment and to the Service, and there is no one in the Brigade who does not mourn him as a friend.

I have also to deplore the death of Honorary Lieutenant L. Manley, as my Commissariat Officer, who had rendered me great assistance, and who died fighting manfully. His loss is a very serious one to the Brigade.

I attach separately for favourable consideration a list of Native Officers, non-commissioned officers and men who have done especially good service, some of whom I have therein recommended for the Order of Merit.

I trust these recommendations will meet with the favourable consideration of His Excellency the Commander-in-Chief.

MALAKAND FIELD FORCE.

Return of casualties in action at Malakand from 26th July to 1st August 1897 inclusive.

SUMMARY.

Officers.

Killed	1
Wounded	19

Non-commissioned Officers and Men.

Killed	22
Wounded	131

No. 728-F —Field Operations. - Malakand, dated Simla, 15th September 1897.

From Major-General G. de C. MORTON, C.B., Adjutant-General in India, to the Secretary to the Government of India, Military Department.

In continuation of my letter No. 727-F., dated 15th September 1897, I have the honour, by direction of the Commander-in-Chief, to forward herewith despatches from Major-General Sir B. Blood, K.C.B., describing the operations at the Malakand and in the Swat Valley from the 1st to 3rd August 1897, including the defence and relief of Chakdara.

2. In submitting these reports His Excellency desires to express his approbation of Sir B. Blood's energy, of the sound dispositions made by him and of the able way in which he was supported by Brigadier-General Meiklejohn, Colonel Reid, and all ranks under his command.

3. The advance from the Malakand to the relief of Chakdara was carried out with skill and judgment. The troops, in spite of the exertions and hardships they had undergone during the past week, advanced with great energy and drove the enemy disheartened and panic-stricken in all directions into the plain, where they were pursued by the cavalry and still further dispersed.

4. The separate report on the defence of Chakdara speaks for itself, but Sir George White wishes to record his admiration of the manner in which this small garrison successfully held their own for six nights and days against overwhelming numbers. He would also specially refer to the patient courage and endurance of the followers, both at the Malakand and Chakdara, during the operations from the 26th July to the 2nd August.

5. Among many other brave acts performed during the defence, Sir George White desires to draw special attention to the gallantry and devotion of the

signallers who, isolated as they were in the signal tower under very trying circumstances, without water to drink, and at times under a heavy fire, continued to perform their duties in a most soldier-like manner.

That the morale of the small garrison of Chakdara was in no degree shaken by the severe strain to which they had been subjected is evident from the brilliant sortie which was made by the party under command of Lieutenant Rattray on the arrival of the Relieving Force.

His Excellency desires to commend the services of Major-General Sir B. Blood, and those mentioned by him in the operations under reference, to the special consideration of the Government of India.

Sir Bindon-Blood closes his despatch describing his relief of Chakdara in the following terms:—

The complete and comparatively easy success of these operations, which I have been privileged to direct, was, chiefly and in the first place, due to the steadfast courage and conduct of our native soldiers under the gallant leading of their British Officers. Not a little was also due to the patient courage of our mule-drivers and other followers, who behaved in the somewhat exciting circumstances of the early morning of the 2nd August, as if they were parading for a peaceful march in the plains of India. Their confidence in us was something touching, especially when we consider the scenes they had witnessed for nearly a week, the heavy and continuous firing at short range which had gone on round two-thirds of our position up to an hour or two before the start of the relieving column, and the constant sight at no great distance of hordes of wild barbarians thirsting for their blood. These circumstances were calculated to unpleasantly affect the steadiest nerves, and the way in which all sorts and conditions of our native soldiers and followers came out of the trial is a source of keen satisfaction to all of us. Truly these men deserve to bear the good old motto *Nec asperat terrent*.

In operations such as those connected with the relief of Chakdara Fort, it is very difficult to select individuals for reward with fairness, and I would accordingly suggest that, if possible, in this case some distribution of rewards should be made to the native ranks at proportionate rates per unit to be allotted in each unit by the British Officers acting as a sort of committee.

I have the honour to invite the special attention of His Excellency the Commander-in-Chief in India to the good services of the following officers during the operations described above, *viz* :—

Brigadier-General W. H. Meiklejohn, C.B., C.M.G., carried out his duties in command of the force which relieved Chakdara Fort with great gallantry and judgment.

Colonel A. J. F Reid, officiating Colonel on the Staff, Malakand Brigade, afforded me valuable assistance by carrying out the re-arrangement of the defensive posts at the Malakand on the 1st August after the Relieving Force had been drawn from them and in making the preparations for Colonel T. H. Goldney's attack on the 2nd.

Colonel T. H. Goldney, 30th Sikhs, disposed and led the troops on the morning of the 2nd in the successful attack on the hill since named after him in a most judicious and satisfactory manner.

Major E. A. P. Hobday, R.A., was most energetic and indefatigable in assisting Colonel A. J. F. Reid and me in carrying out the multifarious work which had to be done at the Malakand and in the Swat Valley on the 1st, 2nd and 3rd.

Brigadier-General Meiklejohn reports favourably on the following Officers who were under his command during the operations above detailed, viz:—

Captain G. F. H. Dillon, 40th Pathans, who acted as Staff Officer to the Relieving Force, showed great readiness and resource, and his assistance was of the utmost value.

Lieutenants C. R. Gaunt, 4th Dragoon Guards, Orderly Officer, and E. Christian, Royal Scots Fusiliers, Signalling Officer, carried out their duties most satisfactorily.

Lieutenant-Colonel R. B. Adams, Queen's Own Corps of Guides, commanded the Cavalry (four squadrons) with the Relieving Force, in the most gallant and judicious manner.

The following Officers commanding Units and Detachments of the Relieving Force are stated by Brigadier-General Meiklejohn to have carried out their duties in a thoroughly capable and satisfactory manner, viz:—

Colonel H. A. Sawyer, 45th Sikhs.
Major Stuart-Beatson, 11th Bengal Lancers.
Major J. G. Ramsay, 24th Punjab Infantry.
Captain A. H. C. Birch, R.A. (8th Bengal Mountain Battery.)
Lieutenant G. de H. Smith, 2nd Regiment, Central India Horse, attached to Queen's Own Corps of Guides (Cavalry).

Lieutenant A. R. Winsloe, R.E. (No. 5 Company, Queen's Own Sappers and Miners).

Lieutenant. P. C. Eliott-Lockhart, Queen's Own Corps of Guides (Infantry).
Surgeon-Captain H. F. Whitchurch, V.C., attended to the wounded under fire throughout the fighting.

The following Officers under Colonel T. H. Goldney's command led their detachments under my own observation with gallantry and judgment, viz:—

Lieutenant-Colonel L. J. E. Bradshaw, 35th Sikhs.
Captain L. C. H. Stainforth, 38th Dogras.

Jemadar Nawab, who commanded two guns of No. 8 Bengal Mountain Battery in support of Colonel Goldney's attack, attracted my favourable notice by his smartness, quickness and thorough knowledge of his work.

I would also wish to bring to His Excellency's notice the good work done by Major H. Burney, Gordon Highlanders, Assistant Adjutant-General; Major H. Wharry, D.S.O., Chief Commissariat Officer, and Captain A. B. Dunsterville, 1st Battalion, East Surrey Regiment, my Aide-de-Camp, the only Officers of the Divisional Staff of my force who had arrived at the Malakand on the 2nd August. These Officers worked very hard and were of great use to me.

Major H. A. Deane, C.S.I., Political Agent, Dir and Swat, was not in any way under my orders during the operations above described, but, notwithstanding, I hope, I may be permitted to express the obligations under which I lie to him for valuable information and general assistance which he gave me.

MALAKAND FIELD FORCE.

Return of casualties in action at relief of Chakdara on 2nd August 1897.

SUMMARY.

Non-commissioned Officers and Men.

Killed 5
Wounded 28

No. 729-F.—Field Operations—Malakand, dated Simla, 15th September 1897.

From Major-General G. de C. Morton, c.b., Adjutant-General in India, to the Secretary to the Government of India, Military Department.

In continuation of my letter No. 728-F., dated 15th September 1897, I have the honour, by direction of the Commander-in-Chief, to submit for the information of the Government of India the accompanying despatch from Major-General Sir B. Blood, K.C.B., Commanding the Malakand Field Force, giving an account of the operations of the force under his command from the 4th to 26th August 1897 inclusive.

2. His Excellency has much pleasure in bringing to the notice of the Government of India the admirable manner in which Sir B. Blood has exercised his command and the skilful way in which that Officer handled his troops at the action of Landaki on the 17th August, when he dislodged the enemy from an extremely strong natural position.

3. Sir George White deeply regrets the loss of Lieutenants R. T. Greaves, Lancashire Fusiliers, and H. L. S. MacLean of the Queen's Own Corps of Guides; and he also desires to record his admiration of gallantry displayed on the occasion of their death by Lieutenant-Colonel R. B. Adams, Queen's Own Corps of Guides, Lieutenant Viscount Fincastle, 16th Lancers, and the Native Officers and non-commissioned officers and men of the Queen's Own Corps of Guides who accompanied them, and whose conduct will form the subject of a separate communication.

4. The Commander-in-Chief cordially endorses the opinions expressed in paragraphs 31 and 35 of the report, and favourably commends to the notice of the Government of India the Officers therein mentioned.

Sir Bindon Blood in his despatch says:—

I would wish to express my admiration of the fine soldierly qualities exhibited by all ranks of the special force which I led into Upper Swat. They fought the action at Landaki in a brilliant manner, working over high hills under a burning sun with the greatest alacrity and showing everywhere the greatest keenness to close with the enemy. They carried out admirably the trying duties necessitated by marching in hot weather with a transport train of more than 2,000 mules, and they endured with perfect cheerfulness the discomforts of several nights' bivouac in heavy rain. The Officers of the Divisional Staff and of my personal staff who were with me, Brigadier-General W. H. Meiklejohn, C.B., C.M.G., and his staff and the several heads of departments and Commanding Officers of Divisional Troops, all carried out their duties in an entirely satisfactory manner.

Major H. A. Deane, Political Agent and his Assistant Lieutenant A. B. Minchin gave valuable assistance in collecting intelligence and supplies.

While the operations above described were in progress a diversion was made towards the southern border of the Buner country from Mardan by the 1st Reserve Brigade, which, on its head-quarters leaving Mardan, came under my command as the 3rd Brigade, Malakand Field Force.

A force under Brigadier-General J. Wodehouse, C.B., C.M.G., was concentrated on the 17th August at Rustam, 18 miles north-east of Mardan and about four miles from the Buner border, with the object of acting as a containing force, and so preventing the sections of the Bunerwals who had not already committed themselves against us from joining in opposition to our advance into Upper Swat.

The presence of this force had the desired effect, and Brigadier-General Wodehouse and his staff made good use of the time they spent at Rustam in acquiring valuable information about several of the passes in the neighbourhood.

Brigadier-General Wodehouse states that throughout the operations of his force, which involved considerable fatigue and exposure to heat and rain, the spirit of his troops left nothing to be desired. He makes special mention of the work of No. 3 Company, Bombay Sappers and Miners, under Captain C. E. Baddeley. R.E. He also reports very favourably on the assistance given him by Lieutenant C. P. Down, Assistant Commissioner, and has expressed to me a high opinion of that Officer's abilities and acquirements, particularly of his proficiency in the local vernacular.

THE BUNER DESPATCH.

Sir Bindon Blood's despatch on the Bunerwal expedition was published in the *Gazette of India* with the following comments :—

The Governor-General in Council concurs in the opinion expressed by the Commander-in-Chief regarding the skill with which the operations of the field force were conducted by Sir Bindon Blood, and the discipline and good conduct displayed by the troops throughout these short but successful operations.

The Adjutant-General in a covering letter wrote :—The celerity with which the successful result was attained is undoubtedly due to the skilful dispositions made by the commander of the force, and to the enterprise, judgment and vigour with which the operations were carried out, particularly in the attack and capture of the Tangao Pass. His Excellency now commends to the notice of the Government the services of Sir Bindon Blood and of the Brigadiers and others mentioned in the despatch. The discipline and conduct of the troops, British and native, have been all that could be desired, and reflect the greatest credit on all ranks.

Sir Bindon Blood in his despatch mentioned between sixty and seventy Officers. He remarked :—The 1st and 2nd Brigades were most ably and efficiently commanded by General Meiklejohn and General Jeffreys respectively, and he recommends these Officers strongly to the consideration of the Commander-in-Chief. The only casualty during the operations was a private of the Highland Light Infantry, mortally wounded.

APPENDIX V.

THE MOHMAND AND MAMUND DESPATCHES.

The despatches from Major-General Sir Bindon Blood and Major-General E. R. Elles dealing with the operations of the Malakand and Mohmand Field Forces in September and October, were published in the *Gazette of India* of the 3rd December.

The Adjutant-General, in a covering letter to Sir Bindon Blood's despatch, says:—The Commander-in-Chief considers that Brigadier-General P. D. Jeffreys's disposition of the troops under his command on the 16th September showed that that Officer had greatly underestimated the fighting power of the Mamunds as regards both numbers and strength of position. His Excellency has, however, much pleasure in endorsing Sir Bindon Blood's commendation of the subsequent operations of this Brigade. Sir George White desires me to express his approval of the general conduct of the operations carried out under Sir Bindon Blood's directions, and of the resource and appreciation of the situation he evinced when confronted with unexpected difficulties. He also concurs in the terms in which Sir Bindon Blood speaks of the services rendered by Brigadier-Generals Meiklejohn and Wodehouse, the latter of whom was severely wounded in the night attack on the 3rd Brigade, on the 20th September. The gallantry and discipline of the troops were, in Sir George White's opinion, conspicuous throughout the operations; especially so in the night attacks made by the enemy on the 14th, 16th and 20th September, as well as during the trying incidents of the 16th September and in the attack on the villages of Agrah and Gat on the 30th September. The valuable reconnaissances made by the 11th Bengal Lancers under Major Beatson when establishing connection with Major-General Elles's force, and the skilful handling of the cavalry of the Corps of Guides by Lieutenant-Colonel R. B. Adams on the 30th September appear to the Commander-in-Chief to be specially worthy of commendation. His Excellency has much pleasure in endorsing the favourable terms in which Sir Bindon Blood has mentioned Colonel A. J. F. Reid, who was responsible for a great portion of the line of communications and for the efficient supply of troops at the front; as well as in commending to the favourable notice of the Government the Staff, Departmental and Regimental Officers named in the despatch. The advance made in knowledge of their special duties evinced by the Transport Officers during the operations now reported on, and the attention that has been paid to the care and treatment of Transport animals, are, in Sir George White's opinion, most satisfactory and creditable. In conclusion, the Commander-in-Chief desires to bring to the notice of the Government the services rendered by Major-General G. de C. Morton, Adjutant-General, and Major-General A. R. Badcock, Quarter-Master-General in India, in the performance of the onerous duties which devolved upon them in connection with these operations.

In a letter from the Government of India it is said that the Governor-General in Council concurs in the Commander-in-Chief's expression of approval of the general conduct of these operations, and of the skill and resource shown by

Sir Bindon Blood. His Excellency in Council also shares with the Commander-in-Chief his appreciation of the gallantry and discipline displayed by all ranks throughout the operations.

SIR BINDON BLOOD'S DESPATCH.

Sir Bindon Blood gives the following reasons for separating his two brigades on the march to co-operate with Major-General Elles in the Mohmand country:—

Some little delay being necessitated by political arrangements with the Jandoul Chiefs and others, the disposition of the force on the 12th September had altered to the following :—

3rd Brigade, Watelai, three miles south-west of Khar on the left bank of the Chaharmung stream.

2nd Brigade, Gosam.

1st Brigade, two battalions and the 10th Field Battery at Panjkora and Serai, the remainder on the Line.

Divisional Head-quarters, with the 3rd Brigade at Watelai.

On the 13th, the 3rd Brigade halted, the 2nd Brigade moved to a point close to south-west of Khar, and I personally examined the Rambat Pass, finding that the country to the south of it was very deficient in water and forage. This being so, I directed Brigadier-General P. D. Jeffreys, C.B., commanding the 2nd Brigade, to encamp on the 14th, north of Markhanai, to improve the Rambat Pass, to cross it into Butkor on the 15th with two battalions, a company of Sappers and Miners, a squadron, and five days' supplies, and to send the remainder of his brigade on the same day, under Colonel T. H. Goldney, 35th Sikhs, to join me at Nawagai, to which place I intended to march on the 14th with the 3rd Brigade. I further directed Brigadier-General Jeffreys to move his special force through Butkor as quickly as possible to Danish Kol, where I promised to join him or send him further instructions. Both brigades carried with them rations for men up to the 23rd September; and I had arranged to drop my communications with the Malakand and draw my next supplies from Shabkadar, where the Mohmand Field Force, under Major-General E. R. Elles, C.B., was waiting to march on the 15th to join me in the Mohmand country, south of Nawagai.

The movements detailed in the foregoing paragraph were duly carried out by the 2nd and 3rd Brigades, so far as the 14th was concerned; the 3rd Brigade, with Divisional Head-quarters, being encamped on the evening of that day about a mile south of the village of Nawagai, while Brigadier-General Jeffreys, with three battalions, a mountain battery and a squadron was on the right bank of the Chaharmung stream, north of Markhanai, having detached the Buffs and the 4th Company, Bengal Sappers and Miners, to the crest of the Rambat Pass to prepare it for the passage of his special force next morning.

At about 8 P.M. on the 14th, while it was still quite dark, before the moon rose, Brigadier-General Jeffreys's camp was suddenly assailed by a heavy musketry fire from the ravines close by. The attack was continued, with little intermission for six hours, being directed at first chiefly against the faces of the camp held by the Guides under Major F. Campbell and the 35th Sikhs under Colonel T. H. Goldney, and afterwards against that defended by the 30th Dogras under Lieutenant-Colonel F. G. Vivian. The enemy showed no inclination to come to close quarters, and ultimately drew off about 2 A.M., doubtless having in view the desirableness of getting beyond reach of cavalry before daylight. This, however, they did not succeed in doing, as they were overtaken in the Mamund Valley about 8 A.M. on the 15th by Captain E. H. Cole and his squadron of the 14th Bengal Lancers, who killed 21 of them and dispersed the rest.

I regret to say that two British Officers were killed * and one dangerously wounded † in this affair. The other casualties were:—*Killed*—two native soldiers and two followers; *wounded* one native officer, five other native ranks and two followers; ninety-eight horses and transport animals were also killed or wounded.

* Captain W. E. Tomkins and Lieutenant A. W. Bailey.
† Lieutenant H. A. Harington.

Meanwhile, on my arrival at Nawagai on the 14th September, I found the Khan disposed to be friendly, and to do all in his power to provide such supplies as we required. The Hadda Mullah was reported to be in the Bedmanai Pass with a small gathering which was said to be increasing in numbers; but the tribes inhabiting the Mittai and neighbouring valleys seemed somewhat half-hearted about opposing us. The tribes south of the Rambat Pass also sent to disclaim hostile intentions; but, notwithstanding this, some of their men joined in the night attack of the 14th-15th on Brigadier-General Jeffreys's camp.

Early in the morning of the 16th I received a brief report by heliograph of the attack on Brigadier-General Jeffreys's camp the night before, and at once sent him orders to concentrate his force and proceed to the punishment of the tribes concerned. Later in the day I received a fuller report of what had happened, together with information from Brigadier-General Jeffreys that he had received my orders and was concentrating his brigade at Inayat Kili in the Mamund Valley, with a view to carrying them out. He had ascertained that the attack on his camp had been made by a small gathering of Mamunds, who had been reinforced by some of Umra Khan's followers from Zagi, a village in the Mamund Valley, and by a few men from the neighbouring tribes.

Naturally the night attack of the 14th-15th, with the consequent turning aside into the Mamund Valley of Brigadier-General Jeffreys's Brigade, made a considerable change in the aspect of affairs in South Bajour and the Mohmand country; and the strategical situation which had now developed itself was interesting. I found myself at Nawagai with a brigade of all arms ‡ in a strongly entrenched position, faced by the Hadda Mullah's gathering in the Bedmanai Pass,—a not very difficult defile, some six or eight miles in length, the mouth of which is about seven miles south-west in a straight line from the site of my camp,—itself about one mile south of Nawagai village. The intervening ground is a plain of which the western half is cut up by ravines, while the rest is favourable for cavalry. East of and behind me lay the road to the camp of the 2nd Brigade at Inayat Kili running for about six miles through a network of deep ravines, and then for the remaining six or seven over a plain. I was not strong enough to attack the Mullah's gathering in their position with sufficient amount of odds in my favour, while I did not think it advisable to rejoin Brigadier-General Jeffreys,—first, because he was strong § enough already for immediate requirements; secondly, because it would have been most unwise to have retired through the ravines above mentioned in face of the Mullah's gathering; thirdly, because I expected that one of Major-General Elles's Brigades would join me in the Nawagai Valley on the 17th or the 18th at latest, and finally, because my support was necessary to keep the Khan of Nawagai with us,—as, if I had deserted him, he would have been compelled by the Mullah's men to throw in his lot with them, which would have been a serious matter on account of his influence in Bajour. Accordingly, I determined to stay where I was until Major-General Elles's advance should make it possible to dispose effectually of the Mullah's gathering, and to clear out the Bedmanai Pass and the Mittai and neighbouring valleys with completeness.

‡ 3 Battalions.
1 Mountain Battery.
3 Squadrons.
1 Company of Sappers.

§ 4 Battalions.
1 Mountain Battery.
1 Squadron.
1 Company of Sappers.

The most interesting part of Sir Bindon Blood's despatch is that which deals with the action of September 16th. It may be well to give it in full, Sir Bindon Blood says:—

At about 6-30 on the morning of the 16th September Brigadier-General Jeffreys moved out from his camp at Inayat Kili with the greater portion of his force in three columns, to deal with the villages of the Mamunds. The right column under Lieutenant-Colonel F. G. Vivian, 38th Dogras, consisting of six companies and a detachment of Sappers was directed along the eastern side of the Mamund Valley on the villages of Shinkot, Chingai, Damadolah and Badam Kili; the central column under Colonel T. H. Goldney, 35th Sikhs, consisting of six companies, four guns, one squadron, and a detachment of Sappers, was directed against the villages of Minar, Hazarnao and Badalai; while the left column under Major F. Campbell of the Guides was composed of five companies and a detachment of Sappers, and was directed along the right bank of the Watelai ravine parallel to the centre column. The right column under Colonel Vivian having advanced by the route ordered as far as Damadolah, found that place too strongly held to be reasonably attempted without artillery, and returned thence to camp arriving at 4 P.M., with two men slightly wounded. The centre column under Colonel Goldney, advanced some six miles up the valley without seeing anything of the enemy, who were first reported at Badam Kili to which place a detachment under Lieutenant-Colonel A. E. Ommanney was sent to dislodge them. The remainder of the column pushed on, and at about 10-30 A.M. two companies of the 35th Sikhs which led the advance occupied a knoll near Shahi Tangi upwards of nine miles from camp. In this movement, however, the two companies advanced too far from their supports and as the enemy promptly attacked them in force they were compelled to retire about a mile with the loss of one British Officer and one sepoy killed and sixteen non-commissioned officers and sepoys wounded. Soon afterwards, the Buffs under Colonel Ommanney coming up, the knoll was again occupied without much opposition, being the furthest point reached by the column during this advance. The guns came into action, first on the spur north of Badalai and afterwards on the north of Chingai (II); they were covered in the first position by two companies of the 35th Sikhs posted to their right, and on their moving towards the second position one-and-a-half of these companies under Captain W. I. Ryder were ordered to cover the movement by climbing to the top of a high ridge to their right and then advancing along it towards the north. Owing to subsequent orders not reaching him, Captain Ryder went further. In the earlier part of the day the left column had remained far behind, being fully occupied for some considerable time in dealing with the numerous villages met with along the road shortly after leaving camp. Towards 9 A.M. it was called up by General Jeffreys, as the enemy began to appear in force on his left near Agrah and it joined the centre column about noon. At about 2-30 P.M., as soon as the fortified villages of Chingai (II) and Shahi Tangi had been dismantled, General Jeffreys ordered the troops to return to camp; Captain Ryder was still on the high ridge above Chingai (II), along which he attempted to retire in a direction which diverged from the line of the retreat of the main body of the force. Soon after the retirement commenced a message was received from him stating that he was hard pressed and could not rejoin the main body, whereupon General Jeffreys ordered Major Campbell with six companies of the Guides Infantry to go to his assistance which they did about 4 P.M., a short time being taken up in assembling the companies which were in extended order. The fact of this movement having to be undertaken so late in the afternoon was a most unfortunate occurrence, since General Jeffreys had to wait until the safety of the Guides and Captain Ryder's detachment was assured; and the consequent delay at that time of the day made it impossible for him to reach camp before dark. The Guides, under Major Campbell, most successfully and gallantly relieved and brought off Captain Ryder's detachment, which had suffered heavy losses.

The combined detachments did not, however, succeed in rejoining General Jeffreys, being prevented by nightfall and a thunderstorm which came on about the same time. Ultimately they made their way to camp without further loss, arriving about 9 P.M. Meanwhile, as soon as the safety of Captain Ryder's detachment was certain, General Jeffreys continued his retirement towards the camp. So long as daylight lasted the enemy kept at a respectful distance from him, but as it got dark they got bold and the ground being broken and difficult they were able to bring a hot fire to bear on the troops, while a heavy thunderstorm which came on at dusk greatly increased the difficulties of the situation. Ultimately, however, by about 8-30 P.M. all the troops had arrived in camp except General Jeffreys, four guns of No. 8 (Bengal) Mountain Battery, a small party of Sappers and a few men of the Buffs and the 35th Sikhs who got separated from the rest in the darkness. About dusk General Jeffreys, then about three miles and a half from camp, decided to occupy a neighbouring village called Bilot for the night, chiefly with a view to sheltering the battery mules with him from the enemy's sharpshooters, and while he was engaged in arranging this the thunderstorm before referred to came on causing sudden and complete darkness. In the consequent confusion the troops got separated and only the detachments above detailed remained with General Jeffreys. He proceeded to occupy and entrench an angle of the village, part of which was burning, while the rest was soon occupied by the enemy, who fired on the General and his detachment from behind walls at a few yards' range, inflicting serious losses on men and animals. This state of things continued, in spite of several gallant attempts to clear the village which were led by Lieutenants Watson and Colvin, R.E., until the arrival about midnight of Major J. F. Worlledge, 55th Sikhs, with two companies of Guides and two of his own regiment. After this the enemy were easily driven off, and gave no further annoyance during the night. Major Worlledge had left camp about 5-30 P.M. in obedience to an order from General Jeffreys, and on joining the General about dark had been sent to find and support the Guides under Major Campbell. Failing to find the Guides in the dark, Major Worlledge tried to retrace his steps to the General but only succeeded in finding him after the moon rose about midnight, although he had been close to him for some time previously without knowing it. General Jeffreys ultimately reached camp at 8 A.M. on the 17th, some of the troops there having been sent out to his assistance and returning with him.

After detailing the losses, 151 killed and wounded, Sir Bindon Blood continues:—The behaviour of the troops throughout this trying day was very good. The steadiness and discipline shown by the Buffs under Colonel Ommanney were admirable, while General Jeffreys has specially commended the gallantry with which the Guides Infantry under Major Campbell brought off Captain Ryder's detachment of the 35th Sikhs, carrying the wounded on their backs under a heavy fire. He has further strongly endorsed Major Campbell's favourable mention of the courage and judgment shown by Captain G. B. Hodson and Lieutenant H. W. Codrington of the Guides who commanded the companies of the battalion which were chiefly in contact with the enemy; the gallantry of Surgeon-Captain J. Fisher who made a most determined though unsuccessful attempt to take medical aid to the wounded of Captain Ryder's detachment through a hot fire; of Surgeon-Lieutenant E. L. Perry; of Jemadar Sikandar Khan of the Guides, and of several non-commissioned officers and sepoys of the same corps. General Jeffreys has also described in very favourable terms the gallant and valuable work done on this day by Captain E. H. Cole and his squadron of the 11th Bengal Lancers. He has commended the conduct of Captain Ryder and Lieutenant O. G. Gunning, 35th Sikhs, who were both wounded, and of Jemadar Narayan Singh, Havildar Ram Singh and Sepoy Karram Singh of the same regiment. He has also brought to notice a gallant act of Captain Birch and his trumpeter Juvan in rescuing a wounded sepoy of the 35th Sikhs, as well as the distinguished gallantry of Jemadars

Nawab and Ishar Singh and several non-commissioned officers and men of the same battery. General Jeffreys further refers in the strongest terms of commendation to the gallant conduct of Lieutenants Watson and Colvin, R.E., and of the handful of men of the Buffs and No. 4 Company, Bengal Sappers, who spent the nights of the 16th and 17th with him in the village of Bijot. The conduct of these Officers and men in entering the village several times in the dark, in the face of a heavy fire directed upon them at close quarters, seems deserving of the highest recognition, and I have consequently made a special communication to you on it. General Jeffreys has also commended the gallant conduct of his Deputy Assistant Adjutant-General, Major Hamilton; and finally he has praised the courage and resolution of Lieutenant Churchill of the 4th Hussars, correspondent of the *Pioneer* newspaper, with the force, who made himself useful at a critical moment.

Sir Bindon Blood, in closing his despatch, pays a high tribute to the work done by the cavalry. The health of the troops was generally good; only seven British and five native soldiers and eight followers died from disease between September 6th and October 27th. The Officers mentioned in the despatch include all the heads of departments, the general staff, Major Deane and Mr. Davis, Political Officers. The commissariat, transport and medical arrangements are all said to have been excellent. The telegraph arrangements were well carried out by Lieutenant W. Robertson, R.E., under the direction of Mr. C. E. Pitman, while the postal service under Mr. H. C. Sheridan was also satisfactory.

Sir Bindon Blood adds :—It will have been gathered from the foregoing narrative that the three brigades of the force were ably commanded by Brigadier-Generals Meiklejohn, Jeffreys and Wodehouse, who were efficiently seconded by their staffs. The line of communications and base were also most efficiently managed by Colonel Reid and by Lieutenant-Colonel V. A. Schalch, Base Commandant, and their respective staffs.

A description is given of the movements about Nawagai, and the account of the night attack on the camp on September 20th, closes in the following words :—

The steadiness of the troops during this somewhat trying action was quite perfect, and the safety of the camp was never in the slightest degree doubtful, although the enemy's swordsmen were so determined that many of them were shot down close to the entrenchment. The fire discipline of the infantry was shown to be excellent, especially that of the 1st Battalion, Queen's (under Lieutenant-Colonel Collins,) who are in all respects an example of what a battalion of infantry should be. The star shells fired by the mountain battery were most useful, and shrapnel and case were also fired at different times with great effect, all under the direction of Lieutenant-Colonel W. Aitken, C.B., commanding the Royal Artillery with my force. In short, the affair was a most satisfactory one, as proving the admirable discipline, confidence and steady shooting of our troops, as well as the efficiency of the simple defensive arrangements which had been made.

The following comments are made on the operations in the Watelai Valley :—

It will have been observed, of course, that there was much more difficulty in dealing with the Mamunds than was experienced with the Swatis, the Masazai Mohmands, or with the Mamund's neighbours, the Salarzai and Shamozai.

Much of this difficulty was due to the fact that our invasion of the Mamund Valley was not preceded by a decisive action like that at the Malakand on the 2nd August, at Ladakai on the 17th August, at Nawagai on the night of the 20th September, or, as in the case of the Salarzai and Shamozai, by such an object-lesson as our operations against the Mamunds themselves.

Besides this, however, the special physical features of the Mamund Valley gave the tribe great advantages, which they utilised with considerable tactical skill. It will be seen that the valley consists of a broad and gently sloping plateau, cut up by ravines, especially towards the top, and with hills rising somewhat suddenly on all sides. This plateau is well cultivated for rain crops, but is practically waterless at this season; the only good water above a point near Inayat Kili being in the ravines on the sides of the hills where many of the most important villages are consequently situated, those on the level depending for their water-supply on tanks or, in one or two cases, on doubtful wells. Thus, as soon as the lower villages had been dealt with, which was done without opposition, it was necessary for our troops to attack those on the sides of the hills, on ground very difficult for assailants and extremely favourable for defenders.

The tribesmen were further much assisted by the circumstances that a great part of their best lands lie in Afghanistan, on the north-western side of the high range of mountains whose crest forms the Afghan frontier in that direction. Thus, much of their property was beyond our reach, while they had a secure refuge to which they could send their movables from our side of the frontier and betake themselves if pressed. They showed commendable skill and patience in adhering to the only tactics which could give them any measure of success, always retiring* before our troops so long as they advanced, and then following them up in skirmishing order as far as the open ground on their withdrawal to their camp, which had to remain low down the valley on account of the difficulty about water higher up. The more credit is due to the Mamunds for holding out so well, as they suffered † severely in every encounter with us, besides undergoing much loss of property and destruction of their defences whose speedy reconstruction, though costly and difficult for them, is necessary to their existence.

* There was an exception at Agrah and Gat on the 30th September.

† It is now known that 220 of the tribes were killed, besides about 150 of their friends who came to help them.

Both in the Nawagai and Mamund Valleys a considerable number of Martini-Henry and other rifles were used against us with apparently unlimited supplies of ammunition.

The conduct and discipline of the troops in the operations under reference was in the highest degree satisfactory. The operations, which extended over seven weeks, were carried on without tents and on a very low scale of baggage, while the rations though abundant and excellent in all respects, were necessarily open to the objection of sameness. Notwithstanding these inconveniences, the troops remained uniformly cheerful, especially when active hostilities were going on.

The despatch closes with the following remarks :—

I have already alluded to the steadiness and gallant bearing of the infantry in the several engagements that took place during the operations under reference, and I would now wish to invite attention to the invaluable nature of the services rendered by the cavalry. At Nawagai three squadrons of the 11th Bengal Lancers, under Major S. B. Beatson, swept the country everywhere that cavalry could go, carrying out reconnaissances, protecting signalling parties, and watching every movement of the enemy. In the Mamund Valley a squadron of the same regiment, under Captain E. H. Cole, took part in every engagement that occurred while they were there, establishing such a reputation that the enemy even when in greatly superior numbers never dared to face them in the open. Afterwards when Captain Cole and his men left the Mamund Valley, the Guides Cavalry, under Lieutenant-Colonel Adams, being in greater strength, acted still more effectually in the same manner, showing tactical skill of a high order, combined with conspicuous gallantry.

A very interesting feature of the operations was the presence of field artillery in the Mamund and Salarzai Valleys, where, although active operations did not go on after their arrival, their presence produced a great effect, while it was amply proved that they could have been brought into most useful action with comparative ease.

The health of the force was remarkably good throughout, only seven British and five native soldiers and eight followers having died from disease between the 6th September and 27th October, out of a force (including Communications and Base Hospitals) which, for nearly a month of that time, included three brigades of infantry, besides a considerable proportion of the other arms.

The Commissariat arrangements under Major H. Wharry, D.S.O., were most successful. The rations were always abundant and of uniformly good quality; and I may here observe that in five previous campaigns I have never seen the supply of bread anything like so continuously good as it has been throughout the operations of the Malakand Field Force. No doubt the excellence of the Commissariat arrangements has had a great deal to do with the good state of health of the troops which I have remarked upon.

The transport was most efficient throughout the operations under reference, and its management under the direction of Captain C. G. R. Thackwell, Divisional Transport Officer, who was most ably and energetically assisted by Veterinary-Captain H. T. W. Mann, Senior Veterinary Officer, was most successful. In proof of this I will cite a report just made to me by Brigadier-General Jeffreys, commanding the 2nd Brigade of my force, that this morning, on inspecting 1,265 mules attached to his brigade, which have just returned from seven weeks in the field, he found fourteen sore backs and four animals otherwise unfit for work, or a total of only 18 disabled animals in all.

The medical service was carried out in a very satisfactory manner. Some difficulties arose on the transfer of Officers and materials to the Tirah Expeditionary Force on its formation, especially as large convoys of sick and wounded were on the line of this force at the time, but these difficulties were successfully overcome by Colonel A. J. F. Reid, who was in charge of the Line, and matters were ultimately restored to smooth working on the arrival of Surgeon-Colonel J. C. G. Carmichael, Indian Medical Service, who is now Principal Medical Officer of the Force.

The telegraph arrangements were well carried out by Lieutenant W. Robertson, R.E., under the direction of Mr. C. E. Pitman, C.I.E. The postal service under Mr. H. C. Sheridan was also satisfactory.

The working of the several departments of the Head-quarters Staff was most satisfactory and successful. The heads of departments were :—

Major H. H. Burney, Gordon Highlanders, Assistant Adjutant-General.

Lieutenant-Colonel A. Masters, 2nd Regiment, Central India Horse, Assistant Quarter-Master-General.

Captain H. E. Stanton, D.S.O., R.A., Deputy Assistant Quarter-Master-General (Intelligence).

Captain E. W. M. Norie, Middlesex Regiment, Superintendent, Army Signalling.

Surgeon-Colonel J. C. G. Carmichael, Indian Medical Service, Principal Medical Officer.

Lieutenant-Colonel W. Aitken, C.B., R.A., Commanding Royal Artillery.

Colonel J. E. Broadbent, R.E., Commanding Royal Engineers—relieved early in October by Lieutenant-Colonel W. Peacocke, C.M.G., R.E.

Captain W. E. Banbury, 25th Madras Infantry, Field Treasure Chest Officer.

Captain W. W. Cookson, R.A., Ordnance Officer.

Major H. Wharry, D.S.O., Staff Corps, Chief Commissariat Officer.

Captain C. G. R. Thackwell, Staff Corps, Divisional Transport Officer.

Veterinary-Captain H. T. W. Mann (wounded in action, 20th September), Army Veterinary Department, Senior Veterinary Officer.

Captain C. L. Robertson, R.E., Survey Officer.

Captain C. G. F. Edwards, 5th Punjab Cavalry, Provost-Marshal.

The Rev. L. Klogh, Chaplain.

Lieutenant W. Robertson, R.E., in charge of Telegraphs.

I am under great obligations to my personal staff—Captain A. B. Dunsterville, 1st Battalion, East Surrey Regiment, Aide-de-Camp; Captain A. R. Dick, 2nd Punjab Cavalry, and Lieutenant Viscount Fincastle 16th (The Queen's) Lancers.

It will have been gathered from the foregoing narrative that the three brigades of the force were ably commanded by Brigadier-Generals W. H. Meiklejohn, 1st Brigade, P. D. Jeffreys, (wounded in action, 16th September), 2nd Brigade, and J. H. Wodehouse (wounded in action, 20th September), 3rd Brigade, who were efficiently seconded by their staffs. The Line of Communications and the Base were also most efficiently managed by Colonel A. J. F. Reid, and by Lieutenant-Colonel A. V. Schalch, 11th Bengal Infantry, the Base Commandant, and their respective staffs.

In my final report on the conclusion of the operations of the force, I shall have the honour to bring the services of the Officers above briefly referred to more fully to the notice of His Excellency the Commander-in-Chief.

Major H. A. Deane, C.S.I., Political Agent, Dir, Chitral and Swat, was in separate and independent charge of the political arrangements connected with the operations I have described as far as Nawagai. He accompanied my headquarters to Gosam, where I left him on the 12th September, and rejoined me at Inayat Kili on the 4th October. He gave much assistance in arranging for the collection of local supplies.

Mr. W. S. Davis was my Political Officer throughout the operations beyond Nawagai and in the Mamund Valley prior to Major Deane's return to my head-quarters on the 4th October. He carried out his duties to my complete satisfaction. His native assistant, Khan Bahadur Ibrahim Khan, also made himself very useful.

Major-General Elles's Despatch.

Major-General Elles in a despatch, dated October 13th, gives a very clear account of the operations in the Mohmand country. The despatch contains the following remarks:—

The expedition proved productive of little fighting, but the splendid force under my command would, I believe, have made little of any possible opposition. I cannot speak too highly of the 20th Punjab Infantry and 21st Gurkhas, on whom the brunt of the work fell. I would wish for no better regiments for hill fighting under their respective commanders. The work done during the expedition by the 28th Bombay Pioneers and No. 5 Company, Bengal Sappers and Miners, is worthy of the highest commendation. The 28th Pioneers also did excellent work in reserve to the 1st Brigade in the attack at Bedmanai, and at Jarobi covered the retirement showing high soldierly qualities in both instances. The main difficulties to contend with were the passes, over which roads had always to be made, and anxiety regarding water as in the western Mohmand country; the supply is almost entirely from tanks, the dams of which had been cut by the Mohmands, and they often only contained a little dirty water.

The Imperial Service Troops under my command proved their fitness to fight in the first line and were utilised exactly the same as the regular native troops. The cavalry escorts of the Patiala and Jodhpore Cavalry did good reconnaissance work on more than one occasion and came under fire. The 1st Patiala Regiment was employed under Lieutenant-Colonel Graves in the operations in the Mittai and Suran Valleys, and covered the retirement of the brigade under fire; their good service was brought to my notice by the General Officer Commanding the 3rd Brigade. The Nabha Regiment, owing to its having been added to my force late in September, had to be kept on the Line of Communications.

I trust the objects of the expedition were fully carried out, thanks to the fine body of troops I had the honour of commanding and to the hearty co-operation of my staff and of all ranks in the Force.

The following subsidiary despatch was published in the *Gazette of India* by General Elles in connection with the Mohmand Field Force in continuation of the despatch of 13th October 1897:—I bring to the notice of the Commander-in-Chief the names of the following for good services during the Mohmand Expedition :—Mr. Merk, Civil Service, rendered very valuable services as Political Officer. The prompt settlement obtained was entirely due to his knowledge of the tribes, his perfect command of their language, which enabled him to deal directly with the *jirgahs*, and his firmness in dealing with the *jirgahs*. His judicious selection of subordinates greatly contributed to the success of the expedition. My movements were almost entirely based on the information obtained by him regarding distances and water. I am under the greatest obligations to Mr. Merk for the manner in which he conducted the political business throughout. Lieutenant Waterfield, Assistant Political Officer, carried out his work very firmly and in great harmony with the Military Officers at the various posts. Captain Cox, in charge of the Imperial Service Troops, the Patiala and Nabha Regiments, carried on all the work connected with them with great smoothness, and was most zealous in his work. Major Bythell, Royal Engineers, Survey Officer, did excellent work under difficulty, marching daily, and was most keen and energetic. Mr. Stowell carried out all the postal arrangements entirely to my satisfaction. Everything was carried on most creditably by him and his subordinates. Mr. Pike, Assistant Superintendent of Telegraphs, ably assisted by his subordinate, Mr. J. C. Murphy, laid the telegraph line rapidly and well. The telegraph work was most satisfactory, all concerned working very willingly.

APPENDIX VI.

THE TIRAH FIELD FORCE.

General object.—The general object of this expedition is to exact reparation for the unprovoked aggression of the Afridi and Orakzai tribes on the Peshawar and Kohat borders, for their attacks on our frontier posts, and for the damage to life and property which has thus been inflicted on British subjects and on those in the British service.

It is believed that this object can best be attained by the invasion of Tirah, the summer home of the Afridis and Orakzais, which has never before been entered by a British force.

Formation of the Force.—The Force which will be styled the "Tirah Expeditionary Force" will be distributed for operations as follows:—

(a) A main column of two Divisions, each consisting of two Infantry Brigades and certain Divisional Troops, will advance on Tirah from the neighbourhood of the Samana Range.
(b) The Line of Communication of the main column between Kohat and Tirah (including the posts on the Samana Range) will be held by a force consisting of one Native Cavalry Regiment and four Native Infantry Battalions.
(c) A mixed brigade, to be styled the "Peshawar Column" will operate, as may be required, from Peshawar.
(d) A force, which will be designated the "Kurram Movable Column" will be formed in support on the Hangu-Parachinar line, for employment as circumstances may require.
(e) A mixed brigade will be formed at Rawalpindi as a Reserve.

Composition of the Force.—These forces will be composed as follows:—

THE MAIN COLUMN.

First Division.

First Brigade.—2nd Battalion the Derbyshire Regiment, 1st Battalion the Devonshire Regiment, 2nd Battalion 1st Gurkha (Rifle) Regiment, 30th (Punjab) Regiment of Bengal Infantry, No. 6 British Field Hospital, and No. 34 Native Field Hospital.

Second Brigade.—2nd Battalion the Yorkshire Regiment, 1st Battalion Royal West Surrey Regiment, 2nd Battalion 4th Gurkha (Rifle) Regiment, 3rd Regiment of Sikh Infantry, Punjab Frontier Force, Sections A. and B. of No. 8 British Field Hospital, Sections A. and C. of No. 14 British Field Hospital and No. 31 Native Field Hospital.

Divisional Troops.—No. 1 Mountain Battery Royal Artillery, No. 2 (Derajat) Mountain Battery, No. 1 (Kohat) Mountain Battery, 2 Squadrons 18th Regiment of Bengal Lancers, 28th Regiment of Bombay Infantry (Pioneers), No. 3 Company Bombay Sappers and Miners, No. 4 Company Bombay Sappers and Miners, one Printing Section from the Bombay Sappers and Miners, the Nabha Regiment of Imperial Service Infantry, the Maler Kotla Imperial Service Sappers, Section A. of No. 13 British Field Hospital, and No. 63 Native Field Hospital.

SECOND DIVISION.

Third Brigade.—1st Battalion the Gordon Highlanders, 1st Battalion the Dorsetshire Regiment, 1st Battalion 2nd Gurkha (Rifle) Regiment, 15th (The Ludhiana Sikh) Regiment of Bengal Infantry, No. 24 British Field Hospital and No. 44 Native Field Hospital.

Fourth Brigade.—2nd Battalion the King's Own Scottish Borderers, 1st Battalion the Northamptonshire Regiment, 1st Battalion 3rd Gurkha (Rifle) Regiment, 36th (Sikh) Regiment of Bengal Infantry, Sections C. and D. of No. 9 British Field Hospital, Sections A. and B. of No. 23 British Field Hospital and No. 48 Native Field Hospital.

Divisional Troops.—No. 8 Mountain Battery Royal Artillery, No. 9 Mountain Battery Royal Artillery, No 5 (Bombay) Mountain Battery, Machine Gun Detachment, 16th Lancers, two Squadrons 18th Regiment of Bengal Lancers, 21st Regiment of Madras Infantry (Pioneers), No. 4 Company, Madras Sappers and Miners, one Printing Section from the Madras Sappers and Miners, the Jhind Regiment of Imperial Service Infantry, the Sirmur Imperial Service Sappers, Section B. of No. 13 British Field Hospital and No. 43 Native Field Hospital.

LINE OF COMMUNICATION.

No. 1 Kashmir Mountain Battery, 22nd (Punjab) Regiment of Bengal Infantry, 2nd Battalion 2nd Gurkha (Rifle) Regiment, 30th (Garhwal Rifle) Regiment of Bengal Infantry, 2nd Regiment of Punjab Infantry, Punjab Frontier Force, 3rd Regiment of Bengal Cavalry, No. 1 Company Bengal Sappers and Miners, No. 42 Native Field Hospital, No. 52 Native Field Hospital, the Jeypore Imperial Service Transport Corps, the Gwalior Imperial Service Transport Corps, Ordnance Field Park, Engineer Field Park, British General Hospital of 500 beds at Rawalpindi, Native General Hospital of 500 beds at Rawalpindi, No. 1 Field Medical Store Depot. (For First Division). No. 2 Field Medical Store Depot. (For Second Division). No 5 Veterinary Field Hospital, No. 11 British Field Hospital, No. 25 British Field Hospital, No. 47 Native Field Hospital, and No 64 Native Field Hospital.

THE PESHAWAR COLUMN.

Second Battalion the Royal Inniskilling Fusiliers, 2nd Battalion the Oxfordshire Light Infantry, Maxim Gun Detachment, 1st Battalion Devonshire Regiment, 9th Gurkha (Rifle) Regiment of Bengal Infantry, 34th Pioneers, 45th (Rattray's Sikh) Regiment of Bengal Infantry, 57th Field Battery Royal Artillery, No. 3 Mountain Battery Royal Artillery, 9th Regiment of Bengal Lancers, No. 5 Company, Bengal Sappers and Miners, No. 5 British Field Hospital, No. 45 Native Field Hospital, A. and B. Sections, No. 54 Native Field Hospital, British General Hospital of 250 beds at Nowshera * and Native General Hospital of 500 beds at Nowshera.*

THE KURRAM MOVABLE COLUMN.

Twelfth Regiment of Bengal Infantry, the Kapurthala Regiment of Imperial Service Infantry, 4 Guns 3rd Field Battery Royal Artillery, 6th Regiment of Bengal Cavalry, one Regiment of Central India Horse, Section D. of No. 3 British Field Hospital, No. 62 Native Field Hospital, Section B. of No. 46 Native Field Hospital and Native General Hospital of 200 beds at Kohat.

THE RAWALPINDI RESERVE BRIGADE.

Second Battalion the King's Own Yorkshire Light Infantry, 1st Battalion the Duke of Cornwall's Light Infantry, 27th Reigment (1st Baluch Battalion of Bombay (Light) Infantry, 2nd Regiment of Infantry Hyderabad Contingent,

---

* These General Hospitals will also receive the sick and wounded from the Force at the Nalakand and in the Swat Valley.

Jodhpur Imperial Service Lancers, No. 12 British Field Hospital and No. 53 Native Field Hospital.

All units which will be concentrated at Peshawar, except such as are detailed for the Peshawar Column, will march from Peshawar to Kohat through the Kohat Pass under the orders of the Lieutenant-General Commanding the Forces, Punjab, under instructions which will be given from Army Head-Quarters. The General Officer Commanding the Expeditionary Force will direct all movements at and beyond Kohat, and he will also direct all movements of the Peshawar Column beyond Peshawar.

Kohat will be the Base of Operations for the First and Second Divisions and the Kurram Movable Column, but the Line of Communication will commence at and include Kushalgarh. Kohat and Kushalgarh will, for the time being, be dissevered from the Punjab Command.

Peshawar will be the Base of Operations for the Peshawar Column, but will remain in the Punjab Command.

COMMANDS AND STAFF.

Army Staff.

Lieutenant-General Commanding the Force.	General Sir W. S. A. Lockhart, K.C.B., K.C.S.I.
Aide-de-Camp	Lieutenant F. A. Maxwell, 18th Bengal Lancers.
Aide-de-Camp	2nd-Lieutenant J. H. A. Annesley, 18th Hussars.
Orderly Officer	Lieutenant G. R. de H. Smith, Central India Horse.
Orderly Officer	2nd Lieutenant E. H. E. Collen, Royal Artillery.
Deputy Adjutant-General, Chief of the Staff.	Brigadier-General W.G. Nicholson, C.B.
Assistant Adjutant-General	Brevet-Lieutenant-Colonel E.G. Barrow, 7th Bengal Infantry.
Assistant Quarter-Master-General	Major G. H. W. O'Sullivan, R.E.
Deputy Assistant Adjutant-General	Captain J. A. L. Haldane, Gordon Highlanders.
Assistant Quarter-Master-General for Intelligence.	Colonel G. H. More-Molyneux, Assistant Quarter-Master-General.
Deputy Assistant Quarter-Master-General for Intelligence.	Captain E. W. S. K. Maconchy, D.S.O., 4th Sikhs.
Field Intelligence Officer	Captain F. F. Badcock, D.S.O., 1st Battalion 5th Gurkhas.
Principal Medical Officer (with the temporary rank of Surgeon-Major-General).	Surgeon-Colonel G. Thomson, C.B., Indian Medical Service.
Secretary to Principal Medical Officer	Surgeon-Major W. A. Morris, Army Medical Staff
Brigadier-General, Commanding Royal Artillery.	Brigadier-General C. H. Spragge, R.A.
Brigade-Major, Royal Artillery	Captain C. de C. Hamilton, R.A.
Orderly Officer, Royal Artillery	Major H F Mercer, R.A.
Brigadier-General Commanding Royal Engineers.	Brevet-Colonel J E. Broadbent, R.E. (with the temporary rank of Brigadier-General).
Brigade-Major, Royal Engineers	Captain S. L. Craster, R.E.
Orderly Officer, Royal Engineers	Lieutenant H. Biddulph R.E.
Superintendent, Army Signalling	Major G. J. N. Logan-Home, 1st Bedfordshire Regiment.

Head-Quarters Commandant	... Captain R. E. Grimston, 6th Bengal Cavalry.
Assistant Judge-Advocate-General	... Captain F. J. S. Lowry, 29th Bombay Infantry.
Principal Provost-Marshal	... Lieutenant-Colonel E. Balfe, Deputy Judge-Advocate-General.
Chief Ordnance Officer ...	... Colonel C. H. Scott, R.A.
Commissariat Transport Officer	... Captain G. W. Palin, Assistant Commissary-General.
Inspecting Veterinary Officer	... Veterinary-Lieutenant-Colonel B. L. Glover.
Comptroller of Military Accounts	... Lieutenant-Colonel W. R. LeG. Anderson, Comptroller of Military Accounts, Punjab Command.
Field Pay-Master ...	... Captain P. G. Shewell, Military Accounts Department.
Chief Survey Officer ...	... Brevet-Colonel Sir T. H. Holdich, K.C.I.E., C.B., R.E.

MAIN COLUMN.

First Division.

Commanding (with the local rank of Major-General).	Brigadier-General W. P. Symons, C.B.
Aide-de-Camp ...	... Captain A. G. Dallas, 16th Lancers.
Extra Orderly Officers ...	... { Lieutenant J. M. Wikeley, 17th Bengal Cavalry. Lieutenant G. H. Badcock, 7th Bengal Cavalry.
Assistant Adjutant-General	... Lieutenant-Colonel C. W. Muir, C.I.E., 17th Bengal Cavalry.
Assistant Quarter-Master General	... Major E. A. G. Gosset, 2nd Derbyshire Regiment
Deputy Assistant Quarter-Master-General for Intelligence.	Captain A. Nicholls, 2nd Punjab Infantry.
Field Intelligence Officer ...	... Lieutenant C. E. E. F. K. Macquoid, 1st Lancers, Hyderabad Contingent
Principal Medical Officer ...	... Surgeon-Colonel E. Townsend, Army Medical Staff.
Lieutenant-Colonel Commanding Royal Artillery.	Lieutenant-Colonel A. E. Duthy, R.A.
Adjutant, Royal Artillery	... Captain W. K. McLeod, R.A.
Divisional Ordnance Officer	... Captain A. R. Braid, R.A.
Commanding Royal Engineers	... Lieutenant-Colonel H. H. Hart, R.E.
Adjutant, Royal Engineers	... Captain O. M. R. Thackwell, R.E.
Field Engineer	... Major J. A. Ferrier, D.S.O., R.E.
Assistant Field Engineer	... Lieutenant J. F. N. Carmichael, R.E.
Assistant Field Engineer	... Lieutenant W. H. Bunbury, R.E.
Assistant Superintendent, Army Signalling.	Captain H. T. Kenny, 2nd Bombay Lancers.
Provost-Marshal ...	... Captain H. W. G. Graham, D.S.O., 5th Lancers.
Commissary-General ...	... Colonel L. W. Christopher, Commissary-General.
Assistant to Commissary-General	... Captain H. S. G. Hall, Assistant Commissary-General.
Chief Transport Officer	... Major H. Mansfield, Assistant Commissary-General.

(xxxi)

Assistant to Chief Transport Officer,	Captain I. H. Smith, 12th Bengal Cavalry.
Principal Chaplain ...	... The Rev. Saunders Dyer, M.A., F.S.A.
Church of England Chaplain	... The Rev. R. M. Kirwan, M.A.
Roman Catholic Chaplain	... The Rev. Father N. J. Winkley.
Divisional Commissariat Officer	... Major W. R. Yielding, C.I.E., D.S.O., Assistant Commissary-General.
Assistant to Divisional Commissariat Officer.	Lieutenant C. H. Corbett, 18th Hussars.
Divisional Transport Officer	... Captain F. C. W. Rideout, Assistant Commissary-General.
Assistant to Divisional Transport Officer.	Captain A. W. V. Plunkett, 2nd Battalion the Manchester Regiment.

First Brigade (First Division).

Commanding ...	... Brigadier-General R. C. Hart, V.C., C.B.
Orderly Officer ...	... Captain C. O. Swanston, 18th Bengal Lancers.
Deputy Assistant Adjutant-General ...	Captain A. G. H. Kemball, 1st Battalion, 5th Gurkhas.
Deputy Assistant Quarter-Master-General.	Captain H. R. B. Donne, 1st Norfolk Regiment.
Brigade Commissariat Officer	... Captain A. Mullaly, Deputy Assistant Commissary-General.
Assistant to Brigade Commissariat Officer.	Lieutenant H. I. Nicholls, 1st Bedfordshire Regiment.
Brigade Transport Officer	... Captain E. de V. Wintle, 15th Bengal Lancers.
Veterinary Officer ...	... Veterinary-Lieutenant W. J. Tatam.

Second Brigade (First Division).

Commanding ...	... Brigadier-General A. Gaselee, C.B., A.-D.-C.
Orderly Officer ...	... Lieutenant A. N. D. Fagan, 1st Lancers, Hyderabad Contingent.
Deputy Assistant Adjutant-General,	Major W. Aldworth, D.S.O., 1st Bedfordshire Regiment.
Deputy Assistant Quarter-Master-General.	Major A. A. Barrett, 2nd Battalion, 5th Gurkhas.
Brigade Commissariat Officer	... Lieutenant C. S. D. Leslie, Deputy Assistant Commissary-General.
Assistant to Brigade Commissariat Officer.	Captain H. de la P. Gough, 16th Lancers.
Brigade Transport Officer	... Lieutenant H. Macandrew, 5th Bengal Cavalry.
Veterinary Officer ...	... Veterinary-Lieutenant W. F. Shore.

Second Division.

Commanding ...	... Major-General A. G. Yeatman-Biggs, C.B.
Aide-de-Camp ...	... Captain E. St. A. Wake, 10th Bengal Lancers.
Orderly Officer ...	... Captain R. G. Brooke, 7th Hussars.
Orderly Officer ...	... Hony.-Lieutenant-Colonel H. H. Maharaja Sir Nripendra Narayan, Bahadur, of Cooch Behar, G.C.I.E., 6th Bengal Cavalry.
Assistant Adjutant-General	... Lieutenant-Colonel R. K. Ridgeway, V.C.
Assistant Quarter-Master-General	... Major C. P. Triscott, D.S.O., R.A.
Deputy Assistant Quarter-Master-General for Intelligence.	Major R. C. A. B. Bewicke-Copley, King's Royal Rifle Corps.

Field Intelligence Officer ...	... Captain H. F. Walters, 24th (Baluchistan) Regiment of Bombay Infantry.
Principal Medical Officer ...	... Surgeon-Colonel G. McB. Davis, D.S.O., Indian Medical Service.
Lieutenant-Colonel Commanding Royal Artillery	Lieutenant-Colonel R. Purdy, R.A.
Adjutant, Royal Artillery	... Captain H. D. Grier, R.A
Divisional Ordnance Officer	... Captain H. F. Head, R.A.
Commanding Royal Engineers	... Lieutenant-Colonel C. B. Wilkieson, R.E.
Adjutant, Royal Engineers	... Captain T. Fraser, R.E.
Field Engineer ...	... Captain F. H. Kelly, R.E.
Assistant Field Engineer	... Lieutenant W. A. Stokes, R.E.
Assistant Field Engineer	... Lieutenant C. B. L. Greenstreet, R.E.
Assistant Superintendent, Army Signalling.	Captain G. C. Rigby, 1st Wiltshire Regiment.
Provost-Marshal ...	... Captain W. C. Knight, 4th Bengal Cavalry.
Field Treasure Chest Officer	... Lieutenant W. M. Grimley, 20th Punjab Infantry.
Church of England Chaplain	... The Rev. H. W. Nelson, B.A.
Roman Catholic Chaplain	... The Rev. Father Vanden Deyssel.
Church of Scotland (attached to Gordons)	The Rev. D. H. Gillan, M.A., B.D.
Church of Scotland (attached to K.O.S.B's,)	The Rev. W. Thomson, M.A.
Wesleyan Chaplain	... The Rev. J. J. Findlater.
Divisional Commissariat Officer	... Lieutenant-Colonel B. L. P. Reilly, Assistant Commissary-General.
Assistant to Divisional Commissariat Officer	Lieutenant A. D. Macpherson, 2nd Punjab Cavalry.
Divisional Transport Officer	... Major H. L. Hutchins, Assistant Commissary-General.
Assistant to Divisional Transport Officer.	Major H. R. W. Lumsden, 3rd Bengal Infantry.
Survey Officer ...	... Mr. E. A. Wainwright, Survey of India Department.

Third Brigade (Second Division).

Commanding (with the temporary rank of Brigadier-General).	Colonel F. J. Kempster, D.S.O.,A.-D.-C.
Orderly Officer ...	... Lieutenant G. D. Crocker, 2nd Royal Munster Fusiliers.
Deputy Assistant Adjutant-General,	Major H. St. Leger Wood, 1st Dorsetshire Regiment.
Deputy Assistant Quarter-Master-General.	Major H. S. Massy, 19th Bengal Lancers.
Brigade Commissariat Officer	... Lieutenant D. H. Drake-Brockman, I.A.C.G.
Assistant to Brigade Commissariat Officer	Lieutenant F. W. Birch, 29th Punjab Infantry.
Brigade Transport Officer	... Lieutenant R. A. N. Tytler, 1st Gordon Highlanders.
Veterinary Officer ...	... Veterinary-Lieutenant C. Rose.

Fourth Brigade Second (Division).

Commanding ...	... Brigadier-General R. Westmacott, C.B., D.S.O.
Orderly Officer ...	... Lieutenant R. C. Wellesley, Royal Horse Artillery.
Deputy Assistant Adjutant-General ...	Captain W. P. Blood, 1st Royal Irish Fusiliers.
Deputy Assistant Quarter-Master-General.	Captain F. J. M. Edwards, 3rd Bombay Light Cavalry.

Brigade Commissariat Officer	... Captain E. Y. Watson, Deputy Assistant Commissary-General.
Assistant to Brigade Commissariat Officer.	Lieutenant N. G. Fraser, 4th Bombay Cavalry.
Brigade Transport Officer	... Captain W. H. Armstrong, 1st East Yorkshire Regiment.
Veterinary Officer ...	... Veterinary-Lieutenant F. W. Wilson.

LINE OF COMMUNICATION.

General Officer Commanding	... Lieutenant-General Sir A. P. Palmer, K.C.B.
Aide-de-Camp ...	... Lieutenant F. C. Galloway, R.A.
Orderly Officer ...	... Lieutenant H. O. Parr, 7th Bengal Infantry.
Assistant Adjutant and Quarter-Master-General.	Captain (temporary Major) J. W. G. Tulloch, 24th Bombay Infantry.
Deputy Assistant Adjutant and Quarter-Master-General.	Captain I. Phillips, 1st Battalion, 5th Gurkhas.
Principal Medical Officer (with the temporary rank of Surgeon-Colonel).	Brigade-Surgeon-Lieutenant-Colonel W. E. Saunders, Army Medical Staff.
Senior Ordnance Officer ...	... Captain Watkins, R.A.
Section Commandant ...	... Captain O. B. S. F. Shore, 18th Bengal Lancers.
Section Commandant ...	... Captain St. G. L. Steel, 2nd Bengal Lancers.
Section Commandant ...	... Captain F. de B. Young, 6th Bengal Cavalry.
Lieutenant-Colonel Commanding Royal Engineers.	Lieutenant-Colonel J. W. Thurburn, R.E.
Adjutant, Royal Engineers	... Captain H. V. Biggs, R.E.
Field Engineer ...	... Captain C. H. Cowie, R.E.
Assistant Field Engineer ...	... Lieutenant H. S. Rogers, R.E.
Assistant Field Engineer ...	... Lieutenant R. P. T. Hawksley, R.E.
Assistant Field Engineer ...	... Lieutenant A. E. Turner, R.E.
Provost Marshal ...	... Major L. S. Peyton, 14th Bengal Lancers.
Chief Commissariat Officer	... Lieutenant-Colonel C. M. Keighley, D.S.O., Assistant Commissary-General.
Chief Transport Officer, L. of C.	... Major C. V. W. Williamson, Assistant Commissary-General.
Church of England Chaplain	... The Rev. W. Pritchett Shaw.
Veterinary Inspector ...	... Veterinary-Captain F. W. Forsdyke.

Staff at the Base.

Base Commandant ...	... Colonel W. J. Vousden, V.C., Indian Staff Corps.
Deputy Assistant Adjutant and Quarter-Master-General.	Major A. J. W. Allen, 1st East Kent Regiment.
Commandant, British Troops Depôt ...	Major A. de B. V. Paget, 2nd Battalion Durham Light Infantry.
Adjutant and Quarter-Master, British Troops Depôt.	Captain A. F. Bundock, 2nd Battalion South Lancashire Regiment.
Commandant, Native Troops Depôts ...	Captain S. M. Edwardes, D.S.O., 2nd Bombay Infantry (Grenadiers).
Base Ordnance Officer ...	... Captain M. W. S. Pasley, R.A.
Officer in Charge of Engineer Field Park.	Captain U. W. Evans, R.E.
Base Commissariat Officer	... Major H. R. Marrett, Assistant Commissary-General.

(xxxiv)

Departmental Assistants to Base Commissariat Officer.	Captain W. H. D. Rich, Assistant Commissary-General. Lieutenant F. W. H. Forteath, Deputy Assistant Commissary-General. Lieutenant L. H. Marriott, Deputy Assistant Commissary-General. Lieutenant H. G. P. Beville, Deputy Assistant Commissary-General.
Departmental Assistant (for Transport) to the Base Commissariat Officer.	Captain H. N. Hilliard, Deputy Assistant Commissary-General.
Regimental Assistants to Base Commissariat Officer.	Captain W. P. M. Pollock, 18th Hussars. Captain H. Smyth, 1st Battalion Cheshire Regiment. Lieutenant T. E. Bayley, 20th Hussars. Lieutenant C. G. E. Ewart, 5th Bengal Cavalry. Lieutenant E. N. Davis, 3rd Infantry Hyderabad Contingent.

THE PESHAWAR COLUMN.

Commanding	Brigadier-General A. G. Hammond, C.B., D.S.O., V.C., A.-D.-C.
Orderly Officer	Lieutenant H. D. Hammond, R.A.
Assistant Adjutant and Quarter-Master-General.	Brevet-Lieutenant-Colonel F. S. Gwatkin, 13th Bengal Lancers.
Deputy Assistant Adjutant and Quarter-Master-General.	Major C. T. Becker, 2nd King's Own Scottish Borderers.
Field Intelligence Officer	Captain F. H. Hoghton, 1st Bombay Infantry (Grenadiers).
Principal Medical Officer	Brigade-Surgeon-Lieutenant-Colonel R. G. Thomsett, Army Medical Staff.
Lieutenant-Colonel Commanding Royal Artillery.	Lieutenant-Colonel W. M. M. Smith, R.A.
Adjutant, Royal Artillery	Captain F. R. Drake, R.A.
Brigade Ordnance Officer	Major T. E. Rowan, R.A.
Field Engineer	Major E. C. Spilsbury, R.E.
Assistant Field Engineer	Lieutenant C. B. Farwell, R.E.
Assistant Superintendent, Army Signalling.	Lieutenant C. E. Cobb, 1st Battalion East Yorkshire Regiment.
Brigade Commissariat Officer	Lieutenant H. H. Jones, Deputy Assistant Commissary-General.
Assistant to Brigade Commissariat Officer.	Lieutenant V. R. Pigott, 1st Battalion Cheshire Regiment.
Brigade Transport Officer	Lieutenant C. Charlton, Royal Horse Artillery.*
Veterinary Officer	Veterinary-Lieutenant F. U. Carr.

THE KURRAM MOVEABLE COLUMN.

Commanding (with rank and pay of Colonel on the Staff).	Colonel W. Hill, Indian Staff Corps.
Orderly Officer	Captain R. O. C. Hume, 1st Battalion Border Regiment.
Deputy Assistant Adjutant-General	Major E. F. H. McSwiney, D.S.O., 1st Lancers, Hyderabad Contingent.

---

* Lieutenant P. Holland Pryor, 13th Bengal Lancers, took over the appointment of Brigade Transport Officer, on October 18th, 1897, two days before the Column left Peshawar and held it throughout the remaining operations.

Deputy Assistant Quarter-Master-General.	Captain C. P. Scudamore, D.S.O., 1st Royal Scots Fusiliers.
Principal Medical Officer ...	Brigade-Surgeon-Lieutenant-Colonel W. R. Murphy, D.S.O., Indian Medical Service.
Brigade Ordnance Officer	... Lieutenant D. R. Poulter, R.A.
Field Engineer ...	... Captain J. A. Gibbon, R.E.
Assistant Field Engineer	... Lieutenant E. A. Tandy, R.E.
Assistant Superintendent, Army Signalling.	Lieutenant C. R. Scott-Elliot, 4th Madras Pioneers.
Brigade Commissariat Officer	... Captain C. F. T. Murray, Assistant Commissary-General.
Assistant to Brigade Commissariat Officer.	Captain P. H. Rogers, 2nd Yorkshire Light Infantry.
Brigade Transport Officer	... Captain H. W. Colquhoun, 24th Madras Infantry.
Veterinary Officer ...	... Veterinary-Lieutenant W. N. Wright.

THE RAWALPINDI RESERVE BRIGADE.

Commanding ...	... Brigadier-General C.R. Macgregor, D.S.O.
Orderly Officer ...	... 2nd-Lieutenant E. W. C. Ridgeway, 29th Punjab Infantry.
Deputy Assistant Adjutant-General ...	Major Sir R. A. W. Colleton, *Bart.*, 1st Royal Welsh Fusiliers.
Deputy Assistant Quarter-Master-General.	Captain H. Hudson, 19th Bengal Lancers.
Brigade Commissariat Officer	... Lieutenant E. G. Vaughan, Deputy Assistant Commissary-General.
Assistant to Brigade Commissariat Officer.	Lieutenant A. P. Trevor, 20th Bombay Infantry.
Brigade Transport Officer	... Lieutenant K. E. Nangle, 3rd Infantry, Hyderabad Contingent.
Veterinary Officer ...	... Veterinary-Lieutenant W. S. Anthony.

APPENDIX VII.

THE SAMANA AND KURRAM VALLEY DESPATCHES.

THE Right Hon'ble the Governor-General in Council is pleased to direct the publication of the subjoined letter from the Adjutant-General in India, submitting despatches from Major-General A. G. Yeatman-Biggs, C.B., Commanding the Kurram-Kohat Force, describing the operations which took place on the Samana Range and in the Kurram Valley in August and September last.

The Governor-General in Council concurs with His Excellency the Commander-in-Chief in his appreciation of the conduct of these operations, and of the behaviour of the troops engaged.

The Governor-General in Council desires especially to express his admiration of the brilliant defence of Fort Gulistan by the 36th Sikhs, and of the post of Saragheri by a party of twenty men of the same regiment under the command of Havildar Ishar Singh, who died fighting to the last, displaying a heroic devotion which has never been surpassed in the annals of the Indian Army.

THE COMMANDER-IN-CHIEF'S COMMENTS.

Major-General G. de C. Morton, C.B., Adjutant-General in India, in forwarding the despatches from the Commander-in-Chief to the Government of India, says:—

His Excellency is of opinion that the operations in question were well planned and skilfully carried out. The march to the relief of Gulistan was performed under very trying circumstances, owing to the heat and to a great scarcity of water *en route*, but the force successfully accomplished its object with the same gallantry and cheerfulness as have been evinced on every occasion by our troops during the various operations which have recently taken place on the North-West Frontier.

The Commander-in-Chief wishes to draw attention to the admirable conduct and steadiness of the 36th Sikhs, under the command of Lieutenant-Colonel Haughton, during the attack on the various posts held by that regiment on the Samana Range.

At Sangar, the small garrison made a sortie and gallantly captured a standard from the enemy while the brilliant defence of Fort Gulistan by the detachment under the command of Major Des Vœux, reflects the greatest credit on that Officer and the garrison of the post.

The Government of India will, His Excellency is assured, appreciate fully the intrepid manner in which the late Havildar Kala Singh led the sortie from the Gulistan Fort, and also the conduct of Havildar Sundar Singh, who assisted his comrades at a critical moment.

The Commander-in-Chief deeply regrets the loss of the garrison of Saragheri, a post held by 21 men of the 36th Sikhs, and he wishes to record his admiration of the heroism shown by those gallant soldiers. Fighting against overwhelming numbers they died at their post, thus proving their loyalty and devotion to their Sovereign, while upholding to the last the traditional bravery of the Sikh nation.

The creditable manner in which the attack of the enemy on the post at Sadda was repulsed is due, in His Excellency's opinion, not only to the steadiness and good discipline of the garrison, but also to the satisfactory arrangements for the protection of his camp which were made by Colonel G. L. R. Richardson, C.I.E.

In conclusion, the Commander-in-Chief recommends to the favourable consideration of Government the services of Major-General Yeatman-Biggs, C.B., and those mentioned by him in his despatch. Among the names brought specially to notice is that of Miss Teresa McGrath, whose heroism is described in terms which His Excellency cordially endorses.

GENERAL WOLSELEY'S COMMENDATION.

Lieutenant-General Sir G. B. Wolseley, K.C.B., Commanding the Forces, Punjab, sent the despatches to the Adjutant-General. In doing so he said :—

These operations seem to have been well planned and carried out. The heroic defence of Saragheri is, in my opinion, worthy of the highest praise, and I deeply lament the loss of the garrison.

I fully endorse the Major-General's commendation on the defence of Fort Gulistan and the behaviour of all ranks Major Des Vœux proved himself a gallant and skilful leader, and the Major-General's remarks on this Officer's conduct appear to be fully deserved.

I have much pleasure in recommending for the Order of Merit all the non-commissioned officers and men the Major-General has brought to notice.

THE ATTACKS ON HANGU AND THE SAMANA POSTS.

Major-General A. G. Yeatman-Biggs, Commanding the Kohat Field Force, writing from Fort Lockhart, the 21st September, says :—

I have the honour to report, for the information of His Excellency the Commander-in-Chief, that news was received by me from reliable sources at Hangu on the 8th instant, to the effect that the Afridis had decided to come and assist the Orakzai in attacks on Hangu and on the Samana posts on Friday, the 10th instant.

Having on the same day received reports that the necessary amount of transport and supplies for putting thirty days' supplies into the Samana posts had been collected, I gave orders to start that night with a column, strength as per margin. The ammunition supply had, ten days previously, been sent up by me to the Samana, making up the total number of rounds to four hundred per rifle, 36th Sikhs.

Margin:
4 guns, 9th Field Battery, Royal Artillery
2 squadrons, 3rd Bengal Cavalry. } To Pat Darband only.
1 squadron, 3rd Punjab Cavalry.
4 companies, Royal Irish Regiment, 300.
1-2nd Gurkhas, 500.
1-3rd Gurkhas, 500.
2nd Punjab Infantry, 500.
Half-company No. 4 Company, Bombay Sappers and Miners.
Sec. No. 8, British Field Hospital.
Sec. No. 42, Native Field Hospital.

Concentrating at Pat Darband at 1 30 A.M. on the 9th instant, the 1-2nd Gurkhas moved up the road as advanced guard, and occupied the plateau on which Dhar is situated before daylight. At 4 A.M. the remainder of the column started. No enemy were reported in sight, and the road was found too bad for guns; so I sent the cavalry and artillery back to Hangu, and the convoy proceeded up the road, arriving at Fort Lockhart about mid-day.

On the 10th I sent the half-company of the Bombay Sappers and Miners to improve the defences of Gulistan.

At 7-30 P.M. Major Bewicke-Copley reported that he had seen clouds of smoke north of the Sampagha Pass, and that the Afridis were coming over the pass.

Hearing that the whole of the Afridi *lashkar* had arrived at Khorappa during the night, I sent a few scouts of the 1-3rd Gurkhas down the spurs towards the Khanki Valley, to ascertain if the information was correct, as Khorappa cannot be seen from the Samana plateau. These scouts were supported by the 1-3rd Gurkhas and two companies of the 2nd Battalion of the Royal Irish Regiment.

About 10 A.M., large numbers of the enemy could be seen marching down the Khanki Valley. I at once recalled the troops by heliograph. Just before receiving the order to retire the 1-3rd Gurkhas fired a few long-range volleys into a party of the enemy, and three were seen to drop. At 1 P.M. Major Bewicke-Copley reported to me from Crag Picket that 22 standards and about 10,000 men had passed down the valley.

It seemed probable that the tribesmen intended to carry out their threat of attacking Hangu, or perhaps Shahu Khel, a small post guarding the Khanki Valley, about four miles north-west of the point where it is crossed by the Kohat-Hangu road.

This post had been reinforced by me with one company of the Royal Irish and 61 rifles of the 15th Sikhs, under command of Major Forster, Royal Irish Regiment.

I ordered the 2nd Punjab Infantry to seize Gogra Hill, supported by the 1-2nd Gurkhas.

The Commandant of the Border Militia Police, Mr. D. Donald, informed me that a large number of the enemy were making for the Darband Kotal, and the Officer Commanding the 1-2nd Gurkhas reported to me (7 P.M.) that seven standards and a considerable number of tribesmen were retracing their steps up the valley.

A convoy with two days' supplies had been ordered out from Hangu to meet me at the Pat Darband Kotal, where I found them when I advanced with the remainder of the column. The supplies had been sent up on 51 camels, as no mules were available.

The advanced guard and main column halted for the night at 9 P.M. on the hill. A few shots were fired at the rear-guard from Gogra Hill, and the whole of the *sarwans*, except one, bolted, and the camels, being left without drivers and without nose-strings, stampeded. The rear-guard, consisting of a wing of the 1-3rd Gurkhas, under Lieutenant-Colonel Pulley, and two companies of the 1-2nd Gurkhas, under Captain Robinson, withstood several determined attacks, and did their utmost to save the convoy. At midnight I sent out two companies of the 2nd Punjab Infantry, under Lieutenant Elsmie accompanied by Captain Scudamore, Deputy Assistant Quarter-Master-General, to assist in bringing the camels in. All but two were found to have thrown their loads, so it was useless, and by 2 A.M. the rear-guard had taken up the position assigned to them in the bivouac. The enemy consisted of Sheikhans, Mishtis, Malla Khels and Ali Khels, and they admit to their losses being over 100 killed and wounded. A leading *malik* of the Sheikhans was wounded and five leading Malla Khels killed.

When morning broke (12th), I sent out Colonel Lawrence, Royal Irish Regiment, with two companies of his Battalion and five companies of each of the remaining corps, to endeavour to recover the camels and stores, but only thirteen camels were recovered, and of these only two had loads. The Royal Irish fired long-range volleys to keep the tribesmen at a respectful distance.

On the return of Colonel Lawrence's reconnaissance, I set the column once more in motion towards Lakka, as being the best position from which both Hangu and Shahu Khel could be protected. I arrived there at 1 P.M., but, finding no water, and having lost our food, I issued orders to commence the march to Hangu at 3 P.M. At 3-30 P.M. I received a message by helio from Fort Lockhart that Saragheri was hard pressed, and at 4-30 P.M. it was helioed that Saragheri had fallen, and that Gulistan was hard pressed.

Four riflemen of the 1-2nd Gurkhas who had been reported missing the previous evening, rejoined, having made their way by the Darband Kotal.

The troops, after their hard day without food or water, had earned a rest, but about 3-30 P.M. on the 13th, a letter was brought to me from Major Des Vœux, 36th Sikhs, Commanding at Gulistan, urgently asking for help. I immediately despatched two guns of the 9th Field Battery and the 3rd Bengal Cavalry with their signallers to gallop along the road at the foot of the hills as far towards Gulistan as they could go, and sent a wire to Doaba to despatch two more guns of the 9th Field Battery and the squadron of the 3rd Punjab Cavalry to join in the demonstration.

The guns from Hangu were accompanied by Mr. D. Donald who knows the country well, and he was able to show them a position from which they could fire a few rounds to encourage the garrison, and Major Middleton, commanding the 3rd Bengal Cavalry, sent through by helio, just before sunset, a message to assure the garrison that they would be relieved by mid-day on the 14th.

The four guns of the Derajat Mountain Battery had reached Hangu the previous day, having marched 35 miles in under thirteen hours, so they were added to our column, and we set out at midnight for Lakka.

At 4 A.M., on the 14th instant, I arrived at Lakka, and sent on two companies of the 1-3rd Gurkhas to occupy the hill on which we had bivouacked on the night of the 11th.

At 5 A.M. we marched for Gulistan. On arrival opposite Tsalai (7 A.M) the advanced guard of the 1-3rd Gurkhas was assailed with a heavy fire. I brought up the guns and shelled the enemy's marksmen out of Tsalai tower at a range of 900 yards, and at once ordered the 1-3rd Gurkhas to attack the enemy's position on Gogra, the 1-2nd Gurkhas following in support. Gogra Hill was quickly taken under cover of the fire of the guns, and one company of the Royal Irish fired long-range volleys at the Orakzai retreating down the Sarmela spur. The strength of the enemy was estimated at about 4,000.

The 2nd Punjab Infantry pressed on followed by the guns, and the Gurkhas held the position until they had passed through.

As we neared Sangar the garrison of that post displayed a white standard which they had captured from the enemy. Sangar and Dhar had been attacked all night, but a sortie had been made from the first-named as soon as our guns opened fire, and Lieutenant-Colonel Haughton, commanding the 36th Sikhs, had joined the party with 12 men of the Royal Irish and 35 Sikhs, and had poured long-range volleys into the foe as they retreated down the Sarmela.

At 10 A.M. I reached Fort Lockhart and reconnoitred the enemy's position from a bastion of the Fort, and found about 8,000 to 10,000 Afridis holding a strong position, which was skilfully occupied with lines of *sangars* on Saragheri ridge.

I ordered up the guns, and by 10-30 A.M. they were playing on the enemy's position with shrapnel, whilst the 36th Sikhs from Fort Lockhart advanced to turn the Afridi right, and the 2nd Punjab Infantry made a frontal attack on their position, supported by the two Gurkha battalions as they arrived on the ground. The Afridis did not wait for the infantry, but fled from their position and made for the Khanki Valley. I pressed on with all possible speed, as I did not know whether Gulistan was holding out or not. On reaching the high ground overlooking Gulistan, I found that the Fort was invested by about 6,000 Orakzais, but they did not wait for the attack of the 2nd Punjab Infantry and 36th Sikhs, which was made under an accurate fire of the guns of the mountain battery, and by 8 P.M. they were in full retreat down the Khandartang spur and Gulistan was relieved, after having been hard pressed by some 7,000 to 8,000 Afridis and Orakzais since the 12th instant. The enemy's casualties are reported over 400 killed.

I wish to bring to the notice of His Excellency the Commander-in-Chief for special recognition the names of—

Major C. H. Des Vœux, 36th Sikhs, who was the life and soul of the defence of Gulistan. He did all that could be done, with the slender means at his disposal, to frustrate each device of the enemy, whose attack was a most determined one, with riflemen ready, on ridges and terraces within fifteen yards of the Fort, to open a heavy fire on any one who exposed himself in the slightest degree. His judgment in permitting the sortie was, in my opinion, good, as the success attending it encouraged the garrison and made the enemy move away from the walls.

Second-Lieutenant H. R. E. Pratt, 36th Sikhs, who, though suffering from dysentery, was always ready for any emergency, and is very highly spoken of be Major Des Vœux.

Surgeon-Captain C. B. Prall, Indian Medical Service, whose care of the wounded was unremitting, and who was often under heavy fire.

Miss Teresa McGrath, who had been previously attached to the hospital by my orders, who rendered most valuable assistance to the Medical Officer. Her conduct is spoken of most enthusiastically by all ranks.

No. 755, Havildar Sundar Singh, 36th Sikhs, who is reported to have been conspicuous for his gallantry throughout the siege, and who, of his own accord, sprang over the wall of the horn-work, carrying with him those who happened to be near him, to the succour of his comrades who had made a sortie to capture a standard, and were in imminent peril of being killed to a man.

Havildar Bishen Singh, 36th Sikhs, who was in command at Saugar, and kept the enemy at bay against heavy odds, who led a successful sortie, capturing a standard.

The rank and file named below, who took part in the sortie made by the 36th Sikhs from Gulistan:—No. 807, Lance-Naick Sadu Singh. No 1078, Sepoy Attar Singh No. 1046, Sepoy Sajin Singh. No. 1380, Sepoy Bakram Singh, No. 1603, Sepoy Chajja Singh. No. 1369, Sepoy Badan Singh. No. 1597, Sepoy Phuman Singh. No. 1741, Sepoy Thaman Singh. No. 1066, Sepoy Sawan Singh. No. 1600, Sepoy Ghuna Singh. No. 1588, Sepoy Bhagwan Singh. No. 1589, Sepoy Harnam Singh. No. 180, Sepoy Rur Singh. No. 368, Sepoy Sher Singh. No. 1632, Sepoy Ralla Singh. No. 1123, Sepoy Kala Singh. No. 1177, Lance-Naick Dewa Singh. No. 817, Lance-Naick Harnam Singh. No. 939, Lance-Naick Jiwan Singh. No. 1167, Sepoy Mihan Singh. No. 823, Sepoy Mehma Singh. No. 1183, Sepoy Hira Singh. No. 1539, Sepoy Nabha Singh. No. 1338, Sepoy Jowahir Singh. No. 907, Sepoy Basawa Singh (since dead). No. 1146, Sepoy Ghulla Singh. No. 1854, Sepoy Jiwan Singh.

No. 2,509, Rifleman Dhanbir Sahai, 1-2nd Gurkhas, for helping in a wounded naick of the same battalion on the night of the 11-12th instant, under heavy fire.

I should also have brought forward the names of Havildar Kala Singh, 36th Sikhs, who volunteered to command the sortie from Gulistan, and Sepoy Gurmukh Singh, 36th Sikhs, for special recognition, but the former has, I regret to say, succumbed to his wounds, and the latter was last seen signalling from Saragheri just before the enemy swarmed in. I trust that in the cases of those brave soldiers who lost their lives at Saragheri and Gulistan, their wives and families may be considered for pension as if they had survived to receive the rewards they so justly deserved.

My thanks are due to the various members of my staff, Majors Bewicke-Copley, King's Royal Rifles, and E. F. H. McSwiney, D.S.O., 1st Lancers, Hyderabad Contingent, and Captains C. P. Scudamore, D.S.O., Royal Scots Fusiliers, and E. St. A. Wake, 10th Bengal Lancers, who, without even the organisation of a Brigade Staff to help them, performed the duties of Divisional Staff to a force larger than a division, scattered over a wide area, to my entire satisfaction. My thanks are also due to His Highness the Maharaja of Cooch Behar, G.C.I.E., Honorary Lieutenant-Colonel, 6th Bengal Cavalry, who accompanied me throughout as Orderly Officer, and to Brigade-Surgeon-Lieutenant-Colonel W. R. Murphy, D.S.O,. Indian Medical Service, Captain C. F. T. Murray, Staff Corps, Commissariat Department, and Captain P. H. Rogers, Yorkshire Light Infantry, Transport Officer, who organised their respective departments under circumstances of exceptional difficulty.

I wish also to favourably mention the following Officers: —Colonel W. W. Lawrence, Royal Irish Regiment, Commanding the Column. Lieutenant-Colonel E. A. Travers, Commanding the 1-2nd Gurkhas. Lieutenant-Colonel C. Pulley, Commanding the 1-3rd Gurkhas. Lieutenant-Colonel J. Haughton. 36th Sikhs, Commanding on the Samana. Lieutenant-Colonel R. R. N. Sturt, Commanding the 2nd Punjab Infantry. Major B. J. C. Doran, Royal Irish Regiment, Staff Officer to the Column. Captain J. L. Parker, R.A., Commanding No. 2 (Derajat) Mountain Battery. Captain J. G. Robinson, 1-2nd Gurkhas, for coolness and gallantry on the occasion of the rear-guard action, 12th instant. Lieutenant A. M. S. Elsmie, Adjutant, 2nd Punjab Infantry, for coolness displayed in assisting to bring in the camels on the night of 11-12th instant. Lieutenant G. W. M. West, 1-3rd Gurkhas, for conspicuous gallantry on the occasion of the rear-guard action, 11-12th instant. Jemadar Harakbir Gurung, 1-3rd Gurkhas, for conspicuous gallantry on the occasion of the rear-guard action, 11-12th instant.

I am also indebted to Mr. D. Donald, Commandant, Border Militia Police, whose unrivalled knowledge of the country and people has been of the greatest service to me.

THE ATTACK ON SADDA.

Major-General Yeatman-Biggs, writing from Fort Lockhart on the 30th September, says:—

I have the honour to report, for the information of His Excellency the Commander-in-Chief in India, that the camp at Sadda was attacked on the night of the 16th and 17th September.

Colonel G. L. R. Richardson, C.I.E., Commanding the Flying Column, had established himself in a well intrenched camp and high ground overlooking Sadda. About 10·10 P.M. on the 16th, a *lashkar*, consisting of Massuznis and Chamkannis, numbering about 2,000, collected in the Khurmandarra and attacked a picket of the 5th Punjab Infantry about a hundred yards outside the south-east corner of the camp. The picket had to abandon their *sangar* and retire into camp, losing the Havildar in so doing. The moon was obscure by passing clouds, and the noise of the water rushing in the *nullah* prevented the patrols of the 5th Punjab Infantry and 1-5th Gurkhas hearing or seeing the approaching enemy.

The enemy's attack was pushed to within twenty or thirty yards of the stone wall with which the camp was surrounded with a certain amount of resolution up to midnight, after which it slackened off considerably. In no case did the enemy come to close quarters, though two standards were brought up to within fifty yards of the camp. They seemed to have lost heart at the last moment in the face of the steady fire which was brought to bear on them

The expenditure of ammunition was as follows :—

	Rounds.
15th Sikhs	525
15th Punjab Infantry	1,200
1-5th Gurkhas	373
Total	2,098

The usual casualty returns have been already forwarded.

FURTHER OPERATIONS ON THE SAMANA.

On the same day Major-General Yeatman-Biggs reported :—

I have the honour to report that on the 27th August last, a large gathering of Orakzai appeared on the Samana Suk, and heavy firing was heard in the direction of Shinawari, which was held by the Border Police. This was reported to me at Kohat.

Reconnaissances were made from Gulistan towards the Samana Suk, and from Hangu to Shinawari.

The enemy was found to be about 4,000 in number, strongly posted on the Samana Suk. In this reconnaissance, I regret to say, Lieutenant A. K. Blair, 36th Sikhs, was wounded in the chest. Reinforcements were sent from Fort Lockhart, but soon after their arrival at Gulistan information was received that the enemy's *lashkar* was assembling to the east of Fort Lockhart, so Lieutenant-Colonel Haughton, 36th Sikhs, Commanding on the Samana, decided to return to Fort Lockhart.

The Officer Commanding the reconnaissance made by a squadron of the 18th Bengal Lancers to Shinawari, returned the same day to Hangu, and reported all well. This was the second reconnaissance made from Hangu to Shinawari (a distance of over twenty miles) within the last few days.

The following day the enemy were discovered to be holding the Chagru Kotal as well as the Samana Suk on the west of the Samana Range, and the Sarmela spur on the east end of the range and during the day they burnt the posts of Gogra and Tsalai, which had been evacuated by the Border Police.

In order to anticipate the enemy, should a second attack be made on Shinawari, I ordered two companies of Gurkhas to march to reinforce the garrison there. One squadron of cavalry accompanied them, with orders to return to Hangu as soon as the Gurkhas had reached the post. Reliable reports were received on the morning of the 29th August that Shinawari had been evacuated by the Border Police, and the post burnt by the tribesmen the previous evening, so the troops *en route* to reinforce the garrison, were recalled.

The Orakzai held a *jirgah* this day, and decided that the Ali Khel, Mamuzai, Alsherzai and Aka Khel should attack Gulistan on Friday, September 3rd, whilst the Mishti, Sheikhan Malla Khel and Rabia Khel attacked Hangu.

During the night of the 29th the post of Sangar was fired into, and a sepoy of the Border Police deserted from the adjacent post of Dhar with his rifle and ammunition. This post was therefore reinforced by one Native Officer and 37 sepoys of the 26th Sikhs, so that all posts on the Samana should be held by Sikhs.

The three following days the enemy remained on the east and west ends of the Samana, but made no further move.

On the 3rd September a *bhisti* from Dhar was murdered by the enemy, and his three mules stolen. Mr. D. Donald, Commandant of the Border Police, proceeded to Dhar to make inquiries into the circumstances, and he and his escort were fired on.

As tribesmen were reported to be advancing on Gulistan and Saragheri in force, these posts were reinforced from Fort Lockhart. Towards evening the enemy, in considerable force, took up a position in and about Picquet Hill '400 yards west of Gulistan, and set fire to the thorn hedge which had been placed as an obstacle a few yards outside the horn-work of the place. The fire was extinguished by volunteers, whose names have been brought to notice by me in a separate letter. At 8 P.M. the bonfire, which had been previously prepared between the horn-work and Picquet Hill, was lit by volunteers, whose names have also been mentioned in the despatch of the 21st September.

The enemy kept up a hot fire until midnight when they retired.

Lieutenant-Colonel J. Haughton and Lieutenant and Adjutant R C. Munn, of the 36th Sikhs, strove hard, with their little handful of men from Fort Lockhart, to succour the many small posts scattered over the Samana Range that were beset on all sides by overwhelming numbers of the enemy.

The expenditure of ammunition between the 27th August and the 3rd September on the Samana was—

Rifles	...	...	...	...	410
Rounds expended	...	...	...	...	3,649

I have not considered it necessary to attach any sketch, as the whole ground is so well known, and has already been mapped by the Survey Department.

APPENDIX VIII.

THE TIRAH DESPATCHES.

The following notification and despatch are taken from the *Gazette of India* :—

The Right Hon'ble the Governor-General in Council is pleased to direct the publication of the subjoined letter from the Adjutant-General in India, submitting a despatch from General Sir W. S. A. Lockhart, K.C.B., K.C.S.I., describing the opperations of the Tirah Expeditionary Force, from the 18th to the 31st October 1897.

His Excellency the Governor-General in Council concurs with his Excellency the Commander-in-Chief in his appreciation of the ability and judgment shown by General Sir William Lockhart in the conduct of the operations recorded in his despatch, and also of the gallant and soldierly behaviour of the Officers, Non-Commissioned Officers and men under his command.

His Excellency in Council, while deeply regretting the loss of life which occurred in the attack on the heights of Dargai on the 20th October 1897, fully shares in the admiration expressed by the Commander-in-Chief of the gallantry displayed by both Officers and men on that occasion.

In the assaults on the Sampagha and Arhanga Passes, the skilful dispositions of the General Commanding and the excellent qualities displayed by the troops, enabled these strong positions to be won with comparatively little loss.

THE COMMANDER-IN-CHIEF'S COMMENT.

Major-General G. de C. Morton, C.B., Adjutant-General in India, in forwarding the despatch to the Secretary to the Government of India, Military Department, said :—

I have the honour, by direction of the Commander-in-Chief, to forward, for the information of the Government of India, the accompanying despatch from General Sir W. S. A. Lockhart, K.C.B., K.C.S.I., describing the operations of the Tirah Expeditionary Force from the 18th to the 31st October 1897.

2. The general object of the expedition was to exact reparation for the unprovoked aggression of the Afridi and Orakzai tribes on the Peshawar and Kohat borderers, in attacking our frontier posts, and for the damage to life and property which had thus been inflicted on British subjects and on those in the British service. The despatch now submitted shows the measures which were taken by General Sir William Lockhart to carry out the orders of the Government of India and to enter Tirah, a country which until now has never been invaded by a British force.

3. The incidents which occurred between the 18th and 20th October, and which immediately preceded the concentration of both divisions of the force at Khangarbur, in the Khanki Valley, are detailed in the despatch. With regard to paragraph 21 thereof the Commander-in-Chief agrees with Sir William Lockhart that a flanking demonstration combined with a frontal attack would in all probability have enabled the Dargai heights to have been taken at less loss of life, but he is confident that the Government of India will share his admiration of the distinguished gallantry and the marked devotion to duty evinced by all ranks in assailing that difficult position, defended as it was by a resolute and well armed enemy.

4. The measures subsequently taken by Sir William Lockhart to force the Sampagha and Arhanga Passes, where it had been anticipated the greatest resistance would be met, were thoroughly successful, and to their skilful conception and the employment of concentrated artillery fire may be ascribed the small loss of life that characterised both operations.

5. His Excellency cordially endorses the remarks which the General Officer Commanding the Force makes regarding the behaviour of the troops engaged in these operations, and he desires to recommend for the favourable consideration of Government the distinguished services of General Sir William Lockhart, and of the Officers, Non-Commissioned Officers and men mentioned by him in the despatch.

SIR WILLIAM LOCKHART'S DESPATCH.

The despatch from General Sir W. S. A. Lockhart to the Adjutant-General in India is dated Head-Quarters, Tirah Expeditionary Force, Camp Bwatoi, the 9th December 1897. It is as follows:—

In compliance with the instructions conveyed in your letter No. 2235-F., dated the 20th November 1897, I have the honour to submit, for the information of His Excellency the Commander-in-Chief in India, the following account of the operations of the force under my command from the 18th to the 31st October 1897.

2. On October 16th, the 2nd Division of the Main Column had concentrated at Shinawari, with the exception of the troops occupying the Samana ridge near Forts Lockhart and Gulistan*; the 1st Division was expected to assemble at the same place on the 19th; and I consequently issued orders for the march of the Main Column on the 20th and following days from Shinawari to Khorappa, each corps being directed to leave behind its tents and heavy baggage under charge of a regimental guard. Meanwhile the road from the Chagru Kotal towards Khorappa was being improved by military and hired labour, working under the protection of covering parties. It was reported, however, that the troops and labourers thus employed were being so molested by the enemy's sharp-shooters who occupied the heights to the west of the Chagru defile, especially by those living in a small village called Dargai, about 1,800 yards to the left of the road shortly after it crosses the crest of the pass, that the improvement of the road could not be continued until the heights had been cleared, while two days' work was said to be necessary to render the road sufficiently good for the passage of laden transport animals. It was further reported that no water was obtainable in the immediate vicinity of Dargai, the inhabitants getting water from the valley below to the west, where there were several rich Ali Khel villages and a number of cattle.

* No. 9 Mountain Battery R.A., 1st Battalion, Northamptonshire Regiment, 36th Sikhs.

3. I therefore determined to attack and destroy the village of Dargai, while by a simultaneous flanking movement I seized the heights overlooking

(xlvi)

the valley to the west, and cleared out the lower villages referred to above. Although I was aware of a hostile gathering in the Khanki Valley, the information I had received through native channels led me to believe that the Orakzai, other than the Ali Khel section of that tribe, did not intend seriously to oppose my advance until I had reached Khorappa, and that the Afridis were too busily engaged in fortifying the Sampagha and Arhanga Passes to be able to assist the Orakzai in any considerable strength.

4. During my stay on the Samana, Major-General Yeatman-Biggs had been in indifferent health, and though he was able to move to Shinawari on October, the 17th, while the troops to be employed were drawn almost exclusively from the 2nd Division, I thought it better to spare him the fatigue of conducting the operations designed to clear the road and punish the Ali Khels. These operations I accordingly entrusted to Lieutenant-General Sir A. P. Palmer, Commanding the Line of Communication.

5. The front attack on Dargai was directed by Brigadier-General Westmacott, C.B., D.S.O., who had the following troops placed at his disposal:—No. 5 (Bombay) Mountain Battery, Rocket Detachment, Royal Artillery, 2nd Battalion King's Own Scottish Borderers, 1st Battalion 3rd Gurkha Rifles.

The Main Column employed on the flanking movement was commanded by Brigadier-General Kempster, D.S.O., and consisted of the following troops :—No. 8 Mountain Battery Royal Artillery, Machine Gun Detachment, 16th Lancers, 1st Battalion Dorsetshire Regiment, 1st Battalion Gordon Highlanders, 1st Battalion 2nd Gurkha Rifles, 15th Sikhs, No. 4 Company Madras Sappers and Miners, Scouts of the 5th Gurkha Rifles. This column was accompanied by Lieutenant-General Sir A. P. Palmer, K.C.B., with an escort of one company of the 3rd Sikhs.

Brigadier-General Kempster's Column left Shinawari at 4-30 A.M., and Brigadier-General Westmacott's at 5 A.M. On the latter reaching the Chagru Kotal at 8-30 A.M., it was joined by No. 9 Mountain Battery Royal Artillery, and the 1st Battalion Northamptonshire Regiment from Fort Lockhart. At 9 A.M. the attack was commenced, the 1st Battalion 3rd Gurkhas leading, with the 2nd Battalion King's Own Scottish Borderers in support and the 1st Battalion Northamptonshire Regiment in reserve. At the same time a working party under Lieutenant-Colonel J. W. Thurburn, Commanding Royal Engineers, Line of Communication, consisting of the 21st Madras Pioneers, the Sirmur Imperial Service Sappers, and the hired labourers, was pushed forward beyond the *kotal* to improve the road.

6. The advance of the troops which was covered by No. 9 Mountain Battery Royal Artillery and No. 5 (Bombay) Mountain Battery, was necessarily slow, the slopes being extremely steep and affording but little cover. The enemy at first kept up a vigorous fire from the walled terraces and rocks in front of the village, but shortly before noon, when the flanking movement began to develop and the tribesmen's line of retreat was threatened, the opposition slackened and the position was carried by a company of the 3rd Gurkhas under Major Rose. About 20 of the enemy's dead were left on the ground, a sure indication of the heavy loss which had been inflicted.

7. Meanwhile the Main Column had moved in a north-westerly direction along a track which had been reported as practicable for baggage animals. At the fifth mile, however, the road was found to be impassable for mules, and No. 8 Mountain Battery Royal Artillery with all laden animals had to be ordered back to Shinawari, escorted by the 1st Battalion Dorsetshire Regiment and two companies of the 15th Sikhs. The remainder continued their march, led by the Gurkha scouts, a few of the enemy's marksmen firing at the advancing troops and wounding two riflemen of the 1st Battalion 2nd Gurkhas.

At 11 A.M., heliographic communication was established with Brigadier-General Westmacott's Column, and shortly before noon the 1st Battalion 2nd Gurkhas, which was leading, reached a commanding position at Khand Talao, about two and a half miles west of Dargai, thus causing the tribesmen hastily to evacuate that village as well as the villages in the valley below. During their retirement the enemy, estimated to number some 800 men, came under the fire of the 1st Battalion 2nd Gurkhas, and suffered considerable loss.

8. At this point, owing to the great difficulties of the road, the Main Column had to be halted to allow of the Gordon Highlanders and 15th Sikhs closing up, and also to cover the return to camp at Shinawari of the Mountain Battery and its escort. At 2-30 P.M. the concentration had been completed, and the Main Column began to move towards Dargai in order to join Brigadier-General Westmacott's force, which in the meantime had destroyed that village. The path was extremely difficult, and in some places precipitous, so that progress was slow, and it was found impossible to reach villages below Dargai which it had been intended to deal with, and near which the water-supply to Dargai was situated. The track to the water was afterwards found to be about three miles in length, so commanded from the adjacent heights, that water could not have been obtained in the presence of an enemy unless these heights as well as Dargai itself had been held.

9. At this time a hostile force, numbering about 4,000 men, was observed advancing from the Khanki Valley up the Narik Darra towards Khand Talao, while another body of the enemy began to ascend the Dargai heights from the same direction. It was clear, therefore, that the gathering of tribesmen near Khorappa, having heard the sound of the guns earlier in the day, had resolved to reinforce the Ali Khels who had just been driven out of Dargai and the neighbouring villages. But before the enemy could come within fighting distance, the junction between the two columns had been effected, the 15th Sikhs covering the climb of Brigadier-General Kempster's Column along the rugged path described above and the retirement of the Sikhs being in turn covered by the Gordon Highlanders and two companies of the King's Own Scottish Borderers, who took up a strong position just below the village of Dargai.

While this was going on, Brigadier-General Westmacott began his withdrawal to the Chagru Kotal, having first posted No. 5 (Bombay) Mountain Battery near the *kotal* itself, and sent No. 9 Mountain Battery Royal Artillery with the 1st Battalion Northamptonshire Regiment to a position on the Samana Suk, which flanked the road from Dargai to the crest of the pass. The enemy pressing on, a hot engagement ensued between them and the rear-guard, our guns making excellent practice, and the Gordon Highlanders with the two companies of the King's Own Scottish Borderers, steadily holding their ground and checking the advance of the tribesmen. The heavy loss inflicted on the enemy caused them to lose heart, no reply being made to a final volley fired by the rear-guard about 7 P.M., after which the withdrawal to the Chagru Kotal and thence to Shinawari was entirely unmolested. Camp was reached by the rear-guard at 11 P.M.

10. Lieutenant-General Sir A. P. Palmer has commented most favourably on the steadiness and gallantry of the troops engaged on October the 18th, and has brought to my special notice the services of the following Officers with Brigadier-General Westmacott's Column:—Major H. Rose, 1st Battalion 3rd Gurkhas; Captain A. P. Bateman-Champain, 2nd Battalion 2nd Gurkhas; and Lieutenant W. G. L. Beynon, D.S.O., 1st Battalion 3rd Gurkhas, who led the attack on Dargai. Also Captain T. G. MacLaren, Captain D. R. Sladen, Captain A. E. Haig, Lieutenant H. F. Pipe-Wolferstan, and 2nd-Lieutenant T. H. Keyes of the 2nd Battalion King's Own Scottish Borderers, who were engaged in supporting the attack and covering the withdrawal.

With Brigadier-General Kempster's Column:—
Lieutenant-Colonel H. H. Mathias, C.B., 1st Battalion Gordon Highlanders.

Lieutenant-Colonel H. A. Abbott, 15th Sikhs.
Lieutenant-Colonel E. A. Travers, 1st Battalion 2nd Gurkhas.
Captain I. Phillips, 1st Battalion 5th Gurkhas, Deputy Assistant Adjutant and Quarter-Master-General, Line of Communication.
Captain F. G. Lucas and Lieutenant the Hon'ble C. G. Bruce, 5th Gurkhas, who were in charge of the Gurkha scouts.
No. 2967, Private W. Rennie, 1st Battalion Gordon Highlanders, who shot down four of the enemy at very close quarters.

11. The casualties on October 18th comprised—
Major R. D. Jennings-Bramly, 1st Battalion Gordon Highlanders, killed.
Lieutenant M. L. Pears, 1st Battalion Scottish Rifles, attached to the Gordon Highlanders, severely wounded.
British Non-Commissioned Officers and men :—Killed 2, wounded 10.
Native ranks :—Killed 6, wounded 21.
Followers :—Wounded 3.

12. I am much indebted to Lieutenant-General Sir A. P. Palmer and Brigadier-Generals Westmacott and Kempster for the skilful manner in which the troops were handled and the operation described above brought to a satisfactory conclusion.

13. Having watched the action from the Samana Suk until Dargai had been captured and the two columns had established communication with each other, I returned to Fort Lockhart, where at 5 P.M. I received a heliogram from Lieutenant-General Sir A. P. Palmer, informing me that the object of the reconnaissance had been attained, and that the troops were returning to Shinawari. I accordingly directed the General Officer Commanding the 2nd Division to continue work on the road the next day, under the protection of two battalions and a mountain battery. At 11 A.M. on October 19th, a heliogram was received from Major-General Yeatman-Biggs, reporting that the troops of his division had reached camp so late on the previous evening that he thought it better not to employ them in the manner indicated, especially as an advance to Khorappa had to be made the next day. I regret that my orders were not carried out even at the risk of fatiguing the troops, as the presence of a force on the Chagru Kotal might have deterred the enemy from re-occupying Dargai, and in any case would have enabled the road to be further improved. But the heliogram reached me too late to allow of the employment of the working party, which otherwise might have been covered by troops detailed from the 1st Division.

14. On October 19th the Dargai heights were observed during the day from the Samana ridge, but there was no sign of a formidable gathering, although a few tribesmen were seen moving about near the village.

15. Late on the evening of the 19th I received a telegram from Shinawari, reporting that Dargai and the adjacent heights were believed to be strongly held by the enemy, and that the General Officer Commanding the 2nd Division proposed to advance the next day to Khorappa *via* Fort Gulistan, the Samana Suk, and the Tsalai spur, instead of down the Chagru defile. For reasons which need not here be detailed, I was unable to accept this suggestion, and in reply desired Major-General Yeatman-Biggs to adhere to the original plan of movement. I remarked that while it would be necessary to clear the Dargai heights overlooking the road to the west, the enemy would probably retire as soon as troops had been pushed on to the point where the Narik Darra joins the Chagru defile, as the enemy's rear would thus be threatened ; and to assist him in the frontal attack, I placed at his disposal two battalions and one mountain battery from the 1st Division. I also informed him that No. 9 Mountain Battery Royal Artillery and the 1st Battalion Northamptonshire Regiment would be directed to co-operate from Fort Lockhart, by taking up a position on the Samana Suk opposite Dargai at 7 A.M.

16. On October 20th the troops of the 2nd Division, as detailed below,* moved as directed, the advance-guard leaving camp at Shinawari at 4-30 A.M. and reaching the Chagru Kotal at 8 A.M. At the latter hour the 1st Battalion Northamptonshire Regiment and No. 9 Mountain Battery Royal Artillery were in position on the Samana Suk. The troops detailed from the 1st Division to assist in the advance of the 2nd Division were No. 1 (Kohat) Mountain Battery, the 2nd Battalion Derbyshire Regiment and the 3rd Sikhs.

The 3rd Brigade under Brigadier-General Kempster began its attack on the Dargai heights at 10 A.M., by a concentrated artillery fire from No. 8 Mountain battery Royal Artillery, and No. 1 (Kohat) and No. 5 (Bombay) Mountain Batteries, these being posted slightly in advance of the *kotal*. No. 9 Mountain Battery Royal Artillery, assisted by shelling the enemy's *sangars* from the Samana Suk. The attack was led by the 1st Battalion 2nd Gurkhas, supported by the 1st Battalion Dorsetshire Regiment. The 2nd Battalion Derbyshire Regiment was in reserve, followed by the 1st Battalion Gordon Highlanders.

By 11-30 A.M. the above force was in formation, under cover, in readiness to capture the heights, but when the 2nd Gurkhas, accompanied by the Gurkha scouts of the 1st Battalion 3rd Gurkhas, made their first rush across the open, they were met by such a hot and well-aimed fire that all they could do was to hold on to the position they had reached, without being able to advance further.

At 2 P.M., the Dorsetshire Regiment was ordered to storm the enemy's entrenchments, but though a few men were able to get across the fire-swept zone, an advance beyond the line held by the 2nd Gurkhas was reported by the Commanding Officer to be impracticable, owing to the large number of tribesmen lining the edge of Dargai plateau and the steepness of the slope leading up to it. The General Officer Commanding the 2nd Division accordingly ordered Brigadier-General Kempster to move up the Gordon Highlanders and the 3rd Sikhs, the former regiment being replaced on the lower spur which it had hitherto occupied by the Jhind Imperial Service Infantry. The Gordon Highlanders went straight up the hill without check or hesitation. Headed by their pipers and led by Lieutenant-Colonel Mathias, C.B., with Major Macbean on his right and Lieutenant A. F. Gordon on his left, this splendid battalion marched across the open. It dashed through a murderous fire and in forty minutes had won the heights, leaving three Officers and thirty men killed or wounded on its way. The first rush of the Gordon Highlanders was deserving

---

* The troops of the 2nd Division referred to above were as follows :—

3rd Brigade.

1st Battalion Dorsetshire Regiment.
1st Battalion Gordon Highlanders.
1st Battalion 2nd Gurkhas.
15th Sikhs
No 24 British Field Hospital.
No. 44 Native Field Hospital.

4th Brigade.

2nd Battalion King's Own Scottish Borderers.
1st Battalion 3rd Gurkhas.
Two sections, No. 9 British Field Hospital.
Two sections, No. 23 British Field Hospital.
No. 48 Native Field Hospital

Divisional Troops.

No. 8 Mountain Battery Royal Artillery.
No. 5 (Bombay) Mountain Battery.
Machine Gun Detachment, 16th Lancers.
21st Madras Pioneers.
No. 4 Company Madras Sappers and Miners.
Jhind Regiment of Imperial Service Infantry.
Sirmur Imperial Service Sappers
One section, No. 13 British Field Hospital.
No. 43 Native Field Hospital.

of the highest praise, for they had just undergone a very severe climb, and had reached a point beyond which other troops had been unable to advance for over three hours. The first rush was followed at short intervals by a second and a third, each led by Officers; and as the leading companies went up the path for the final assault, the remainder of the troops, among whom the 3rd Sikhs were conspicuous, streamed on in support. But few of the enemy waited for the bayonet, many of them being shot down as they fled in confusion.

17. The position was won at 3-15 P.M., with the loss of three Officers killed, namely:—Major C. B. Judge, 1st Battalion 2nd Gurkhas; Captain W. E. C. Smith, 2nd Battalion Derbyshire Regiment; and Lieutenant A. Lamont, 1st Battalion Gordon Highlanders; and nine wounded, namely:— Lieutenant-Colonel H. H. Mathias, C.B., 1st Battalion Gordon Highlanders; Major F. Macbean, 1st Battalion Gordon Highlanders; Captain H. P. Uniacke, 1st Battalion Gordon Highlanders; Lieutenant M. F. M. Meiklejohn, 1st Battalion Gordon Highlanders; Lieutenant K. Dingwall, 1st Battalion Gordon Highlanders; Lieutenant G. S. G. Craufurd, 1st Battalion Gordon Highlanders; Captain W. R. Arnold, 1st Battalion Dorsetshire Regiment; Captain J. G. Robinson, 1st Battalion 2nd Gurkhas (since dead); Lieutenant G. E. White, 3rd Sikhs; of other ranks 35 were killed, and 158 wounded.

18. The enemy's loss has not been ascertained, but must have been heavy. Nearly every section of the Afridis was represented, but not in full strength; and there were about 1,500 Sheikhans, Mishtis, Mallakhels and Akhels, besides contingents from the Mamozai, Massozai and Akhels.

19. The General Officer Commanding the 2nd Division has brought to my special notice the gallant conduct of Lieutenant-Colonel Mathias, C.B., Commanding the 1st Battalion Gordon Highlanders, in leading his battalion to the assault of a most difficult position at a critical period of the fight, when previous attempts had failed. I recommend this Officer for the Victoria Cross.

Major-General Yeatman-Biggs has also reported most favourably on the behaviour of the following British and Native Officers and soldiers:—

Major F. Macbean, 1st Battalion Gordon Highlanders, who was the first to spring out of cover and lead his company to the attack, and who, being immediately afterwards wounded, continued to cheer his men on while lying on the ground.

Lieutenant-Colonel E. A. Travers, 1st Battalion 2nd Gurkhas, who led the first rush of his men.

Captains D. C. F. Macintyre and J. G. Robinson, 1st Battalion 2nd Gurkhas; and Lieutenant A. B. Tillard, 1st Battalion 3rd Gurkhas, commanding the Gurkha scouts of his regiment.

No. 2951, Piper G. Findlater, 1st Battalion Gordon Highlanders, who, after being shot through both feet and unable to stand, sat up under a heavy fire playing the regimental march to encourage the charge.

No. 3456, Private E. Lawson, 1st Battalion Gordon Highlanders, who carried Lieutenant Dingwall, when wounded and unable to move, out of a heavy fire, and subsequently returned and brought in Private McMillan, being himself wounded in two places in so doing.

Subadar Kirpa Ram Thapa, 1st Battalion 2nd Gurkhas, who, though wounded in two places, continued to discharge his duties in the front line.

I recommend Piper Findlater and Private Lawson for the Victoria Cross.

20. The General Officer Commanding the 2nd Division has also brought to notice the services of the following Officers, Non-Commissioned Officers and men as deserving of recognition:—

Major G. T. F. Downman, 1st Battalion Gordon Highlanders.
Captain C. C. Miller-Wallnut, 1st Battalion Gordon Highlanders.
Captain and Adjutant W. Campbell, 1st Battalion Gordon Highlanders.
Lieutenant G. D. Mackenzie, 1st Battalion Gordon Highlanders.
Lieutenant G. E. E. G. Cameron, 1st Battalion Gordon Highlanders.

No. 1771, Colour-Sergeant J. Craib, 1st Battalion Gordon Highlanders.
No. 2025, Colour-Sergeant T. Mackie, 1st Battalion Gordon Highlanders.
No. 2021, Sergeant F. Richie, 1st Battalion Gordon Highlanders.
No. 3056, Sergeant D. Mathers, 1st Battalion Gordon Highlanders.
No. 1952, Sergeant T. Donaldson, 1st Battalion Gordon Highlanders.
No. 2465, Sergeant J. M'Kay, 1st Battalion Gordon Highlanders.
No. 3711, Lance-Corporal (piper) G. Milne, 1st Battalion Gordon Highlanders.

Captain W. R. Arnold, 1st Battalion Dorsetshire Regiment, who led the first rush of his battalion.

No. 3937, Private S. Vickery, 1st Battalion Dorsetshire Regiment, who ran down the slope, rescued a wounded comrade, and brought him back to cover. This soldier has subsequently greatly distinguished himself during the withdrawal of Brigadier-General Kempster's Column from the Waran Valley, and I propose in due course to recommend him for the Victoria Cross.

Lieutenant H. S. Pennell, 2nd Battalion Derbyshire Regiment, who endeavoured to bring in Captain Smith's body, and only desisted on finding that Captain Smith was dead.

Captain C. E. de M. Norie, 1st Battalion 2nd Gurkhas, who was conspicuously forward at the commencement of the action.

21. In recording my acknowledgments to Major-General Yeatman-Biggs, C.B., and Brigadier-General Kempster, D.S.O., for the success of the operations on October 20th I think it necessary to point out that the advance was not conducted in the manner in which I had intended, and as I thought I had clearly indicated. The General Officer Commanding the 2nd Division restricted himself to a frontal attack on the Dargai heights, without employing a portion of the large force at his disposal to turn the enemy's rear by pushing on as rapidly as possible to the point of junction of the Narik Darra with the Chagru defile. Undoubtedly the troops would have been under fire and might have suffered some loss in moving along the road below the heights; but if full advantage had been taken of the inequalities of the ground, I am of opinion that the loss would not have been heavy, and I feel confident that, as soon as their line of retreat was threatened, the tribesmen would have begun to disperse.

At the same time, I recognise that the enemy's defeat was rendered more complete and decisive by their being encouraged to hold on to the last, and the result of the action must be regarded as satisfactory, inasmuch as the movement of the troops, baggage and supplies from Shinawari to Khorappa, subsequent to the capture of the Dargai heights, was almost unmolested.

22. On the night of October 20th, Dargai was held by the 1st Battalion Dorsetshire Regiment and 3rd Sikhs, supported by the 1st Battalion Gordon Highlanders, while the remainder of the troops bivouacked on or near the Chagru Kotal.

23. At daybreak on the 21st, the march of the 2nd Division to Khorappa, or, more properly, to Khangarbur, on the left bank of the Khanki stream, was resumed, while in order to avoid a block on the main road, I proceeded from Fort Lockhart to the same point *viâ* Fort Gulistan and the Tsalai spur, taking with me No. 9 Mountain Battery Royal Artillery, the 1st Battalion Northamptonshire Regiment, the 36th Sikhs, and No. 3 Company Bombay Sappers and Miners. The track from the village of Tsalai down to its junction with the main road was so bad, that none of the baggage of the troops accompanying me reached camp at Khorappa until late the next day, that of the 36th Sikhs not arriving until mid-day on the 23rd.

24. The 4th Brigade and some of the Divisional troops of the 2nd Division arrived at Khorappa towards the evening of the 21st October. The remainder of the division coming in the next day; but owing to the steepness and narrowness of the road, and the inferiority of a considerable proportion of the transport

animals, several days elapsed before all the baggage of the division had come up. On October 24th, the troops of the 1st Division began to move from Shinawari to Khorappa, and by the evening of the 27th the Main Column, with its supplies and transport, had concentrated in readiness for a further advance. Advantage was taken of the halt at Khorappa to improve the road from the Chagru Kotal, to complete the organisation of the transport service, and to adjust the loads of the several classes of animals employed, namely, mules, ponies and donkeys.

25. And here I may mention that during the halt at Khorappa, though every military precaution was taken, the camp was fired into every night, sometimes by large bodies of the enemy. and our foraging parties were pertinaciously opposed and followed up by the tribesmen. The losses from this cause were heavy, aggregating three British Officers, twenty-five British soldiers, and twenty-one native ranks, killed or wounded. The names of the Officers are given below :—

Lieutenant-Colonel R. C. Hadow, 15th Sikhs, severely wounded.
Captain F. F. Badcock, D.S.O., 1st Battalion 5th Gurkhas, dangerously wounded.
Lieutenant G. D. Crocker, 2nd Battalion Royal Munster Fusiliers, wounded.

26. On October 28th, in accordance with instructions issued on the previous evening, the force marched in two columns to Gundaki, the 1st Division across the plain and the 2nd Division up the bed of the Kandi Mishti stream, while a detached column consisting of the 1st Battalion Northamptonshire Regiment and the 36th Sikhs occupied the hills to the right of my line of advance As the left column was threatened from the west, I also occupied three hills which commanded that flank with the 2nd Battalion Yorkshire Regiment, a wing of the 2nd Battalion 4th Gurkhas, and a wing of the 3rd Sikhs, respectively. This display of force led the enemy to believe that I intended to turn their right, which they at once began to strengthen, and during the night of the 28th the detachment of the 4th Gurkhas, which in the evening had been reduced to two companies, was continuously attacked at close quarters, suffering, however, but slight loss owing to the care taken in the day time to protect the position by *sangars*. The strong flanking parties which had pushed out enabled me to reconnoitre the Sampagha Pass, and having settled on my plan of action, I directed the whole force to bivouac near Gundaki, and issued orders for the attack on the following day.

Our casualties on October 28th were :—
Lieutenant-Colonel C. A. R. Sage, 2nd Battalion 1st Gurkhas, severely wounded. Other ranks :—Killed two, wounded 10.

27. Here it may be noted that, previous to my advance, on October 28th, I had to detach two battalions to strengthen the force on the Line of Communication. The 30th Punjab Infantry was detailed to hold the Dargai heights, and the 21st Madras Pioneers to form part of the Khorappo garrison.

28. On October 29th, at 5 A.M., the 1st Brigade moved out of camp to cover the advance to the Sampagha. The 1st Battalion Devonshire Regiment seized the village of Nazeno, thus protecting my right. Lieutenant-Colonel Yule quickly brushed away all opposition on that side. The 2nd Battalion 1st Gurkhas covered my left by occupying the village of Kandi Mishti and met with no opposition The 2nd Battalion Derbyshire Regiment, advancing in the centre, occupied without resistance a low rocky hill stretching across the plateau between the Kandi Mishti and Sampagha ravines, which I had chosen as my first artillery position.

At 5·15 A.M., the 2nd Brigade, preceded by the Gurkha scouts, left camp with orders to enter the Sampagha ravine, and to advance by a path leading towards the enemy's position up a long bare spur as soon as the guns should have sufficiently silenced the fire from the *sangars ;* this advance to be supported in succession by the 4th and 3rd Brigades.

At 6·30 A.M. the first shots were fired by the enemy, but the action did not really begin until 7·30 A.M., when the three mountain batteries of the 1st Division opened fire on the *sangars* from the first artillery position above mentioned. Their fire was effective, the range being 1,850 yards, and the enemy quickly evacuated the entrenchments which commanded the lower slopes of the pass, these being seized by the 2nd Brigade at 8 A.M. The three batteries of the 2nd Division, together with the rocket detachment, were now pushed on, and opened fire on the crest of the pass at a range of 2,200 yards. The fire of the guns was, however, soon masked by the rapid advance of the 2nd Brigade which, with the 1st Battalion Royal West Surrey Regiment (the Queen's) leading, reached the summit of the pass at 9·45 A.M. The artillery was again ordered up in support, No. 5 (Bombay) Mountain Battery in front. On reaching the crest this battery did excellent service in assisting the infantry of the 2nd Brigade to dislodge the tribesmen from the heights they were holding on either flank, but while engaged on this duty I regret to report that Captain De Butts, Royal Artillery, Commanding the battery, was mortally wounded. The heights on the north-east of the pass were eventually cleared by the 1st Battalion Royal West Surrey Regiment and the 3rd Sikhs, while those on the north-west were stormed by the 36th Sikhs, supported by six companies of the 2nd Battalion King's Own Scottish Borderers. The last shots were fired at 11·30 A.M., and the 15th Sikhs were then sent on as an advance-guard into the Mastura Valley, where I proposed to bivouac.

29. While the troops were moving down into the valley some slight resistance was met with, but this ceased as soon as the hills commanding the camping ground had been occupied by pickets.

The 1st Brigade remained on the Sampagha for the night, with a view to protecting transport animals and baggage.

30. The casualties during the action were:—
Captain F. R. McC. De Butts, Royal Artillery, killed.
Major R. T. Hanford-Flood, 1st Battalion Royal West Surrey Regiment, slightly wounded.
Other ranks:—Killed one, wounded three.

31. On October 30th, the Main Column, with the exception of the 1st Brigade, which continued to hold the Sampagha Pass, remained in camp on the right bank of the Mastura stream. In the morning I made a reconnaissance of the Arhanga Pass, and issued orders for the attack on the following day. My great difficulty was the want of food, some corps having absolutely nothing in hand and the steep and narrow track over the pass delaying the arrival of supplies. But by redistributing what there was, and making use of what could be collected in the neighbouring villages, each man was eventually provided with two days' rations. I therefore determined not to postpone the attack on the Arhanga Pass, as I was convinced that a protracted halt in the Mastura Valley, expedient as it might seem from a commissariat point of view, would not only encourage the Afridis and give them time to collect their fighting men, but also enable them to destroy, hide, or remove the forage and grain stored in their villages, and thus render our stay in Tirah a matter of extreme difficulty.

32. On October 31st, the 4th Brigade crossed the Mastura stream at 6 A.M. and advanced towards the Arhanga Pass across a broken plain up to a low detached mound, in rear of which the brigade was massed at 8 A.M. Shortly afterwards the three batteries of the 2nd Division opened fire from this mound, at a range of 1,300 yards, on the enemy's main position along the crest of the pass. Meanwhile the 2nd Brigade had moved up on the right, and the 3rd Brigade was disposed in *echelon* on the left, with the object of threatening the enemy's right and joining the central attack when ordered to do so. The 2nd Brigade began the action by a flank movement on the right up two rocky spurs and an intervening ravine, thus gaining the crest east of the pass; while the 4th Brigade attacked in the centre, supported by the 3rd Brigade. The

2nd Brigade's attack was led by the 2nd Battalion Yorkshire Regiment and the Gurkha scouts, each gallantly racing up the steep slope, the summit of which was reached by both simultaneously at 10 A.M. The main attack was led by the 2nd Battalion King's Own Scottish Borderers. Neither attack met with serious opposition, and shortly after 10 A.M. the pass was in our hands, and all opposition had practically ceased.

The casualties were:—Killed none, wounded two.

I may here mention that the road up the Arhanga Pass though short, was the steepest and worst that had yet been encountered.

33. Immediately after the action I gave orders for the concentration of the force in Maidan with the exception of the 1st Brigade, which I had to leave behind for the purpose of dominating the Mastura Valley and of guarding the Line of Communication between Tirah and Khorappa.

34. During the period dealt with in this report the troops under my command were subjected to much privation and fatigue, to great variations of temperature, to heavy losses in action, and to continual night alarms. No body of men could have shown a better spirit.

That a more formidable resistance was not offered in the passes leading respectively into Orakzai and Afridi Tirah, I attribute to the lesson taught those tribes at Dargai in the actions of October 18th and October 20th. They then learnt that their strongest positions could not avail them against the valour of British and Native troops.

35. In submitting this report, I desire to record my acknowledgments to the General Officer Commanding the Line of Communications, the General Officers Commanding Divisions and Brigades, the Chief of the Staff, and the Brigadier-Generals Commanding the Royal Artillery and Royal Engineers, the Heads of Departments, especially those of Ordnance, Supply and Transport, the Officers of the Head-Quarters, Divisional, and Brigade Staffs, and the Commanding and other Officers, Non-Commissioned Officers and men of the several corps under my command, all of whom have done their duty in a manner befitting Her Majesty's Army.

My recommendations for the recognition of the services of individual Officers, Non-Commissioned Officers and soldiers, subsequent to the action of October 20th, will be embodied in my final despatch on the termination of the present expedition.

General Sir William Lockhart's despatch describing the operations of the Tirah Expeditionary Force from November 1st to January 26th, was published in a later issue of the *Gazette of India*, together with comments as follows:—

SIR GEORGE WHITE'S LETTER TO GOVERNMENT.

In a covering letter the Adjutant-General on behalf of the Commander-in-Chief writes:—

"No campaign on the frontiers of India has been conducted under more trying and arduous circumstances than those encountered by the Tirah Expeditionary Force. Its operations have been carried out in a country destitute of roads, the physical configuration of which is such as to present the maximum of difficulty to the movement of regular troops. The enemy were for the most part skilled marksmen, exceptionally active and well armed, and expert in guerilla tactics. While avoiding serious resistance to the advance of our troops, they have lost no opportunity of harassing them both on the march and in bivouac: a system of fighting admirably suited to the nature of the country, and which has necessarily occasioned us considerable loss not only in action, but also from toil and exposure. In spite of these difficulties severe punishment has been meted out to the tribes concerned, with the result that the entire

Orakzai tribe has submitted and complied with the terms of the Government, as have also a portion of the Afridis; and it seems probable even now that the remainder of this tribe will not force a repetition of offensive operations, but will tender their submission at an early date. During the operations the fighting qualities and endurance of the troops have been highly tested, and it is with no small sense of gratification and pride that the Commander-in-Chief brings to the notice of the Government of India the soldierly conduct and discipline of the troops amidst all the hardships and exposure which fell to them; both Officers and men having, whether in action or in bivouac, conducted themselves in a manner thoroughly befitting the traditions of Her Majesty's Army. His Excellency deplores the loss to the Army of the many brave Officers and men who have died in the performance of their duty, and amongst them such distinguished soldiers as the late Major-General Yeatman-Biggs, Lieutenant-Colonel Haughton, 36th Sikhs, and others whose careers were so full of promise.

"The Commander-in-Chief would specially commend to the favourable notice of the Government the distinguished Officer selected for the command of the expedition, who has exercised an exceptionally difficult and responsible command with much skill, vigour and judgment; and His Excellency takes this opportunity of expressing his own acknowledgments to Sir William Lockhart for the able manner in which he has directed the operations of the Force under his command. The Commander-in-Chief also endorses the commendatory remarks made by Sir William Lockhart on the services of General Sir A. Power Palmer, General Symons and General Nicholson, and the Officers and others mentioned in paragraphs 22 to 31 of the despatch. His Excellency fully shares Sir William Lockhart's appreciation of the assistance rendered by the Imperial Service troops, whose association with our own troops has given them an opportunity of gaining valuable military experience which cannot fail to result in increased efficiency.

"Sir George White has much pleasure in commending to the notice of the Government the services of Lieutenant-Colonel Sir Partab Singh, who accompanied the force throughout the expedition as extra Aide-de-Camp to Sir William Lockhart; of Lieutenant-Colonel the Maharaja of Cooch Behar and of Major the Maharaj Rana of Dholpur, who were employed as extra Orderly Officers to the Divisional Commanders.

"As this despatch will probably be the last that Sir George White will submit during his tenure of command, he desires to take this opportunity of bringing to the notice of the Government the valuable services rendered by the following Officers and Departments in connection with the recent operations."

The Officers named are: Sir George Wolseley, Commanding the Punjab; General Morton, Adjutant-General; General Badcock, Quarter-Master-General; Colonel Duff, Military Secretary; Surgeon-Major-General Gore; Major Mullaly, D.A.Q.-M.-G. for Mobilisation; Veterinary-Colonel Thomson; Major-General Hobday, Commissary-General-in-Chief; Major-General Wace, Director-General of Ordnance; Mr. Reynolds, Director-General of Telegraphs; the Postal, Telegraph and Survey Officers and subordinates with the Field Force; Colonel Brackenbury, Manager, Mr. Jacob, Traffic Superintendent, and the subordinate staff of the North-Western Railway.

It is further remarked:—" It has been ascertained that between the 1st July and the 31st October the additional trains on the North-Western Railway required for military traffic amounted to 4,544, or an average of 37 trains per diem in excess of the normal traffic. Any breakdown of the railway arrangements during the period when troops and supplies were being pushed to the front would have had a very serious effect on the military operations; and that no such failure occurred, is due, in His Excellency's opinion, to the able administration of his railway system by the Manager and to the untiring efforts of his subordinates."

The following are some of the observations in detail:—

"On Lieutenant-General Sir G. Wolseley and the Staff of the Punjab Command devolved the duty of carrying out the preliminary concentration of the various forces which have been placed in the field. This has been no light task, but it has been successfully performed. Of the staff at Army Head-Quarters I am to mention General Morton, Adjutant-General in India, who has throughout proved himself zealous and untiring in the performance of the duties which, especially during the war, pertain to his responsible position, and has at all times afforded to the Commander-in-Chief all the assistance in his power. I am especially to bring to notice General Badcock, Quarter-Master-General in India, for his supervision of all the arrangements for the mobilisation of the large forces now and recently in the field. The difficulty of the task has been greatly enhanced by the fact that we were not only engaged in active operations in several directions at one and the same time, but were also compelled to be in readiness to meet any further complication which might suddenly arise along any portion of the North-West frontier. That we have been able to mass the necessary troops without delay on the point threatened by each successive rising as it occurred, and that our mobilisation arrangements have worked smoothly and without friction, have been very largely due to the Quarter-Master-General's constant and assiduous work. Sir George White also wishes to bring to the special notice of the Government of India the services of Lieutenant-Colonel Duff, Military Secretary, in whom His Excellency has always found a Staff Officer of the very highest ability, most earnest sense of duty and soundest judgment, who has done all that a direct personal assistant could do to lighten the work and anxiety of the Commander-in-Chief in a time of exceptional difficulty."

SIR WILLIAM LOCKHART'S DESPATCH.

Sir William Lockhart, in his despatch, describes the military operations in November, December and January.

Regarding Sir Henry Havelock Allen's death, for which he expresses deep regret, Sir William Lockhart says:—"Every precaution had been taken to ensure his safety, and on bidding him good-bye at Lala China, I had impressed on him the necessity of invariably remaining with the troops detailed for his protection."

The despatch continues:—

"During the operations described I have received every possible support and assistance from the General Officer Commanding the Line of Communication, his Staff and the troops under his command. The requirements of the Main Column have been promptly and fully met, while the arrangements made to protect the long and exposed line between Kohat and the Sampagha Pass and afterwards to transfer the base from Kohat to Peshawar have been all that I could have desired.

"In bringing this narrative to a close I wish to record my high appreciation of the conduct of the British and native troops serving with the Tirah Expeditionary Force. Up to the present date their losses have amounted to 1,050 killed and wounded. They have been subjected to great hardship and exposure, harassed at night by assaults at close quarters or by distant rifle fire, and engaged in long and trying rear-guard actions. Their duties on picket and in guarding foraging parties, have been specially onerous. Hardly a day or night has passed without casualties, and whether we advanced or retired, every soldier had to be constantly on the alert against the enemy, who made no stand in the open but were unrivalled as skirmishers and marksmen. The operations were carried out in a country which offered every natural advantage to the tribesmen and imposed on regimental Officers and rank and file the necessity for individual initiative, unremitting watchfulness and personal activity. I am glad to say the troops responded nobly to the call made upon them. Cheeerful and soldier-like under exceptionally trying conditions, Officers and men upheld to the utmost the traditions of their corps and the honour of Her Majesty's Army.

"The advance into Tirah was delayed, and the subsequent movements of the force were impeded, by the inferiority of a large proportion of the transport animals and the want of proper discipline and training amongst many of the transport drivers and Kahars. But it must be remembered that a peace organisation which has to be rapidly expanded when war breaks out takes time to render it efficient, and that the requirements elsewhere had already absorbed much of the better class of pack transport which would otherwise have been available.

"The results attained by the expedition may be summarised as follows:—The troops under my command have marched everywhere within the Orakzai and Afridi limits and the whole of Tirah has now for the first time been accurately surveyed. Our enemies, wherever encountered, have been punished, and their losses are stated on unimpeachable evidence to have been extremely severe. The towers and walls of almost every fortified village in the country have been levelled to the ground, and the winter supply of grain, fodder and fuel of both tribes has been consumed by the force. The Orakzai have been completely subdued and have complied with the terms prescribed for them; but the Afridis still hold out, although I have strong hopes that they may before long submit and thus save their country from a fresh invasion in the spring.

"During the present expedition the scouts, drawn from the 3rd and 5th Gurkhas, have proved especially valuable. Being trained mountaineers and accustomed to guerilla warfare, they were able to climb most precipitous hills, lie in ambush at night, and surpass the tribesmen in their own tactics.

"The Imperial Service Corps attached to the force have taken their full share in the hardships of the campaign, and fighting side by side with their comrades in the regular army have given a tangible proof of their readiness and that of their rulers to assist in the defence of the Empire.

"During the expedition the Mountain Artillery had an important part to play, and fully sustained its reputation as one of the most efficient branches of that arm of the service.

"Much work of a responsible and arduous nature, principally road-making and the destruction of village defences, devolved on the corps of Royal Engineers, the companies of Sappers and Miners and the Pioneer regiments. This work was carried out in a creditable manner."

Sir William Lockhart praises the administration of the Army and Civil Departments, and says that medical officers fully maintained their high reputation by their attention to the sick and wounded under fire and in hospital; also that the signalling and survey work were well done. He acknowledges the public spirit evinced by Mr. Dhanjiboy, who by tonga service facilitated the transport of the sick and wounded to the base hospital.

In recording his obligations to the General Officers, Sir William Lockhart writes:—"Sir A. Power Palmer has commanded the Line of Communication to my entire satisfaction, and has displayed administrative talents of a high order. Major-General Symons has commanded the 1st Division with marked ability, and in a manner which has gained the confidence of all ranks. Major-General Yeatman-Biggs was in a very bad state of health from the outset, but his indomitable spirit carried him through the whole of the operations, only to die at Peshawar on January 5th. I would fain have sent him back to India from the Samana or subsequently from Korappa, but the responsible medical officers considered him fit to remain in the field: a decision which gratified him, although I personally could not agree with it. Owing to a regrettable accident to Brigadier-General Hamilton, Brigadier-General R. Hart was sent to relieve him. General Hart joined the 1st Brigade on October 24th, and has commanded it throughout the expedition with great ability and energy. Brigadier-General Gaselee has fully maintained his high reputation and proved himself to be an admirable leader in mountain warfare. Brigadier-General Westmacott has performed excellent service, more particularly when withdrawing from the Bara Valley on December 13th and 14th. Brigadier-General Hammond, though until lately he has not participated in the active operations of the force, has commanded the Peshawar Column to my satisfaction. I am also much indebted to the Officer Commanding the Kurram Movable Column, Colonel Hill, who has shown energy, capacity and judgment in the performance of his duties. His troops were well handled, both in the reconnaissance to Hissar and during the operations against the Khani Khel Chamkannis.

"I desire to bring to the notice of the Commander-in-Chief and the Government of India the following Officers who have rendered exceptionally good service:—Brigadier-General Nicholson, chief of the staff, an officer of brilliant abilities, fertility of resource and experience in war, the value of whose assistance it is difficult for me to acknowledge in adequate terms. I would very specially put forward his services for recognition and reward. Lieutenant-Colonel Barrow, Assistant Adjutant-General and Major G. H. W. O'Sullivan, Assistant Quarter-Master-General, have fully justified their selection for their important post on the Army Staff. I consider these Officers are well deserving of advancement. Captain Haldane, Deputy Assistant Adjutant-General, is a staff officer of high promise, great ability and untiring mental and physical energy."

Other Officers included in this special list are Brigadier-General Spragge, C.R.A., and his Brigade-Major Captain C. De C. Hamilton; Brigadier-General Broadbent, C.R.E., and his Brigade-Major Captain Craster; Surgeon-Major-General Thomson, Principal Medical Officer, and his Secretary Surgeon-Major Morris; Colonel Scott, Senior Ordnance Officer; Colonel Christopher, Commissary-General of the Force; Major Mansfield, Chief Transport Officer, and his Assistant Captain Hall; Lieutenant-Colonels Dixon, King's Own Scottish Borderers; Abbott, 15th Sikhs; Travers, 2nd Gurkhas; Haughton, 36th Sikhs (who are said to have commanded their battalions in a manner which merits high approbation), Mr. Van Someren and Mr. Truninger, Postal Department; Sir Pratab Singh, Extra Aide-de-Camp. Sir William Lockhart says, his acknowledgments are due also to Lord Methuen, Press Censor; Colonel Holdich, Chief Survey Officer; Veterinary-Colonel Glover; Lieutenant-Colonel Anderson, Military Accounts; Mr. Pitman, Chief Superintendent of Telegraphs, Punjab Division; Lieutenant Davie, 3rd Sikhs, Commanding the Personal Escort; and Subadar-Major Bishan Singh.

The following list includes the names of Officers whose good services came under Sir William Lockhart's personal notice:—"Officers whose good services came under my personal notice:—

Army and Personal Staff.—Colonel More-Molyneux, Lieutenant-Colonel Balfe, Major Logan-Home, Captain Maconchy, Captain Swanston, Major Mercer, Captain Grimston, Surgeon-Captain Morgan, Captain Shewell, Major Scallon, in charge of Imperial Service troops, Captain Bajee (Baroda State Artillery), Lieutenants Maxwell and Annesley (Aide-de-Camps), Lieutenants Collen and Smith (Orderly Officers), Risaldar-Major Khan Bahadur Risaldar Kadam Khan, Jemadar Abdul Ghani.

1st Division.—Surgeon-Colonel Townsend, Lieutenant Macquoid, Captain Leshi; Royal Surrey Regiment, Lieutenant-Colonel Collins; Devonshire Regiment, Lieutenant-Colonel Yule; Yorkshire Regiment, Lieutenant-Colonel Franklyn; No 2 Derajat Mountain Battery, Captain Parker, Bengal Sappers, Captain Sergeant; 3rd Sikhs, Lieutenant-Colonel Tonnochy; 4th Gurkhas, Lieutenant-Colonel Browne; Gurkha Scout, Lieutenant Tillard.

2nd Division.—Lieutenant-Colonel Martin Surgeon-Colonel Davies, Major Lyons Montgomery, Captain Grier, Veterinary-Lieutenant Rose; No. 8 Mountain Battery, Major Shirres; Royal Scots Fusiliers, Captain Northcott; King's Own Scottish Borderers, Captain Macfarlane and Captain Maclaren;

Dorsetshire Regiment, Captain Clarkson; Gordon Highlanders, Major Downman; No. 5 Bombay Mountain Battery, Lieutenant Edlmoun; 15th Sikhs, Captain Rowcroft; 2nd Gurkhas, Captains Macintyre and Norie; 3rd Gurkhas, Lieutenant-Colonel Pulley and Major Rose; 2nd Punjab Infantry, Lieutenant-Colonel Sturt; 36th Sikhs, Lieutenant-Colonel Des Vœux and Lieutenant Munn; Gurkha Scouts, Captain Lucas and Lieutenant Bruce; Surgeon-Majors Whitehead, Bevor, Gerard, Shearer.

Line of Communications.—Colonels Vousden, Keighley, Thurburn, Lieutenant Tomkins, Surgeon-Colonel Saunders.

The following list is given of Officers favourably mentioned by the different Generals :—

1st *Division.*—Lieutenant-Colonels Muir and Hart, Majors Ferrier and Yielding, Captains Rideout and Dabas, the Maharaj Rana of Dholpur.

1st *Brigade*—Major Donne and Captain Kemball; 5th Gurkhas, Deputy Assistant Quarter-Master-General, Captain Mullaly.

2nd *Brigade.*—Major Aldworth, Major Barret, Lieutenant Abadie. Regimental: Royal West Surrey Regiment, Captain King King; Yorkshire Regiment, Major Bowles and Lieutenant Noble; Derbyshire Regiment, Lieutenant-Colonel Dowseard, Major Smith-Dorrien; No. 1 Kohat Mountain Battery, Captain St John; 21st Madras Pioneers, Lieutenant-Colonel Huggins; 1st Gurkhas, Lieutenant-Colonel Sage and Major Martin; 3rd Sikhs, Major Quin and Lieutenant Taylor; 4th Gurkhas, Captain Carnegy; 30th Punjab Infantry, Lieutenant-Colonel Maisey.

Army Medical Staff.—Brigade-Surgeon Lieutenant-Colonels Swayne and King, Surgeon-Major Priggs and Corker.

2nd *Division.*—Major Triscott, Major Bewicke Copley, Lieutenant-Colonel Purdy, Major Kelly, Captains Knight, Hilliard and Wake, the Maharaja of Cocch Behar, Mr. Wainright, Survey Department.

3rd *Brigade.*—Majors St. Leger Wood and Massy.

4th *Brigade.*—Major Doran, Captain Edwards, 3rd Bombay Cavalry. Regimental: Royal Scots Fusiliers, Lieutenant-Colonel Spurgin, Captain Powes; King's Own Scottish Borderers, Major Mayne, Captains Sladen and Haig; Dorsetshire Regiment, Lieutenant Shonbridge; Gordon Highlanders, Lieutenant-Colonel Mathias, Captains Uniacke and W. Campbell, Lieutenant A. F. Gordon; 15th Sikhs, Lieutenant Gordon; 3rd Gurkhas, Lieutenant West (since deceased); 28th Bombay Pioneers, Major Chase and Lieutenant Moore; 2nd Punjab Infantry, Captain Eales; 36th Sikhs, Captain Custance and Lieutenant Van Someren; Sirmur Sappers, Lieutenant Chancellor, Surgeon-Lieutenant-Colonel Bourke, Surgeon-Major Granger, Surgeon-Captains Burtchnell and Selby.

Line of Communication.—Major Tulloch, Captain Philipps, Major Allen, Lieutenant Galloway, Captain Steel Shore, Young, Biggs, Watkins, Major Bond, Veterinary-Captain Forsdyke, Lieutenant-Colonel R. Gordon (22nd Punjab Infantry); Lieutenant-Colonel Graves (39th Garhwal Rifles); Captain Denne, Captain Hollway, Surgeon-Lieutenant-Colonel H. Hamilton, Surgeon-Major Bigger.

Peshawar Column.—Lieutenant-Colonel Gwatkin, Captain Bretherton, Lieutenant Holland, Lieutenant-Colonel Plowden and Captain Davies, Oxfordshire Light Infantry; Colonel Sawyer, 45th Sikhs.

Kurram Movable Column.—Major McSwiney, Captain Scudamore, Brigade-Surgeon Lieutenant-Colonel Murray, Assistant Commissary-General, Captain Rogers, Colonel-Lieutenant Gordon, Captain Shakespear, 6th Bengal Cavalry, Lieutenant-Colonel Money, Central India Horse, Major Kettlewell, Surgeon-Major Willis.

In addition to the transport officers mentioned in the preceding paragraphs, the Commissary-General with the Tirah Expeditionary Force brought to special notice the services of the following regimental officers :—Captains Weller, S. D. Browne, Cookson, C. Davies, Pollock, Cotgrave.

Sir William Lockhart further records his acknowledgments to the Native Commanding Officers of the various Imperial Service Corps. Among the honorary commissioned and warrant officers mentioned are: Assistant Surgeons O'Connor, Charters, Hussey, Captain Bennett, Conductors Land and Thorne, Ordnance Department; Lieutenant Ezechiel, Conductor Falkland, Commissariat Transport Department; Lieutenant J. McDermott, Conductor Morrison, Sub-Conductor Wiggins, Miscellaneous Departments. The Non-Commissioned Officers mentioned are: Sergeant-Major Diblett, Sergeants Howell, Payne, Blaker, Tibbs, G. C. White, A. White, Pepper and Ashworth. The Rev. A. S. Dyer and the chaplains of all denominations were mentioned as having performed their duties satisfactorily.

Sir William Lockhart concludes by recording his indebtedness for advice and assistance to Sir Richard Udny, Colonel Warburton, Mr. King and other Officers attached to the force in a political capacity.

Comprehensive lists of Non-Commissioned Officers and men, British and native, who have shown conspicuous gallantry, and whom it is intended to recommend for the Distinguished Conduct Medal or Order of Merit, will be submitted in a supplementary despatch.

THE VICEROY'S REMARKS.

The Governor-General in Council, in directing the publication of the above despatch, remarks :—" These operations have been conducted in a country of great natural difficulty and against an enemy of extraordinary boldness and activity, armed moreover with weapons of precision, of which they thoroughly understood the use. The withdrawal from Tirah necessitated by the season formed part of the plan of operations from the outset, but it was nevertheless an operation of great difficulty under circumstances requiring not only most careful dispositions, but also a very high degree of discipline, courage and endurance on the part of the troops. The Governor-General concurs with the Commander-in-Chief in his opinion that the manner in which the campaign has been conducted reflects very great credit on Sir William Lockhart's skill and judgment, and shares His Excellency's admiration of the devotion to duty and soldierly spirit displayed by the troops on all occasions. His Excellency tenders to all Officers and men of the Tirah Expeditionary Force the cordial congratulations and thanks of the Government of India. His Excellency also fully shares in Sir George White's appreciation of the assistance rendered by the Imperial Service Troops, and takes this opportunity of acknowledging the ready loyalty of the chiefs who have placed their regiments and transport trains at the disposal of the Government and the personal services rendered by Sir Partab Singh, the Maharaja of Cooch Behar, and the Maharaja Rana of Dholpur. His Excellency further desires to acknowledge the services rendered during the operations by the Officers of the Staff at Army Head-Quarters and of the Departments under the Government of India mentioned by the Commander-in-Chief, and cannot allow this opportunity to pass without conveying to Sir George White his sense of the distinguished ability with which on this occasion and throughout his term of office the responsible duties of Commander-in-Chief have been performed."

A despatch from Sir William Lockhart describing the operations of the Tirah Expeditionary Force from the 27th January to the 5th April, was published still later with comments :—

The Governor-General in Council agrees with the Commander-in-Chief in his appreciation of the services of the Officers named in the Adjutant-General's letter, and of the conduct of the troops during the period in question.

The Commander-in-Chief endorses the commendatory remarks made by Sir William Lockhart on the services of Brigadier-General Hamilton, Commanding the 3rd Brigade, Brigadier-General Ottley, Commanding the Royal Engineer Force, and the others named in the despatch, as also the soldier like conduct shown by the troops.

Sir William Lockhart in his despatch describes the Shinkamar action, and adds:—" Among the killed the country has to deplore the loss of Lieutenant-Colonel Haughton, 36th Sikhs, an officer whose able and gallant leading of the fine regiment which he commanded had repeatedly come under my notice."

Sir William Lockhart, in concluding his despatch, remarks: " The Afridis are now most desirous of resuming their former friendly relations with the British Government, and admit that the recent operations in Tirah have convinced them of the folly of their unprovoked attack on the Khyber and the Samana posts and other hostile acts. They express contrition for their misconduct and acknowledge the justice of their punishment. I trust that these tribesmen who have proved themselves as brave foes as the Sikhs did, may like the latter become our firm friends. No finer fighting material can be found on the borders of India, and if by firm yet sympathetic treatment we succeed in gaining the confidence and affection of these hardy mountaineers, we may hope to utilize their services more fully than before in the defence of the Empire.

" In bringing this narrative to a close I would wish to record my appreciation of the soldier-like behaviour of the troops under my command, not only while actively engaged in the field, but also while employed on the tedious and monotonous duties of a blockade. Their conduct during the second phase of the campaign has been as creditable as were their gallantry and endurance during the first. The force can congratulate itself on having carried out in the most thorough manner the task entrusted to it. In no previous campaign on the north-west frontier of India has a more exemplary punishment been inflicted, or a more complete submission been enforced. I have to record my obligations to Brigadier-General Hamilton, who has performed his duties with marked ability and energy; also to Brigadier-General Ottley, who has rendered valuable service as commanding the Royal Engineers of the force, more particularly in connection with the improvement of communications and the restoration of the Khyber posts.

"During the period dealt with in this despatch the following Officers have been brought to my notice as deserving of favourable mention: Major C. St. L. Barter and Captain H. Wells Cole, King's Own Yorkshire Light Infantry; Lieutenant A. K. Robb, Durham Light Infantry (attached to King's Own Yorkshire Light Infantry); Surgeon-Lieutenant M. Dick, Indian Medical Service.

" Since the publication of my previous despatches the under-mentioned Officers, whose names were omitted in the first instance, have been specially recommended for their good services by the general officers concerned:—Lieutenant-Colonel C. H. W. Cafe, Royal Sussex Regiment; Major G. F. A. Morton, Commanding No. 1 Mountain Battery Royal Artillery; Major E. Hegan, 5th Dragoon Guards, Deputy Assistant Quarter-Master-General; Major H. R. Marrett, Base Commissariat Officer; Major A. B. Helyar, Commanding 57th Field Battery; Surgeon-Major Spence, Army Medical Staff; Captain H. B. H. Wright, Commanding No. 4 Company Madras Sappers; Surgeon-Captain J. B. Jameson, Army Medical Staff; Captain A. M. Lloyd, Base Transport Officer; Captain A. Nicholls, Deputy Assistant Quarter-Master-General for Intelligence; Captain U. W. Evans, in charge of the Engineer Field Park; Captain F. H. Hoghton, Field Intelligence Officer; Captain G. W. Palin, Commissariat Transport Officer; Veterinary-Captain Richardson; Captain H. Smyth, Cheshire Regiment, Transport Officer; Captain H. F. Walters, Field Intelligence Officer; Captain Birdwood, Orderly Officer; Captain G. C. Rigby, Assistant Superintendent, Army Signalling; Captain W. S. Nathan, Field

Engineer; Captain H. J. M. MacAndrew, Brigade Transport Officer; Lieutenant Hill, 15th Sikhs; Lieutenant C. S. D. Leslie, Brigade Commissariat Officer; Lieutenant Beatty, Transport Officer; Lieutenant H. O. Pan, Orderly Officer; Lieutenant Ballard, Transport Officer; Lieutenant Herbert, Royal Horse Artillery, Transport Officer; Lieutenant Sheppard, Bengal Sappers; Lieutenant A. E. Turner, Assistant Field Engineer; Lieutenant Hammond, Orderly Officer (dangerously wounded and since dead); Second-Lieutenant Young, attached to the Gordon Highlanders.

"I am much indebted to Subadar-Major Yasin Khan, 24th Punjab Infantry, for his assistance in dealing with the Afridi representatives, and I trust his services may be duly recognised."

Sir William Lockhart forwards lists of British, Non-Commissioned Officers and men and of native ranks who have shown conspicuous gallantry in the field during the operations subsequent to the 26th January, whom he recommends for the Distinguished Conduct Medal and the Order of Merit.

(lxiii)

CASUALTY LIST.

Statement showing the number of casualties reported to the Adjutant-General in India from 10th June 1897 to the 10th January 1898, during the recent Field Operations on the North-West Frontier of India.

FORCE.	Staff and Departmental Officers.			British Troops.							Native Troops.												
				Officers.			Warrant, Non-Commissioned Officers and Men.				British Officers.			Native Officers.			Rank and File.				Followers.			
	Killed.	Died of wounds.	Wounded.	Killed.	Died of wounds.	Wounded.	Killed.	Died of wounds.	Wounded.	Missing.	Killed.	Died of wounds.	Wounded.	Killed.	Died of wounds.	Wounded.	Killed.	Died of wounds.	Wounded.	Missing.	Killed.	Died of wounds.	Wounded.	Missing.
Tochi Field Force (includes attack on escort at Maizar)	...	...	...	...	...	...	...	...	2	...	3	1	3	...	...	3	21	3	33	...	2	...	1	...
Malakand Field Force	1	...	4	2	2	8	6	1	37	...	9	2	18	1	...	14	71	5	305	...	1	...	7	...
Peshawar	...	...	...	1	...	3	7	...	11	...	...	...	...	...	...	...	9	...	55	...	...	...	...	...
Mohmand Field Force	...	...	...	...	...	...	...	...	...	...	...	...	1	...	...	1	2	...	29	...	1	...	...	...
Kohat-Kurram	1	...	...	...	...	...	...	...	...	...	...	...	2	...	...	4	36	6	74	...	1	...	5	...
Tirah Expeditionary Force	...	...	...	9	...	24	75	11	323	5	8	1	17	5	...	14	141	10	368	3	4	...	11	1
Total	2	...	8	12	2	35	88	12	373	5	20	4	41	6	...	36	280	24	864	3	9	...	25	1

SUMMARY.

	Killed.	Wounded.	Missing.
Staff and Departmental Officers	2	8	...
Regimental Officers	36	76	...
British Non-Commissioned Officers and Men	100	373	5
Native Officers	6	36	3
Native Non-Commissioned Officers and Men	304	864	3
Followers	9	25	1
Total	457	1,382	9

* Includes those who died of wounds.

www.ingramcontent.com/pod-product-compliance
Lightning Source LLC
Chambersburg PA
CBHW030007240426
43672CB00007B/860